SOLDIERS
OF
CHRIST

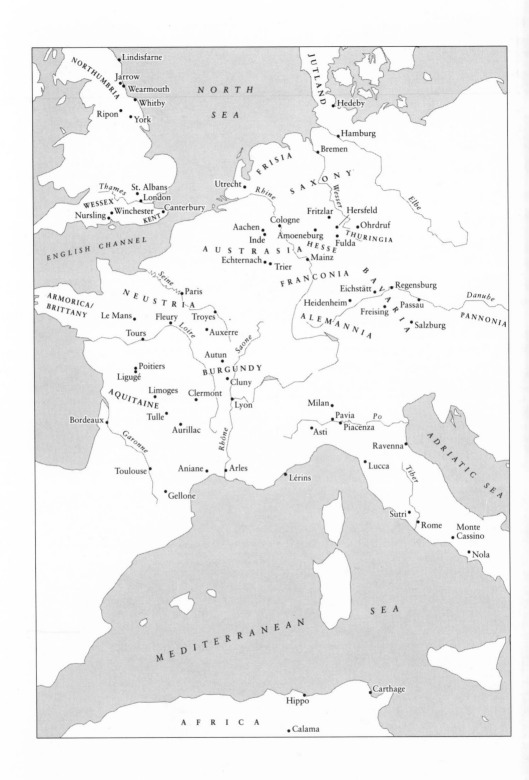

SOLDIERS
OF
CHRIST

Saints and Saints' Lives
from
Late Antiquity
and the
Early Middle Ages

Edited by
Thomas F. X. Noble
and
Thomas Head

Sheed & Ward
London

Copyright © 1995 The Pennsylvania State University
Published in the United States of America by The Pennsylvania State University Press,
University Park, PA 16802-1003

First published in the U.K. in 1995 by
Sheed & Ward Ltd
14 Coopers Row
London EC3N 2BH

Printed and bound in the U.S.A. by Braun-Brumfield Inc., Ann Arbor, Michigan.

ISBN 0 7220 8350 5

FRONTISPIECE: Western Europe in the Early Middle Ages

To
Giles Constable
and
Richard Sullivan

CONTENTS

A NOTE ON THE TEXTS

Apart from the *Life of Willehad*, which was prepared especially for this volume, all of the lives included here have been translated before and published elsewhere. Although we have not provided new translations of most of these texts, we have taken some steps to make them more accessible to readers.

Each text is preceded by an introduction that supplies both essential details about the author as well as interesting or important matters pertaining to the text's composition and its transmission to today. Generally, we leave the texts to speak for themselves; that is, we do not offer extensive introductory comments that reveal *our* ideas about what is significant, noteworthy, interesting, and distinctive. We prefer to let readers discover these works for themselves. Each introduction is followed by a brief section "Texts and References." These sections provide a handy reference to the best or most accessible critical Latin edition of each life and also identify a few crucial works of relevant scholarship. Our intention is to help readers get started on additional reading and research, not to provide comprehensive bibliographies. The Guide to Further Reading that follows the texts serves to acquaint readers with the literature of hagiography; many of the titles cited in the Guide contain extensive, and often precisely focused, bibliographies. Where possible, works in English have been cited.

The notes that accompany each text do not take the form of full historical or literary commentaries. Their aims are more modest: identifying for readers potentially unfamiliar personal and place names; explaining ecclesiastical terminology; defining certain terms and phrases that are peculiar to the late antique and early medieval worlds.

The texts are presented here in the order in which they were written, which differs from the order in which their subjects actually lived. We organized the texts in this way to give readers an opportunity to follow developments in hagiography as a literary genre while learning something about the saints who are the subjects of hagiographical writing.

Readers who are familiar with the original translations of these texts will notice that we have revised them in certain respects. The prologues to Huneberc's *Hodoeporicon of Saint Willibald* and Willibald's *Life of Boniface* have been completely retranslated. The preface to Alcuin's *Life of Willibrord* is here translated for the first time. In almost all the texts the original translations of technical terms, personal names, and place-names have been revised to make them more accurate and more consistent with present-day scholarly usage. The chapter divisions of the Latin editions were, for no apparent reason, omitted from some of the original translations. We have restored them.

Finally, biblical quotations and allusions have been extensively revised. As far as we could tell, the original translators did not adopt (or adapt) any known Bible translation in preparing their versions. Where the authors of the following texts are clearly quoting Scripture, we have "normalized" all their quotations according to the wording of the Revised Standard Version. Once in a while this may mean that we have been more "accurate" than the authors whose works we are editing. It is important to remember that the biblical culture of these authors was immense and omnipresent, but that they frequently worked from memory, and memory is a powerful but fallible guide. Think of how many scriptural verses, lines of poetry, or popular lyrics we have in our own memories, but remember all too imperfectly. It is also important to remember that late antique and early medieval authors had their biblical memories formed by two primary agents: the Bible itself and the liturgy. Where the former is concerned, the Latin Vulgate, the version prepared by Saint Jerome between 382 and 405, was dominant but by no means exclusive. Where the latter is concerned, passages that monks or clerics recited very frequently were often slightly altered from the actual wording of the biblical texts in order to serve the ritual or syntactical needs of the moment. Thus, and ironically, intelligent people could accurately remember similar things differently. Allusions that were not obvious or putative quotations provided us with another problem. An example from the *Life of Germanus* will illustrate the point. In chapter 8 Constantius says, "They found him immune thanks to the breastplate of faith" (indutum fidei lorica inexpugnabilem repperissent). This could be a quotation, or else a vague allusion to 1 Thes. 5.8, Eph. 6.11, or Is. 59.17. We take it as the latter and thus identify it with a parenthetical reference in the text. Generally, we have been stricter than the original translators in identifying both quotations and allusions.

As aids to comprehension, two further comments are in order. First, many of the following texts sprang from or were deeply influenced by the monastic world. Most monastic communities lived under some form of rule. A rule was a set of written guidelines, more or less detailed depending on time and place, that governed the daily life of monks and nuns. The Rule of Saint Benedict eventually became the most prestigious and widely disseminated of all rules. But between its composition around 520 and its imposition on virtually all monasteries by Charlemagne and Louis the Pious—a process that readers will encounter in the *Life of Benedict of Aniane*—it enjoyed no special status. Benedict's Rule was, until the late sixth century, largely confined to his own monastery of Monte Cassino some eighty miles south of Rome. Then, slowly at first, the Benedictine Rule began to appear in monasteries in Gaul and by 665 it had been introduced at Ripon in Northumbria. Still, before the Carolingian "normalization" of monastic usages, a regime of "mixed rule" prevailed. This means that most communities observed a locally confected recipe of monastic practices that derived from many sources. Occasionally the original translators of these texts mistook a vague reference to a rule for a specific reference to the Rule of Saint Benedict. We have changed these references so that they read simply "rule," or "holy rule," with no broader implication. Where Benedict's Rule is unquestionably at issue, we say so, though usually in a note.

Second, and again because of the monastic source and inspiration of so many saints' lives, readers continually will encounter references to the canonical hours of the monastic day. The "canonical hours" are the times each day when the community gathered for the prayers that, taken together, are called the Divine Office (*Opus Divinum*). They are, in order: Matins (of which Lauds is a part in most cases), celebrated in the middle of the night; Prime, celebrated at the first hour—roughly dawn; Tierce, the office for the third hour; Sext, the office for the sixth hour; None, the office for the ninth hour; Vespers, the evening office; and Compline, the prayers said before retiring for the night. Hours were not reckoned as equal amounts of a total day, but as hours of daylight. Thus the length of time between offices was greater in summer than in winter.

INTRODUCTION

The history of the late antique and early medieval west is the story of one of
the most ambitious experiments in the integration of varied cultures ever
undertaken. Edward Gibbon's familiar tale of the "fall of the Roman empire"
to the Germanic tribes is also the story of the "rise of Europe." The Germanic
migration into and subsequent conquest of lands that constituted almost half
of one of the greatest empires of human history was not, however, an unam-
biguous triumph. Beginning with the sack of the city of Rome in 410 by Alaric
and the Visigoths, the Germanic peoples inexorably gained a military and even
a political victory over their onetime rulers. They in turn accepted and slowly
came to be dominated by the culture—the law, the government, the language,
and perhaps most important, the religion—of the Romans.

The invaders did not simply pillage the lands they had won; rather, they
sought, and even forced, entrance into the halls of government. As Theodoric,
the king of the Ostrogoths who ruled most of Italy, wrote to Emperor Anastasius
of the eastern Roman (or Byzantine) empire in 505, "My kingdom is an imitation of yours, the form of good order and the unique exemplar of an empire."[1]
Indeed the statement should be in part ascribed to Cassiodorus, a Roman of senatorial rank, who wrote on Theodoric's behalf as one of his chief ministers.
Throughout the western part of the empire, the new German rulers often employed Romans like Cassiodorus in positions of governmental and ecclesiastical
power, offices for which they were suited by their culture and learning. Slowly,
through both the imitation and the interaction implied in the passage just
quoted, the culture of the Germanic peoples was transformed. So too was that of

---

1. Cassiodorus Senator, *Variae*, ed. Theodor Mommsen (Monumenta Germaniae Historica,
Auctores Antiquissimi, 12; Berlin, 1894), 1.1, p. 10.

the native Roman population, for the Germans in turn imposed their notions of sacral kingship, gift-giving, and feuding on their new homelands. European civilization was the product of this grand experiment in multiculturalism.

The most important driving force in this process of cultural interchange and transformation was Christianity. It was the conversion of the Germanic tribes that most effectively Romanized those peoples. It was Christian ideology that remained the most effective weapon, and the most seductive ploy, of the old rulers. The Roman aristocracy dominated the institutions of the Christian church longer than they were able to control any other base of power under the new order. Thus the Christian religion became the primary means through which Roman culture survived. In time the term "Rome" came to refer not so much to the ancient imperial capital as it did to the religion of Latin Christianity. The importance of Christianity is perhaps the most surprising aspect of this entire experiment, for that religion had gained official acceptance and freedom from persecution in the Roman Empire less than a century before the imperial capital fell to the Visigoths.

Christian Sanctity and the Cult of Saints

To understand these processes of acculturation and with them the development of European culture and society in the Middle Ages it is therefore essential to understand the role of Christianity. And there is no better way to understand that role than to study that religion's greatest human heroes, the saints. For if Christians regarded God as their king, then the saints were the Christian nobility, human members of the divine court. To use one much-repeated phrase, they served as "the soldiers of Christ" (*militia Christi*). More specifically saints were those persons who had been judged by God to be worthy of entrance to the kingdom of heaven immediately after death. The word used to designate a saint in Latin (*sanctus* or *sancta*) had as its root meaning a "holy person." Over time the word slowly acquired the status of a title. While many Christians were considered "holy," only a limited number came to be regarded as "saints."

A Christian community in practice conferred such an honor on a person by celebrating a feast day in their memory. The day chosen was the date, or the presumed date, of that person's death, a date which for Christians represented the saint's birth into eternal life as a member of the kingdom of God. It is important to recognize that a person could not in this official sense become a saint either in isolation or while still alive, but that he or she had to be posthumously recognized as holy by a Christian community.

It is the purpose of this volume to present in English translation some of the most significant records of the lives of those people considered to be saints. In exploring these works, the reader will be presented with rich evidence about the development of religion and society in western Europe from the late Roman Empire to the great changes that transformed European society around the year 1000.

The saints were, both during their lives and after their deaths, key members not only of the Christian community, but of western society as a whole. As "friends of God" or "soldiers of Christ" saints possessed—or, perhaps more accurately, had delegated to them by God—enormous power. This power allowed them to give gifts and distribute favors, that is, in Roman terms, to act as patrons for their followers. As the texts that follow demonstrate, Christians thought that saints were regularly capable of performing miracles: they could cure disease, counter famine, quell storms, extinguish fires, and defeat enemies. Even the prayers of a holy man or woman were more effective than those of more ordinary Christians. All this was God's doing, for the miraculous powers did not belong to the saints themselves, but were divine actions performed through them. Such divine favor sometimes provided the saints with positions of social or political prominence. On the strength of their sacred aura, provided by both asceticism and miracles, they could mediate disputes, dispense charity, advise the emperor, or influence the army.

Nonetheless, the posthumous patronage of the saints was, if anything, more impressive. As residents of the divine kingdom, they could directly present petitions on behalf of the living to God in order to win favor for them in God's court. Christianity preached the universality of sinfulness, as well as of the divine judgment and punishment that was the result of sin. If a person wished to undo the consequences of their sins, they sought the aid of a saint. Perhaps a person was thought lame as a result of sin; a friend of God could ask that the limb be made whole. Or perhaps a person had been possessed by a demon; a saint had the power to drive that demon away. Or perhaps a person simply feared being sent to hell; there was no better ally to have on the Day of Judgment than someone already living in heaven. Such intercessory prayer was deemed in many ways more appropriate for ordinary humanity than direct approach to God. The universal creator and judge was envisioned as a remote and awesome figure. It was more effective to approach the divine throne through the intermediate agency of God's human friends.

The living expected effective intercession or miracles when they petitioned the holy dead. The posthumous power that saints possessed was a direct result of the manner in which they had lived. It is no accident that in Latin one can refer both to the holy actions of a saint's life and to the miracles performed by that saint posthumously with the same word—*virtus*—which can be rendered in English as either virtue or power. It is important to remember, however, that this power was thought to come directly from God and that the honor shown to the saints was considered a means of worshiping God. Augustine of Hippo (d. 430) remarked, "When we make our offerings at shrines, it is to God. The martyrs have their place of honor . . . but they are not adored in the place of Christ."[2]

The patronage provided by the saints made sense in different ways to Christians of both Roman and German background. Romans were accustomed to the obligations that wealthy senators or landowners felt toward their clients. They provided aid and advice to those who served them faithfully. In times of crisis, too, they helped, dispensing protection in time of war, food in time of famine. This very traditional sense of the gains to be had from friendship (*amicitia*) and solidarity (*unanimitas*) with the aristocracy was easily translated into the new Christian idiom of the ties formed around the friends of God (*amici Dei*). Similarly Germans residing in the western provinces of the empire knew the responsibilities that leaders of bands of warriors had to their followers. Power and authority were to be wielded for the good of all, not just the ruler. Once again Christian parallels were easily formed. Versions of the New Testament in Germanic vernaculars, such as the ninth-century *Heliand*, portrayed Christ as the son of the Chieftain of humanity and the apostles as his military companions (*gisidos* in Saxon, *comitatus* in Latin).[3] Similarly the idea of intercessory prayer could readily find translations in both cultural idioms. The Roman aristocracy had regularly interceded on behalf of their more humble followers in civic law courts or before the emperor. Similarly it was the German king who mediated on behalf of his warriors with external powers, most notably the Roman Empire.

Both peoples also knew that clients and warriors had even greater responsibilities to their patrons and leaders. It was through prayers and feasts, gifts and services that the living sought to gain the patronage of the saints. We collectively call these efforts the cult of the saints. It took two primary forms. The first was liturgical. Each Christian community celebrated the memory of various saints on the feast of that saint's death. Such commemorations included prayers, readings taken from the life of the saint, and sometimes even

2. Augustine of Hippo, *Sermones*, 273.7 in *Patrologia Latina*, ed. Jacques-Paul Migne, 221 vols. (Paris, 1844–64), 38:1251 (hereafter cited as *PL*).

3. For a translation, see *The Heliand*, trans. G. Ronald Murphy (Oxford, 1992).

processions in which the bodies of the saints were carried around the church that sheltered their remains. The other form the veneration of saints assumed involved their relics, that is, the physical objects associated with the saints. The most significant relics were the saints' bodies or fragmentary parts of those bodies, although other objects—possessions of the saint, such as clothing or crosses, or tokens that had touched the saint's corpse, such as bits of cloth or vials of water—also assumed the status of relics. Relics were not merely a symbol of the saint, but rather the continued physical presence of the saint in this world. As a fifth-century inscription at the tomb of Martin of Tours (d. 397) read, "Here is Bishop Martin of sacred memory, whose soul is in the hand of God. But he is completely present here, made manifest to everyone by the goodwill of his miracles."[4] Relics thus provided a physical link between the spiritual realm of heaven, where the saint's soul resided, and the material world, where the shrine guarded the saint's corporeal remains.

A vast part of medieval literature, primarily in Latin but also in the vernacular languages, was devoted to the saints. Such writings are known to modern scholars as hagiography, a term compounded from Greek words (*hagios* and *graphē*) meaning "holy" and "writing," that is "writings about the saints." The most common works of hagiography were the lives of saints that recorded the ways in which these residents of heaven had developed and demonstrated their holiness. Other types of hagiography included collections of stories of miracles performed at a saint's tomb or accounts of the history of their relics. The present volume includes only lives of saints.

Above all else, such works instructed the faithful in the virtues of the Christian life. Authors stressed that the lives of the saints were intended to provide their audience with exemplars of conduct. As Gregory of Tours (d. 594), one of the most prolific and influential hagiographers of the early Middle Ages, introduced one of his works, "I have recently discovered information about those who have been raised to heaven by the merit of their blessed conduct here below, and I thought that their way of life, which is known to us through reliable sources, could strengthen the Church . . . because the life of the saints . . . encourages the minds of listeners to follow their example."[5] This theme of imitation was echoed many times. A ninth-century hagiographer, Bertholdus of Micy, described the purpose of his *Life of Saint*

4. "Inscriptions from the *Martinellus*," in Raymond Van Dam, *Saints and Their Miracles in Late Antique Gaul* (Princeton, 1993), 315. (We have employed, where available, published translations of the passages we have cited in order to aid the student in finding further reading.)

5. Gregory of Tours, *Life of the Fathers*, trans. Edward James (Translated Texts for Historians, Latin Series 1; Liverpool, 1985), 27.

Maximinus as follows: "What has been said and done by the saints ought not be concealed in silence. God's love provided their deeds to serve as a norm of living for the people of their own times as well as of those years which have since passed; they are now to be imitated piously by those who are faithful to Christ."[6] The lives of the saints thus provided a model, albeit an extraordinary and almost unattainable one, of the Christian life. The records of the lives of the saints were a template of Christian virtue, a map of the path to salvation. Just as epics such as *Beowulf* or the Norse sagas provide a key to understanding the ideals of Germanic culture, so too the texts that follow will help unlock the ideals of early medieval Christianity.

Like epic, medieval hagiography was also prone to the use of stereotypic forms. It is important to keep in mind that the primary aim of the authors included here was not to compose a biographical record of the saint, but rather to portray the subject as an exemplar of Christian virtue. Hagiographers also sought to show how the saints themselves had imitated such norms, particularly those provided by the life of Christ and previous saints. Just as they encouraged their audience to imitate the example of the saints, so too they employed the literary models offered them by the Bible and by earlier hagiographic works. Stories, themes, and motifs were repeated from the life of one saint to that of another, each hagiographer adapting a traditional pool of material to the needs of the narrative at hand. Hagiographers even went so far as to repeat phrases and whole passages verbatim from earlier works. The effect, largely intentional, was in part to subsume the particularity of a given saint's life into a generalized type of sanctity, such as the martyr, the virgin, or the holy bishop. Such use of models aided the moral and didactic purpose of hagiography. As André Vauchez has noted, hagiography was a genre that "aims precisely at blurring the individual's traits and transforming his or her lifetime into a fragment of eternity."[7] At the same time, the traditional character of hagiography can be overstated. The models of sanctity changed considerably over time, as each new author used and thus altered extant tradition.

To this point we have considered the place of saints in Christianity and of hagiography in the literature of the early Middle Ages only in the most general terms. We would now do well to consider briefly the development of the ideals and practices associated with the Christian notion of sainthood. This

6. Bertholdus of Micy, *Vita s. Maximini*, chap. 1 in *Acta sanctorum ordinis sancti Benedicti*, ed. Luc d'Achéry and Jean Mabillon, 1st ed., 9 vols. (Paris, 1668–1701), 1:592.

7. André Vauchez, "The Saint," in *Medieval Callings*, ed. Jacques Le Goff, trans. Lydia Cochrane (Chicago, 1990), 313.

sketch is intended to provide a broad context into which the reader might place the various texts of the collection. More specific information on each individual text is included in the prefatory introductions.

The Cult of the Martyrs and the Triumph of Christianity

The cult of saints was forged in the crucible of persecution to which the Roman government subjected early Christians. While the varied religions of the ancient Mediterranean world had their own diverse concepts of heroes and holy persons, scholarly attempts to locate the origins of Christian sanctity in specific facets of Roman religion or of Judaism have failed. To be sure, various aspects of the cult of saints bear functional similarities to antecedent religious practices and concepts, such as curing shrines associated with the Greco-Roman divinity Asclepius, sanctuaries dedicated to heroes such as Hercules, family feasts at the tombs of deceased ancestors, the popular cult of good luck, or Jewish ideas of sacred place. The Christian ideas of sanctity and saintly patronage, however, were intimately tied to unique Christian notions of the afterlife, an eschatology that involved an ultimate divine judgment of each person either to eternal salvation or to eternal damnation. It was those promises and perils that encouraged the earliest Christians to persevere in their faith during almost three centuries of periodic but often severe attacks by local and imperial authorities.

Those Christians who suffered execution because of their faith were called martyrs (from the Greek *martus*, "witness") because in the manner of their deaths they bore the ultimate witness to the name of Jesus Christ. Martyrs were the first Christians to be honored as saints. Christian communities began at an early date to collect and preserve stories of the sufferings they endured. By the middle of the second century, independent works were circulated concerning the martyrdoms of specific individuals. It is in these "passions" or "acts" of the martyrs that we find the origins of later hagiography.

The earliest extant example of the genre is an anonymous work in Greek, *The Martyrdom of Saint Polycarp*. Polycarp (c. 69–c. 155) was a bishop of Smyrna in the province of Asia Minor (Izmir in modern Turkey). Some writings of the bishop survive, attesting to the great stature he had attained in both his own and neighboring communities. The *Martyrdom* provides a vivid eyewitness testimony to Polycarp's suffering and death recorded by his disciples. The bishop was remembered as having answered the Roman governor,

"The fire you threaten me with burns merely for a time and is soon extinguished. It is clear you are ignorant of the fire of everlasting punishment and of the judgment that is to come, which awaits the impious." The Christian eschatological equation could not be rendered more simply or directly. For Polycarp and other martyrs, it was preferable, indeed desirable, to accept the proximate sufferings and tortures offered by the Roman government in order to avoid the punishments ordained by divine judgment.

The account of Polycarp's martyrdom goes further, for it records how the Christians of Smyrna gathered up the bishop's bodily remains "dearer to us than precious stones and finer than gold [which] we buried in a fitting spot." They then gathered together as a community each year "to celebrate the anniversary day of his martyrdom, both as a memorial for those who have already fought the contest and for the training and preparation of those who will do so one day." Quite likely they recited an early version of the *Martyrdom* as part of these liturgical celebrations. Here we glimpse the very origins of the cult of saints. For Polycarp was not regarded as holy in the manner of ordinary martyrs; his community had subtly but definitively changed the meaning of that term by raising him to the rank of a designated "holy person," that is, a saint, through commemoration of a shrine to his relics and a feast day in his memory. Already they urged future generations to imitate the heroic example offered by the executed bishop.[8]

Although mainstream Christianity accepted much of the general misogynism of the Roman world virtually from its inception, a large number of the earliest saints were women. Martyrdom, after all, was little dependent on gender, for Roman authorities made few attempts to treat women differently than men when sending Christians to the lions. Significantly one of the earliest passions known in Latin records the martyrdom of Perpetua and her slave Felicity around the year 200 in Carthage. Although assembled by an authoritative redactor, probably a male cleric, the work contains Perpetua's own account of the visions she experienced in prison during the days leading to her execution. These visions include a moving account of the afterlife that awaited Perpetua and her fellow Christians. Her prophetic powers had given her a leading role in her community at Carthage. Posthumously they served to validate her sanctity. Thus the record of her visions and her death was preserved.

Over the course of the next century the varied Christian communities of the

---

8. *The Martyrdom of St. Polycarp*, in Herbert Musurillo, ed. and trans., *The Acts of the Christian Martyrs* (Oxford, 1972), 2–21. For the quoted passages, see chaps. 11 and 18, pp. 11 and 17.

Roman Empire came to do what those of Smyrna and Carthage had done: raise up the memory of select martyred heroes from their own ranks. Cities large and small had their favored sons and daughters. That notable center of learning Alexandria honored its virgin-martyr Catherine as an opponent of pagan philosophers, while tiny Nola near Naples in Italy nurtured the memory of its bishop Felix. Multiple cults were common. That of the bishop Cyprian, for example, came to eclipse the memory of Perpetua in Carthage. Rome, as the imperial capital, had more celebrated martyrs than any other community. Greatest of its saints, from an early date, were Peter, chief of the apostles and first bishop of Rome, and Paul, the great convert and Apostle to the Gentiles. The former was allegedly buried on a hill across the Tiber that became the site of the Vatican. The latter was memorialized at a suburban grave that became known as Saint Paul's Outside the Walls. By unintentionally giving the impetus for the cult of martyrs, the imperial persecutors unwittingly provided one of the chief means through which Christian communities created a sense both of identity and of historical consciousness.

In the second decade of the fourth century, in the wake of one of the most severe of all persecutions, the fortunes of Christianity changed. Beginning with a victory over a rival at the Milvian Bridge in 312, Constantine gradually gained control over the Roman Empire. The following year an imperial edict granted Christians freedom of religious expression. Persecutions, at least within the empire, were at an end. Although it is difficult to say exactly when the new emperor converted to Christianity, he was consistently supportive of the religion and used it as part of his strategy of consolidating and maintaining control of the empire. Christianity quickly achieved a position of dominance among the creeds and philosophies of the Roman world. Traditional religion was in retreat. In 382 the statue of Victory, the divinity symbolic of Rome's military power and success, was removed from the meeting hall of the Senate. Temples to the old gods were closed in the imperial capital and elsewhere, frequently transformed into Christian churches. In 392 an edict of the emperor Theodosius effectively rendered the practice of the Roman religion illegal.

The triumph of Christianity was virtually complete. In little over a century, what had been a persecuted minority sect had come to be the imperial state religion. Victory was not, however, total. Throughout the empire there were still, and would be for some time, adherents of the ancient divinities, but their religion came to be known as paganism, that is, the religion of the *pagenses* or countryfolk. Bishops launched campaigns designed to root out such idolatry. As Maximus of Turin (died c. 415) remarked in a sermon, "Hardly anyone's field is unpolluted by idols, hardly any property is kept free from the cult of demons."[9]

The official expansion of Christianity over the course of the fourth century led to a similar growth in the cult of the martyrs, which had hitherto remained fragmented and local. A calendar of Christian feasts dedicated to these saints developed, a cycle of sacred time that intentionally rivaled the old Roman calendar of secular festivals. The list of people honored on these feast days was called the canon of the saints. While it varied to some degree from region to region, many feasts—such as those of Peter the chief apostle or of Stephen the first martyr—became universal among all Christian communities. Following traditions established in Roman North Africa, bishops exercised authority over the canon used in their own diocese.

Shrines were also built over the tombs of the sainted martyrs. These *martyria* were located in cemeteries scattered outside city walls, for Roman law and custom both militated against the burial of human remains within the urban community of the living. The Theodosian Code, for example, had required that all corpses be removed from Constantinople. The ritual pollution and physical stench of the dead had been traditionally banished to fields outside the urban walls. Constantine himself sponsored a church over the traditional site of the tomb of Peter on the Vatican hill. The patronage of the martyrs was closely associated with the region in which they had died. As Maximus of Turin noted, "All the martyrs, therefore, are to be very devoutly honored, but the ones whose relics we possess are to be especially venerated by us. For they all help us by their prayers, but these help us also by their suffering."[10] Slowly, nonetheless, relics were brought from the suburban cemeteries to the cities themselves. One of the first instances occurred in Milan, where in 385 Bishop Ambrose (340–397) announced the discovery of the relics of the martyrs Gervasius and Protasius. He soon moved their bodies to a newly completed cathedral in the city center, thus openly challenging the deep-rooted Roman taboo. Now Christians were inviting their holy dead back within the community of the living.

Feast days and shrines, both in suburban cemeteries and urban cathedrals, were the public expression of the cult of the martyrs. There were private expressions as well. People strove to have the bodies of their relatives buried close to the tombs of those recognized as saints. On the Day of Judgment those

---

9. *The Sermons of St. Maximus of Turin,* trans. Boniface Ramsey (Ancient Christian Writers 50; New York, 1989), 91.2, p. 212.

10. *The Sermons of St. Maximus of Turin,* 12.2, p. 32.

bodies were to be reunited with the souls of the saints. Would it not be prudent to have one's own body and the body of those one loved in the same vicinity? Moreover, the power of the martyrs extended well beyond the boundary of the grave. When Paulinus of Nola (353–431) decided to inter the corpse of his son near the shrines of martyrs in his native land, he remarked, "We have sent [the body of my son Celsus] to the town of Complutum [Alcalá in modern Spain] so that he may be joined near to the martyrs in his tomb and so that in proximity to the blood of the saints he may draw forth that which refines our souls like fire."[11]

Nonetheless the flames of such a refiner's fire had to be fanned. Families gathered at the tomb of the martyrs to hold banquets in their honor. These feasts were in some sense a continuation of the Roman custom of the *refrigium,* meals shared at the graves of the ancestors. The calculus was, however, crucially altered. The Romans held their picnics on the shores of the hereafter in order to provide sustenance to the pathetically suffering shades of their forefathers and foremothers. Meat and drink were poured out on the ground, real food for unreal, or at least insubstantial, people. Where "pagans" had once given succor to their dead, Christians partook of their feasts in order to celebrate, and hence to gain the assistance of, deceased martyrs. Now it was the dead who would aid the living. The clergy, however, sometimes demurred at lay practices. In the *Confessions* (6.2), Augustine recalled how Bishop Ambrose of Milan had criticized the homage Monica made at the tombs of the martyrs, although there was no one closer to Augustine's heart than his own mother. Later, as bishop of Hippo, Augustine complained about people who returned home drunk from feasts held at martyrs' shrines.

The Changing Face of Sanctity in the Late Roman Empire

While the legends, feasts, and shrines of the martyrs certainly formed the foundation for the cult of the saints, by the fourth century martyrs were no longer the only saints. The end of the official persecution of Christianity within the empire had greatly reduced the opportunities for martyrdom. To be sure, Christians would continue to suffer death as witnesses to their faith in the wake of foreign invasions and raids, or during the course of missions to non-Christians, or even as the result of violent disagreements among Chris-

---

11. Paulinus of Nola, *Carmina,* no. 34 in *PL,* 61:689.

tian sects. The churches of the fourth century, however, were generally secure and powerful communities that had a need for new ideals to add to the exemplar offered by the martyrs. These communities now had to learn to live with success. They also had to learn to live with dissent, as a variety of controversies splintered Christian communities into rival sects. Those who considered themselves to be the upholders of traditional orthodoxy, or "correct teaching," branded groups like the Arians and the Donatists as heretics.

The orthodox found appropriate new models of heroic Christianity in the monastic movements, which at that time were experiencing spectacular growth throughout the Mediterranean world. The strict self-denial of asceticism had always played a significant role in Christianity. It was in monasticism, however, that its role became institutionalized. Disillusioned with what they perceived to be the vanity of ordinary society, monks (the word comes from the Greek *monachos*, "he who lives alone") abandoned the settled life of towns and cities in favor of the Egyptian desert and other desolate places. There they created an alternative society devoted to prayer and rigorous ascetic discipline. They sought to purify their souls and their bodies through spare diet, frequent fasts, lifelong chastity, lack of personal property. Their life was passed in a silence that was often broken for prayer but rarely for personal conversation. Others adapted the monastic life to varied circumstances. Some women, for example, lived as consecrated virgins or widows, alone or as part of small communities, thus creating their own desert within the city. In the highlands of Anatolia and Syria, some men went to even further extremes than the desert monks, erecting small platforms on the tops of pillars. There these stylites (from the Greek *stulites*, "column") practiced their ascetic discipline literally nearer to God, as well as in full view of any who came to observe. Varied and extraordinary acts of self-denial marked ascetics as holy and also separated them from the sometimes suffocating ties of family and community, from the petty power of bureaucrats and professionals. Villagers and townspeople, jaded by their own dull routine, perceived the ascetic friends of God to be charismatic figures possessing great sacred power. Removed from society, the ascetics came to influence it by settling disputes, dispensing charity, counseling the troubled, and healing the sick.

Some of those who endured the so-called white (that is, bloodless) martyrdom of the ascetic life came to be celebrated as saints. One of the earliest was Anthony (d. 356), a young man from a wealthy family who abandoned his inheritance to become a hermit in the desert wastes and abandoned pagan temples of Upper Egypt. Anthanasius of Alexandria (c. 295–373) celebrated his story in a work designed to teach both the monastic life and orthodox

Christianity to others: "Read these things now to the other brothers so that they may learn what the life of the monks ought to be. . . . And if the need arises, read this to the pagans as well, so they may understand by this means that our Lord Jesus Christ is God."[12] Many other hagiographic works about the Egyptian monks came into circulation, including the anonymous collection *The Lives of the Desert Fathers* and Palladius's *Lausiac History*. They helped to spread monasticism east to Palestine and Syria and then, via Latin translations, west to the provinces of Gaul (modern France) and Iberia (modern Spain). The heart of the new hagiography was didactic; the new type of saints came to be known as confessors, those who confessed or taught the faith.

By the early fifth century still more types of Christians came to be included in the canon of the saints under the rubric of confessor. Most were clerics: bishops and other men who held an official position within church hierarchies. This clericalization of sanctity occurred more fully in the Latin west than in the Greek east, where only a few great patriarchs of this period, such as Athanasius, were considered as saints.

This process points to the ways in which gender helped to construct ideals of sanctity, for women were completely excluded from such clerical offices. As noted above, women such as Agnes, Cecilia, and Lucy stood alongside their male counterparts in the lists of martyrs. The shift to an ascetic ideal of sanctity, however, began to narrow the access of women to the canon of saints; in the late antique world women were viewed as being by nature less capable of living such a spiritual life than were men. Despite misogynist social attitudes and ecclesiastical regulations, however, there were many women involved in the ascetic movement. Some of these in turn came to be regarded as saints. The theologian Gregory of Nyssa, for example, composed a work about his sister Macrina who had become a learned student of Scripture while living as a consecrated virgin. But he and others who composed the lives of saintly women stressed that their heroines had to overcome the natural incapacities inherent to their gender. One common element of the hagiography of this period was a much-repeated story in which a female saint was forced to disguise herself as a man in order to live the monastic life. Another, which in part recalled the biblical story of Mary Magdalene, concerned repetent prostitutes who left the city to live ascetically in the desert and thus to remove the stain of their sexual sins. With the change to a more clerical ideal of sanctity in the west, women were even more fully excluded from the paths of sainthood during the fifth and sixth centuries.

12. Athanasius, *The Life of Antony*, trans. Robert Gregg (New York, 1980), chap. 94, p. 99.

The first two saints included in this collection—Martin of Tours and Augustine of Hippo—belonged to the new breed of saintly bishop. Both, however, were also formed in a profound manner by asceticism. When Martin converted to Christianity, he abandoned his military career for life as a monk, becoming a bishop only later as a result of the renown he gained from his ascetic discipline and charismatic powers. The influence of Athanasius's life of Anthony also reached Augustine, who, in his *Confessions*, tells us that he avidly read the text and that he consciously modeled his own experience of conversion on that of the Egyptian monk. The two men do not appear in these lives as ascetic recluses, but rather as pastors who tirelessly protected their flocks. Stories about Martin's efforts to uproot idolatry in the countryside or Augustine's struggles against heretics showed how the soldiers of Christ did battle on behalf of ordinary people entrusted to their care.

These two saints had very different posthumous careers. Augustine's prolific writings made him the most influential theologian in western Christianity for many centuries. He was quickly and widely recognized as a saint, but there was no shrine for his relics and no major cult dedicated to his memory. Martin's posthumous reputation, on the other hand, was based on his miraculous powers. Pilgrims flocked in increasing numbers to his tomb outside of Tours, which soon became the most important shrine in the province of Gaul. The cult of Martin was also dispersed throughout the west in the form of numerous churches dedicated to his name. Similarly Sulpicius's life of the saint, a work of great literary sophistication but also of palpable excitement and zeal, became perhaps the most influential of all works of Latin hagiography. As Athanasius had provided a model to Sulpicius, so he provided a model to all later authors, in a work that became in the process a virtual mine of stereotypic phrases and themes.

The fall of Rome to the Goths and the great Germanic settlements of the fifth century permanently changed the character of life in the western Roman Empire. The mantle of imperial rule was gradually replaced by a patchwork quilt of small kingdoms dominated by individual tribes. Augustine himself was profoundly affected. In the last decades of his life he produced the towering *City of God* as a reply to pagans who blamed Rome's downfall on its conversion to Christianity. The bishop died before the Vandals captured and destroyed his city. He thus escaped, and probably never fully envisioned, the full effects of the migrations. Roman imperial authority passed remarkably quickly in these lands. In 476 a German general deposed Romulus Augustulus, the last to claim the title of emperor in the west.

By the end of the fifth century the descendants of the imperial aristocracy had become the subjects of Gothic, Vandal, and Frankish kings. In this new world order, men from the old Roman elite turned to ecclesiastical careers as a means of retaining and exercising power. The saints of the fifth and sixth centuries were largely bishops of this sort who guarded the Roman population against their new German overlords, succeeding with the use of divine power where the secular power of the empire had failed. Germanus of Auxerre (c. 380–448) not only battled metaphorically against Pelagian heretics, as had Augustine, but literally took to the battlefield against an invading army of Alans who had been given permission by a Roman general to pillage part of Gaul. Anianus of Orléans (died c. 453) used miraculous powers and visions to defy Attila and his Huns until a Roman army arrived to relieve the siege of his city. Fulgentius of Ruspe (468–533) forged his theological opposition to Arianism into a powerful political weapon to be wielded against the Vandal rulers of North Africa. The saintly patrons of this age were not, however, exclusively bishops. Geneviève of Paris (420–512), a consecrated virgin who had been inspired to follow the religious life by Germanus of Auxerre, rallied the people of her city against the invading Huns in 451.

The growing stress on patronage also affected the memory of older saints. In the middle of the fifth century the posthumous cult of Martin began to grow in popularity and importance at Tours. The saint was remembered not so much as the gaunt ascetic celebrated by Sulpicius Severus, but as a powerful bishop still capable of aiding his flock. A new church was built over Martin's tomb. An inscription addressed the hopes of the pilgrims who came there, "You who have knelt on the ground, lowered your face to the dust, and pressed your moist eyes to the compacted ground, lift your eyes, and with a trembling gaze look at the miracles and entrust your cause to the distinguished patron. . . . Seek [Martin's] protection; you do not knock at these doors in vain."[13] It was an enticing message to a Roman populace who found themselves falling ever more completely under barbarian domination.

The works of Gregory of Tours confirm the growing importance attached to the miraculous powers of the saints in sixth-century Christianity. A man of proud lineage who counted a martyr and a saintly bishop among his ancestors, Gregory himself was a bishop and one of the leaders of the Roman population of Gaul, now ruled by the Franks (who gave their name to the kingdom of France). A prolific author, he produced the monumental *Ten Books of Histories* and eight linked collections of miracle stories. While he recorded the lives of many saints, it was the posthumous presence of long-dead men like Martin

---

13. "Inscriptions from the *Martinellus*," in Van Dam, *Saints and Their Miracles*, 314.

of Tours and Germanus of Auxerre that dominated his world. The shrines of saints were special places: their walls were adorned with hangings and murals depicting scenes from the lives of the saints; candles and incense burned ceaselessly before the shrine; pilgrims jostled one another for physical contact with the holy tomb, going so far as to spend the night sleeping over the remains. People did not only come into the presence of the saints to be cured, they also swore oaths to end feuds or begged the saint's support on Judgment Day. In return the faithful presented their prayers, deposited offerings, or provided service to the saints. Gregory saw his own writings as a means of repaying what Martin had done for him, "If only the worthlessness of my mind will allow him to be honored as is proper for a friend of God! For whenever different kinds of serious illnesses afflicted me, he often restored me to health."[14]

Romans were not the only clients of the saints discussed by Gregory. The Franks had, beginning with their king Clovis (b. 465, r. 481–511), converted to orthodox Christianity. Clovis himself endowed the church of Martin at Tours, while his widow Clothild retired to that city to be close to Martin's tomb. Martin was slowly transformed from the patron of Tours to the patron of the Frankish kingdom. The relic of the saint's cloak, cut in two to clothe a beggar in a famous episode recorded in his life, came into the possession of the Frankish royal family. It was jealously guarded by the clerics of the palace, where it gave its name (*cappa*) to the private church or "chapel" where it was enshrined. Over the course of the sixth century, the Frankish nobility followed this royal example and gave lavishly to the saintly patrons celebrated by Gregory. The cult of the saints became one of the main avenues through which the Franks became enmeshed in the practice of Christianity. A Frankish author would later boast, "After the knowledge of baptism, the Franks, having found the bodies of the blessed martyrs whom the Romans had mutilated with fire or sword, decorated them with gold and precious stones."[15]

If Gregory of Tours was one of the most eloquent expositors of the logic of saintly patronage, the logic of saintly asceticism still had its proponents in the west, none stronger than Pope Gregory the Great (b. 540; pope, 590–604). In a rambling and endlessly fascinating collection of stories known as the *Dialogues*, Gregory celebrated the memory of the holy men, and less commonly

14. Gregory of Tours, *The Miracles of the Bishop St. Martin*, preface to book 4 in Van Dam, *Saints and Their Miracles*, 285.

15. *Lex Salica Karolina*, prologue in *The Laws of the Salian Franks*, trans. Katherine Fischer Drew (Philadelphia, 1991), 171. This prologue was added to the text of the *Salic Law* sometime in the eighth century. The repetition of the quoted sentence in the translation is a misprint.

women, of central Italy. They were ascetics who abandoned the cities for lives as hermits and monks in the wild valleys of the Appenines. Typical of their conversion was that experienced by Benedict of Nursia (c. 480–c. 547), author of the famed Rule for monks and later celebrated as the father of western monasticism: "[His] parents sent him to Rome for a liberal education. But when he saw many of his fellow students falling headlong into vice, he stepped back from the threshold of the world in which he had just set foot. For he was afraid that if he acquired any of its learning he, too, would later plunge, body and soul, into the dread abyss. In his desire to please God alone, he turned his back on further studies, gave up home and inheritance and resolved to embrace the religious [that is, monastic] life."[16] At first glance, Benedict and the other subjects of Gregory's work look much like Anthony and the monks of the Egyptian desert. Their world, however, was much different. Living in a land dominated by Goths and Lombards—who had converted to Arian, rather than orthodox, Christianity—their asceticism served as a form of political protest that strengthened the resolve of the Roman community. Like the bishop of Tours, the bishop of Rome dwelt at length on the miraculous powers possessed by his heroes. Benedict, for example, worked miracles to cure the sick, chastise lax monks, and free the prisoners of Arian overlords. Moreover, Gregory emphasized that Benedict continued to work these miracles after his death. Thus was patronage married to asceticism.

In the eastern Mediterranean, which was less affected by the Germanic migrations, the pre-invasion traditions of ascetic sanctity survived. There the Roman Empire continued to flourish as the predominantly Greek-speaking state ruled from Constantinople, known to us as the Byzantine Empire. Eastern saints of the sixth and seventh centuries were largely of well-established types: stylites (such as Daniel of Anaplos and Alypios), monastic leaders (such as Sabas and Theodosius the Cenobiarch), charismatic bishops (such as John of Alexandria and Theodore of Sykeon), female virgins who disguised themselves as male monastics to protect their chastity (such as Anastasia), and martyrs who died in the course of invasion or religious persecution (such as the female martyrs of Najran or Maximus the Confessor). Many widely disseminated collections of saints' lives, such as the *Spiritual Meadow* of John Moschos or the *Lives of the Eastern Saints* of John of Ephesus, consciously hearkened back to the tradition of the legends of the Egyptian desert. While the cult of relics was well developed in Byzantium, even more important was the veneration of

16. Gregory the Great, *Dialogues*, trans. Odo Zimmerman (The Fathers of the Church 39; Washington, D.C., 1959), prologue to book 2, 55–56.

icons of the saints. These images, usually paintings but some in other media, contained and projected the posthumous power of the saints in ways similar to relics. In the eighth century, however, widespread opposition to icons grew, splitting Byzantine Christians into iconoclast (anti) and iconodule (pro) factions. The agony of the Iconoclast controversy—which ended by supporting the orthodoxy of the veneration of images and thus securing the central place of icons in eastern Christianity—led to a reexamination of the function of sanctity and ultimately to new ideals of sainthood.

An ascetic sanctity also flourished far to the west, in Celtic Ireland. Through the efforts of Patrick and others that land was converted to Christianity in the first half of the fifth century. Monasticism was quickly adopted along with the new faith and came to be the focus of Christianity in Ireland, recruiting large numbers of both men and women. The ideals of the Egyptian desert mingled with native concepts of holiness, such as the magical powers of the druids and the charismatic poetry of the bards. What emerged was a unique form of monasticism, especially severe in its ascetic rigor, but tempered by a boundless enthusiasm for the wonders of the natural world. On the plains of eastern Ireland, for example, a sanctuary dedicated to the fertility goddess Bríg was replaced by St. Brigid and the community which she founded at Cell Dara. The nuns served, like the priestesses before them, as custodians of an eternal flame. Another distinctive aspect of Irish monasticism was its itinerant character. In contrast to the Continental tradition, where a fixed abode was the norm, many Irish monks and nuns undertook long pilgrimages in which they wandered from place to place spreading the message of the monastic life and of Christianity itself.

Over the course of the sixth and seventh centuries Irish monks crossed over to Scotland and England, where they helped to convert the Celts and Anglo-Saxons to Christianity and to found a native monastic tradition; to the Frankish kingdom on the Continent, where Saint Columbanus and his followers implanted a distinctive new brand of monasticism; and on to Italy, where those monks helped to convert the Lombards from Arian to orthodox Christianity.

The hagiographic tradition that recorded the saints of Irish monasticism, in both the Latin and Irish tongues, was itself a unique blend of Mediterranean literature and Celtic folklore. Alongside stories derived from the traditions of Anthony and Martin, one encounters wonder-working animals such as otters who loyally served the saints, as they once had served the heroes of bardic verse, as messengers to the otherworld, retrieving sacred books lost in a lake or tenderly drying a holy man's body after a night of ascetic immersion in the frigid ocean. There were also tales of epic journeys in which saints traversed the vividly portrayed seas and coastlines of the North Atlantic, encountering terrifying monsters, edifying visions, and venerable hermits. In *The Voyage of Saint Brendan*, for example, the abbot and his "co-warriors in Christ" sailed leather boats called coracles for seven years "glorifying God in all things" and learning lessons of the religious life.[17] The holy men and women, such as Brendan and Brigid, who founded the great centers of Irish monasticism would never be mistaken for the aristocratic Roman saints celebrated by Gregory of Tours.

CHRISTIAN SAINTS AND GERMANIC KINGDOMS

Until the end of the sixth century, sainthood in western Christendom remained (at least on the Continent) largely a Roman domain, despite the political and military dominance of the Germanic rulers. Gregory of Tours was an aristocratic Roman who wrote about Roman saints. Saints of Germanic heritage were conspicuous by their virtual absence from his works. Over the course of the seventh century, however, the situation began to change as numerous men and women of the Frankish aristocracy came to be viewed as saints. They represented a new type of sainthood, dubbed by German scholars *Adelsheiligkeit* or "noble holiness," which was representative of and attractive to the ruling elite.

One of the first of these new saints was Queen Radegund (518–587). When she learned of her husband Clothar I's plans to murder her brother, she abandoned him and life at the royal court for a politically and religiously acceptable retirement at the convent of the Holy Cross, which she founded in Poitiers. There she pursued a life of ascetic service to her fellow nuns and the poor of the surrounding community, while retaining and often using her ties to the leading ecclesiastics of the realm. Her life was recorded by two writers, the second a nun of her own community named Baudinovia who was almost certainly the first female hagiographer. The Frankish female saints of the seventh century were, like Radegund, largely abbesses; the men were almost all bishops.[18] Many had distinctly Germanic names: Balthild, Sadalberga, Rictrude, Wandrille, and Arnulf. Others bore traditional Roman names:

17. *The Voyage of Brendan*, chap. 26 in *The Age of Bede*, ed. David Farmer (Harmondsworth, 1983), 241.

18. The lives of the female Frankish saints of the late sixth and seventh centuries have been translated and studied in *Sainted Women of the Dark Ages*, ed. and trans. Jo Ann McNamara and John Halborg, with E. Gordon Whatley (Durham, N.C., 1992).

Sulpicius, Eligius, and Caesaria. This evidence suggests that the old Roman elite had by now been almost entirely absorbed through intermarriage into the Frankish ruling classes. In the process the Franks had largely adopted a form of Latin as their spoken tongue, known as a Romance vernacular. Although literacy itself was confined to the clergy and to the elite among the lay aristocracy, the stories of the lives and miracles of these saintly Frankish nobles would have been understood by the laity when read out as part of the liturgy.

Sprung from aristocratic stock, these saints occupied positions of power within the church and society at large. Their efforts were to provide some semblance of Christian order in an often brutal world: denouncing the abuses of kings, organizing the distribution of charity, settling disputes, converting the countryside, providing sanctuary. These were people of action who tempered their often turbulent careers with a rigorous dose of asceticism learned from wandering Irish monks. Noble blood and ascetic self-denial provided twin roots to a considerable charisma. These were figures whose blessings and curses carried weight among their contemporaries. Their words could destroy the trees sacred to pagans or save fellow travelers from shipwreck. In these men and women, the memory of Martin had been updated and transformed. An ideal of Germanic sanctity had been born.

Such saints were not limited to the Frankish kingdom, although the thirty-odd saints' lives that were written there between 600 and 750 easily outnumber those extant from the rest of Europe. The Visigoths of Spain were converted from Arianism to orthodox Christianity in the last years of the sixth century. The Lombards of Italy followed suit in the early seventh century, in some part due to the efforts of Irish monks. Some native saints were celebrated in both lands. The list of hagiographers even includes the Visigothic king Sisebut (d. 620).

The religious landscape of the western Mediterranean, however, was irrevocably changed with the expansion of Islam in the last decades of the seventh and first decades of the eighth century, military campaigns that extinguished Christian rule in North Africa and much of the Iberian Peninsula. The boundaries of Latin Christendom were thus slowly being defined by geopolitical change. To the north, however, those boundaries had long been expanding. Among their other accomplishments, some of the Frankish *Adelsheilige* undertook missionary activities along the boundaries of their kingdom. In Flanders and Frisia to the north and Bavaria to the east, followers of Columbanus and his Irish monastic ideal such as Amand of Noyon, Emmeram of Regensburg, and Kilian of Wurzburg replanted Christianity in formerly Roman lands where the Germanic migrations had largely uprooted it. The process of conversion had a secular aspect as well: it paved the way for absorption of these lands into the Frankish kingdom.

Nowhere were missionary efforts more successful, however, at producing a Germanic Christian culture than in England. The Roman province of Britain had been home to a lively Christian community. In the middle of the fifth century Germanus of Auxerre was welcomed there as a champion of orthodoxy, while its native son Patrick brought Christianity to Ireland. The invasions of the Angles and Saxons, however, threatened the practice of Christianity in much of the island. Unlike the Goths and Franks who entered Roman territory on the Continent, these tribes did not soon convert to any form of Christianity. In the late sixth century missionaries came to the Anglo-Saxon kingdoms from two sources. One group were wandering Celtic monks, who founded monasteries in the north. The second were Roman priests sent by Pope Gregory the Great, who established a beachhead of sorts in the south around Canterbury. Despite bitter disputes between the two parties, the Christianity that took over England in the course of the next century was a creative fusion of Continental and Irish ideals.

One result of that fusion was the development of a native tradition of sanctity. Later generations remembered the founders of new Christian communities and institutions as saints. Unlike the Continent, there are few shrines that survived from the Roman past. The cult of the saints had to be reinvented from the ground up. These new saints included a wide variety of types: abbots who founded monasteries (Benedict Biscop), monks who were called to work as missionary bishops converting the countryside (Wilfrid and Cuthbert), kings who were martyred by pagan rivals (Oswald and Edwin), hermits who wrestled demons in fetid bogs (Guthlac), queens who retired to monasteries (Etheldreda). They were the creators of a new Christian tradition. Their relics were enshrined in an effort to create a Christian topography of sacred places. The memory of their lives was recorded primarily by monks, for the most vibrant spiritual and intellectual centers of Anglo-Saxon Christianity were monasteries such as Jarrow and Whitby where Celtic asceticism merged with Roman learning. These produced a remarkable cadre of scholarly hagiographers. Head and shoulders above the rest stands Bede (673–735) who brought to his lives of saints like Cuthbert and Benedict Biscop the same discerning eye and polished style that marks his *Ecclesiastical History of the English People*. While one can certainly identify Roman, Celtic, and even Frankish elements in this Anglo-Saxon hagiography, it is a novel and surprisingly independent tradition. Its heroes are just that, men and women who share much in common with the aristocratic protagonists of such Old English epic poems as

Beowulf and the *Battle of Maldon*. They moved in a world little formed by the Roman Empire, structured rather by the obligations of blood and caste, gift-giving and pillaging, feasting and feuding. It is no accident that the earliest hagiography composed in a Germanic tongue is to be found in the Old English of the Anglo-Saxon kingdoms.

One trait common to the traditions of sanctity from the late Roman, the Frankish, and the Anglo-Saxon worlds is nobility. The great majority of saints came from the families of the aristocracy. In both late Roman cities and Germanic kingdoms, it was largely people of high birth who were allowed to pursue careers of power and prestige. The society of western Christendom was governed by secular and clerical hierarchies that cooperated closely. When the Anglo-Saxon aristocrat Wilfrid decided that he could no longer bear to remain in his father's entourage because of the abuses of his stepmother, he undertook an ecclesiastic career. This he began not as a priest serving a church, but as a noble with an entourage of fellow warriors in the court of Queen Eanfled where "he requested that he be allowed to serve God with her counsel and under her patronage."[19] The traditions of hagiography and the practices of the cult of saints reaffirmed connections among holiness, charisma, and noble blood that were deeply rooted in both Roman and German societies. The saints' lives of late antiquity and the early Middle Ages assumed that spiritual virtue could not be easily developed by those who did not also possess an illustrious lineage. Thus did Christianity help to legitimize the dominance of a hereditary elite over other groups, both free and unfree.

This collection does not contain any examples from the seventh-century traditions of hagiography in the Frankish and Anglo-Saxon realms. Those works serve, however, as the background to many of the saints' lives that follow. Over the course of the eighth century, Frankish aristocrats and Anglo-Saxon monks collaborated in two mutually dependent undertakings of enormous scope and momentous achievement: first, the conversion to Christianity of those Germanic peoples who had remained largely outside the Roman sphere of influence; and second, the creation of a new empire in the west based on Roman traditions, but ruled by Germanic emperors. The creative mixture of Roman, Christian, and Germanic elements was continuing.

Beginning in the last decade of the seventh century, Anglo-Saxon monks and nuns migrated in great numbers to the Continent where they preached Christianity to still-pagan Germanic tribes. They worked among peoples—the

---

19. Eddius Stephanus, *The Life of Bishop Wilfrid,* chap. 2 in *Anglo-Saxon Saints and Heroes,* ed. Clinton Albertson (New York, 1967), 91.

Frisians, the Thuringians, and, most important, the Saxons—spread in an arc along the boundaries of the Frankish kingdom from the North Sea to Bavaria. The missionaries were inspired in part by a sense of kinship with these peoples and in part by the wandering ideals of Celtic monasticism, in essence taking up the missionary project from the disciples of Columbanus. The Anglo-Saxon monks were also true to the Roman side of their dual Christian ancestry, however; in these regions they established new bishoprics with close ties to Rome. A pattern to this work soon developed. The missionaries first constructed small churches served by monks, both Anglo-Saxons and native converts. These were often located on pagan sanctuaries or in the remains of long-abandoned Roman and Christian foundations. Next came more ambitious monasteries for the training of more missionaries, communities such as Fulda and Korvei. Nunneries were also established as the regions became pacified. Finally, the monastic leaders became bishops of newly created dioceses, journeying to Rome to receive their blessings and regalia from the pope.

The task was not an easy one. Tribal leaders resisted the changes, often violently. They recognized that conversion was simply a prelude to political domination by Christian kings. The Saxons destroyed some thirty missionary churches in 752 alone. Opportunities for heroism and even martyrdom were easily found by this new generation of soldiers of Christ. Not surprisingly, many were recognized as saints. For lands newly Christianized, a local, if not precisely native, saintly canon was thus established. The subjects of no less than five of the lives included in the present collection were Anglo-Saxon missionaries who left their English homes for work on the Continent: Willibrord of Northumbria (658–739), Boniface of Crediton (675–754), Willibald of Essex (d. 786), Leoba of Wessex (d. 780), and Willihad of Northumbria (d. 789). The presence of Leoba among them, as well as the presence of Huneberc—an Anglo-Saxon nun from the German nunnery of Heidenheim—among their hagiographers, signals the important role played by women in the second generation of the movement. The work begun by Anglo-Saxons was carried on by Continental Germans, some from neighboring regions, others local converts. Sturm (d. 779), whose life is also to be found in this collection, was from a Bavarian Christian family; as a disciple of Boniface, he labored as a missionary in Hesse and then was consecrated by his mentor as the first abbot of Fulda.

The posthumous presence of these recently deceased saints was also important in lands that lacked a long Christian heritage. Boniface's monastery at Fulda, for example, went to great lengths to secure the bones of its founder after his martyrdom. His tomb became the focus of its church, which also functioned as a cathedral for the surrounding region. The monks continued to enshrine more recently deceased saints, such as Sturm and Leoba. But throughout these borderlands, newly founded monasteries and episcopal sees also eagerly sought to obtain relics of saints of an older vintage, most especially martyrs. They obtained these from the ancient Roman cities of Italy, Spain, and France. The monks and clergy of these regions recognized the spatial and temporal distance that separated them from the venerable traditions of the saints within the Roman Empire. When the monastery of Korvei in Saxony obtained relics of Saint Vitus from Saint-Denis, the Frankish royal monastery located near Paris, one of the monks remarked that, since his brothers had constructed their community "among barbarian peoples" and so had no relics of a saintly patron, they had turned westward "for there are many relics in the land of the Franks."[20]

THE CAROLINGIAN ACHIEVEMENT

It was not only bones that came to Saxony from the lands of the Franks. Through the efforts of the Anglo-Saxon and German missionaries, the vast lands between the Rhine and Elbe rivers had been largely Christianized and pacified by the last decade of the eighth century. The missionaries had worked with the enthusiastic patronage and support of the Frankish kings. In the process, closer ties had been forged between the Frankish court and the popes in Rome.

In the middle part of the eighth century, a momentous dynastic change took place in the Frankish kingdom. The Carolingian family replaced the Merovingian dynasty that had ruled since the time of Clovis. The papacy in turn provided the sacred means of justification required by the upstart Carolingians when Stephen II consecrated Pepin as king of the Franks in 754. Even before that date the Carolingians had begun to expand their territories. Lands were added to the Frankish realm in every possible direction: to the east in Burgundy and Bavaria, to the south across the Alps and the Pyrenees in the Italian and Iberian Peninsulas, to the north in Frisia and Saxony. In these latter regions, conversion had led more or less inexorably to annexation. On Christmas Day in the year 800, Charlemagne, the greatest leader of the Carolingian dynasty, was acclaimed emperor in the city of Rome. He was the first man in

20. *Translatio sancti Viti martyris in Saxoniam*, chap. 13 in *Acta sanctorum ordinis sancti Benedicti*, 4.1:531.

more than three hundred years to bear that title in the west; he was also the first German ruler to be bold and confident enough to assume that Roman title. A German empire had been born in the west, but it had deep Roman and Christian roots.

The Carolingian rulers undertook an ambitious reform of both the machinery of government and the practice of Christianity within their lands. To aid them in formulating, articulating, and achieving their goals, they recruited scholarly clerics from all corners of Christendom. The circle of learned advisers that gathered around the Carolingian court—men such as Alcuin (a Northumbrian), Einhard (An Austrasian Frank), Theodulf (a Visigoth), Paschasius Radbertus (a Neustrian Frank), Walahfrid Strabo (an Alemann), and John Scottus Eriugena (an Irishman)—served as an important addition and even counterweight to the power of the military aristocracy. The reforming measures were promulgated in documents known as capitularies, as they were divided into chapters (Latin, *capitula*). In March 789 at Aachen Charlemagne issued the first, and probably the most programmatic, of his capitularies on ecclesiastical matters, the *Admonitio Generalis*. The emperor claimed that he sought to recall the peoples of his empire to the proper practice of Christianity through "visitation," "correction," and "admonition." All three paths firmly reinforced the control of the clergy over lay religious practices. The education and training of the clergy was presented as an overriding concern, one in which the composition, copying, and distribution of trustworthy texts was of paramount importance. The cult of the saints was not forgotten. The legislation mandated that "the false names of martyrs and the uncertain memorials of saints should not be venerated."[21] Five years later, the bishops whom the emperor gathered at Frankfurt were more explicit: "No new saints should be honored or invoked, nor shrines to them erected on the roads. Only those saints are to be venerated in a church who have been chosen on the authority of their passion or on the merit of their life."[22] The emperor was to play a role, along with the bishops, in controlling this aspect of religious practice. The Synod of Mainz declared in 813 that no new saint was to be recognized without "the council of the prince or license from a holy synod of bishops."[23] The effect of such legislation was an examination and sharp reduction of the canon of saints honored in most regions. To be sure, Alcuin and other court

21. *Admonitio Generalis*, c. 42 in *Capitularia Regum Francorum*, ed. Alfred Boretius, 2 vol. (Monumenta Germaniae Historica, Legum Sectio 2; Hannover, 1883–97), 1:56.

22. *Synodus Franconofurtensis*, c. 42 in *Capitularia Regum Francorum*, 1:77.

23. *Concilium Moguntinense*, c. 51 in *Concilia Aevi Karolini*, ed. Albert Werminghoff, 2 vols. (Monumenta Germaniae Historica, Legum Sectio 3, Concilia, 2; Hannover, 1906–8), 1:272.

scholars undertook to write the lives of such heroes of the missionary movement as Willibrord. Outside of the recently Christianized lands, however, few contemporaries came to be newly recognized as saints over the course of the ninth century.

There were some exceptions, notably Benedict of Aniane (d. 821). An abbot from Aquitaine famed for both his asceticism and his learning, he was chosen by Emperor Louis the Pious to spearhead the reform of monasticism. This Benedict chose the Rule composed long before by his namesake, Benedict of Nursia, to be the basic legislation for monastic life. The parallels between the efforts of the two abbots did not escape contemporary observers. Bishop Theodulf of Orléans wrote, "What Benedict [of Nursia] was as director in Italian lands, so you, Benedict [of Aniane] will be in our lands."[24] His reform program, however, did not consist simply of traditionalism or antiquarianism. Benedict of Aniane interpreted, expounded, and even expanded the sixth-century text at great length in a capitulary issued in 817. Indeed, his text was so novel that it in turn needed commentaries provided by Benedict himself and by Abbot Smaragdus of Saint-Mihiel. The emperor appointed visitors who were charged with seeing that the reforms were implemented in the individual abbeys of the realm. Ardo's life of Benedict—contained in this volume—was intended not only to celebrate the reforming abbot as a saint on the basis of his personal holiness, but also to serve as a template of and a gloss on his reforming program. Thus reform, scholarship, and hagiography worked hand in hand to achieve the goals of the *Admonitio Generalis*.

Despite the relative lack of contemporary saints, the ninth century was a great age of hagiography; in response to the need for texts that guaranteed the sanctity of traditional patrons as required by the legislation promulgated at Aachen, Frankfurt, and Mainz, Carolingian clerics produced many works that celebrated the saints of a now-distant Roman past. To cite only two examples by well-known authors, Hilduin of Saint-Denis (died c. 855) wrote about Denis (third-century bishop of Paris) and Hincmar of Reims (d. 882) about Remigius (sixth-century bishop of Reims). They pieced together bits of written and oral tradition, along with stereotypic stories borrowed from ancient and respected works of hagiography such as Sulpicius Severus's (died c. 420) life of Martin. These works were intended in part as spiritual reading for clerics and in part for a liturgical purpose, that is, to be recited on the feast days

---

24. Theodulf of Orléans, "Ad monachos sancti Benedicti," lines 23–24 in *Poetae Latini aevi Karolini*, ed. Ernst Dümmler, Ludwig Traube, Paul de Winterfeld, and Karl Strecker, 4 vols. in 6 (Monumenta Germaniae Historica, Poetae Latini medii aevi, 1–4; Berlin, 1881–1923), 1:520.

of such patron saints. In the ninth century Latin could still be understood, at least in a rough and ready way, by the lay populace in those regions where a Romance, rather than a Germanic, vernacular language was spoken. Laypeople were still part of the audience of hagiography. Hilduin composed his life of Denis at the request of Emperor Louis the Pious. Hincmar recognized the dual clerical and lay audiences of his work when he marked his life of Remigius with two symbols, one indicating those passages to be recited to the laity, the other indicating those reserved for the learned.

The ninth century also witnessed the widespread composition of hagiographic works that concerned the posthumous veneration of saints' relics. Monks compiled numerous collections of miracles performed at the shrines of the patron saints of their communities. They also recorded numerous ritual transfers—technically called translations—in which relics were moved from one shrine to another. An excellent example of a monastic shrine may be found in that of Saint Benedict of Nursia located at the monastery of Fleury on the Loire river near the city of Orléans. Such a shrine was central both to the spiritual identity and to the economy of the house. Legal documents specified the abbey as "the place where St. Benedict rests." In theory nobles made their donations not to the monks themselves, but to their patron saint. The number of pilgrims who came to the shrine could be quite large, particularly on the feast day of the saint. An abbot of Fleury later recalled, "A multitude turns out on [Benedict's] feastdays . . . some devoutly, others for pleasure, from all over they come to his most holy tomb. Not only countryfolk, but even people from the city, a mingling of noblemen and clerics, as well as some puffed-up sorts, they stream together rejoicing and devoutly seeking [the saint's] patronage."[25] Many monastic churches, including that of Fleury itself, however, remained closed to women. Special arrangements, such as the construction of chapels outside the cloister, had to be made in order to allow female pilgrims access to relics. Saints not only provided cures and mediation to their friends, but were thought capable of wreaking miracles of chastisement on those nobles who chose to steal their property. A monk of Fleury recorded how the community had brought the relics of Benedict to Count Odo of Orléans in a vain attempt to stop that local magnate from plundering their lands. When Odo died in battle, his demise was interpreted as an expression of the judgment of God. The saintly patron inherited from the late Roman Empire was changing into a saintly lord who defended his or her property—that is, ecclesiastical property, which consti-

25. Odo of Cluny, *Sermo de sancto Benedicto* in *PL*, 133:722.

tuted part of the kingdom of God on this earth—against the attacks of earthly lords. The battle lines were already being drawn for later, epic conflicts between religious and secular power.

TOWARD THE YEAR 1000

By the early ninth century Charlemagne had placed virtually all of western Christendom on the European continent at least nominally under a single political hegemony. The great islands to the west were no less Christian and they became closely tied to this Carolingian cultural world, although the Celtic and Anglo-Saxon kingdoms remained politically fragmented. Over the course of the ninth and tenth centuries, however, various non-Christian peoples began to raid these Christian lands: from the north, Scandinavians, known variously as Vikings, Norse, or Normans; from the east, Magyars and Slavs; from the south, Muslims. All came in search of plunder or slaves. In the process, monasteries and cathedrals were pillaged or destroyed and the relics of patron saints often had to be moved to new homes. The tale of the monks of Noirmoutier who wandered up the Loire river as far as Tournus carrying the relics of their patron, Saint Philibert, is one of the best known. They feared that "faithless men [that is, the Normans] would dig up the grave of the blessed Philibert and scatter whatever they found in it hither and yon, or rather throw it into the sea."[26] Non-Christians did not appreciate the value of the bones of the holy dead; they did, however, consider the reliquaries that housed those bones, adorned as they were with jewels and precious metals, to be valuable loot.

Unable to rely on the military protection of their kings and lords, clerics often looked instead to the miraculous powers of their patron saints. They recounted numerous stories in which those saints drove off or even killed attackers. A village near Angers celebrated how Saint Albinus—patron of their parish church and an early bishop of Angers—had appeared among them armed as a knight and led a successful defense against the raiding Normans. The monks of Fleury displayed a kind of trophy on the side of their church, a sculpture of the head of a warlord allegedly killed by the powers of their patron Benedict. A monk of Saint-Germain in Paris, recounting the exploits of his

---

26. Ermentarius, *The Miracles of St. Philibert* as translated in *The History of Feudalism*, ed. David Herlihy (New York, 1970), 9.

patron, had a Norman lord tell his king that "in Christian lands the dead have greater power than the living."[27] The power of the holy dead, at least in the stories put about by monks, was great indeed, a sacred bulwark against military threats.

Invasion and devastation, however, constituted only one side of the story; over the same period of time many of the peoples to the north and east of the western Christian world were being converted to Christianity. New bishoprics and monasteries were established in Poland, Bohemia, Hungary, and Denmark over the course of the tenth and early eleventh centuries. Scandinavian settlers in England, Ireland, and France were slowly drawn into Christian society. As in eighth-century Saxony, this new movement of conversion produced its own saintly heroes and martyrs, such as Archbishop Anskar of Bremen (801–865), King Edmund of East Anglia (841–869), Duke Wenceslas of Bohemia (907–929), and Archbishop Adalbert of Prague (d. 981). Relics of older saints were also translated to the new churches and shrines of these lands. Sometimes these took the form of gifts by Christian monarchs to the newly converted rulers of neighboring lands. The dukes of Bohemia received bones of Saint Vitus from the Ottonian rulers of Germany, while the kings of Poland accepted a copy of the Holy Lance that had pierced the side of Christ.

By the last quarter of the ninth century the Carolingian empire began slowly to dissolve, wracked by feud and civil war, as well as by the often devastating effects of Scandinavian, Muslim, and Slav raids. As one contemporary observer remarked, "After the death [of Emperor Charles the Fat in 888] the kingdoms which had remained under his control—as soon as they were deprived of a legitimate heir—broke apart at the seams and did not wait for a natural lord, but each one arranged to create a king for itself out of its own entrails."[28] By the year 1000 two kingdoms that would attain greatness— Germany (originally the east Frankish realm) and France (originally the west Frankish realm)—had been established in the rubble of the Carolingian empire. Meanwhile the many Anglo-Saxon kingdoms were being unified into a truly English realm, albeit one that would soon fall prey to foreign conquerors, the Danes in 1016 and the Normans in 1066. At the same time the fabric of these societies was being radically altered in a process historians have variously

27. Monk of Saint Germain, *Miracula sancti Germani in Normannorum adventu facta*, ed. Georg Waitz, chap. 30 in Monumenta Germaniae Historica, Scriptores in folio, 15.1:16.

28. Regino of Prüm, *Chronicon*, ed. Friedrich Kurze (Monumenta Germaniae Historica, Scriptores rerum Germanicarum in usum scholarum 11; Hannover, 1890), sub anno 888, p. 129.

labeled the "feudal transformation," the "making of the Middle Ages," or the "birth (awakening, crucible, childhood, ascent) of Europe."[29]

These political and social changes brought with them changes in the ideals of sanctity expressed in the hagiography of the tenth century.[30] To be sure, on the Continent, the Carolingian project of writing and rewriting the lives and miracles of long-dead patrons from the past continued, although with somewhat less urgency and vigor. Clerics from sees scattered across the old empire—Limoges and Trier, Liège and Metz, Perigueux and Toul—turned their attention to their early bishops, hoping to enhance the power and prestige of the contemporary episcopate. Similarly monks considered the careers of male and female monastic leaders—such as Abbot Ursmar of Lobbes, Abbess Rictrude of Marchiennes, and Abbess Glodesindis of Metz—who had served in the seventh and early eighth century, a period that came in the process to be portrayed as a kind of "golden age" of Frankish monasticism. Such hagiography tended to the traditional.

Innovation lay rather in the depiction of recently deceased figures. That a number of contemporary figures—most particularly those who were neither missionaries nor martyrs—came to be regarded as saints over the course of the tenth century departed from the traditional practice of the Carolingian ecclesiastical hierarchy. In the western Frankish kingdom (that is, France) and Lotharingia these contemporary saints tended to be abbots of leading communities in the monastic reform movement, such as Cluny and Fleury.[31] In Lotharingia, not only reforming abbots, but bishops sympathetic to such re-

---

29. See the titles of some of the surveys of this period: Jean-Pierre Poly and Eric Bournazel, *La mutation féodale, Xe–XIIe siècles* (Nouvelle Clio 16; Paris, 1980), English translation as *The Feudal Transformation, 900–1200,* trans. Caroline Higgitt (New York, 1991); Richard Southern, *The Making of the Middle Ages* (New Haven, 1953); Klaus Randsborg, ed., *The Birth of Europe* (analecta Romana Instituti Danici, supplementum 16; 1989); Philippe Wolff, *The Awakening of Europe,* trans. Anne Carter (Baltimore, 1968); Geoffrey Barraclough, *The Crucible of Europe: The Ninth and Tenth Centuries in European History* (Berkeley and Los Angeles, 1976); Robert Fossier, *L'Enfance de l'Europe (Xe–XIIe siècles). Aspects économiques et sociaux,* 2 vols. (Nouvelle Clio 17; Paris, 1982); Karl Leyser, *The Ascent of Latin Europe* (Oxford, 1986). For a critique of this thesis, see Dominique Barthelemy, "La Mutation féodale a-t-elle eu lieu?" *Annales E. S. C.* (1992): 367–77.

30. On Europe after the collapse of the Carolingian empire, two particularly interesting surveys are Poly and Bournazel, *The Feudal Transformation,* and Heinrich Fichtenau, *Living in the Tenth Century: Mentalities and Social Orders,* trans. Patrick Geary (Chicago, 1991). Both have perceptive comments about saints and their cults; the former also has an excellent bibliography.

31. For example, Abbot Odo of Cluny, Abbot Maiolus of Cluny, and Abbot Abbo of Fleury. A study of the cult of saints that spans the Carolingian and post-Carolingian periods in one important region may be found in Thomas Head, *Hagiography and the Cult of Saints: The Diocese of Orléans, 800–1200* (Cambridge, 1990).

form were regarded as saints.[32] In England the saints tended to be members of the supreme secular or ecclesiastical hierarchy, that is, royalty or bishops.[33] In the east Frankish realm (Germany), the newly installed Ottonian dynasty in essence combined these trends. Their saints were members of the royal family or the episcopal hierarchy, but their lives were composed and their cults promulgated by monastic reformers.[34]

One of the most important examples of tenth-century hagiography may be found below in the life of Gerald of Aurillac (855–909). He was a count, that is, the chief minister of the Carolingian monarch for a large region. Although not himself a monastic reformer, as were most tenth-century French saints, he was sympathetic to the reform movement and his life was composed by one of the most important members of that movement, Abbot Odo of Cluny (879–942), who was himself later celebrated as a saint. Gerald numbered aristocrats and, allegedly, saints among his forebears. It was local magnates such as Gerald whose power was at this time increasing, as the stature of the Carolingian kings declined. Odo portrayed this count as a soldier of Christ not just in a metaphorical sense, but literally as a knight who turned his warfare into a Christian way of life. Like a monk, Gerald practiced a life of prayer and asceticism, but he used his political and military power to protect the clergy and the poor. Odo's message was clear: an aristocrat might lead a life pleasing to God by providing for the peace and defending God's church. It was a message geared to a time of violent confrontation between the secular and ecclesiastic aristocracies. But it was a clerical ideal, and one intended largely for a clerical audience; by the middle of the tenth century the number of laypeople who could still comprehend Latin, even as a spoken language, was sharply diminishing.

The year 1000 will serve us in this collection, as it does many students of

32. For example, Abbot Gerard of Brogne, Bishop Gerard of Toul, Abbot John of Gorze, and Bishop Adalbero of Metz.

33. For example, King Edmund of East Anglia, Bishop Aethelwold of Winchester, Archbishop Dunstan of Canterbury, Archbishop Aelfege of Canterbury, and, a bit later, Queen Emma and King Edward the Confessor. The best guides to this hagiography are David Rollason, *Saints and Relics in Anglo-Saxon England* (Oxford, 1989) and Susan Ridyard, *The Royal Saints of Anglo-Saxon England: A Study of West Saxon and East Anglian Cults* (Cambridge, 1988).

34. For example, Duchess Oda (grandmother of Henry I), Queen Mathilda (wife of Henry I and mother of Otto the Great), Archbishop Brun of Cologne (brother of Emperor Otto the Great), Empress Adelaide (wife of Otto the Great), Bishop Wolfgang of Ratisbon, Bishop Ulrich of Augsburg, and, a bit later, Emperor Henry I and Empress Cunigunda (his wife). Little is available in English on Ottonian hagiography, but see Patrick Corbet, *Les saints ottoniens: Sainteté dynastique, sainteté royale et sainteté féminine autour de l'an mil* (Sigmaringen, 1986).

history, as both a convenient and a valid terminus. On the one hand, an enormous temporal and cultural distance separates the Roman province of Gaul in which Martin of Tours served as a bishop from the Carolingian counties such as the Auvergne that were governed by Gerald of Aurillac and his fellows in the Germanic military elite. By the year 1000 a new social world was forming, a world dominated by that elite. In that world new ideals of sanctity and new ways of utilizing the patronage of traditional saints would be forged. In a number of episcopal synods held around the year 1000, for example, the relics of local patron saints were gathered to serve as witnesses for the oaths that members of the military aristocracy would take to observe the so-called Peace of God.[35] On the other hand, there were substantial similarities in the stories told about Martin of Tours and Gerald of Aurillac. Both were soldiers who underwent a profound experience of conversion in which they consciously altered their lives to be more like Christ. Odo of Cluny doubtless had the work of Sulpicius Severus in mind and perhaps even in hand when he sat down to compose his account of the life of a Germanic warrior holding a Roman office and imbued with Christian virtue. To trace the similarities and differences in the ideas of Christian sanctity over the course of some six hundred years is to trace the processes by which the European identity was formed from its Roman, Christian, and Germanic elements.

35. On this movement, and the place of the relics of saints in it, see Thomas Head and Richard Landes, eds., *The Peace of God: Social Violence and Religious Response in France Around the Year One Thousand* (Ithaca, N.Y., 1992).

Sulpicius Severus

THE LIFE OF SAINT MARTIN OF TOURS

Translated by F. R. Hoare

Sulpicius Severus was born in about 363 to a well-off but not senatorial family from Aquitaine. After securing his primary education, perhaps at Bordeaux, Sulpicius went on to the study of law as a route into the imperial administration—a career that his social background was insufficiently exalted to assure him without such further training. A very good marriage also improved Sulpicius's social prospects.

By 392, after the early death of his wife, Sulpicius retired to a house owned by his mother-in-law and began there a form of ascetic retreat. Sulpicius seems to have fallen under the influence of his old friend Paulinus, who is best known in Christian history as Saint Paulinus of Nola (c. 355–431). Paulinus was the first of many Gallic aristocrats who renounced their possessions and worldly station to embrace a life of asceticism and withdrawal. Paulinus was healed of an eye ailment by Martin of Tours in about 389. His own retreat should be dated to this time or just a little later.

Eventually he settled at Nola in Italy where, from 395 to 404, he carried on a correspondence with Sulpicius.

In 393 or 394 Sulpicius visited Martin at Tours and was captivated by the personal charisma and spiritual power of this extraordinary holy man. He returned to his house-monastery at Primuliacum and began writing Martin's *Life*. By 395 Sulpicius was definitely a monk, although he seems to have adopted a less rigorous form of ascetic life than the one he encountered at Tours. The *Life of Martin* was probably issued in 396, in the year before Martin's death. Sulpicius may have been ordained a priest at some point (Gennadius, *De viris illustribus*, 19). He was involved in minor ways in some of the theological quarrels that disturbed the church in late antique Gaul. The date of Sulpicius's death is not known but he seems to have lived until at least 420.

Sulpicius, to whom the censorious Edward Gibbon attributed a "style not unworthy of the Augustan age," was a product of a great time of literary achievement in Gaul. His education was superb and his Latin style reveals a complete familiarity with the most up-to-date metrical and rhythmic conventions of the day. In addition to his *Life of Martin*, Sulpicius wrote three letters occasioned by the saint's death, the third of which movingly relates that death; a collection of *Dialogues* that contain accounts of Martin's miracles; and a *Chronicle* that is a history of the church from creation to the year 400. Sulpicius's writings reveal considerable familiarity with classical Latin authors, especially historical writers. Evident too are the Bible, the writings of some Latin Church Fathers, and earlier saints' lives. Sulpicius clearly knew Athanasius's *Life of Anthony*, a work written in 357 and at least twice translated into Latin, plus three saints' lives written by Jerome (342–420) who was, along with Ambrose and Augustine, among the greatest of the Church Fathers.

It is important to note that Sulpicius wrote at a time of great confusion. Gaul was, in his lifetime, the scene of civil wars, peasant uprisings, barbarian incursions, and dramatic imperial reorganization. This turbulent secular world serves as a backdrop to the apparently odd career patterns of men like Paulinus and Sulpicius. No less contentious was the ecclesiastical world of fourth- and fifth-century Gaul. As the church grew in importance, aristocratic factions struggled for its control. Theological controversies also appeared with regularity.

This was Martin's world too and some part of Sulpicius's task was to find a place in it for this strange ascetic holy man. Martin, after all, was the first ascetic to appear in Gaul. Tales about Martin, and Sulpicius's *Life*, popularized the monastic life, but Martin himself had no forerunners. Likewise, despite the Gospels, a few saints' lives, and some general conventions in Latin literature, Sulpicius had no firm guidelines for writing the life of a Gallic saint. One of his goals may have been to elevate Martin to the status of the heroic figures of the Egyptian desert. To some extent in the *Life*, and even more clearly in the *Dialogues*, Sulpicius may have been responding to Gallic critics of the strange, uncouth Martin. Gallic bishops were generally cultivated gentlemen, not wonder-working recluses.

Sulpicius's Martinian writings, the *Life* chief among them, were immensely popular, frequently copied, and deeply influential. Other texts in this collection will show some of the influence of Martin and his cult, and recent scholarship has traced the continuing influence of Martin well into the thirteenth century. The *Life* set a standard for saints' lives for a long time and helped to popularize monasticism in Rome's western provinces.

Martin was born circa 336 in Roman Pannonia (modern Hungary). He entered the army but soon regretted having done so. He longed for a life of Christian withdrawal and finally received permission from his superiors to leave the forces. Then, in a fairly traditional pattern, he experienced individual asceticism, learned from spiritual masters, and wound up as a master to others. Martin became bishop of Tours circa 372 and was regarded as something of an oddball by the cultured, elegant bishops of late antique Gaul. Undaunted, Martin carried on with his ascetic ways. He died in 397.

Texts and References

The preferred text of Martin's *Life* is Sulpice Sévère, *Vie de Saint Martin*, ed. and trans. Jacques Fontaine, 3 vols., Sources Chrétiennes, nos. 133, 134, 135 (Paris, 1967, 1968, 1969). Vol. 1 contains a general and literary introduction plus Latin texts and French translations of the *Life* and the *Letters*. Vols. 2 and 3 contain an extensive commentary. An outstanding introduction to Sulpicius is Claire Stancliffe, *St. Martin and His Hagiographer* (Oxford, 1983).

SEVERUS TO HIS MOST DEAR BROTHER DESIDERIUS[1]

Yes, brother and second self, I have written a little book on the life of our holy Martin, but I had decided to keep it uncopied and within the walls of my house. For I am the weakest of creatures and was loath to submit it to the

---

1. A friend and fellow monk of Sulpicius who received a letter from Paulinus. Probably the man who visited Jerome in Bethlehem in 398 and returned with texts for Sulpicius.

world's judgment, for fear that an all too unpolished diction should prove displeasing to the reader (as indeed I think it will) and that I should be deemed the proper object of general reprobation for having had the effrontery to annex a subject that should have been reserved for writers of competence. But when it is you who ask, and ask so often, I cannot say no. For what could I refuse to your affection, whatever the injury to my self-respect? Besides, I have let the book go to you with some confidence because I cannot think that you will betray it to anyone else, since that is what you have promised.

Nevertheless I have a fear that you may prove to be a gateway for it and that, if it once passes through, it can never be recalled. If that should happen, and you see it being read by others, will you, in your kindly indulgence, ask the readers to attend to the matter rather than to the language and not to take it too much to heart if a faulty locution should impinge upon their ears; for the Kingdom of God comes not by eloquence but rests upon faith. Let them remember also that salvation was not preached to the world by orators (though Our Lord could assuredly have arranged for that too, if it would have served His purpose), but by simple fishermen.

For my part, indeed, from the day that I set myself to write (thinking it a sin that the miracles of so great a man should remain unknown), I made up my mind to feel no shame for solecisms. For I had never attained to any great knowledge of these matters; and, if I had ever gleaned anything from the study of them, I had lost it all by long disuse. Spare me, however, the necessity for these painful excuses by letting the book be published, if you are agreeable, with the name suppressed. To make this possible, please erase it from the title-page, so that the silenced page announces (and what more is wanted?) the book's subject and does not announce the author.[2]

1

PREFACE

Many mortals, in the empty quest of earthly glory, have looked to win what they thought would be enduring remembrance for their own names by penning the lives of men of eminence. By so doing, they certainly gathered in, if nothing enduring, at least a little of the fruit for which they hoped, for they perpetuated their own memory, however uselessly; and their readers, too, were stirred to no little emulation by the pictures of great men thus set before them.

---

2. This introduction depends heavily on the conventions of ancient rhetoric. It is marked by an extended "humility (or modesty) topos." The author's protestations about his lack of ability are not to be taken seriously. In fact, they are to be taken in a sense almost exactly opposite to that expressed by the author.

But none of this anxiety of theirs was for the blessed and eternal life beyond; and how do they profit if their writings win a glory that must perish with this world? And what does posterity gain by reading of Hector fighting or Socrates philosophizing, seeing that it is not only folly to imitate them but madness to do less than wage strenuous war against them? For by valuing human life for its present activities only, they committed their hopes to romances, their souls to the tomb. Yes, they trusted for their immortality solely to the memories of men, whereas it is the duty of man to seek enduring life rather than enduring remembrance and to seek it, not by writing or fighting or philosophizing, but by a life of devotion, holiness and piety.

This common error, when perpetuated in literature, has had sufficient influence to send many questing after empty philosophy or that silly valor. For this reason I think it worth my while to write the life of a very holy man, to serve hereafter as an example to others and to rouse in the reader a desire for true wisdom, for the heavenly warfare and for a valor inspired by God. And I reckon that I too shall be the gainer by the work, in being able to look, not to a futile remembering by men, but to an eternal reward from God. For though I have not myself so lived that I can be an example to others, I have at least taken pains to ensure that one who really should be imitated does not remain unknown.

I shall proceed, then, to write the life of the holy man, Martin, as he lived it, first before he was a bishop and then during his episcopate, in spite of having been quite unable to ascertain all the facts. Thus, the things to which he himself was the only witness are not known at all, for he did not look for praise from men and, if it had rested with him, all his mighty works would have remained unknown. For matter of that, even of what I have ascertained I have omitted much, deeming it sufficient to record only what is outstanding. There was the reader also to be considered, who might be wearied by the accumulated mass of material. But I do ask those who are intending to read to give credence to what is said and not think that I have written anything not duly ascertained and tested. Rather than utter falsehoods, I would have chosen to say nothing at all.

2

Martin, then, was born[3] at the town of Sabaria, in Pannonia,[4] but was brought up in Italy, at Pavia. His parents were somewhat above the lowest

---

3. Probably in 336. He died in 397.
4. Now Szombathely in Hungary.

grade in worldly dignity, but were pagans. His father had begun life as a common soldier and rose to be a military tribune.[5] Martin himself in his youth served in the soldiery that uses earthly weapons, in the cavalry of the Imperial Guard under the Emperor Constantius,[6] and afterward under the Caesar Julian.[7] But it was not voluntary service, for, from almost the earliest years of his hallowed childhood, this remarkable boy aspired to the service of God.

At the age of ten, against the wish of his parents, he took himself off to a church and asked to be made a catechumen. He was soon in the most wonderful way wholly taken up with the work of God and at the age of twelve longed for the desert. His tender age prevented him from fulfilling his desire, but his mind, ever fixed on hermitages and the church, continued to dream, even in these boyhood years, of the life to which he was afterward consecrated.

But the emperors had issued an edict that the sons of veterans were to be registered for military service and his father, who grudged him his auspicious occupations, betrayed him to the authorities. Thus at the age of fifteen, as a prisoner in chains, he bound himself by the military oath. He was content with only one servant to attend on him and even then, topsy-turvy fashion, it was the master who performed the services, often to the extent of taking off the servant's boots himself and cleaning them. They took their meals together and it was generally the master who waited.

He was in the army nearly three years before his baptism but kept himself free from the vices in which men in that position are apt to indulge. Great was his kindness toward his fellow-soldiers, and wonderful his charity, while his patience and humility were more than human. As for abstemiousness, it is superfluous to praise it in him. He practiced it to such an extent that even at that time he was regarded as a monk rather than as a soldier.

In these ways he so won the hearts of all those serving with him that they felt for him a quite extraordinary affection, amounting to veneration. Though not yet reborn in Christ, he acted as one already robed in the good works of baptism—caring for the suffering, succoring the unfortunate, feeding the needy, clothing the naked, keeping nothing for himself out of his army pay beyond his daily food. For even then he was no deaf hearer of the Gospel, and he took no thought for the morrow.

---

5. A responsible position as the six tribunes in a legion each commanded several hundred men.
6. Constantius II, Roman emperor, 337–361.
7. Julian, "the Apostate," reigned 361–363.

3

So it came about that one day when he had nothing on him but his weapons and his uniform, in the middle of a winter that had been fearfully hard beyond the ordinary, so that many were dying of the intense cold, he met at the city gate of Amiens a coatless beggar.[8] This beggar had been asking the passers-by to take pity on him but all had gone past the unfortunate creature. Then the God-filled man understood, from the fact that no one else had had pity, that this beggar had been reserved for him. But what was he to do? He had nothing with him but the cape he had on, for he had already used up what else he had, in similar good works. So he took the sword he was wearing and cut the cape in two and gave one half to the beggar, putting on the rest himself again.

This raised a laugh from some of the bystanders, for he looked grotesque in the mutilated garment; but many had more sense, and sighed to think that they had not done something of the kind; indeed, having more to give, they could have clothed the beggar without stripping themselves. And that night, in his sleep, Martin saw Christ wearing the half of his cape with which he had clothed the beggar. He was told to look carefully at Our Lord and take note that it was the garment he had given away. Then he heard Jesus say aloud to the throng of angels that surrounded Him: "Martin is still only a catechumen but he has clothed Me with this garment."

But Our Lord Himself had once said: "As you did it to one of the least of my brethren, you did it to me" (Mt 25.40), and He was only acting on His own words when He declared that He had been clothed in the person of the beggar and reinforced His testimony to so good a deed by graciously showing Himself in the very garment that the beggar had received. But this most blessed man was not puffed up with vainglory by the vision but saw God's goodness in his own good deed. And being then twenty-two years old, he flew to be baptized. But he did not immediately abandon the military life, for he was overborne by the entreaties of his tribune, on whose personal staff he was serving and who promised him that when his term as tribune was over he would abandon the world. Buoyed up by this hope, Martin remained a soldier, though only in name, for nearly two years after his baptism.

8. This is the most famous scene in Martin's *Life*. It has been depicted in art countless times.

4

Meanwhile the barbarians were making incursions into Gaul and the Caesar Julian concentrated his army at Worms. There he began to distribute a bonus to the soldiers. They were called up one by one in the usual way until Martin's turn came. But he thought it would be a suitable time for applying for his discharge, for he did not think that it would be honest for him to take the bonus if he was not going to fight. So he said to the Caesar: "I have been your soldier up to now. Let me now be God's. Let someone who is going to fight have your bonus. I am Christ's soldier; I am not allowed to fight."

These words put the tyrant in a rage and he said that it was from fear of the battle that was to be fought the next day that he wanted to quit the service, not from religious motives. But Martin was undaunted; in fact he stood all the firmer when they tried to frighten him.

"If it is put down to cowardice," he said, "and not to faith, I will stand unarmed in front of the battle line tomorrow and I will go unscathed through the enemy's columns in the name of the Lord Jesus, protected by the sign of the Cross instead of by shield and helmet."

So he was ordered to be removed into custody so that he could prove his words and face the barbarians unarmed. The next day the enemy sent envoys to ask for peace, surrendering themselves and all they had. Who can doubt in these circumstances that this victory was due to this man of blessings and was granted to him so that he should not be sent unarmed into the battle? The good Lord could have kept His soldier safe even among the swords and javelins of the enemy but, to spare those hallowed eyes the sight of other men's deaths, He made a battle unnecessary. For Christ could not rightly have granted any other victory for the benefit of His own soldier than one in which the enemy were beaten bloodlessly and no man had to die.

5

After leaving the army he sought out the holy Hilary, bishop of Poitiers,[9] a man well known at that time for his proved fidelity in the things of God. He stayed with him for a while and Hilary tried to attach him more closely to himself and to bind him to the sacred ministry by conferring the diaconate[10] upon him. But he refused again and again, vehemently protesting his unwor-

---

9. C. 315–367, became bishop c. 353. He was involved in several bitter theological disputes.
10. The "major orders" of clergy were bishops, priests, deacons, and, sometimes, subdeacons.

thiness, until this deeply understanding man saw that there was only one way of keeping a hold on him and that was by conferring on him an office that could be taken as a slight on him. He therefore told him that he must be an exorcist,[11] and Martin did not resist ordination to this office for fear that it might look as if he regarded it as beneath him.

Not long after this he was prompted in a dream to pay a visit, in the cause of religion, to his native land and to his parents, who were still in the bondage of paganism. The holy Hilary gave his consent but by his many tearful entreaties laid him under an obligation to return. So he set off; but it is said that he felt depressed as he entered upon this journey, and called the brethren to witness that he would meet with many misfortunes, which did in fact come about.

First, he lost his way in the Alps and fell among brigands. One of them lifted his axe and poised it for a blow at his head but the other one checked his hand as he was striking. Eventually his hands were tied behind his back and he was handed over to the first as his prisoner, to be plundered. The brigand took him to a more secluded spot and began questioning him as to who he was. He replied that he was a Christian. Was he not afraid? asked the other. But he declared with the greatest firmness that he had never felt safer, since he knew that the Lord's compassion is never closer than when the trial comes; in fact, he was much more sorry for the other man, who was disqualifying himself for Christ's compassion by a life of brigandage.

Thus embarked upon a discussion of the Christian religion, he preached to the brigand the Word of God. But why make a long story of it? The brigand became a believer, escorted Martin back and put him on his way again, asking him to pray to Our Lord for him. He was seen afterward leading a pious life; indeed, the story I have just related is told as it came from him.

6

So Martin went on his way. He had passed Milan,[12] when the devil, taking human form, met him on the road and asked him his destination. Martin replied that his destination was where God was calling him.

---

11. There were four traditional "minor orders" of clergy: doorkeepers, lectors, acolytes, and exorcists. The usual role of the latter was to pray special prayers over catechumens, persons who were preparing to enter the church.

12. For much of the fourth century Milan in northern Italy was the location of the imperial court and the de facto capital of the western half of the empire.

"Then wherever you go," said he, "and whatever you attempt, you will have the devil against you."

To which Martin answered in the words of the Prophet: "With the Lord on my side I do not fear. What can man do to me?" (Ps. 117.6). And at once the enemy of souls vanished. Thus he carried out his purpose and plan and liberated his mother from the errors of paganism, though his father persisted in its evil ways. Moreover, he brought many to salvation by his example.

Now, the Arian heresy[13] had been making headway all over the world and particularly in Illyricum,[14] and presently Martin was contending most strenuously, almost single-handed, against infidelity in the episcopate. He suffered severely for this, for he was publicly flogged and in the end forced to leave the city. Returning to Italy, he learned that the church in Gaul was in a disturbed state also, with the departure of the holy Hilary, whom the heretics had forcibly driven into exile.[15] He therefore made himself a hermitage at Milan. But there too he became the object of the harshest persecution, at the hands of Auxentius,[16] the fountainhead and leader of Arianism there, who, after inflicting on him much ill-treatment, drove him from the city.

He now judged it best to accept the situation and retired to an island named Gallinaria,[17] with a priest of many virtues as his companion. Here he lived for some time on roots, and during this period he made a meal of hellebore, a plant that they say is poisonous. But when he felt the strength of the poison working in him, and death was imminent, he met the threatening danger with prayer and at once all the pain vanished.

Not long after this he learned that the emperor had repented, and had granted the holy Hilary leave to return. He therefore set out for Rome in the hope of meeting him there.

---

13. Arianism takes its name from Arius (c. 250–c. 336), a priest of Alexandria, who taught that Jesus Christ was "the first born of all creation," that is, not equal in time and substance to God the Father. His teachings were condemned at the Council of Nicaea in 325. Arianism, however, lasted well into the fifth century because some members of the imperial court favored it and because several barbarian peoples were converted to this form of Christianity.

14. Roughly, the lands that were until recently Yugoslavia.

15. Constantius II expelled many Catholic bishops from their sees. Hilary was banished to Phrygia in Asia Minor in 356. He so disturbed the Arians there that he was finally sent back to Gaul in 360. It is not known when or how he recovered the see of Poitiers.

16. An ardent Arian who was made bishop of Milan in 355 by Constantius II, himself an avowed adherent of the sect. Despite condemnations by popes and church councils, Auxentius held his bishopric until his death in 373/4.

17. Now Gallinare, a tiny island off the northwestern coast of Italy.

7

Hilary, however, had already passed through the city, so Martin followed in his track. He was given a very warm welcome by him and made himself a hermitage not far from the town.[18]

It was during this period that a certain catechumen joined him, who wished to be trained by this most holy man. After a few days he fell ill and lay racked by a high fever. Martin happened to be away at the time and when he returned on the third day he found a corpse; death had come so suddenly that he had departed this life without baptism.

The body had been laid out and was surrounded by sorrowing brethren, who were performing the sad rites, when Martin came hurrying up, weeping and uttering lamentations. But, with his whole soul possessed by the Holy Spirit, he ordered the others out of the cell where the body lay, fastened the door, and stretched himself out over the lifeless limbs of the dead brother. For some time he gave his whole self to prayer. Then, made aware by the Spirit of God that divine power was present, he raised himself a little, fixed his eyes on the dead man, and awaited without misgiving the outcome of his prayer and of the Lord's mercy. Hardly two hours had gone by before he saw the dead man stir slightly in all his limbs, then blink, as his eyes opened again to see. Then indeed he turned to the Lord with shouts of gratitude and filled the cell with the sound of them. The brethren standing outside the door heard and at once ran in. And what a marvellous sight! The man they had left dead, they saw alive.

Thus restored to life, he at once received baptism and lived for many years afterward. He was the first among us to be the subject of Martin's miracle-working and to bear witness to it. He was in the habit of relating how, when he was out of the body, he had been brought before the tribunal of the Judge and had heard the dismal sentence of consignment to a place of gloom among the generality of men.[19] Then two angels had represented to the Judge that he was the man for whom Martin was praying. He was therefore ordered to be taken back by these same angels and to be restored to Martin and to his former life.

The immense renown of this man of blessings dates from this time. He was already regarded by everybody as a saint; now he was looked upon as a man of power and in very truth an apostle.

---

18. At Ligugé.

19. This is one of the first references to Limbo, the place to which the souls of the unbaptized were consigned.

8

Not long after this he was passing by the farm of a man of good position by this world's reckoning, named Lupicinus,[20] when his attention was caught by the cries and wailings of a crowd of mourners. Much concerned, he stopped and enquired the reason for this weeping. He was told that a young servant belonging to the household had hanged himself. Hearing this, he went into the hut where the body lay, shut everybody out, laid himself upon the body and prayed for a while. Presently the dead man's features showed signs of life and his faded eyes looked into Martin's face. He made a long slow effort to raise himself, then took the hand of the man of blessings and stood upright on his feet. In this way, with all the crowd looking on, he walked with him up to the front of the house.

9

It was somewhere about this time that Martin was wanted as bishop of Tours.[21] But it was difficult to get him to leave his hermitage, so a citizen of Tours named Rusticus came and knelt at his knees and got him to come out by pretending that his wife was ill. A number of the townsmen had previously been posted along the road, and it was practically as a prisoner that he reached the city.

Incredible numbers had assembled in the most extraordinary way, not only of the people of Tours but also from neighboring towns, to give their votes. There was but one purpose among them; all had the same desire and the same opinion, which was that Martin was the fittest to be bishop and that the church would be fortunate to get such a priest. There were a few, however, including some of the bishops who had been summoned to consecrate the new prelate, who were so abandoned as to oppose. They said, if you please, that Martin was a despicable individual and quite unfit to be a bishop, what with his insignificant appearance, his sordid garments and his disgraceful hair. But the folly of these men, who in their very efforts to vilify this remarkable man were singing his praises, was laughed at by the people, whose judgment was sounder than theirs. Nor were they permitted to do anything contrary to what the people, by God's will, were purposing.

20. Surely an aristocrat (*honoratus secundum saeculum vir*) but nothing else is known about him.
21. Between 370 and 372.

Nevertheless, particularly strong resistance was offered, it is said, by one of the bishops present, named Defender.[22] It was much remarked, therefore, that he received unpleasant mention in the reading from the Prophets on that occasion. For it so happened that the lector whose turn it was to read had been held up by the crowd and was not in his place and, in the confusion among the ministers during the wait for the absentee, one of the bystanders picked up a psalter and plunged into the first verse he saw. It was: "By the mouths of babes and infants thou hast founded a bulwark to still the enemy and the avenger [that is, defender]" (Ps. 8.3). When these words were read, the congregation raised a shout and the opposition was put to shame; and it was generally thought that God had prompted the reading of this particular psalm in order that Defender should hear its condemnation of his proceedings. For while the praise of the Lord had been brought to perfection out of the mouths of babes and sucklings in the person of Martin, he himself had been exposed as an enemy and destroyed at the same time.

10

What Martin was like, and his greatness, after entering the episcopate, it is beyond my powers to describe. For with unswerving constancy he remained the same man as before. There was the same humble heart and the same poverty-stricken clothing; and, amply endowed with authority and tact, he fully sustained the dignity of the episcopate without forsaking the life or the virtues of the monk.

For a time he occupied a cell next to the cathedral. Then, when he could no longer endure the disturbance from his many visitors, he made himself a hermitage about two miles from the city.[23] The place was so secluded and remote that it had all the solitude of the desert. On one side it was walled in by the rockface of a high mountain, and the level ground that remained was enclosed by a gentle bend of the River Loire. There was only one approach to it, and that a very narrow one.

His own cell was built of wood, as were those of many of the brethren; but most of them had hollowed out shelters for themselves in the rock of the overhanging mountain. There were about eighty disciples there, being trained in the pattern of their most blessed master. No one possessed anything of his

---

22. Bishop of Angers.
23. At the site that became Marmoutier.

own; everything was put into the common stock. The buying and selling that
is customary with most hermits was forbidden them. No craft was practiced
there except that of the copyist, and that was assigned to the younger men.
The older ones were left free for prayer.

It was seldom that anyone left his cell except when they assembled at the
place of worship. All received their food together after the fast was ended. No
one touched wine unless ill health forced him to do so. Most of them wore
clothes of camel's hair; softer clothing was looked upon as an offense there.
This must be regarded as all the more wonderful because there were many
among them of noble rank, who had been brought up to something quite
different before forcing themselves to this lowliness and endurance. Many of
them we have since seen as bishops. For what kind of city or church would it be
that did not covet a bishop from Martin's monastery?[24]

11

But I must come to his other miracles, performed during his episcopate.

Not far from the town, and near the monastery, there was a place to which
sanctity had been mistakenly attributed with the idea that martyrs were buried
there. There was even an altar there, erected by previous bishops. But Martin
did not lightly give credence to uncertainties, and made constant efforts to get
from the older priests and clerics the name of the martyr and the occasion
when he suffered. He explained that he felt grave doubts of conscience, seeing
that no certain and settled tradition had come down to them.

For some time, therefore, he kept away from the place, not condemning
such veneration, since he was not sure of his ground, but at the same time not
lending his authority to popular opinion, in case he should be strengthening a
superstition. Then one day he took with him a few of the brethren and went to
the place. Standing on the grave itself, he prayed to Our Lord to make it
known who was buried there and what his character had been. Then, turning
to the left, he saw a ghost standing close by, foul and grim. He ordered him to

---

24. This passage relates more to the 390s, when Sulpicius visited Martin, than to the 370s,
when Martin was just beginning his episcopal and monastic careers. It is important to see that
Martin progressed from living alone in a cell or hermitage to a life in community with his
brethren. Martin, the solitary, had become a proponent of "cenobitic" (from Greek *koinos bios*,
"common life") monasticism as opposed to "eremitic" (from Greek *heremos*, "desert," implying
solitude, seclusion) monasticism. Throughout late antiquity and the early Middle Ages there was
tension between individual and communal forms of monastic life.

give his name and character. He gave his name and confessed to a guilty past. He had been a robber, and had been executed for his crimes, but had become an object of devotion through a mistake of the common people. In reality he had nothing in common with martyrs; glory was their portion, punishment his.

The others who were present had heard a voice speaking in an inexplicable manner but had seen no one. Martin now described what he had seen and gave orders for the altar that had stood there to be removed. Thus he rid the population of a false and superstitious belief.

12

Some time after this he happened, when on a journey, to encounter the corpse of a pagan being carried to its grave with superstitious rites. He had seen the approaching crowd from a distance and stopped for a little, not knowing what it was, for there was nearly half a mile between them and it was difficult to distinguish what he saw. He made out, however, a band of rustics, and linen cloths (that had been spread over the body) fluttering in the wind. He supposed, therefore, that unhallowed sacrificial rites were being performed, for it was the custom of the Gallic rustics, in their lamentable infatuation, to carry round their fields the images of the demons covered with white veils. With uplifted hand, therefore, he made the sign of the cross before the approaching crowd and ordered them not to move from where they were and to put down what they were carrying.

Then indeed there was a wonderful sight to be seen. First the unfortunate creatures turned as rigid as rocks. Then they tried with all their might to advance but, being quite unable to move forward, they kept turning round in the most ridiculous whirligigs. Finally, completely beaten, they put down the body they were carrying and, looking at one another in their bewilderment, silently speculated as to what had happened to them. However, when the man of blessings found that the assemblage was a funeral procession and not for sacrifices, he raised his hand again and set them free to pick up the body and go on. Thus, when he wished, he made them halt and when he chose he let them go.

13

Again, in a certain village he had demolished a very ancient temple and was proceeding to cut down a pine tree that was close to the shrine, when the priest of the place and all his pagan following came up to stop him. These same people had been quiet enough, at Our Lord's command, while the temple was being thrown down but they were not prepared to see the tree felled. He painstakingly explained to them that there was nothing sacred about a tree trunk and that they had much better be followers of the God he himself served. As for the tree, it ought to be cut down because it was dedicated to a demon.

Then one of them, more audacious than the rest, said to him: "If you have confidence in the God you say you worship, stand where the tree will fall, and we will cut it down ourselves; and if your Lord, as you call Him, is with you, you will not be harmed."

Martin, with dauntless trust in God, undertook to do this. Thereupon all the assembled pagans agreed to the bargain, reckoning the loss of their tree a small matter if, in its downfall, it crushed the enemy of their religion. And as the pine leaned to one side, so that there was no doubt on which side it would fall when cut through, Martin was bound and made to stand on the spot chosen by the rustics, where they were all quite sure that the tree would come down. Then they began to cut down the tree themselves with great joy and delight. A wondering crowd stood at a little distance.

Gradually the pine began nodding and a disastrous fall seemed imminent. Standing at a distance, the monks grew pale; and, so frightened were they as the danger drew near, that they lost all hope and courage, and could only await the death of Martin. He, however, waited undaunted, relying on the Lord. The tottering pine had already given a crack, it was actually falling, it was just coming down on him, when he lifted his hand and met it with the sign of salvation.

At that—and you would have thought it had been whipped like a top—the tree plunged in another direction, almost crushing some rustics who had ensconced themselves in a safe place. Then indeed a shout went up to heaven as the pagans gasped at the miracle, the monks wept for joy, and all with one accord acclaimed the name of Christ; and you may be sure that on that day salvation came to that region. Indeed, there was hardly anyone in that vast multitude of pagans who did not ask for the imposition of hands,[25] abandoning his heathenish errors and making profession of faith in the Lord Jesus.

It is certainly a fact that before Martin's time very few, in fact hardly anyone, in those parts acknowledged Christ but now His name, thanks to Martin's miracles and example, has gained such a hold that there is no district there not filled with crowded churches or with monasteries. For he immediately built a church or a monastery in every place where he destroyed a pagan shrine.

25. A rite performed by exorcists (see note 11). The implication is that these pagans were being admitted as catechumens.

14

It was somewhere about this time that in the course of this work he performed another miracle at least as great. He had set on fire a very ancient and much frequented shrine in a certain village and the flames were being driven by the wind against a neighboring, in fact adjacent, house. When Martin noticed this, he climbed speedily to the roof of the house and placed himself in front of the oncoming flames. Then you might have seen an amazing sight—the flames bending back against the force of the wind till it looked like a battle between warring elements. Such were his powers that the fire destroyed only where it was bidden.

In a village named Levroux, however, when he wished to demolish in the same way a temple that had been made very rich by its superstitious cult, he met with resistance from a crowd of pagans and was driven off with some injuries to himself. He withdrew, therefore, to a place in the neighborhood where for three days in sackcloth and ashes, continuously fasting and praying, he beseeched Our Lord that the temple that human hands had failed to demolish might be destroyed by divine power.

Then suddenly two angels stood before him, looking like heavenly warriors, with spears and shields. They said that the Lord had sent them to rout the rustic host and give Martin protection, so that no one should hinder the destruction of the temple. He was to go back, therefore, and carry out faithfully the work he had undertaken. So he returned to the village and, while crowds of pagans watched in silence, the heathen sanctuary was razed to its foundations and all its altars and images reduced to powder.

The sight convinced the rustics that it was by divine decree that they had been stupefied and overcome with dread, so as to offer no resistance to the bishop; and nearly all of them made profession of faith in the Lord Jesus, proclaiming with shouts before all that Martin's God should be worshiped and the idols ignored, which could neither save themselves nor anyone else.

15

I will also relate what happened in the country of the Aedui.[26] He was demolishing a temple there also, when a frenzied mob of rustic pagans made a rush at him and one of them, more audacious than the rest, drew his sword and went for him. Throwing back his cloak, Martin offered his bare neck to the stroke.

26. The area around modern Autun, a long way from Tours.

Nor was the pagan slow to strike but, when his hand was well above his head, he fell flat on his back. Stricken with the fear of God, he asked for pardon.

Nor was the following incident dissimilar. Once, when he was destroying some idols, someone planned to stab him with a large knife. But in the very act of striking, the weapon was struck from his hand and disappeared. More often, however, when the rustics were protesting against the destruction of their shrines, he so subdued their pagan hearts by his holy preaching that the light of the truth penetrated to them and they themselves threw down their own temples.

16

He had the gift of healing in such a degree that a sick man hardly ever came to him without at once being cured, as may easily be seen from the following example. There was a girl at Trier[27] who was suffering from such acute paralysis that for a long time she had been altogether without the use of her body. She was as good as dead in every part of her and drew only a fluttering breath. Her grieving relatives surrounded her, only awaiting her death.

Suddenly it was announced that Martin had come to the city. When the girl's father heard the news, he ran breathlessly to plead for his daughter. It happened that Martin had already entered the cathedral. There, with the congregation looking on and many other bishops present, the old man with loud lamentations clasped his knees.

"My daughter," he said, "is dying of a disease of the most pitiable kind and—worse than death—is alive only in her breathing; her body is already a corpse. Please come to her and bless her. I am sure that you are the one to make a cure."

Dumbfounded and embarrassed by such language, Martin tried to refuse. He protested that the matter was not in his province; the old man was mistaken about him and he was quite unworthy to be used by Our Lord for such a manifestation of power. But the weeping father continued to insist passionately and to beg him to come and see the lifeless body. In the end he was overborne by the bishops standing by, and went with him to the girl's home.

A huge crowd was waiting at the street door to see what the servant of God would do. First he resorted to his usual weapons in cases of this kind and

---

27. A Roman administrative center in the Rhineland that was from 361 to 392 the effective capital of the western Roman Empire.

prostrated himself on the ground in prayer. Then, after looking at the sick girl, he asked to be given some oil. This he blessed, then poured the hallowed liquid, now a powerful remedy, into the girl's mouth. At once her voice came back to her. Then, at his touch, little by little each of her limbs began to recover its life. Finally, in the sight of all, she rose and stood firmly on her feet.

17

On this same occasion, a servant of a man of proconsular rank named Tetradius,[28] having been entered by a demon, was dying pitiably in agonies. Martin was therefore asked to lay his hands on him. He ordered the man to be brought to him, but it proved impossible to get the wicked spirit out of the hut where he was, such frenzied attacks did he make with his teeth on anyone who approached.

Tetradius then came and knelt at the knees of the man of blessings and begged him to come himself to the house where the demoniac lived. Martin, however, protested that he could not go to the unhallowed house of a pagan. For Tetradius at that time was still held fast in the errors of paganism. He therefore promised that, if the demon were expelled from the boy, he would become a Christian. Martin then laid his hands on the boy and drove the evil spirit out of him. Tetradius, on seeing this, made profession of faith in the Lord Jesus. He became a catechumen at once and was baptized not long afterward. He always cherished an extraordinary affection for Martin as the instrument of his salvation.

At this same time and in the same town he was entering the house of a certain householder when he stopped on the threshold, saying that he saw a frightful demon in the hall. When he ordered it to go, it took possession of the master of the house, who was waiting for Martin in the interior of the house. The unhappy man began to gnash his teeth and to maul everyone who approached him.

The house was thrown into disorder, the slaves were all confused and there was a rush to get out of the way. Martin placed himself before the frenzied man and began by ordering him to stand still. But he still kept gnashing his teeth and opening his mouth to bite. Martin then put his fingers into the gaping mouth, saying: "If you have any power at all, devour these." At this the man drew his jaws back wide apart, as if he had a red-hot iron between

---

28. An aristocrat and high imperial official from the region of Trier.

them, trying to avoid touching the fingers of the man of blessings. Eventually he was forced by penalties and torments to abandon the body he occupied and, not being allowed to go out through the mouth, was discharged in the excrement, leaving filth behind him.

18

Meanwhile the city had been alarmed by a sudden rumor of a movement and inroad of the barbarians, so Martin ordered one of the demoniacs to be brought to him and told him to say whether the report was true. He admitted that there had been ten demons besides himself who had spread this rumor through the population, in the hope that by the ensuing panic, if by nothing else, Martin might be driven from the town; there was nothing further from the minds of the barbarians than an invasion. This admission was made by the evil spirit before everybody in the cathedral and freed the city from the disquieting fears that had been overhanging it.

Then again, at Paris he was passing through the city gates accompanied by a great crowd when, to everybody's horror, he kissed the pitiable face of a leper and gave him his blessing. The man was at once cleansed from all trace of his affliction, and coming to the cathedral the next day with a clear skin he gave thanks for his recovered health. And I must not omit to mention the frequent miracles that threads pulled from Martin's clothing or hairshirt worked on the sick. When tied round a finger or hung round the neck of the patient, they often banished his malady.

19

Arborius[29] was a man of prefectorial rank and of conspicuous holiness and strong faith. He had a daughter who was wasting away from the acute fevers of a quartan ague. A letter from Martin happened to be brought to him and he placed it in her bosom at the very moment when her temperature was rising and at once the fever left her. This made such an impression on Arborius that he immediately made an offering of his daughter to God and dedicated her to perpetual virginity. He then set off to visit Martin and presented the girl to

29. A man of senatorial rank, the highest. It is important to note the kind of people with whom Sulpicius associates Martin.

him as concrete evidence of the extent of his powers, seeing that she had been cured by him from a distance; nor would he allow the ceremony of her clothing and consecration as a virgin to be performed by anyone but Martin.

A man named Paulinus,[30] who was afterward to be an example to all, had begun to suffer from acute pain in one eye and a fairly thick film had by now grown over the pupil. Martin, by touching the eye with a fine paintbrush, restored it to its former state and at the same time banished all the pain.

Martin himself once by some accident fell from an upstairs landing and rolled down a rough uneven staircase, receiving many injuries. As he lay half-dead in his cell in extreme pain, an angel appeared to him during the night and washed his wounds and dressed his bruises with a healing ointment. By the next day he was so sound and well that you would have thought he had not been injured at all.

But it would be tedious to go through all the instances; and these few out of a great number must suffice. Let it be enough if in things so surpassing I have told the whole truth, and among so many have never been wearisome.

20

In the midst of these great matters I must insert some lesser ones—though, in truth (such is the general depravity and corruption of our times) it must be reckoned a sufficiently remarkable occurrence when the firmness of the churchman does not give place to the fawning of the courtier.

Many bishops, then, from various parts of the world had assembled to meet the Emperor Maximus,[31] a man ferocious by nature and, moreover, elated by his victory in a civil war. The foul fawning of all of them upon the sovereign was much remarked, and the dignity of the priesthood with unworthy weakness lowered itself to win imperial patronage. Martin alone retained apostolic authority. For even when he had to petition the Emperor on somebody's behalf, he commanded rather than requested and, though frequently invited to his banquets, he kept away, saying that he could not sit at table with a man who had robbed one emperor of his throne and another of his life.

Maximus, however, maintained that he had not become emperor of his own

---

30. This is Paulinus of Nola (mentioned above, page 1), an aristocrat from Bordeaux.

31. Ruler in Gaul, 383–388, he had been commander of Roman troops in Britain. His soldiers were intensely loyal to him and he invaded Gaul in an attempt to improve their lot. He was ardently Catholic and earned Martin's displeasure by putting to death for sorcery an obscure Spaniard named Priscillian. Martin, and others, seem to have thought Priscillian guiltless.

accord but had simply been defending by the sword the burden of rule that had been thrust upon him by the soldiers at God's prompting. And God's will could hardly be against a man who, by such an unbelievable turn of events, had ended victorious. He added that none of his opponents had fallen except in battle. In the end Martin was so far overcome by his arguments and entreaties as to attend a banquet, to the enormous delight of the emperor at having gained his point.

Invitations were sent out as if for a great festival and among the guests were men of the very highest rank, including Evodius,[32] who was prefect, and consul also, and one of the most upright men that ever lived, and two counts wielding immense authority, the brother and the uncle of the emperor. Between these sat one of Martin's priests, Martin himself occupying a stool placed next to the emperor. Toward the middle of the meal a servant, in accordance with custom, brought a goblet to the emperor. He ordered it to be given instead to our most holy bishop and waited expectantly to receive it from the bishop's own hands. But Martin, after drinking himself, passed the goblet to his priest, holding that no one had a better right to drink immediately after himself and that it would not be honest of him to give precedence over the priest either to the emperor or to those who ranked next to him.

The emperor and all who were present were so struck by this action that the very gesture by which they had been humiliated became for them a source of pleasure. And the news went all around the palace that Martin had done at the emperor's table what no other bishop would have done even when dining with the least of his magistrates.

He also foretold, long beforehand, to this same Maximus that if he made an expedition into Italy, where he was wanting to go, in order to make war on the Emperor Valentinian,[33] he could count on being victorious at the first onset but also on utter destruction a little later. And this we saw come to pass. For at his first approach Valentinian fled; then, less than a year later, on taking up arms again, he captured and killed Maximus within the walls of Aquileia.

21

It is certain that Martin actually saw angels very often, even to the extent of engaging in continuous conversation with them. As for the devil, it was so

32. Praetorian Prefect (second-in-command) to Maximus and consul for 386.
33. Valentinian II, western Roman emperor, 375–392.

fully within his power to see him that he recognized him under any form, whether he kept to his own character or changed himself into any of the various shapes of "spiritual wickedness."

When the devil found that he could not avoid recognition, then, since stratagems failed to deceive, he frequently assailed him with violent abuse. Once he burst into his cell with a tremendous clatter, holding in his hand a bloodstained ox-horn. Fresh from committing crime, he displayed his right hand covered with blood. "Martin," he said gleefully, "where is your power? I have just killed one of your people." Martin thereupon called the brethren together and told them what the devil had revealed and ordered them to go carefully through all the cells to see who had been the victim of the tragedy. They reported that none of the monks was missing but that a rustic hired to cart wood was gone into the forest. He told some of them, therefore, to go and meet him. Thus he was found not far from the monastery, already almost lifeless. But, though at his last gasp, he made it plain to the brethren how he came by his mortal wound. He was tightening up some thongs that had got loose on his team of oxen when an ox had tossed its head and dug a horn into his groin. And before long he was dead.

You must judge for yourself of God's reasons for permitting the devil to wield such power. As regards Martin, the marvel lay in the fact that, in the instance just related and also in many others of the same kind, no matter how often they happened, he foresaw the event far in advance or else was given news of it and announced it to the brethren.

22

Quite often, however, the devil, resorting to a thousand malicious tricks to score off the holy man, would thrust his visible presence upon him under forms of the utmost diversity. Sometimes he presented himself with features disguised to resemble Jupiter, very frequently Mercury, often even Venus or Minerva. Against him, Martin, undaunted always, would protect himself with the sign of the cross and the power of prayer. Very frequently, violent scolding could be heard, when a crowd of demons was abusing him in impudent language; but Martin, knowing that it was all false and baseless, remained unmoved by their accusations.

Some of the brethren used even to tell how they had heard a demon in impudent language wanting to know why Martin had admitted into the monastery after their repentance certain brethren who had lost the grace of baptism by various misdeeds—and he specified the crimes of each. Martin had defended himself against the devil most firmly, saying that former offenses could be wiped out by leading a better life and that the Lord in His mercy had ordained that absolution from their sins was to be given to those who had left off sinning. To this the devil had retorted that there was no problem for the guilty and it was impossible for the Lord to extend His mercy to those who had once fallen away.

At this Martin exclaimed (so it is said): "If you yourself, wretched being, would cease to prey upon mankind and would even now repent of your misdeeds, now that the Day of Judgment is at hand, I have such trust in the Lord Jesus Christ that I would promise you mercy."

What a holy boldness, so to presume on the loving-kindness of Our Lord! For even though he could quote no authority for this, he showed where his feelings lay.

And, as we are on the subject of the devil and his wiles, it would seem not out of place, though not strictly relevant, to relate the following incident, partly because Martin's miraculous powers do to some extent appear in it and partly because a situation that was deemed worthy of a miracle may well be put on record, to serve as a warning should anything of the kind occur anywhere again.

23

There was a young man of most noble birth named Clarus, who afterward became a priest and is now entitled by his happy end to be numbered among the blest. He had left all and gone to join Martin and very soon was a shining example of the highest degree of faith and of all the virtues. He had established himself in a hut not far from the bishop's monastery and had many brethren living round him. Thus there came to him a youth named Anatolius, who used the monastic way of life to make a false display of humility and innocence, and for a time shared the common life with the others.

Then, as time went on, he began to speak of angels that were in the habit of conversing with him. As nobody would credit this, he produced certain manifestations that did induce a number to believe. Eventually he reached the point of asserting that angelic messengers passed between himself and God; and it was now his ambition to be regarded as one of the Prophets.

But nothing could persuade Clarus to believe in him. Anatolius began threatening him with the wrath of God and immediate chastisement for not believing in a saint. He is said to have burst out finally into this speech:

"I tell you, this very night God will give me a shining robe from out of heaven and I will make my abode among you clad in it, and it shall be a sign to you that in me dwells the Power of God, who has presented me with His garment."

This declaration roused everybody to the highest pitch of expectation. And indeed, about midnight, the heavy thudding of dancing feet seemed to shake the ground under every hermitage in the place. You could see, too, the cell that housed this young man ablaze with a mass of lights; and there was heard the thudding of feet running about in it, and what might have been the murmur of many voices.

Then came silence and he emerged and called one of the brethren, named Sabatius, and showed him the tunic he was wearing. The brother in amazement called the rest to come, and even Clarus came hurrying up. A light was brought and all carefully inspected the garment. It was exceedingly soft, with a surpassing luster, and of a brilliant scarlet, but it was impossible to tell the nature of the material. At the same time, under the most exact scrutiny of eyes and fingers it seemed to be a garment and nothing else.

Meanwhile Clarus[34] had been urging the brethren to pray their hardest to be shown by the Lord what it was. The rest of the night, therefore, was spent in singing hymns and psalms. At daybreak he took Anatolius by the hand with the intention of taking him to Martin, being well aware that Martin could not be taken in by a trick of the devil. At this, the wretched man began to resist and protest loudly, saying that he had been forbidden to show himself to Martin. And when he was being forced to go against his will, between the hands of those who were dragging him the garment disappeared. Who, then, can doubt that Martin had this power also, that the devil was unable to keep up his illusions or conceal their nature when they were to be submitted to Martin's eyes?

24

It was remarked, however, about this same time that a youth in Spain acquired some authority by a number of manifestations and this so turned his head that he gave himself out to be Elijah. When many were so rash as to believe this, he went further and said that he was Christ. Even then he took some people in, and a bishop named Rufus adored him as God, for which we afterward saw him deposed from his office.

---

34. A well-born local man, one of Martin's earliest disciples. He became a priest in Tours and died shortly before Martin.

Again, many of the brethren have told me that at the time period there was someone in the East who boasted that he was John. We can infer from this that, with false prophets of this kind about, the coming of Antichrist is at hand; for in them he is already active, as the mystery of iniquity.

Nor do I think I should pass over a very skillful ruse that the devil tried on Martin about this period. One day, announcing himself by a salutation, he came and stood before Martin as he was praying in his cell. He was enveloped in a bright red light, thinking to deceive more easily if he shone with borrowed splendor. He wore, too, a royal robe and was crowned with a diadem of gems and gold, and gold gleamed upon his shoes. His face was serene and his expression joyful, so that he should be thought anything rather than the devil.

At the first sight of him, Martin was staggered and for a long time there was complete silence between them. The devil spoke first.

"Martin," he said, "you see me. Acknowledge me. I am Christ. I am about to come down upon the earth and I wished first to manifest myself to you."

Martin received this in silence and made no kind of response, and the devil had the audacity to repeat his daring claim.

"Martin," he said, "why so slow to believe, now that you see? I am Christ."

Then, enlightened by the Holy Spirit, Martin knew that it was the devil and not Our Lord.

"The Lord Jesus," said he, "did not say that he would come in purple robe and glittering diadem. I will only believe in a Christ who comes in the garments and the lineaments of His passion, who comes bearing upon Him the wounds of the cross."

At these words the devil immediately vanished like smoke, filling the cell with such a stench as to put it beyond doubt that it was the devil indeed. And should anyone think that I am romancing, I had the story, just as I have told it, from Martin's own lips.

25

You must understand that I had previously heard accounts of his faith, his life, and his powers and burned with the desire to know the man himself. I therefore undertook as a labor of love a pilgrimage to see him. At the same time I was all on fire to write his life and I collected part of my information from him, so far as it was possible to question him, and learned the rest from those who had firsthand knowledge.

You would never credit the humility and kindness with which he received me on that occasion. He congratulated himself and praised the Lord because I had thought so highly of him that I had undertaken a long journey especially to see him. And poor me!—I hardly dare say it—when he condescended to let me sit at his sacred board, it was he who fetched the water for me to wash my hands and, in the evening, it was he who washed my feet. Nor had I the courage to remonstrate or resist. I was so overborne by his authority that I would have felt it impious to do anything but acquiesce.

But all his talk while I was there was of the necessity of renouncing the allurements of the world and the burdens of secular life in order to follow the Lord Jesus freely and unimpeded. He quoted as an outstanding example in our own day the case of his excellency Paulinus, whom I mentioned earlier. He had abandoned immense wealth to follow Christ and was almost alone in our times in fulfilling the evangelical counsels. "There," Martin kept exclaiming, "there is someone for you to follow. There," he cried, "is someone to imitate." He held that our generation was blessed in possessing such an example of faith and virtue. For a rich man with great possessions, by selling all and giving to the poor, had illustrated Our Lord's saying, that what is impossible to do is in fact a possibility.

But what seriousness there was, what dignity, in Martin's words and conversation! And how eager he was, and forceful, and how promptly and easily he solved scriptural problems. I know that many are skeptical on this last point; indeed, I have seen some still incredulous even when it was I myself who told them. I therefore call Jesus to witness, and the hope we all hold in common, that never from any other lips have I heard so much knowledge, so much natural talent, and such purity of diction. It is little enough praise when we remember Martin's miracles, but it may surely rank as a wonder that not even this gift was lacking in a quite uneducated man.

26

But my book is asking to be ended, my story must be brought to a close, not because there is no more to be said about Martin, but because I, like an indolent craftsman,[35] growing careless as his task is ending, have abandoned the effort, beaten by the weight of the material. For although it was possible to depict his outward actions in words (after a fashion), no language at all—none,

35. The feigned humility here echoes that of the introductory chapters. This is a commonplace of ancient literature taken over by hagiographers. It is to be taken seriously but not literally.

I can say with truth—could ever depict his interior life, his everyday behavior and his mind ever fixed upon heaven. I say again, not even Homer, if, as the saying goes, he returned from Hades, could do justice to his perseverance and self-discipline in abstinence and fasting; to his capacity for night vigils and prayer; to the nights, and days also, spent by him without any time taken from the work of God for indulgence either in recreation or in business, or even in sleep or food except insofar as nature insisted—it was all so much greater in Martin than words can express.

Not an hour, not a moment passed without his either giving himself to prayer or applying himself to reading. But in truth, even during his reading or anything else he happened to be doing, he never let his mind relax from prayer. Blacksmiths have a way of striking on their anvils while working, as a kind of relief from the strain; that was precisely how Martin, when he seemed to be doing something else, was praying all the time. A truly blessed man, "in whom there was no guile"—judging no man, condemning no man, never returning evil for evil. Indeed, he had armed himself with such patience in the face of every injury that, although he was a prelate, he could be wronged with impunity by the lowest of his clergy. He never dismissed them from their posts for such offenses nor, so far as it lay with him, did he exclude them from his charity.

27

No one ever saw him angered, no one saw him excited, none saw him grieving, none saw him laughing. He was always just the same, with a kind of celestial joy shining in his face, so that he seemed more than human. There was never anything on his lips but Christ, nor anything in his heart but kindness, peace, and mercy. He was constantly weeping, too, for the sins of those whom he believed to be his calumniators—men who, with poisoned tongues and the bite of adders, used to pick him to pieces in his retired and peaceful life.

Indeed, I have come across some who were so envious of his spiritual powers and his life as actually to hate in him what they missed in themselves but had not the strength to imitate. And—oh, grievous and lamentable scandal!—nearly all his calumniators—there were not a great many—nearly all his calumniators were bishops. There is no need to mention names, though several of them are barking now at me. It will serve the same purpose if any of them who reads this and recognizes himself is made to blush. For his anger will be an admission that it applies to him, though I might, in fact, have had someone else in mind.

Besides, if such people exist, I have no objection to being hated by them in the company of such a man as Martin. I can be quite sure that this little work will give pleasure to all good Christians. I will only add that if anyone reads it skeptically he will be sinning. I am clear in my own conscience that my motives for writing were the certainty of the facts and the love of Christ and that I have only related what is well known, only said what is true. As for the reward prepared (as I hope) by God, not he who reads, but "he who believes" shall have it.

Possidius

THE LIFE OF SAINT AUGUSTINE

Translated by F. R. Hoare

Possidius is a puzzle. He was evidently a North African and a pupil of Augustine at Hippo. He became bishop of Calama in Numidia where he served until he fled before the Vandal onslaught in 428. He returned to Calama in 435 but was expelled definitively by the Arian king Geiserich in 437. The date and place of his death are unknown.

Possidius shared Augustine's battles against pagans, Manichaeans, Pelagians, and Donatists (see notes 4, 12, and 31). He regularly attended North African church councils and at least once, in 410, he went to the imperial court in Italy as a representative of the African church. He wrote his *Life of Augustine* between 432 and 435. No other writings of Possidius are known.

If the earliest saints' lives were devoted to ascetics, then Possidius's *Life of Augustine* is the first account devoted to a bishop as a public man of the church. This life does not present Augustine as a miracle-worker and reveals little of his spiritual life. Possidius declined to tackle Augustine's beliefs and early life because the prolific Church Father had recounted them himself, not least in his *Confessions*.

Possidius's *Life* differs from other saints' lives in formal qualities as well as in topics, tone, and feeling. Possidius clearly had not received the kind of education that Augustine himself, or Sulpicius Severus, had received. He indulges in little of the rhetorical artifice and embellishment that were the hallmarks of his age. Some have suggested that his Latin betrays "vulgar" characteristics. This means that it approached the popular tongue and departed sharply from the refinements of literary Latin. Striking too are Possidius's constant references to the written records of the North African church and to the many writings of Augustine. From this *Life* one can form a good impression of the kinds of materials that enabled one generation of ecclesiastical figures to write the history of another generation. That this text survived at all is due entirely to the fame of its subject. For centuries readers seem to have preferred to read Augustine's own writings. Few manuscripts of Possidius's *Life* survive, none older than the eleventh century.

On Augustine, a few details may be provided. He was born in Roman North Africa, then a thriving region. His was a modest family that sacrificed much for his education. He became a professor of rhetoric, first in Carthage, later in Rome, and finally in Milan. While in Milan he fell under the influence of Ambrose, bishop of the city. After a years-long search for truth and certainty, Augustine converted to Christianity in about 386. A few years later he was ordained a priest, and later consecrated a bishop. In addition to serving the church in North Africa as a solid administrator, Augustine issued a torrent of writing on almost every imaginable subject. He is the greatest of the Latin Church Fathers and, after Saint Paul, the most influential thinker in the history of western Christianity.

Texts and References

An accessible Latin text is in *Patrologia Latina*, vol. 32, cols. 33–66. Herbert T. Weiskotten prepared an edition with introduction, notes, and an English version: *Sancti Augustini vita scripta a Possidio episcopo* (Princeton, 1919). A new edition with an Italian translation is not a notable improvement over Weiskotten but its commentary and bibliography are very useful: A. A. R. Bastiansen, ed., *Vita di Agostino*, in *Vita dei santi*, vol. 2, ed. Christine Mohrmann (Verona, 1975). Brief notices are those by F. R. Hoare accompanying the original publication of this English version (*Western Fathers*, pp. 191–92) and by R. K. Poetzel, "Possidius," *New Catholic Encyclopedia* (New York, 1967), 11:630–31.

Preface

I write at the prompting of God, the Maker and Ruler of all things, and in accordance with my resolution, first as a layman and now as a bishop, to serve in the faith, by the grace of the Savior, the omnipotent and divine Trinity, desiring to use such talents and literary gifts as I possess to promote the welfare of the true and holy Catholic Church of Christ Our Lord. My subject is the life and character of that best of bishops, Augustine, a man predestined from eternity to be given to us when his time came, and I must keep back nothing of what I saw in him and heard from him.

And indeed we may learn from our reading that the same kind of thing was repeatedly done in times past by the most devout sons of our Holy Mother, the Catholic Church. Inspired by the Holy Spirit, but in their own language and style, by speech or by pen they addressed similar narratives to the ears or the eyes of those who wished to be informed, and thus enabled the student to learn of the great and remarkable men who were privileged to share in the grace of the Lord while living amidst the affairs of men, and to persevere in it to the end of their days.

I, too, therefore, though the least of God's stewards, but in that unfeigned good faith with which the Lord of Lords wishes all good Christians to serve and please Him, have undertaken to trace, so far as He allows me, the beginnings, the career and the fitting end of this venerable man, as I have learned them from him or observed them for myself through many years of close friendship. And I beseech the infinite Majesty that in the execution and completion of the task I have begun I may neither sin against the truth as it is known to the Father of all enlightenment (see Jas 1.17) nor appear at any point to depart from charity toward good sons of the Church.

I have no intention of entering into all those things that the most blessed Augustine recorded of himself in his *Confessions*,[1] concerning the kind of man he was before he received grace and the kind of life he lived afterward. He wrote as he did in order that (as the Apostle says) no man should believe or imagine anything better of him than he knew for himself or had heard about him (see 2 Cor 12.6). So, with his customary holy humility, he would deceive in nothing. It was not his own glory but his Lord's that he sought in respect of the benefits he had already received—his own deliverance and vocation; and, for what he hoped to receive further, he looked to the prayers of his brethren.

---

1. *Confessions* (see the English translation by R. S. Pine-Coffin in the Penguin Classics [Harmondsworth, 1961]), written in 397–398, is Augustine's probing account of his own youth and early manhood. The work focuses on Augustine's spiritual development.

For we have it on the authority of the angel: "It is good to guard the secret of a king, but gloriously to reveal the works of God" (Tb 12.7).

1

He was born, then, in the city of Tagaste in the province of Africa.[2] His parents were of good standing, and of senatorial rank, and Christians. They carefully attended to his upbringing themselves and he was educated at their expense, chiefly in secular literature; in other words, he took all the subjects that are included in what we call a liberal education. Thus equipped, he first of all taught literature in his own town and then oratory at Carthage, the capital of the province, and, later still, overseas, in Rome and at Milan, where at that time the emperor, Valentinian the Younger, had established his court.

In this city the office of bishop was then held by Ambrose,[3] a priest most dear to God and outstanding even among men of the first quality. From time to time Augustine, standing in the congregation, used to listen with fixed attention to the discourses frequently delivered in the church by this preacher of God's word. Now, at one time, when only a youth at Carthage, he had been attracted by the Manichaean heresy.[4] For that reason he was, more than most people, on the lookout for anything said either for or against it; and the day came when God so worked upon the heart of His priest that certain problems of the divine law were solved that bore upon those errors.

Thanks to this instruction, the heresy was slowly and step by step driven out from Augustine's soul. Then, as soon as he was convinced of the truth of the Catholic faith, there was born in him a burning desire to go forward in it, and with the coming of the holy season of Easter he received the saving waters of baptism. In this way it came about, through God's ordering, that he received both the saving truths of the Catholic Church and the divinely instituted sacraments through that great and remarkable prelate Ambrose.

2. Augustine lived from 354 to 430. His natal city was a minor one and his parents were of modest station despite Possidius's remark to the contrary. Although Augustine's mother Monica was a devout Christian, his father was a pagan.

3. C. 339–397; bishop of Milan, 374–397. A highborn Roman and one of the greatest Latin Church Fathers.

4. Manichaeans were followers of the Persian prophet Mani (c. 216–276). Mani taught a radical dualism symbolized by a cosmic battle between the forces of light and of darkness. To achieve light, or purity, severe asceticism was necessary. Manichaeanism was an offshoot of ancient Persian Zoroastrianism and recurred several times in the Middle Ages, most notably as Catharism, or Albigensianism.

2

Soon after this, with every fiber of his being he renounced all his ambitions for this world. He no longer thought of wife or children[5] or wealth or worldly honors but resolved to serve God among God's people, desiring to be one of that "little flock" whom the Lord was addressing when He said: "Fear not, little flock, for it is your father's good pleasure to give you the kingdom. Sell your possessions and give alms; provide yourselves with purses that do not grow old, with a treasure in heaven that does not fail" (Lk 12.32–33) and so on. And what Our Lord said on another occasion, this holy man conceived the desire to act on: "If you would be perfect, go sell what you possess and give to the poor, and you will have a treasure in heaven; and come follow me" (Mt 19.21). It was on the foundation of faith that he wished to build; not on wood or hay or straw, but on gold and silver and precious stones.

He was then more than thirty years old. Only his mother[6] was surviving and still close to him, for his father had died some time before this, and she had more joy in his resolution to give himself to the service of God than in the thought of grandchildren. And he duly gave notice to his pupils in oratory that, as he himself had decided to enter God's service, they must find another teacher.

3

His next step after being admitted to the sacrament, was to return to Africa and his own house and estate, in the company of some fellow countrymen and friends of his who were joining him in God's service. On arriving there, he settled down there for about three years, selling his property and, with his companions, giving himself to God in a life of fasting, prayer, and good works, and "on his law he meditates day and night" (Ps 1.2). And what God revealed to his understanding as he reflected and prayed, he taught by sermons to those who were with him and by books to those who were not.

Now, it so happened that during this period his good name and his teaching came to the knowledge of one of those people known as "public executive

---

5. In fact, Augustine never married, although he lived faithfully for some fifteen years with the mother of his equally obscure son.

6. Saint Monica, c. 331–387.

officers,"[7] appointed to Hippo-Regius,[8] a man living as a good Christian in the fear of God. He conceived a strong desire to see Augustine and asserted that he could defy all the lusts and allurements of this world if only he might, some time or other, have the privilege of hearing the Word of God from his lips.

A report of this came to Augustine from a reliable source and he longed for this soul to be rescued from the dangers of this life and from eternal death. So without being asked he went at once to the city now so famous, and saw the man. He had several talks with him and urged him, with all the force God gave him, to see that his promises to God were kept. The man kept promising from day to day to do this but never carried it out during this visit of Augustine. But we may be certain that there was some benefit and profit derived from the action of divine providence, which was now operating everywhere through this "vessel for noble use, consecrated and useful to the master of the house, ready for any sort of work" (2 Tm 2.21).

4

At this time the office of bishop in the Catholic Church at Hippo was held by that holy man Valerius. He was now impelled by the pressing needs of the church to address his flock and impress upon them the necessity of finding and ordaining a priest for the city. The Catholics were by now aware of the holy Augustine's teaching and way of life and they seized hold of him—he was standing in the congregation quite unconcerned and with no idea of what was going to happen to him. (While a layman, as he used to tell us, he used to keep away from churches where the bishopric was vacant but only from these). Holding him fast they brought him, as their custom was, to the bishop for ordination, for they were unanimous in asking for this to be done then and there. And while they were demanding this with eager shouts, he was weeping copiously.

At the time, indeed, some of them, as he told us himself, attributed his tears to wounded pride and, by way of consoling him, told him that the priesthood, though he was certainly worthy of something better, was not much below the episcopate. But the man of God, as he told us, was viewing the situation with more understanding and was bemoaning the many great

7. "Agentes in rebus," minor but sometimes influential officers of the imperial administration who were assigned tasks ad hoc.
8. Hippo Regius, approximately 100 miles west of Carthage, was the second most important secular and ecclesiastical center of late antique North Africa.

dangers to his way of life that he anticipated would come crowding on him if he had to govern and direct the church, and that was why he was weeping. But they had their way.[9]

5

Once [he was] a priest, it was not long before he established a monastery[10] within the precincts of the church and entered upon a life with the servants of God in accordance with the method and rule established under the holy apostles. Above all, no one in that community might have anything of his own but they were to "hold everything in common" and it was to be "distributed to each one as he had need of it" (Acts 2.44–45, 4.35). He himself had done this before, when he returned from across the sea to his own home.

The holy Valerius, who had ordained him and was a devout man living in the fear of God, was filled with joy and gave God thanks. He used to tell people how the Lord had heard the prayers he had so often sent up to Him that heaven would send him just such a man as this, who would help to build up the Lord's church by his invigorating teaching of the word of God. For this was a work for which he knew himself to be less fitted, being a Greek by birth and less versed in the Latin language and literature.

He even gave his priest permission to preach the Gospel in his presence in the church and very frequently to hold public discussions also, contrary to the custom and practice of the churches of Africa.[11] Some bishops found fault with him for this. But this venerable and far-seeing man, who knew for certain that this was the practice in the eastern churches and thought only of the good of the church, cared nothing for nagging tongues so long as the priest was getting done what the bishop could see could never be done by himself.

Thus, lit and burning and "raised upon a candlestick" Augustine continued to "give light to all who were in the house" (Mt 5.15). Presently the news of it got about everywhere and, such was the force of good example, other priests were given permission by their bishops and began to hold forth to the people in their bishop's presence.

9. In 391.
10. Possidius was a member of this monastery.
11. Actually it was uncommon anywhere for officers other than bishops to preach and teach publicly.

6

Now, at the time we are speaking of, in this city of Hippo the plague of Manichaeanism had infected and taken hold of both citizens and visitors in great numbers. They had been attracted to it and ensnared by a certain priest of that heresy named Fortunatus, who had settled there. In due course the Christian citizens and visitors to Hippo, Catholics and even Donatists,[12] came to our priest and demanded that he should meet this Manichaean priest, whom they regarded as a learned man, and hold a discussion with him about the law of God. He made no objection to this, being, in the words of Scripture, "prepared to make a defense to anyone who calls [him] to account for the hope that is in [him]" (1 Pt 3.15) and "able to give instruction in sound doctrine and also to confute those who contradict it" (Ti 1.9). But he inquired whether Fortunatus would agree to this.

They at once reported the position to Fortunatus, asking, pressing, and indeed demanding that he should on no account refuse. But this Fortunatus had known the holy Augustine before this, at Carthage, when he had been involved with him in the same errors, and dreaded an encounter with him. However, hard-pressed and embarrassed by this insistence, particularly from his own people, he promised to meet him face to face and oppose him in debate.

So a day and place were fixed[13] and they met in the presence of a large and interested audience and a crowd drawn by curiosity. The shorthand reporters opened their notebooks and the debate was opened on one day and concluded on the next. In the course of it, as the record of the proceedings shows, the exponent of Manichaeanism could neither refute the Catholic case nor succeed in proving that the sect of the Manichaeans was founded upon truth. When he broke down in his final reply, he undertook to consult his superiors about the

---

12. During Emperor Diocletian's persecution of Christianity (303–305), some North African bishops collaborated with the persecutors. One such was Caecilian, bishop of Carthage. When the persecution ended, most of the compromised clergy made peace with their communities and returned to office. Caecilian's opponents, who supported Donatus, refused to accept any tainted members of the clergy. By Augustine's day there was still a lively "Donatist" movement in North Africa. By then it had come to involve a debate over the efficacy of sacraments celebrated by unworthy members of the clergy. Augustine and the anti-Donatists represented the majority view within the whole Catholic Church, but probably a minority view in Africa, that the power of sacraments depended on God, not on the spiritual condition of the clergy. With or without the Donatist label, movements calling into question the validity of the works of morally impure clergy have recurred constantly in Christian history.

13. 28 August 392.

arguments he had been unable to answer and, if by any chance they failed to satisfy him, well, he would look to his own soul.

The result was that this man, whom everybody had thought so great and learned, was considered to have entirely failed in the defense of his sect. His embarrassment was such that, when soon afterward he left Hippo, he left it never to return. Thus, through this remarkable man of God, these errors were uprooted from the minds of all, whether they had been present at the debate, or had not been present but had heard about the proceedings; and the Catholic religion was admitted to be manifestly the genuine one.

7

Augustine continued to teach and preach the message of salvation both privately and publicly, in his home and in the church. He opposed with the fullest confidence the African heresies and especially the Donatists, the Manichaeans, and the pagans, in carefully finished books and in extempore sermons. The Christians admired him beyond words and were full of his praises. They could not keep silent about it but made it known wherever they could. In fact, by God's good gift, the Catholic Church in Africa began to lift its head again after a long period during which it had lain prostrate—led astray, overpowered and oppressed, while the heretics grew strong, especially the rebaptizing Donatist party, which comprised the majority of Africans.

As for these books and pamphlets of his, which by the marvelous grace of God issued from his pen in a constant flow, they were founded upon an abundance of reasoned argument and the authority of Holy Scripture, and the heretics themselves used to come hurrying with the Catholics with intense eagerness to hear them read aloud. Those who wished to have what they heard taken down, and could afford to do so, brought shorthand writers with them. Thus the splendid teaching and the sweet odor of Christ was spread abroad and made known through the length and breadth of Africa; and the church of God across the seas rejoiced also when they heard of it. For "if one member suffers, all suffer together; if one member is honored, all rejoice together" (1 Cor 12.26).

8

That man of blessings, the aged Valerius, rejoiced over all this even more than the rest and thanked God for the special favor conferred upon him. But he began to be afraid, such is human nature, that Augustine might be wanted as bishop by some other church, which had lost its own, and thus taken away from him. Indeed, this would actually have happened if our bishop had not got to know of it and succeeded in hiding him, so that he was not found by the searchers. After this, the venerable old man grew still more nervous and, realizing how very infirm he had become through old age, he approached the primate of the bishops of the diocese of Carthage[14] by a private letter in which he pleaded his bodily weakness and the weight of his years and asked that Augustine might be consecrated as a bishop of the church at Hippo, not so much to succeed him in the see as to serve with him as co-bishop. And what he hoped for, and had taken such trouble to get, was formally granted.[15]

Accordingly when, after this, Megalius, bishop of Calama, the then primate of Numidia,[16] came by invitation to visit the church of Hippo, Bishop Valerius surprised the bishops who happened to be present, as well as all the clergy of Hippo and his whole flock, by intimating to them his intention. His audience was delighted and clamored eagerly for the business to be put through then and there. But our priest refused to receive the episcopate contrary to the practice of the church, while his bishop was still living.

All set to work to persuade him that the thing was constantly done and appealed to examples from churches across the sea and in Africa, which he had not known about. Under this pressure and constraint he gave in and received consecration to the higher office. In later years he said, and wrote, that they ought not to have done this to him, namely, consecrate him while his bishop was living, since he had been prohibited by a general council, as he had discovered after his consecration.[17] As he did not want others to have done to them what he had been sorry to have done to himself, he made efforts to have it decreed by an episcopal synod that the canons[18] relating to priests should be brought to the knowledge of ordinands[19] and already ordained priests by the ordaining bishops, and this was done.[20]

14. Aurelius, bishop of Carthage, 388–423.

15. This happened in 395.

16. Metropolitan bishops in the North African church were the most senior bishops in a province, not the bishop of a specific see. Thus, Possidius succeeded Megalius as bishop at Calama, but was not metropolitan.

17. Either Augustine or Possidius is confused here. The Council of Nicaea (325) had forbidden two bishops to hold the same see simultaneously but did not prevent a bishop from naming an auxiliary to assist, and perhaps to succeed, him.

18. Decrees of church councils, hence canon law.

19. Candidates for ordination.

20. At the Third Council of Carthage, 397.

9

As bishop he preached the message of eternal salvation more insistently and fervently than ever and with greater authority, and no longer in one district only but in others where he went by invitation; and the church of the Lord blossomed and expanded, briskly and busily.

He was always ready to give an account, to anyone who asked, of the faith and hope he had in God (see 1 Pt 3.15); and Donatists in particular, if they lived in Hippo or one of the neighboring towns, used to bring along to their bishops things they had heard him say. When the bishops had heard these, and perhaps made some sort of reply, either they were answered by their own followers or their replies were brought to the holy Augustine. He used to examine them patiently and gently (as Scripture says, in fear and trembling he worked for men's salvation) and showed how these bishops were neither willing nor able to attempt a proper refutation and how true and clear are the things we hold and learn in the faith of the church of God.

He labored at this task day and night continually. He even wrote personal letters to some of the bishops of that heresy—the more prominent, that is to say—and to laymen, trying to persuade them by reasoned argument that they ought either to alter their perverse opinions or else meet him in debate. But they had too little confidence in their own case even to answer his letters, but merely raged against him in their anger, denouncing him in private and in public as a seducer and deceiver of souls. They used to say, and argue at length, that he was a wolf to be killed in defense of their flock and that there could be no doubt whatever that God would forgive all the sins of those who could achieve this feat; for they felt neither fear of God nor shame before men. Augustine for his part took pains that everyone should know of their lack of confidence in their own cause and they, when they met him on public bodies, dared not enter into a discussion with him.

10

These same Donatists had in almost all their congregations men of an unheard-of kind, perverted and violent, who made a profession of celibacy and were called Circumcellions.[21] They were very numerous, and there were organized bands of them all over Africa. Evil teachers had inspired them with an

21. So named by Augustine because they "went around" (*circum*) the "dwellings" (*cella*) of rural people. They were fanatical Donatists who worked more by terror than by persuasion.

insolent audacity and a reckless lawlessness. They spared neither their own people nor strangers and interfered with justice in defiance of all law and right. If they were not obeyed, they inflicted fearful loss and injuries, for, armed with various weapons, they ran raving over the farmlands and estates, restrained by no fears from going as far as bloodshed. And though the word of God was unremittingly preached and with those who hated peace, peacemaking was attempted, against him who spoke of it they made war without a reason (see Ps 120.6–7).

Nevertheless, when the truth began to make headway against their teaching, there were some who were glad to break away from them as opportunity arose, either openly or by stealth, and to enter the peace and unity of the church with as many as they could bring with them. Seeing their heretical congregations growing smaller as a result, and envious of the growth of the church, they became more angry and inflamed than ever and banded themselves together in an intolerable persecution of the undivided church. They made daily and nightly attacks even upon Catholic priests and clerics, plundering them of all their goods. Many servants of God they beat till they crippled them. They even threw lime mixed with vinegar into people's eyes, and others they killed outright. In the end, these rebaptizers[22] came to be hated even by their fellow Donatists.

11

As divine truth made headway, those who had been serving God in the monastery with the holy Augustine, and under his rule, began to be ordained as clergy for the church at Hippo. The result was to make better known and more evident every day the truths preached by the Catholic Church, the way of life of the holy servants of God, their chastity, and their utter poverty. Then, in the church of peace and unity, there grew up a strong desire for bishops and clergy from the monastery founded by, and flourishing under, this remarkable man. They began to be asked for, and presently what was asked was obtained.

For no less than ten men, known to us as holy and venerable, chaste and learned, were supplied by the most blessed Augustine to various churches, including some of the most important, in response to requests. These in their turn, having come from the religious life, founded fresh monasteries as the

---

22. Because Donatists, whether Circumcellions or not, rejected the sacraments of unworthy clergy, they rebaptized converts to their point of view.

churches of the Lord multiplied; and then, as zeal for the spread of God's Word went on growing, they supplied brethren to yet other churches for promotion to the priesthood.

Thus through many agents and to many hearers, the saving faith, hope, and charity taught by the church became known, not only through every part of Africa, but also across the seas, especially through his books that were published and translated into Greek; and it was from this one man, and to the many through him, that all this knowledge flowed. And, as Scripture says: "The wicked man sees it and is angry; he gnashes his teeth and melts away" (Ps 112.10). But, as it says again, your servants with those who hated peace played the peacemaker; and against them, when they spoke of it, they made war without a reason (see Ps 120.6–7).

12

Now, the Circumcellions we have been speaking of lay in wait by the road with weapons several times for God's servant Augustine, when he happened to have been asked to go and pay a visit, or to instruct or preach to Catholic congregations, as he very often was. On one occasion they failed to capture him although they had come out in full force; for, as it turned out, by the providence of God acting through a mistake of the guide, the bishop and his companions reached their destination by the wrong road and, as he learned afterward, by this mistake had just missed falling into the hands of the wicked, for which they all gave thanks to the God who delivers us. For it was certainly not the way of the Circumcellions to spare either laity or clergy, as the public records bear witness.

In this connection it is impossible to pass over in silence certain measures taken and carried through, to the glory of God, against these rebaptizing Donatists through the energy of this outstanding churchman and his "zeal for the house of God."

On this occasion one of the bishops he had provided for the church from the clergy of his monastery was making a round of the diocese of Calama, of which he had charge, and for the peace of the church was preaching against this heresy what he had learned from Augustine. In the course of his journey he fell into one of their ambushes. He and all his companions got away but their beasts and their baggage were taken and he himself was most seriously injured.

This time, to remove a real hindrance to the church's peace and progress, the church's representative appealed to the law; and Crispinus, who was bishop of the Donatists in the city and district of Calama and for a long time had a reputation for learning, was pronounced liable to a fine of gold under the state's laws against heretics.[23] He appealed against this and, when he appeared before the proconsul, denied that he was a heretic.

The church's representative had by this time withdrawn from the case but this plea made it absolutely necessary for Crispinus to be opposed by the Catholic bishop and convicted of being what he denied he was. For if his pretense had been allowed to stand, the Catholic bishop might have been taken by the simple to be a heretic, since the heretic denied that he was one, so that letting the case go by default would have created a hindrance to the faith of the weak.

Indeed, that unforgettable prelate Augustine firmly insisted on this course, so both bishops of Calama came into the case—the third clash that had occurred between them in connection with their religious differences. Vast numbers of Christians, not only in Carthage but all over Africa, awaited the result of the trial, which was that Crispinus was pronounced a heretic by a written judgment of the proconsul.

The Catholic bishop, however, interceded on his behalf with the judge, to remit the fine of gold; and this favor was granted. But the ungrateful man appealed to the most gracious sovereign and his statement of his case duly brought from the emperor a general ruling, in conformity with which an injunction was issued to the effect that the Donatist heretics were not to be tolerated in any place and that all the laws passed against heretics were to be enforced against them everywhere. It also ordered the judges and officers of the court and Crispinus himself, since he had not been fined before, to pay ten pounds weight of gold apiece to the credit of the imperial treasury.

However, speedy steps were taken by the Catholic bishops, and particularly by Augustine of holy memory, to get this sentence on all of them remitted by a pardon from the sovereign and this, by the Lord's help, was achieved. And all this vigilance and holy zeal contributed greatly to the growth of the church.

13

For all this work in the cause of peace in the church, Our Lord rewarded Augustine with triumphs here on earth and kept a crown for his well-doing in readiness for him in heaven. More and more every day, unity in peace—the

23. Theodosius I (379–395) passed a series of repressive measures against persons who denied the teachings of the councils of Nicaea (325), Constantinople (381), or the popes of Rome.

true brotherhood of the church of God grew and spread widely (see Acts 12.24). This was particularly the case after the conference that was held at Carthage some time later between all the Catholic bishops and the bishops of the Donatists by the orders of the most glorious and gracious Emperor Honorius,[24] who had sent Marcellinus, a military officer and secretary, to Africa as his personal representative to act as judge and see the thing through.

In the debates[25] on this occasion the Donatists were completely outargued. They were convicted of heresy by the Catholics and formally censured by the arbitrator. They appealed against this, and these evil men were then condemned as heretics by the decision of the most gracious sovereign himself. The effect of this was to make it a more common event than before for their bishops, as well as their clergy and laity, to enter the Catholic communion; and these men, being now at peace with the church, endured much persecution from the Donatists, even to the loss of life and limb. And all this good work was, as I said, begun and carried through by this holy man, with our fellow bishops glad to play their part.

14

However, after this conference with the Donatists there were some to be found who said that their bishops had not been allowed to put their case fully before the magistrate who presided, since the arbitrator belonged to the Catholic communion and favored his church. As a matter of fact they only put forward this excuse after they had failed and been defeated, for these heretics had known before the discussion began that he belonged to the Catholic communion, yet, when they had been summoned by him to the public proceedings for the trial of strength, they had agreed to it. After all, if they had mistrusted him, they could have declined the encounter.

However, the providence of Almighty God brought it about that some time afterward Augustine of revered memory was staying in the city of Caesarea in Mauretania.[26] A letter from the Apostolic See[27] had obliged him and some of

---

24. Western emperor, 395–423. Note here and elsewhere the prominence of the imperial authorities in questions of religious controversy.

25. This occurred in 411. Possidius himself was one of the Catholic participants. The raging split in the African church can be grasped from the presence at Carthage of 286 Catholic bishops as opposed to 279 Donatists. Virtually every city in North Africa had one of each.

26. Roughly modern Morocco.

27. That is, from the pope at Rome.

his fellow bishops to go there to settle some other difficulties of the church. In this way he met Emeritus, the Donatist bishop of the place, who was looked on as having been the chief defender of their sect at the conference. He reasoned with him publicly in the church on this very point with people of both communions present, and challenged him to a trial of the issues, to be conducted in the church, so that, if (as they said) there was something that Emeritus could have put forward at the conference but had not been allowed to, he need have no anxiety about saying it there and then, with no magistrate present to prohibit or obstruct, and he should not refuse to defend his own communion boldly in his own city with all his fellow citizens present.

In spite of this appeal and the pressing requests of his relations and townsfolk, he was unwilling to do this, though they promised him that they would return to his communion, even at the risk of losing their property and their temporal prosperity, if he refuted the Catholic arguments. He was neither willing nor able to add anything to the former proceedings except to say: "The records of the bishops' meeting at Carthage are enough to show whether we won or lost." And when from another direction came a warning from a reporter that he had better make some reply, he said, "Do what you like!" His subsequent silence and the publicity given to his doings through his lack of confidence in his own position caused the growth of the church, and the strength of its case, to stand out plainly.

But anyone who would like to know more of the care and industry that Augustine of blessed memory devoted to upholding the dignity of the church of God should read those proceedings. He will discover there the nature of the arguments he brought forward in challenging and appealing to that learned, eloquent, and illustrious man to say whatever he wished in defense of his faction and he will see Emeritus vanquished.

15

Here is an incident, known not only to me personally but also to other brethren and fellow servants of God who at that time were living with us in the church at Hippo with this holy man. He said to us as we were seated at table:

"Did you notice in my sermon in church today that the beginning and ending went differently to my usual method? Because I did not continue my explanation of the subject to the end, but left it in the air."

"Yes," we replied, "we know, and we remember that we wondered at it at the time."

"I should not be surprised," he said, "if the Lord was wanting some wanderer from the flock to be taught and cured through my own forgetfulness and wandering. We are all in His hands, and our sermons too. I was when I was dealing with something on the borderline of my subject that I went off from my sermon to something else. That is why I never brought my explanation of the question to a proper conclusion but ended with an argument against the errors of the Manichaeans, which I had had no intention of discussing, instead of with what I had planned to say."

It was after this and, if I am not mistaken, within the next day or two, that there came, if you please, a certain businessman named Firmus. The holy Augustine was in the monastery, sitting with us round him, and the man flung himself down on his knees at his feet and, with tears falling, asked the bishop to intercede, together with the saints, with the Lord for his sins. He confessed that he had been a follower of the Manichaean sect and had lived in it for many years, which meant that he had spent a great deal of money on the Manichaeans and their so-called elect[28] that was all wasted. He had just lately, by the mercy of God, been shown his errors by Augustine's arguments in church and been made a Catholic.

Our revered Augustine and those of us who were present carefully enquired of him what exactly in the sermon had especially satisfied his mind. He told us, and it brought back to all of us the whole course of the sermon. We contemplated with wonder and stupefaction the depth of God's plans for the salvation of souls; and we glorified and blessed the holy Name of Him who brings about the salvation of souls just at the time He wishes, just from the direction He wishes, and just by the method He wishes, through those who know what they are doing and through those who know it not.

From that day the man followed the way of life of the servants of God. He gave up his business and made such progress as a member of the church that, in another land, by the will of God he was summoned and even constrained to enter the priesthood. He continued faithfully in the religious life and, for all I know, is still alive and active among men across the seas.

16

To go back to Carthage, a certain financial officer of the imperial household named Ursus, a Catholic by faith, had a visit of inspection paid to a gathering

---

28. The highest grade of Manichaean.

of Manichaeans of the kind they call the elect, both men and women. They were removed by him to the church, where they were examined by the bishops, a record being taken of the proceedings. Among the bishops was Augustine of holy memory, who knew the abominable sect better than the rest and could produce their damnable blasphemies from passages in books that they acknowledge. By this means he brought them to confess these blasphemies; and the shameful and foul rites that they practice to their utter undoing were brought to light in the ecclesiastical proceedings through the disclosures of these women.

Thus, through the vigilance of its shepherds, the Lord's flock grew in numbers and an adequate defense was maintained against the thieves and robbers.

Augustine held a public debate also with a man named Felix, another of those the Manichaeans call the elect. This was in the church at Hippo, with the people present and reporters taking it down. After the second or third session, when the unrealities and fallacies of the sect had been laid bare, the Manichaean was converted to the faith of our church, as the records in question will show if consulted.

17

There was also an officer of the imperial household named Pascentius, who was an Arian.[29] He was a ruthless collector of the imperial taxes and used his position to wage cruel and continuous war upon the Catholic faith. Both by his sarcasms and his official powers, he used to harass and distress great numbers of God's priests who were living lives of faith in all simplicity. Through certain men of noble rank who acted as intermediaries, Augustine had been challenged by him, and met him publicly at Carthage.

But this heretic absolutely refused to have notebook or pen in the place, though our master expressed the strongest desire for it both before and at the encounter. And he persisted in his refusal, on the ground that he did not want to run the risk of written records for fear of the state's laws, and appealed to the intermediaries. Eventually Bishop Augustine agreed to hold the discussion, as his colleagues who were present thought that there had better be a private debate without reporters. But he prophesied what did afterward come about, that, once the conference had dispersed, anyone would be free to say, in

---

29. On Arians, see page 10, note 13.

the absence of written proof, that he had said what perhaps he did not say, or had not said what he did say.

He then plunged into the argument. He stated his own beliefs, heard from his opponent what *he* held, and then brought forward solid arguments and the authority of scripture to teach and demonstrate the foundations of our faith. He also explained how the assertions of his opponent were unsupported either by the truth of reason or by the authority of Holy Scripture and thereby showed their worthlessness. Then, when the two parties had gone their separate ways, the Arian's anger worked itself up into a frenzy and he began hurling about numbers of lies in support of his false faith and proclaimed that Augustine, the much-praised Augustine, had really been vanquished by him.

All this was bound to become public and Augustine was compelled to write to Pascentius himself. In deference to the latter's fears he omitted the names of those present at the conference but in this letter he set out faithfully all that had passed between the two parties. If his assertions were denied he had, in readiness to prove them, plenty of witnesses, namely, the illustrious men of rank who had been present. But Pascentius, in reply to the two letters addressed to him, wrote one, and what was hardly a reply at all. In it he contrived to offer insults rather than to present the case for his sect, as anyone can verify who is willing and able to read it.

Augustine also held a debate with a bishop of these same Arians. This was Maximin, who had come to Africa with the Goths.[30] It was held at Hippo, at the wish and request, and through the mediation, of a number of distinguished men; and what was said on either side was taken down. Anyone who is sufficiently interested to read the report carefully will undoubtedly get a good idea of what this plausible but illogical heresy puts forward to ensnare and deceive, and also of what the Catholic Church holds and teaches about the divine Trinity.

But when this heretic got back to Carthage from Hippo he boasted that, thanks to his interminable flow of speech in the debate, he had come away from it victorious. He was lying but, of course, he could not easily be cross-examined and exposed by people ignorant of theology. Our revered Augustine, therefore, subsequently put into writing a summary of all the points made and answers given in the course of the debate. Moreover, how completely unable

---

30. The Goths, in this instance Visigoths, had entered the Balkans in 376, defeated the Roman emperor Valens at Adrianople in 378, moved to Italy in 406, sacked Rome in 410, and, finally, settled under Roman auspices in southern Gaul between 411 and 418. The Goths were Arians. Only individual Goths crossed to North Africa, but one of them was Maximin, the Arian bishop of Hippo who debated Augustine in 427 or 428.

Maximin had been to answer objections was shown in a supplementary section containing matter that it had been impossible to introduce and have taken down in the short time available at the conference. For the malice of the man had contrived that all that remained of the day had been taken up with his last and by far his longest speech.

18

The most recent heresy of our times is that of the Pelagians,[31] plausible debaters, still more subtle and pernicious writers, and untiring talkers in public and in the homes of the people. Against these, Augustine labored for nearly ten years, writing and publishing many books and frequently holding debates in the church with people holding those errors. When these perverted minds tried by flattery to force their false faith upon the Apostolic See, the most urgent measures were taken by councils of the holy bishops of Africa, to impress upon the holy pope of Rome, first on the venerable Innocent, then on his successor, the holy Zosimus,[32] how strongly this sect should be reprobated and condemned by the Catholic faith. And the bishops of that great See did, at various times, censure them and cut them off from the body of the church and sent letters to the African churches of the west and to the churches of the east decreeing that they should be anathematized, and shunned by all Catholics.

Moreover, the most gracious Emperor Honorius, when he heard of this judgment passed on them by the Catholic Church of God, followed its lead. He condemned them by his own laws and decreed that they should be treated as heretics. As a result, some of them returned to the bosom of holy mother church, out of which they had flung themselves; and others are still returning, as the truth of the orthodox faith stands out ever more clearly and victoriously against their abominable errors.

But indeed, this unforgettable man, this outstanding member of the Lord's body, was unceasingly solicitous and vigilant in all that concerned the welfare of the church universal. And God granted him the joy of seeing even in this

31. Followers of Pelagius, a British monk who taught in Rome in the late fourth and early fifth centuries. Pelagius has long been accused of believing that humans, thought sinful, could take the first steps on the path to their own salvation. Augustine attacked an extreme form of Pelagianism that, he believed, rendered God's grace—the divine assistance necessary for humans to respond to God's offer of salvation—almost unnecessary. Recent research suggests that Pelagius actually aimed at holding all Christians—ascetics, secular clergy, and laypeople alike—to the same high standard. He believed that all Christians should strive for "perfection."

32. Popes, respectively, from 402 to 407 and 417 to 418.

life the fruit of his labors, first in the establishment of unity and peace in the diocese of Hippo, his own particular charge, then in other parts of Africa. There he could see the church of the Lord budding and extending, either through his own action or through that of others (including priests he had himself provided), and rejoice over Manichaeans, Donatists, Pelagians, and pagans losing much of their strength as numbers of them returned to the church of God.

He loved to see enterprise and zeal, and delighted in all that was good. He had a kind and holy patience with the irregularities of the brethren and sighed over the wickedness of evil men, both those within the church and those outside it, for, as I said, the Lord's gains always brought him joy and His losses grief.

As for all that he dictated and published, and all the debates in the cathedral that were taken down and revised, some were against heretics of various kinds, others were expositions of the canonical books for the instruction of holy sons of the church, but there are so many that there is hardly a student who has been able to read and get acquainted with them all. However, not to be thought in any way to fail those who are particularly eager for the words of truth, I have decided, if God furthers it, to append to this little work of mine a catalogue of these books, pamphlets, and letters.[33] Anyone who reads it, and who cares more for God's truth than for earthly riches, will be able to pick out for himself the book he wants to read. If he wants to make himself a copy of it, he should apply to the church at Hippo, where the best texts can generally be found. Or he may make inquiries anywhere else he can and should make a copy of what he finds and preserve it and not grudge lending it in his turn to someone else asking to copy it.

19

In another matter also he followed the teaching of the Apostle: "When one of you has a grievance against a brother, does he dare go to law before the unrighteous instead of the saints? Do you not know that the saints will judge the world? And if the world is to be judged by you, are you incompetent to try trivial cases? Do you know that we are to judge angels? How much more, matters pertaining to this life! If then you have such cases, why do you lay

33. This *Indiculus*, which is neither complete nor accurate in all respects, survives in an edition by André Wilmart, *Miscellanea Agostiniana* 2 (Rome, 1931), 149–233.

them before those who are least esteemed by the church? I say this to your shame. Can it be that there is no man among you wise enough to decide between members of the brotherhood, but brother goes to law against brother, and that before unbelievers?" (1 Cor 6.1–6).

When, therefore, he was appealed to by Christians or men of any sect,[34] he used to listen carefully and conscientiously, keeping in mind the maxim of someone who said that he would rather hear cases between strangers than between friends, because he could gain one of the strangers as a friend when he gave a just decision in his favor but would lose one of his friends when the judgment had gone against him.

And he would always go into these cases until he had settled them, even though it meant fasting till dinner-time or sometimes all day long. He studied in them the movements of Christian souls, and how one would be advancing in faith and morals and another falling back. When the business in hand provided an opportunity, he would teach the parties to the actions truths about the law of God and impress these upon them, and remind them how to obtain eternal life. The only payment he asked of them for giving up his time to them was the Christian obedience and devotion they owed to God and men. Sinners he would "rebuke . . . in the presence of all, so that the rest may stand in fear" (1 Tm 5.20).

He did all this as one appointed by the Lord as "a watchman for the house of Israel" (Ez 3.17), as one appointed to "preach the word, be urgent in season and out of season, convince, rebuke, and exhort, be unfailing in patience and teaching" (2 Tm 4.2). He took special pains to train those who might be suitable for teaching others (see 2 Tm 2.2). He used also, in response to requests, to write letters to various people about their temporal affairs. But this he regarded as forced labor that took him away from better things. What he really enjoyed was addressing or conversing with the brethren about the things of God in the intimacy of the home circle.

20

We know, also, how he refused requests to write letters petitioning the civil authorities even on behalf of his dearest friends. He used to say that one

---

34. Fourth- and fifth-century imperial legislation assigned bishops wide-ranging jurisdiction in cases involving minor sums of money or modest problems. This jurisdiction is one measure of the prominence of bishops in late antique towns and of that age's admixture of secular and religious business.

should go by the wisdom of a certain sage of whom it is recorded that he had too much regard for his own reputation to vouch for his friends. But he used to add a reason of his own, which was that an official of whom you ask favors generally becomes overbearing.

Nevertheless, when he saw that the intervention for which he was asked was really required, he conducted it with such dignity and reasonableness that, so far from being regarded as giving trouble or annoyance, he actually aroused admiration. Thus, he interceded once in his usual way in a case of necessity, on behalf of a petitioner, in a letter to a vicar of Africa[35] named Macedonius. The latter, in acceding to the request, wrote in this strain:

"I am amazingly impressed by the wisdom I find, first in the books you have published, and now in this letter you have not thought it too much trouble to send me, interceding for people in trouble. The books show a penetration, a learning and a piety to which nothing can be added; and the letter is written with such delicate restraint that, if I did not do what you tell me, I should have to put the blame on myself and not on the case. For you, my lord—'venerable' indeed—and most esteemed father in God, do not, like most men in your position, insist on extracting everything the petitioner wants, but confine yourself to what you think can rightly be asked of a judge with so many responsibilities, and recommend it with that accommodating tact that is the best way of settling difficulties among men of good will. For this reason I have given immediate effect to your recommendations, as, indeed, I had given you reason to expect."

21

Whenever he could, he attended the councils of the holy bishops held in the various provinces, not seeking his own interests but those of Jesus Christ (see Phil 2.21) as, for example, in preserving inviolate the faith of the holy Catholic Church, or in absolving or casting out priests and clerics rightly or wrongly excommunicated. When it came to ordaining priests and clerics, he thought it best to follow the common opinion of our Christian ancestors and the custom of the church.

---

35. The Roman Empire was divided administratively into four prefectures, under praetorian prefects. Each prefecture was divided into dioceses, which consisted of several provinces. Dioceses were under vicars.

22

His clothes and food, and bedclothes also, were simple and adequate, neither ostentatious nor particularly poor. For it is in these matters, more than in most, that men are apt either to show off or to demean themselves, in either case seeking their own interests, not Jesus Christ's (again, see Phil 2.21). So he, as I said, held a middle course, turning aside neither to the right hand nor to the left (Prv 4.27). His diet was frugal and economical. With the herbs and pulse he sometimes had meat for the sake of his guests or the delicate brethren, and always wine, for he recognized and taught that, as the Apostle says, "everything created by God is good and nothing is to be rejected if it is received with thanksgiving; for then it is consecrated by the word of God and prayer" (1 Tm 4.4–5). As Augustine himself put it in his *Confessions:* "It is defilement from greed, not defilement from food, that I fear. I know that Noe had permission to eat any kind of flesh fit for food, that Elias was refreshed by flesh-food, and that John, who was capable of marvelous austerity, was not defiled by the animals (the locusts, that is) which fell to his lot for food. I know that Esau, on the other hand, *was* ensnared by a craving for lentils, that David found fault with himself for wanting water, and that, when our King was tested, it was not with meat but with bread. Similarly, when the people earned a rebuke in the wilderness, it was not because they desired meat but because, in their desire for meat, they muttered against God" (10.31.46).

As regards taking wine, there is the dictum of the Apostle writing to Timothy, and saying: "No longer drink only water, but use a little wine for the sake of your stomach and your frequent ailments" (1 Tm 5.23).

Only his spoons were of silver; the dishes in which the food was served were either earthenware or wood or marble, not under the compulsion of poverty, but from choice. And he was always hospitable. Moreover, what he loved at table was not feasting and drinking but reading and discussion; as a preventative against a common pest of human intercourse he had these words inscribed on it:

> Let him who takes pleasure in mauling the lives of the
>   absent
> Know his own is not such as to fit him to sit at this table.

By this he warned all the company to refrain from wanton and damaging anecdotes. And once, when some most intimate friends among his fellow bishops forgot the inscription and broke the rule, he was so upset that he rebuked them really sharply, saying that either those lines must be erased from the table or he would get up from the middle of the meal and go to his own room. I myself and others who were with him at table were witnesses of this.

23

He never forgot his companions in poverty; and what he spent on them came from the same fund as supported him and those who lived with him, namely, the income from the church's property and the offerings of the faithful. When, as often happened, this property roused the envy of the clergy, he would address his flock and tell them that he would rather live on the contributions of the people of God than be burdened with the care and administration of this property and that he was quite ready to hand it over to them and let all God's servants and ministers live in the way we read of in the Old Testament, that those who serve the altar share in its offerings.[36] But the laity were never willing to undertake it.

24

He used to delegate the care of the church house and all the property to the more capable clergy, entrusting it to them in turn. He never kept the keys or wore the signet-ring, and all the accounts were kept by these household stewards. At the end of the year they were read to him so that he could know the amount received and spent and the balance in hand. Many documents he took on trust from the steward instead of checking and inspecting them for himself.

He was never willing to buy a house or land or an estate. If, however, anything of that sort happened to be given to the church by someone of his own accord, or came as a legacy, he would not refuse it and gave orders for it to be accepted. But I have known him refuse to be the heir to inheritances, not because they could not be used for the poor, but because it seemed only right and fair that they should go to the children or relatives or connections of the deceased, even though the latter had not wanted to leave them to them.

Once one of the leading citizens of Hippo, who was living at Carthage, wished to present his estate to the church at Hippo. Retaining the income from it for himself, he sent, quite spontaneously, the title-deeds duly executed to this same

---

36. Presumably a reference to Dt 18.1–6 on what was done to the tribe of Levi.

Augustine of holy memory. The latter gladly accepted his offering and congratulated him on thinking of his eternal salvation. But some years later, when I
happened to be staying with him, what should the donor do but send his son
with a letter requesting that the title-deeds should be handed over to the son and
giving directions for distributing one hundred gold pieces to the poor.

When the holy man was told of this he was deeply grieved, for either the
original donation had been a sham or the man had regretted his good deed.
In his distress of mind at this perversity, he gave utterance as far as he could
to what God put into his heart to say, by way of censuring and reproving
him. Moreover, he immediately returned the deeds (which the man had sent
of his own accord, unasked and under no necessity) and at the same time
refused to touch the money. He wrote a letter, too, in which he reprimanded
and reproached him, as was only right. He warned him that he had better
atone to God by doing humble penance for what was either double-dealing
or a wanton injury, so as not to depart from this life with so heavy a burden
of sin.

He used also quite often to say that the church could accept legacies much
more confidently and safely than she could succeed to inheritances, that might
bring anxiety and loss. Furthermore, the legacies themselves should be offered, not extracted. Nor would he himself accept property to be held in trust,
though he would not stop his clergy doing so if they wished.

But in none of these holdings or possessions[37] of the church did he allow his
affections to become fixed or entangled; all that happened was that, with the
whole bent of his mind upon higher and spiritual things, he did occasionally
relax from the contemplation of things eternal to turn to these temporal affairs;
then, once they had been settled and put in order, in mind drew back from them
as if from a sting or an irritant and reverted to interior and higher thoughts,
either to discover new truths of theology or to dictate what he had discovered or
perhaps to revise what had previously been dictated and transcribed.

He got through it all by living laborious days and working far into the
night. He was a type of the church in heaven, like that ever glorious Mary of
whom it is written that she sat at the feet of the Lord listening intently to His
words; and, when her sister complained of her that she got no help from her
when she was overwhelmed by all the household work, she heard Him say:

37. As churches acquired more responsibility they needed the secure income that landed
wealth could provide. These passages also show that late antique bishops needed formidable
administrative skills in addition to theological ability and personal sanctity. We are also reminded
here of the property disputes into which the church could be dragged.

"Martha, Martha . . . Mary has chosen the good portion and it shall not be taken away from her" (Lk 10.41–42).

He never had the passion for erecting new buildings, not wishing to have his mind taken up with them. He liked to have it always free from all mundane anxieties. Nevertheless he did not stop those who wished to build from doing so, unless they did it to excess.

Occasionally, when the funds of the church gave out, he would announce this to his flock, telling them he had nothing to bestow upon the needy. He would even order some of the sacred vessels to be broken up and melted down, for the benefit of captives and of as many of the poor as possible, and to be distributed to them. I would not have mentioned this if I had not seen that it was done against the all too human judgment of some. I may add that Ambrose of revered memory said and wrote that it was unquestionably a thing that ought to be done in such extremities. So, too, if the faithful had been neglecting the collections for the sacristy (for supplying the needs of the altar), he would sometimes speak warningly in church about it, and he once told us how he had been present in the church when the most blessed Ambrose had dealt with the same subject.

25

The clergy and he were all fed and clothed in the same house, at the same table and from a common purse.

In view of the danger of slipping from thoughtless swearing into perjury, he used to tell the people in his sermons in church, and made it a rule for his own household, that no one should swear, and certainly not at table. If anyone offended against this, he lost one drink from his allowance (for there was a fixed number of cups allowed to each person living and dining with him). So, too, with irregularities among his household and offenses against rules or good manners, whether he rebuked them or overlooked them, it was to the extent that was fitting and right. He was particularly insistent, in such matters, that no one should lower himself to petty lies in making excuses for his sins.

Again, "so if you are offering your gift at the altar, and there remember that your brother has something against you, leave your gift there before the altar and go; first be reconciled to your brother, and then come and offer your gift" (Mt 5.23–24). But if he had grounds for complaint against his brother, he ought to "go and tell him his fault, between you and him alone. If he listens to you, you have gained your brother. But if he does not listen, take one or two others along with you, that every word may be confirmed by the evidence of two or three witnesses. If he refuses to listen to them, tell it to the church; and if he refuses to listen even to the church, let him be to you as a Gentile and a tax collector" (Mt 8.15–17).

He used to add that a brother who sins and asks forgiveness for his offense should be pardoned "not seven times but seventy times seven" (Mt 18.22), just as each of us asks the Lord for pardon for himself every day.

26

No woman ever lived in his house, or stayed there, not even his own sister, who as a widow in the service of God lived for many years, to the very day of her death, as prioress of God's handmaidens. It was the same with his brother's daughters, who were also enrolled in God's service, although the councils of the holy bishops had allowed an exception to be made of them. He used to say that even though no suspicion of evil could arise from his sister or his nieces stopping with him, *they* would have to have other women attending on them and staying with them, and other women again would be coming to see them from outside, and all this might give scandal or prove a temptation to the weak. Thus, the men who happened to be staying with the bishop or with one of the clergy, when all these women were stopping there together or coming and going, might fall victims to the common temptations of mankind and would certainly suffer the grossest defamation by suspicious people.

For these reasons he used to say that the servants of God, however chaste they might be, ought never to have women staying in the same house with them, for fear (as I have said) of setting an example that might give scandal or prove a temptation to the weak. Even when women asked to interview him, or just to pay their respects, they might never come into his room unless there were clergy there as witnesses. He would never talk to them alone even if the matter were strictly private.

27

In the matter of visiting, he held to the rule laid down by the Apostle, to visit only widows and orphans in their affliction (see Jas 1.27). If he were specially asked by people who were ill to pray to the Lord for them in their presence and lay his hands on them, he would go at once. He would only visit convents of nuns if there were urgent need.

He used also to quote, as a rule to be observed in the life and conduct of every man of God, what he had learned from the practice of Ambrose of holy memory: never ask a woman's hand for another man; never give a recommendation to a man who wants to join the army or advise him to accept an invitation to a banquet in his hometown. And he would give his reasons in each case. Thus, when a married couple quarrel, they are likely to curse the man who brought them together. (But of course, if the two parties have already agreed to marry and have asked the priest, he ought to be there, so that their compact and consent may be ratified and blessed.)[38] As to military service, the man who has been recommended and then misconducted himself is likely to say that it is the fault of the man who recommended him. Finally, by constant attendance at banquets with fellow citizens, the habit of temperance is easily lost.

He once told us how he had heard of the very wise and very pious reply which the above-mentioned man of blessed memory made in the last moments of his life; and he used often to praise and commend it. When that venerable man was on his deathbed, the leading members of the church were standing round his bed. Seeing that he was on the point of passing from this world to God, they were full of grief that the church was being deprived of the teaching and the administration of the sacraments by so great and remarkable a prelate, and they tearfully asked him to petition God for an extension of his life.

"I have not lived in such a way," he said, "that I am ashamed to be living among you; at the same time, I am not afraid to die, for we have a very good God."

Our Augustine, when he was an old man himself, used to marvel at, and praise, the lapidary and balanced phrases of this reply. Ambrose (he said) must be understood to have added the words "I am not afraid to die, because we have a very good God" so that it should not be thought that it was from overconfidence in the immaculateness of his own character that he had said first, "I have not lived in such a way that I am ashamed to be living among you." When he said that, he had been referring to what men could know of a fellow man, but when it came to the scrutiny of divine justice, for any goodness he preferred to trust to God, to whom, indeed, he said in his daily prayer, "Forgive us our sins."

In the same connection he was constantly repeating toward the end of his

38. Before the twelfth century, when marriage definitively became one of the church's sacraments, the clergy generally had an insignificant role in marriages.

life the words of a certain fellow bishop and most intimate friend. He had been
going frequently to visit him as his death drew near, and his friend by a
gesture of the hand had indicated that he was on the point of leaving the
world. Augustine had replied that his life was perhaps still necessary to the
church; but he answered, so as not to be thought to be clinging to this life,
"Yes, if I need never die; but, if some day, why not now?"

Augustine marveled at the saying and used to praise the man who uttered
it—a God-fearing man, certainly, but brought up on a country estate and
without much education or reading. Contrast the attitude of another sick
bishop, of whom the holy martyr Cyprian[39] told this story in the letter he
wrote on mortality:

"One of our colleagues in the episcopate, worn out by illness and disturbed
by the approach of death, was praying for an extension of his life. As he
prayed, and was almost on the point of death, there stood before him a youth
of such awe-inspiring dignity and majesty, and so tall and radiant, that human
vision and mortal eyes could hardly have looked upon him as he stood there if
the one who looked had not been about to leave this world. With a certain
disgust in his expression and voice the youth sighed and said: 'You are afraid to
suffer; you are unwilling to die. What am I to do with you?' "

28

Shortly before his death he made a survey of the books he had dictated and
published, some in the early days of his conversion, when he was still a layman,
some as a priest and some, again, as a bishop. Whenever he found anything in
them that he had dictated or written when he had had comparatively little
knowledge and understanding of the church's tradition and which was not in
accordance with the church's mind, he censored and corrected it himself.

In this way he wrote two volumes entitled *A Survey of My Books*.[40] He used
to complain, however, that some of his books had been carried off by certain
brethren before they had been properly revised, though he had meant to revise
them later. Some of his books he was prevented by death from correcting. But
in his desire to be of service to all, whether they could read lots of books or
whether they could not, he made a selection from both the Holy Testaments,

39. C. 210–258, a pagan rhetorician who converted to Christianity, became bishop of Carthage
c. 250, and was martyred in 258.

40. His *Retractationes*, published in 427. Note that the force of "retract" in Latin is to go back
over again, not to withdraw or take back.

Old and New, of precepts and prohibitions constituting a rule of life. He prefixed a preface to them and made one volume of them, which anyone who wished might read, and learn from it how obedient or disobedient he was to God. He wanted this book to be called *The Mirror.*

It was not long after this, however, that, by God's will and permission, there poured into Africa from across the sea in ships from Spain a huge host of savage enemies armed with every kind of weapon and trained in war. There were Vandals and Alans, mixed with one of the Gothic peoples, and individuals of various nations.[41] They overran the country, spreading all over Mauretania and passing on to our other provinces and territories. There was no limit to their savage atrocities and cruelties. Everything they could reach they laid waste, with their looting, murders, tortures of all kinds, burnings, and count-less other unspeakable crimes. They spared neither sex nor age, nor the very priests and ministers of God, nor the ornaments and vessels of the churches, nor the buildings.

Our man of God did not view all this running riot and devastation by a ferocious enemy in the same light as other men. He brought to its origin and progress loftier and profounder considerations. He saw in it chiefly the danger and the death it brought to souls and, more than ever, "tears became his food by day and night" (Ps 42.3) ("more than ever," because "he who increases knowledge increases sorrow" (Eccl 1.18) and "passion makes the bones rot" (Prv 14.30).

These days, therefore, that he lived through, or endured, almost at the very end of his life, were the bitterest and most mournful of all his old age. A man such as he had to see cities overthrown and destroyed and, with them, their citizens and inhabitants and the buildings on their estates wiped out by a murderous enemy, and others put to flight and scattered. He saw churches denuded of priests and ministers; holy virgins and others vowed to chastity dispersed, some among them succumbing to tortures, others perishing by the sword, others taken captive and losing innocence of soul and body, and faith itself, in evil and cruel slavery to their foes.

He saw the hymns and divine praises ceasing in the churches, the buildings themselves in many places burned down, the solemn sacrifices owed to God no longer offered in the appointed places, the holy sacraments no longer wanted, and, if they were wanted, ministers of them hard to find. He saw

41. These Germanic peoples had crossed the Rhine near Metz and Trier on the last day of 406, carved a swath of destruction across Gaul, settled for a time in Spain, and then headed for North Africa in 428 and 429.

men taking refuge in forests on the mountains, in caves in the rocks, in dens, or in any strong places; others forced out of them and their escape cut off; others, again, stripped and deprived of all means of subsistence and slowly perishing of hunger; the very bishops and clergy of the churches (if, by God's favor, they did not encounter the enemy or escaped from the encounter) robbed and denuded of everything and begging in the utmost need, when there was no possibility of supplying them with all that was necessary for their support.

Of the countless churches, he saw only three survive, those of Carthage, Hippo, and Cirta, which by God's favor were not uprooted; and their cities still stand, buttressed by human and divine support. After his death the city of Hippo was burned to the ground by the enemy after being abandoned by its inhabitants. And amid these calamities he used to console himself with the maxim of a certain wise man who said: "No great man will think it a great matter when sticks and stones fall and mortals die."

Over all these events, then, in his own wise way, he daily and deeply mourned. Then, to his other griefs and sorrows, there was added the arrival of this same enemy to besiege Hippo-Regius itself, which had so far been left alone. Their reason was that a certain Count Boniface with an army of allied Goths[42] had taken up his position there to defend it. For nearly fourteen months their investment of the city was complete, for their lines even deprived it of its seacoast.

I myself, and other bishops from neighboring regions, had taken refuge there and were in the city during the whole of the siege. We had many talks together, therefore, saying, as we pondered the dread judgments of God that were being executed before our eyes: "Just are you, O Lord, and righteous are your judgments" (Ps 119.137). And as we sorrowed, sighed, and wept together, we implored the Father of mercies and the God from whom all consolation comes (see 2 Cor 1.3) that He would see fit to support us in our present tribulation.

29

One day, when we happened to be at table with him and talking about these matters, he said to us:

---

42. Much of the late Roman military establishment consisted of Germanic troops who were either regulars or allies.

"You ought to know that, in these days of disaster for us, my prayer to God is that He will either consent to liberate this besieged city or, if He thinks otherwise, will give His servants strength to go through with what He wills for them or, so far as I am concerned, will take me from this world."

Then, using the words he gave us, we joined him in making the same petition to God on high for ourselves and for all our flocks and for those who were in the city with us. And what should happen but that in the third month of the siege he went to bed with a fever and entered upon his last illness. The Lord was not going to withhold from His servant the answer to his prayer. He obtained in due time what he had asked for through his tears both for himself and for his city.[43]

I know, too, that both as a priest and as a bishop, when asked to pray for sufferers from demon-possession, he has petitioned God with many tears and the demons have gone out. Again, when he was ill and in bed, someone came to him with a sick patient and asked him to lay his hand on him, so that he might recover. He replied that if he had any powers of that kind he would surely have used them on himself first. But the man insisted that he had a vision and had been told in his dream: "Go to Bishop Augustine and get him to lay his hand on him and he will recover." Informed of this, Augustine acted on it without further delay and the Lord at once enabled the sick man to leave his presence healed.

30

I must certainly record, in connection with these events, how, when the enemy I have been speaking of was threatening us, Augustine was consulted by letter by that holy man, our colleague Honoratus, bishop of Thiabe,[44] as to whether the bishops and clergy ought to leave their churches when the enemy were approaching, or not. In his reply he brought out clearly what was most to be feared from these subverters of Romanity. I want this letter to him included in this memoir as a very useful and much needed guide to conduct for God's priests and ministers.

"From Augustine, to his holy brother and colleague, Bishop Honoratus, greetings in the Lord."

43. The siege of Hippo finally ended in 431 after Augustine's death.
44. A small town, evidently near Hippo but not yet satisfactorily identified.

1. "I had thought that the copy sent to your Grace of the letter I wrote to our brother and colleague Quodvultdeus would have relieved me of the task you have laid upon me in asking my advice as to what you ought to do in these perilous circumstances in which we are living. For although I wrote only a short letter, I think that I omitted nothing that the writer of the reply needed to say or the questioner to hear. For I said that, while those who wished to withdraw, while they could, to fortified centers, should not be prevented, at the same time we have no right to throw off the fetters of our ministry, with which the love of Christ has bound us, and desert the churches that we have the duty of serving. These, in fact, are the words I used in that letter: 'I say, then, in conclusion, that our ministrations are so necessary to even the smallest of God's congregations that, when it is staying on in the place we are in, it ought not to be left without them. It is for us, therefore, to say to the Lord; Be to us a God who protects, a city fortified (see Ps 31.1–3).

2. "But you are not satisfied with this advice because (you say in your letter) we would be resisting the teaching and example of Our Lord, where He advises us to fly from city to city. And, of course, we remember His words; 'When they persecute you in one town, flee to the next' " (Mt 10.23).

"But who supposes that Our Lord meant by this that the flocks that He bought with His own blood were to be left without the ministrations necessary to their very life? Was He Himself doing that when He fled to Egypt as an infant in His parents' arms, before He had gathered any congregations He could be said to be deserting? Or when the apostle Paul, to avoid capture by his enemy, "was let down in a basket through a window in the wall, and escaped his hands" (2 Cor 11.33), was the church there left without the ministrations necessary to it? Were not all that were needed supplied by other brethren resident there? Indeed, it was at their wish that the apostle was doing it, in order to preserve for the church the particular person that that persecutor was trying to seize.

"Let the servants of Christ, then, the ministers of His message and His Sacrament, do just what He has commanded or permitted. By all means let them fly from city to city when someone is specially wanted by the persecutors, so long as there are others not so much wanted who are not deserting the Church and can supply spiritual nourishment to their fellow servants, who they know could not live without it. But when all—bishops, priests, and laity alike—are in the same danger, then those who need the others must not be abandoned by those they need. Either let them all go off together to fortified centers or, if some are obliged to remain, let them not be deserted by those through whom their spiritual needs have to be met. Thus they will either survive together or suffer together, whichever their heavenly Father wishes to be their lot.

3. "And should it be their lot to suffer, whether in unequal or in equal measure, it will then become apparent which are those who are suffering on behalf of others. They will be those who could have avoided these calamities by flight but preferred to remain and not abandon others in their need. This, indeed, is the great proof of that charity which the apostle John is recommending to us when he says: As Christ laid down His life for us, so we should lay down our lives for the brethren (see 1 Jn 3.16).

"In other words, when those who take to flight, or are prevented from doing so only by their own concerns, are caught and made to suffer, they suffer, of course, for themselves, not for their brothers. But those who suffer because they were not willing to desert the brethren who needed them for their health as Christians are laying down their lives for the brethren without a doubt.

4. "What, then, of what I once heard a bishop say, that if Our Lord told us to take to flight even in those persecutions in which the crown of martyrdom can be won, we ought all the more to fly from the fruitless sufferings that come from an invasion of barbarian enemies? That is very true and sound advice for those who have no ties of ecclesiastical duty. But if their reason for not flying from a murderous enemy when they might have done is that they do not wish to desert Christ's ministry, without which men cannot live as Christians or become Christians, then their charity receives a greater reward than if they had fled on their own account and not on their brethren's and had then been caught and suffered martyrdom for not denying Christ.

5. "But what was the point you made in your first letter? You said: 'If we are to stay with our congregations, I cannot see what good we shall be doing either to ourselves or to the people. All that will happen will be that the slaughter of men, the outraging of women, and the burning of churches will take place under our eyes and we ourselves will die under torture when they are trying to get from us something we have not got.' Well, God is quite able to hear the prayers of His children and ward off these things they are dreading; and dangers that are, therefore, at the worst uncertain cannot justify us in what would certainly be a dereliction of duty and would certainly inflict fatal injuries on our flocks, not in this life, but in that other life so incomparably better worth our anxious thought and care.

"You see, if those calamities, which we fear may come upon us where we are, were certain, all those for whose sake we ought to stay would have already fled from there and freed us from any obligation to remain. For no one says that ministers have to stay on where there is no one needing their ministry.

That is why some of the holy bishops of Spain fled, after their flocks had in some cases melted away in flight, in others had been slaughtered, in others had been starved in sieges or dispersed in captivity. But many more stayed on in the thick of the dangers, because those they stayed for were staying on. And if some did desert their flocks, that is what I say should not be done. For they were not being guided by divine authority but were blinded by human error or in the bondage or human fears.

6. "And how is it that they think they must give undiscriminating obedience to precepts when they read about fleeing from one city to another, and have no horror of the hireling who sees the wolf coming and flies, because he is not concerned for the sheep? (see Jn 10.12–13). Here are two pronouncements, both by Our Lord and both true, one permitting and even ordering flight, the other rebuking and condemning it. Why do they not try to find interpretations for them that will show them to be consistent with each other, as indeed they are? And how can this be found without stressing the point I have just been making, that the time for us ministers of Christ to fly from the places where we happen to be, in face of persecution, is when Christ has no people there who need our ministrations, or the necessary ministrations can be supplied by others who have not the same reason for flight?

"It was like that in the case I have just quoted, when the apostle was let down in a sack and fled because the persecutor was looking for him particularly. Since there were others for whom no such necessity existed and who were responsible for the ministry there, God forbid that we should suppose the church deserted. It was the same when the holy Athanasius,[45] bishop of Alexandria, fled, for the Emperor Constantius had given orders for the arrest of him particularly, and the Catholic congregations resident in Alexandria were by no means deserted by the other ministers.

"But when the people stay on and the ministers take to flight and their ministrations cease, what is that but the damnable flight of hirelings who are not concerned for the sheep? For the wolf will come, in the form not of a man but of the devil, who has often persuaded the faithful to apostatize when the Lord's Body ceased to be ministered to them daily; and thus the weak, for whom Christ died, will perish, not through your knowledge but through your ignorance, my brother (see 1 Cor 8.11).

7. "As for those who, in this matter, are not so much deceived by fallacies as overcome by terror, why should they not, by the mercy and aid of the Lord,

---

45. C. 296–373, the great battler against Arianism who several times earned the displeasure of the Arian emperor Constantius II.

make a brave struggle against their fears, rather than incur calamities incomparably graver and far more to be dreaded? That is what men do when they burn with the flames of charity, not with the fumes of this world's lusts. For charity says, "who is weak and I am not weak? Who is made to fall and I am not indignant?" (2 Cor 11.29). But charity is the gift of God. Let us pray, then, that He who orders it will give it.

"And in our charity toward God's sheep, who must all die some day, some way, we should be more afraid of a butchery of their minds by the sword of spiritual evil than of their bodies by a sword of steel. We should be more afraid of their losing the purity of the faith through the corrupting of the interior life than of women being defiled by violence done to their bodies. For violence cannot violate chastity if the mind preserves it. Even the chastity of the body is not violated when she who suffers is not voluntarily abusing her body but is enduring, without consenting, what another is perpetrating.

"We should be more afraid of 'living stones' being extinguished when we have abandoned them than of the stone and wood of earthly buildings being set on fire under our eyes. We should be more afraid of the members of Christ's body being destroyed, starved of the food of the spirit, than of the members of our own body being tortured, gripped in the clutch of the enemy. Not that such things as these are not to be escaped when they can be; but when they cannot be escaped without irreligion they are better endured—unless, of course, one is going to argue that a minister is not irreligious who withdraws the ministrations necessary for religion at the very time when the need is greatest.

8. "But perhaps we do not think of the scene when the peril has come to a climax and all chance of flight has gone—of the church packed, as it always is, with a throng of both sexes and all ages, some clamoring for baptism, others to be reconciled to the church, others, again, to be given penance, and all for consolation and for the consecration and distribution of the sacraments. And if the ministers of the sacraments are not there, what a catastrophe for those who depart from this world either unregenerated by baptism or unabsolved from sin! What a grief for their Christian relatives not to have them with them when they enter the repose of life eternal! And lastly, what groans from all, and what blasphemies from some, at the absence of these ministrations and their ministers.

"You see what the fear of temporal calamities can do, and how great an increase of eternal calamities springs from it. But if the ministers are there, they are a help to all, in proportion to the strength which the Lord supplies to them. They baptize some, others are reconciled to the church, none are deprived of the Communion of the Lord's Body. All are consoled, strengthened, and encouraged, so that, when they pray to God, who is able to avert all the ills they fear, they are prepared for either event and able to say, if this cup cannot pass from them, His will be done, who cannot will any evil.

9. "I am sure you can see now what you wrote that you could not see, how much the Christian congregations stand to gain if, in their present troubles, they have Christ's ministers among them. You can see also how much is lost if they are absent seeking their own ends and not Jesus Christ's (cf. Phil 2.21), not possessing that charity of which it was said it seeks not its own ends (cf. 1 Cor 3.5), and not imitating the one who described himself as "not seeking my own advantage, but that of many, that they may be saved" (1 Cor 10.33), and who would never have fled from the plots of that persecuting prince if there had not been others to whom he was a necessity for whom he wished to preserve himself. That is why he says, "I am hard-pressed between the two. My desire is to depart and be with Christ, for that is far better. But to remain in the flesh is more necessary on your account (Phil 1.23–24).

10. "Possibly at this point someone may say that God's ministers ought to flee, when such calamities are threatening, so as to preserve themselves to be of use to the church in calmer times. It is quite right for some people to do this when there are others to carry on the church's ministry, so that it is not abandoned by all. Athanasius did this, as I said above. For the Catholic faith, which he defended, by his words and his love, against the Arian heretics, bears witness to how necessary it was for the church, and how profitable, to have him still in the flesh. But when all are in the same danger, the probability is that anyone taking to flight will be regarded as doing it from fear of death rather than from the wish to be helpful and will do more harm by setting an example of fleeing than he can do good by performing the service of living; and then flight should be out of the question.

"Finally, when holy David would not entrust himself to the chances of battle for fear (as the narrative puts it) 'lest the lamp of Israel be quenched' (2 Sm 21.17), he was taking the course urged by others, not taking it upon himself to decide. Otherwise he would have had many imitators among the cowards, who would have supposed him to be acting thus, not out of regard for the good of others, but under the pressure of his own fears.

11. "But another point arises which we have no right to pass over. If we admit that questions of utility cannot be altogether disregarded, so that some ministers ought to escape when some great disaster threatens so as to minister to those whom they find left after the slaughter, what should be done when it looks as if all are going to perish unless some take to flight? Again, what if the destruction has been checked to the extent that only the church's ministers are being persecuted?

"What can one say? Is the church to be left desolate by the flight of her ministers because it would be more wretched for her to be left desolate by their deaths? Besides, if the laity are not being hunted to death themselves, they can hide their bishops and clergy in such ways as God makes possible, who has everything under His control and is able to save by His most marvelous power even those who do not run away—only we are inquiring what we ought to do, because we do not want to be thought to be experimenting with God by looking to Him for a miracle every time.

"Certainly the case when laymen and clergy are in the same danger cannot be compared with one of those storms when merchants and seamen are in the same danger on a ship. God forbid that this ship of ours should be valued at so little that it could be right for the sailors, and even for the pilot, to abandon it in its dangers, just because they can escape by jumping into the ship's boat or even by swimming. For what is it we fear for those who we fear may perish by our desertion? It is not temporal death, which must come some time or other, but eternal death, which can come if precautions are not taken but need not come if they *are* taken.

"Moreover, if the temporal dangers are really the same for all, why should we suppose that every time the enemy break in, the clergy are all going to die, but the laity are not? And, if the laity do all die, there will be an end for everyone at the same time of the life for which the clergy are necessary. Alternatively, why should we not hope that, if some of the laity survive, some of the clergy will survive also and be in a position to provide them with the ministrations they will need?

12. "But how much better it would be if the contention between God's ministers were as to who should stay and who should fly to ensure that the church should be desolated neither by the flight of all nor by the death of all! That will be the contest between them when on both sides charity is the impulse and on both sides charity is the aim.

"And if there is no other way of ending that argument, then, so far as I can see, it must be decided by lot who shall stay and who shall go. For those who say that it is their duty to go will either seem timid because they do not want to face the threatened disaster, or conceited because they think that they are the ones most necessary to preserve for the church. Then again, the best of them will probably choose to lay down their lives for their brethren, so that the ones preserved by flight will be those whose lives are less useful because they are less skilled as counselors and rulers. But these, in their turn, if they have a sense of what is fitting, will contest the choice of those who much prefer death to flight but are obviously the ones who ought to live.

"And thus, as Scripture says, "the log puts an end to disputes and decides between powerful contenders" (Prv 18.18). For in these doubtful cases it is better for God than for men to judge whether it is more fitting to call the best to receive the crown of martyrdom and to spare the weak or, alternatively, to give the weak the strength to undergo those sufferings and so take from this world those whose lives could not benefit the church as much as the lives of the others. No doubt to draw lots would be an unusual course to take but, if it were taken, who would dare to find fault with it? Who, except from ignorance or malice, would not lavish on it the praises due to it?

"But if there is reluctance to take a course without precedent, at least let no one by taking to flight cause the church's ministrations to cease, least of all when such great perils make them more than ever a necessity and a duty. Let no one have such regard for himself that, just because he seems to excel in some quality, he says he is the fittest to live, and so to fly. Whoever *thinks* that, is much too pleased with himself; whoever *says* that, is displeasing to everyone else.

13. "There are some, to be sure, who think that bishops and clergy who do not take to flight amid such dangers, but stay where they are, mislead their flocks who, when they see their pastors staying, will not go themselves. But it is easy to avoid these malicious reproaches by addressing these same flocks and saying to them: 'Do not be misled by the fact that we are not leaving this place. It is on your account, not on our own, that we are choosing to stay here, so as not to fail you in the ministrations we know to be necessary to the salvation you have in Christ. So if you want to leave yourselves, you will at the same time be releasing us from the bonds that hold us.'

"This is what I think *should* be said when it really seems expedient to withdraw to safer localities. But, even after hearing this, all or some may say: 'We are in the hands of Him whose anger no one can escape, no matter where he goes, and whose mercy anyone can find, no matter where he is, if he is reluctant to go elsewhere, either because he is tied by definite obligations or because he is unwilling to spend great toil on finding a dubious refuge and changing the danger without ending it.' If they say this, they certainly must not be neglected by the Christian ministry. But if, after hearing the bishops, they prefer to leave, those who were staying on their account are no longer bound to stay, because there is no one there any longer whom they are bound to stay for.

14. "Whoever, then, flees in such circumstances that the ministrations necessary to the church are not brought to an end by his flight, does what Our Lord ordered or allowed. But whosoever flees in such a way that the nourish-

ment from which Christ's flock draws its spiritual life is withdrawn from it, is 'the hireling who sees the wolf coming and who flies because he is not concerned for the sheep.'

"I have written to you in this way, dearest brother, in truth and true charity, because you have asked my advice and because it is what I think. But if you can find a better opinion, I claim no priority for my own. But a better thing to do in these dangers we shall never find than to pray to the Lord our God that He will have mercy on us. As for this intention of not deserting the churches, there are wise and holy men who, by God's grace, have been privileged to entertain it and to act on it, and, in the teeth of obloquy, have persevered in their set purpose."

31

God granted that the life of this holy man should be a long one, for the benefit and happiness of holy church, and he lived seventy-six years, nearly forty of them as priest or bishop. In the course of them he often told us in intimate conversation that the reception of baptism did not absolve Christians, and especially priests, however estimable, from the duty of doing fitting and adequate penance before departing from this life. And he acted on this himself in his last and fatal illness. For he ordered those psalms of David which are specially penitential to be copied out and, when he was very weak, used to lie in bed facing the wall where the sheets of paper were put up, gazing at them and reading them, and copiously and continuously weeping as he read.

Moreover, so as not to have his thoughts distracted by anyone, about ten days before his death he asked those of us who were with him not to let anyone go in to him, except at the times when the doctors came to see him or food was brought to him. This was attended to and carried out, and during the whole of that time he gave himself to prayer.

Right up to his last illness he had preached God's Word in the church unceasingly, vigorously, and powerfully, with sound mind and sound judgment. Now, with all his limbs and organs unimpaired, and sound in sight and hearing, while we stood by and watched and prayed, he, in the words of Scripture, "slept with his fathers" (1 Kgs 2.10), in the ripeness of "a good old age" (1 Chr 29.28). In our presence the Holy Sacrifice was offered up commending his body to the earth, and he was buried.

He made no will because, as one of God's poor, he had nothing to leave. It was a standing order that the library of the church and all the books should be carefully preserved for posterity. Whatever the church possessed in the way of funds or ornaments he handed over in trust to the priest who had been in charge of the church house in his lifetime.

As for his relatives, whether they were in the religious life or not, neither in life nor in death did he treat them as most people treat their relations. While he was still alive he would give to them, when they needed it, as he would give to anyone else, not so as to make them rich but so that they might not be in want, or be less in want.

To the church he left an adequate body of clergy, as well as convents for men and for women, full of celibates under their appointed superiors. He left also a library with books containing writings by himself and other holy men. It is through these, thanks be to God, that his quality and stature in the church is known to the world; and in these he will always live among the faithful. To quote an epitaph that one of the secular poets composed for himself when directing that after his death a monument should be erected to him in a public place:

> Traveler, would you like to know
> How poets live on after death?
> As you read aloud, it is I who speak;
> Your voice is sounded by my breath.[46]

His writings, indeed, show us as clearly as the light of truth ever permits one to see, that this priest, so acceptable and so dear to God, lived rightly and sanely in the faith and hope and charity of the Catholic Church; and no one can read what he wrote on theology without profit. But I think that those were able to profit still more who could hear him speak in church and see him with their own eyes and, above all, had some knowledge of him as he lived among his fellow men. For he was not only "a scribe who was trained in the kingdom of heaven . . . who brings out of his treasure what is new and what is old" (Mt 13.52) or "like a merchant in search of fine pearls who, on finding one pearl of great value, went and sold all that he had and bought it" (Mt 13.45–46). He was also one of those in whom is fulfilled the text "So speak and so act" (see Jas 2.12) and of whom the Savior said: "he who does them and teaches them shall be called great in the kingdom of heaven" (Mt 5.19).

46. This fine poem partakes of the ancient poetic tradition that the poet lives on in his poetry. Both Horace and Ovid wrote similar verses, but there does not appear to be a single, direct source for these lines.

And now I earnestly ask you who read these words that in your charity you will join me in giving thanks to Almighty God, for "I bless the Lord who gave me counsel" (Ps 16.7) and with it the will and capacity to bring these things to the knowledge both of those who are with us and those who are far from us, of men of our times and men of times to come. And join me also in praying for me myself, that having been allowed by God to live with this man, no longer with us, in a lovely intimacy without a single bitter disagreement for nearly forty years, I may be his emulator and imitator in this world and may share with him in the world to come the joys promised by Almighty God.

Constantius of Lyon

THE LIFE OF SAINT GERMANUS OF AUXERRE

Translated by F. R. Hoare

Constantius of Lyon is an extremely shadowy figure. He reveals virtually nothing about himself in his *Life of Germanus* and in our quest for details we are reduced to conjectures based upon scattered references. Sidonius Apollinaris (c. 430–c. 480), a cultivated Gallic aristocrat, imperial officer, man of letters, and bishop of Clermont, refers to Constantius several times in his letters. In a letter written around 469 (*Letters*, 1.1), Sidonius referred to Constantius as "My highly honored master" (*Domine maior*) and it may be that Constantius was actually Sidonius's teacher. He may therefore have been twenty or more years older than his pupil. Both men did come from Lyon. An epitaph long assumed to be Constantius's says only that he lived eighty-four years. Supposing that he was born around 410, it would be possible to conclude that he lived into the 490s. Sometime between 470 and 475 Sidonius thanked Constantius for coming to Clermont after a barbarian attack (*Letters*, 3.2) despite being old and sick. Sidonius also tells us (*Letters*,

2.10) that Constantius was a gifted poet, but no surviving texts permit corroboration of that assertion. We are thrown back on the *Life of Germanus*.

Consensus holds that the *Life* was composed between 475 and 480. Constantius himself tells us that he wrote it on the request of Bishop Patiens of Auxerre. It seems that Germanus had become the object of considerable popular devotion and that his successor as bishop of Auxerre desired to have a proper saint's life prepared. Surely it is a measure of the esteem in which Constantius was then held that Patiens turned to him to write this life. Constantius had no discernible connection with Auxerre and does not seem to have known Germanus.

The polished Latin of the text confirms Patiens's good judgment while also making clear why so stern a cultural arbiter as Sidonius would have admired Constantius. The author observes well the emerging conventions of hagiography, and the immense popularity of this text attests to its own influential role in the development of the genre. Later writers in Gaul, such as the poet Venantius Fortunatus (c. 530–c. 610), in Italy, such as Ennodius of Pavia (c. 473–521), in Spain, such as Isidore of Seville (560–636) and Braulio of Saragossa (585/90–651), and in England, such as Bede (673–735) drew from or were influenced by this *Life*. More than one hundred manuscripts survive, many of the best ones from the ninth century.

This text shows both similarities and differences to the two preceding ones. Again, the life of a bishop is told. But Germanus is a wonder-worker, like Martin, rather than a scholar, controversialist, and administrator, like Augustine. Unlike Martin and Augustine, Germanus is an aristocrat. We meet him as a high imperial official and leave him after his triumphal visit to the imperial court. Hagiographical texts may be conventional, but conventions, like the subjects to which they are applied, permit infinite variation.

Germanus (375–446), a Gallic aristocrat, served in the imperial administration and as a soldier before entering the clergy. It was his class of people who found the likes of Martin of Tours uncouth. He traveled twice to Britain to combat heresy and on one occasion used his military skills to help the British repel a barbarian attack. No writings by Germanus have survived.

Texts and References

Outstanding is Constance de Lyon, *Vie de Saint Germain d'Auxerre*, ed. and trans. René Borius, Sources Chrétiennes 112 (Paris, 1965). Borius's lengthy introduction (pp. 7–106) remains unsurpassed. Recent and challenging, but emphasizing one aspect of Germanus's career is E. A. Thompson, *Saint Germanus of Auxerre and the End of Roman Britain* (Woodbridge, Suffolk, 1984).

Dedications To His Most Blessed and Apostolic Lordship and My Perpetual Patron Patiens,[1] Father in God,[2] from Constantius, a Sinner

Among the virtues, the first place is rightly claimed by obedience; and, though it makes many of us attempt what we cannot accomplish, those who obey orders regardless of their powers merit praise at least for their devotion. Now you, most reverend Father in God, desiring to secure for a holy man the fame due to his virtues and to publish the witness of his miracles for all to profit by, have again and again commanded me to preserve both for our own and for future generations, in such language as I can, the life of the holy Bishop Germanus,[3] hitherto shrouded in silence. In boldly approaching this task I know myself to be guilty of presumption. But grant me your pardon; perhaps some blame attaches to your own judgment; you should have chosen for so great a topic a worthier narrator. But since we have both sinned out of charity, you in thinking me able to do what I cannot and I in deferring with goodwill to your authority, pray for me that my service may through your intercession earn the favor that it cannot win by its own merits.[4]

May you long prosper. Remember me always.

To His Most Blessed Lordship, whom I Revere as an Apostle, Censurius,[5] Father in God, from Constantius, a Sinner

It is my first care to preserve intact a sense of humility and, if now I break violently through the barriers it imposes, the blame attaches to those who lay

---

1. Bishop of Lyon, c. 451–491.

2. Constantius uses *Patiens papa*. Eventually this word was reserved to the pope, but in late antiquity it was applied to many bishops as a term of affection and respect.

3. C. 375–446, bishop of Auxerre after 418.

4. Here is the humility (or modesty) topos (or commonplace) that we already met in Sulpicius and Possidius.

5. Bishop of Auxerre, 472–502.

commands upon me, rather than to myself. When I strung together, far from completely, the life and deeds of the blessed Bishop Germanus, it was the authority of your holy brother-prelate Patiens that brought it about; I was obeying his commands, if not as I ought, at least as best I could. And now that my obedience has come to the knowledge of your beatitude, it seems that I must once more be overbold. For you have commanded that my poor pages, which hitherto have been for little more than private circulation, are to go abroad bearing my name; and I am, so to speak, to incriminate myself and surrender myself to execution. For plainly I shall fall under condemnation if my rustic idiom[6] is brought to learned ears. However, I have cast aside the veil of modesty, obeyed your order, and sent you this pledge of the devotion I bear you. I ask only this as a token of your charity, that in your kindness you say two prayers for me: may my readers not scrutinize my words too closely and may my service be brought by your intercession to the knowledge of my holy master Germanus.

PREFACE

Most people are drawn to writing by an abundance of materials, and wits are supposed to be enriched where there is much to say; but for myself, as I begin to recount, far from completely, the life and deeds of that most illustrious man, Bishop Germanus, I am filled with trepidation at the number of his miracles. Just as the brightness of the sun brought to bear upon stupefied humans blunts the keenness of the eyes, and light throws light into confusion, so my feeble mind shrinks from so much to praise, heaped up before its impotence. Thus, within my breast, two courses are in conflict. On the one side, my knowledge of my impotence says "No"; on the other side, the sight of such piety, and the witness borne by countless miracles, drive me to record and bring to light matters that it would be impious to hide under a veil of silence from those who might profit by a knowledge of them. I have chosen, therefore, to shut my eyes to my own shame rather than allow the works of God to grow old in a prolonged oblivion. The materials must excuse the narrator. Those who are displeased by my rustic idiom will at least find pleasure in the beauty of the deeds it recounts. Nor need I fear that I shall be regarded as having pushed myself forward into such a task as this, for so many cycles of the seasons have gone round that a knowledge of the facts, dimmed by long silence, can now only be acquired by labor. Indeed, I should have preferred that another than myself should have been the historian

---

6. More rhetorical artifice: Constantius's Latin is highly polished.

of such good things, for whoever he was he would have been more worthy than I. But, since this has not come about, better myself than no one.

1

Germanus, then, was a native of the town of Auxerre,[7] born of parents of the highest rank, and was from earliest childhood given a liberal education. In this, the instruction he received was matched by the abundance of his talent and together these gave him learning doubly assured, by nature and by industry. Moreover, that nothing should be lacking to complete his education, when he had done with the lecture rooms of Gaul he added in Rome a knowledge of law to the completeness he had already attained.

Next, practicing as a barrister he became the ornament of the law courts. While he was thus engaged and dazzling all by the praises he drew upon himself, he took a wife, whose birth, wealth, and character were all of the highest. Then, when he was at the height of his reputation in the legal profession, the state promoted him to official rank by conferring on him the supreme office of dux[8] and the rule over more than one province. Assuredly his training was being directed by the hidden wisdom of God so that nothing should be lacking to the completeness of the apostolic pontiff-to-be. Eloquence was provided to equip the preacher, legal learning as an aid to justice, and the society of a wife to witness to his chastity.

2

Suddenly divine authority intervened and universal consent executed its decrees. For all the clergy, the whole nobility, the townsfolk and the countryfolk, with one accord demanded Germanus for their bishop. A war was declared by the people against their magistrate, who was easily overcome, since even his own staff turned against him. Thus he received the fullness of the priesthood[9]

---

7. Auxerre was a modest town about 100 miles southeast of Paris on the Yonne River.

8. Military governor of a turbulent frontier region, in this case Armorica (modern Brittany).

9. Like the great Church Father Ambrose of Milan, Germanus was promoted from the laity directly to the episcopate. It is reasonable to suppose some period of training and then ordination to the priesthood before his episcopal consecration. Though not usual, this did happen with some frequency in late antiquity as communities sought spiritual leaders who could replace the patronage and protection formerly provided by lay leaders. Note well that it was personal connections and public distinction that first recommended Germanus as bishop, not sanctity.

under compulsion, as a conscript; but, this done, immediately he made the change complete. He deserted the earthly militia to be enrolled in the heavenly; the pomps of this world were trodden underfoot; a lowly way of life was adopted, his wife was turned into a sister, his riches were distributed among the poor, and poverty became his ambition.

3

But no words can describe the fierceness with which he did violence to himself and the crucifixions and penances with which he persecuted his own body. I will summarize them briefly, with strict fidelity to the truth. From the day upon which he entered upon the fullness of the priesthood until the end of his life, he persisted in nourishing his soul by starving his body, even to the extent of never taking wheaten bread, nor wine, nor vinegar, nor oil, nor pulse, nor even salt for seasoning. It is true that on Easter and Christmas Day a drink was served in which there would have been a taste of wine if it had not been destroyed by excessive dilution in the way one tempers with quantities of water the harshness of vinegar! At meals he first took a taste of ashes, then bread made of barley which he himself had pounded and ground. And this food, acknowledged to be more trying than fasting, was never served until evening, except sometimes on a Wednesday and generally on Saturdays.

4

His clothing was a cloak and tunic, regardless of the seasons, for winter brought no addition to it nor was summer allowed to lighten it. These two garments continued to be used, unless one was given away, until they fell to pieces from hard wear. Under them there was always a hair-shirt.[10] Narrow rough-hewn planks formed a framework for his bed, the space between them being filled to the brim with ashes. These, by being constantly compressed by his weight, became as hard as unbroken earth. His only bedclothes were a piece of sacking spread beneath him and a single military cape over him; there was nothing in the way of a pillow to place under his neck to support his head.

Lying flat like this, he condemned his limbs to be stretched out along the

10. A rough, harsh garment made of cloth woven directly from animal hair and worn next to the body as a form of penitence.

ground. He never removed his clothes at night and seldom either his girdle or his shoes, and he always had round his neck a leather strap with a box containing relics. His groans were continual and prayer unceasing, for he could get little sleep in such acute discomfort. Everyone must have his own opinion; mine is quite definitely that the blessed Germanus, amid all these crucifixions, endured a drawn-out martyrdom. But how wonderful is the power and goodness of our God! for He gave His servant, traveling faithfully along the true road, a twofold recompense. Such errors as he may formerly have committed were purged away and in the process a refined sanctity was rapidly acquired; and, though he may have been a debtor by reason of past sins, he was presently able to draw for the benefit of others upon a stock of accumulated virtues.

5

He was especially punctilious in hospitality. His house was open to all without exception and he entertained them at his table without breaking his own fast. He washed the feet of all his guests with his own hands, following the example of the Lord whose servant he was.

6

Thus this man of blessings achieved something very difficult: amid all the coming and going he lived the life of the solitary, and inhabited the desert while dwelling in the world.

Furthermore, for the advancement of religion he provided two roads to Christ, by founding a monastery within sight of the town, across the river Yonne, so that the surrounding population might be brought to the Catholic faith[11] by contact with the monastic community as well as by the ministrations of the church.[12] This was all the more likely to succeed since the flame of faith was fanned by such a bishop and such a teacher, to say nothing of the miracles.

11. Rural people were still largely pagan, that is, adherent of their ancestral religion, while the local military administration was in the hands of the Arian (see above, page 49, note 30) Visigoths.

12. With Martin of Tours, Germanus was a great promoter of cenobitic monasticism. By Germanus's day the monastery founded at Lérins (an island in the Mediterranean just offshore from Cannes) in 410 was popularizing "eremitic" monasticism of a harsh variety. It seems probable that Germanus's monastery was dedicated in honor of Saints Cosmas and Damian, two extremely shadowy martyrs of the early church.

As for these, when, as his holiness grew, he came to make proof of his spiritual powers, his motive was not presumption but mercy.

7

There was at that time a man of high character named Januarius who was in the governor's service as head of his office staff and used to bring him the gold collected in taxes from the province. One day he broke his journey to visit the bishop and mislaid his handbag. It was accidentally found, when no one was looking, by a man who was frequently the victim of demoniacal possession. Presently the traveler resumed his journey and discovered his loss. He filled the city with his lamentations and demanded the money back from the holy bishop just as if he had entrusted it to him. The latter, as if he had really been his debtor, promised in the name of God that it should be restored.

Now, the day on which the man had rushed all over the city in his frantic search had been a Saturday. The next day, when there was still no trace of the gold, the man who was looking for it clasped the bishop's knees with tears in his eyes, assuring him that it would mean the death penalty for him if the state's money were not found. The bishop enjoined patience, promising that all would be well. Soon afterward, before setting out for Mass, he gave orders for one of the sufferers from demoniacal possession to be brought before him privately; and who should be brought to him but the man responsible for the theft.

He put him through a strict examination, saying that it was impossible for a crime on his conscience to remain concealed. Then he ordered the enemy of souls who had been prompting these evil deeds to admit the truth of the matter without delay. But the wicked spirit, from sheer malice, denied having committed the crime. At this the bishop, in righteous anger, ordered the liar to be produced in front of the congregation and, without further delay, set out to celebrate Mass.

He gave the solemn salutation to the people, then prostrated him at full length in prayer. All at once the unhappy man, the captive and at the same time the servant of the demon, was lifted high into the air. The church was filled with his screams, the whole congregation was in confusion and the man himself, yelling out the bishop's name as if he were in the midst of flames, confessed his crime.

Then at last the man of blessings rose from his prayer and came down to the steps of the sanctuary. He called up the raving man, cross-examined him and learned the whole truth. The coins were brought out of their hiding-place, the acclamations of the people resounded, and with one accord they proclaimed the sanctity of Germanus and the power of God. By one and the same miracle the man who had been robbed had got back his money and the demoniac his sanity. Germanus had, indeed, cured many before this, but always under a veil of secrecy. What made this occasion so notable was its publicity.

8

At one time there was a fearful conspiracy of demons to wage a kind of war on the man of blessings himself. When they found him immune, thanks to the breastplate of faith, to all their assaults, they contrived a device for the destruction of his flock. First the children, then their elders, began to succumb to a swelling in their throats that brought death after an illness of less than three days. His congregation was being wiped out as if they were being slaughtered by the sword. No human measures brought any relief and, when it was almost too late, the panic-stricken people appealed to their bishop for divine aid.

Immediately he blessed some oil and, at its touch, the internal swelling went down and a passage was thereby opened for breathing and swallowing. The heavenly remedy effected a cure as rapidly as the onslaught of the disease had brought death. One of those who had been possessed bawled out when he was being exorcised that all this had been brought about by the entry of demons, and acknowledged that they had been put to flight by the holy man's prayer.

9

The man of blessings made it his practice, as leader of the soldiers of God, to stay alternately at the monastery and the church, to set the goal of perfection before each of the rivals in this warfare. On one occasion, when he had been invited to the monastery, he was detained by business and excused himself from coming. A little later, however, when the cause of the delay had been disposed of, he set off to give the brethren a surprise. Now, some of them were troubled by demons and it happened that just then one of the sufferers was in the grip of one. Suddenly he announced at the top of his voice: "Germanus is at the river but cannot cross because he has no boat."

For a long time the abbot gave no credence to this assertion, supposing the evil spirit to be lying, since the bishop had excused himself and would not be coming. But he persisted in his cries and one of the brethren was sent and reported that the demon was right. A boat was sent and the bishop crossed and was received with the usual fervor. He fell at once to praying and the community knelt with him.

Suddenly the demoniac rose in the empty air, held by invisible cords. There was no more delay than was necessary for the bishop to rise from prayer, and all that he required of the demon was that it should go out of the man with some bodily weakness of his. Thus adjured it departed, leaving filth behind it and a stench worthy of it.

10

He was once making a journey in winter and had gone fasting and weary all day long. It was put to him that the approach of night made it necessary to make a stop somewhere. There was a house at a little distance, obviously uninhabited, with its roof partly fallen in, and all overgrown owing to the neglect of the neighbors. In fact it almost looked as if it would be better to pass the night in the cold in the open air than to face the dangers and horrors of that place, particularly as two old men declared that it was so terribly haunted as to be quite uninhabitable. But as soon as the man of blessings heard this, he made for the horrible ruin as if it had been a most desirable residence. He found in it, among what had once been a great many rooms, one that was still something like one, and there his little party and their slender packs were deposited and a short supper was taken; but the bishop would eat nothing at all.

Presently, when the night was well advanced, one of the clergy had begun to read aloud, as his duty was, but the bishop, worn out by fasting and fatigue, had fallen asleep. Suddenly there appeared before the reader's eyes a dreadful specter, which rose up little by little as he gazed on it, while the walls were pelted with a shower of stones. The terrified reader implored the protection of the bishop, who started up and fixed his eyes upon the fearful apparition. Then, invoking the name of Christ, he ordered it to declare who he was and what he was doing there.

At once it lost its terrifying demeanor and, speaking low as a humble suppliant, said that he and a companion after committing many crimes were lying unburied, and that was why they disturbed the living, because they could not rest quietly themselves. It asked the bishop to pray to the Lord for them that He would take them to Himself and grant them eternal rest.

Moved to pity, the holy man told the apparition to show him where they lay. Then, with a torch carried in front, the ghost proceeded to lead the way and, in spite of great difficulties due to the ruins and the stormy night, pointed out the place where they had been thrown. With the return of day the bishop persuaded some of the neigbors to come, and himself stood by to urge on the work. Rubble that had accumulated haphazard in the course of time was raked up and cleared away. The bodies were found, thrown down anyhow, the bones still fastened together with iron fetters. A grave was dug in accordance with the church's law, the limbs were freed from the chains and wrapped in winding sheets, earth was thrown upon them and smoothed down, and the prayers for the dead were recited. There was repose for the dead and quiet for the living. From that day onward the house lost all its terrors and was restored and regularly occupied.

11

Another incident deserves to be recounted that took place some days later on the same journey. Oncoming darkness had compelled the bishop to seek hospitality, and his hosts were quite humble people, a thing which he greatly preferred, as he shunned ostentation. When he had spent the night according to his custom in the recitation of the Divine Office, the sun rose, but no crowing of cocks heralded it, although there were numbers of these birds about the place. He inquired as to the cause of this novelty and was told that, for a long time now, the natural habits of the cocks had given way to a melancholy silence. Everybody asked for his help, so he made return for their hospitality. He took some corn and seasoned it with a blessing and when the birds had eaten it they wearied the ears of the household almost to distraction by their constant crowing. Thus the power of God reveals its greatness even in the smallest things.

12

About this time a deputation from Britain came to tell the bishops of Gaul that the heresy of Pelagius[13] had taken hold of the people over a great part of the country and help ought to be brought to the Catholic faith as soon as possible. A large number of bishops gathered in synod to consider the matter and all

13. On Pelagius, see above, page 50, note 31. This happened in 429.

turned for help to the two who in everybody's judgment were the leading lights of religion, namely Germanus and Lupus,[14] apostolic priests who through their merits were citizens of heaven, though their bodies were on earth. And because the task seemed laborious, these heroes of piety were all the more ready to undertake it; and the stimulus of their faith brought the business of the synod to a speedy end.

13

Thus they embarked upon the ocean under the leadership and inspiration of Christ, who, in the midst of danger, kept His servants safe and proved their worth. At first, when the ship put out to sea, she ran before light breezes blowing from the Bay of Gaul until she was in midchannel where, gaze as you might, you could see nothing but sky and water. Then it was not long before the ocean was assaulted by the violence of demons, haters of religion, who were livid with malice at the sight of such great men hastening to bring salvation to the nations. They heaped up dangers, roused the gales, hid the heavens and the day under a night of clouds, and filled the thick darkness with the terrors of the sea and air. The sails could not resist the fury of the winds and the fragile craft scarcely sustained the weight of the waters. The sailors were powerless and abandoned their efforts; the vessel was navigated by prayer and not by muscles. And at that point the leader himself, the bishop, his body worn out, in his weariness went to sleep.

Then indeed did the storm put forth its strength; it was as if a restraining hand had gone. Before long the vessel was actually being swamped by the waves that swept over it. At last the blessed Lupus and all the excited throng aroused their chief, to match him against the raging elements. He, all the more steadfast for the very immensity of the danger, in the name of Christ chided the ocean, pleading the cause of religion against the savagery of the gales. Then, taking some oil, he lightly sprinkled the waves in the name of the Trinity and this diminished their fury. Consulting his colleague, he now called upon everybody; and prayer was poured out by their united voice.

And there was God! The enemies of souls were put to flight, the air became clear and calm, the contrary winds were turned to aid the voyage, the currents flowed in the service of the ship. Thus great distances were covered and soon all were enjoying repose on the desired shore.

14. Bishop of Troyes, c. 426–478.

There great crowds had gathered from many regions to receive the bishops, whose coming had been foretold by the enemies of souls, for the spirits of evil were heralds of what they feared. And, as they were being cast out of the bodies of the possessed by the prelates, they acknowledged that they had contrived the storm and its dangers, and could not deny that the holiness and the authority of the prelates had vanquished them.

14

And now it was not long before these apostolic priests had filled all Britain, the first and largest of the islands, with their fame, their preaching, and their miracles; and, since it was a daily occurrence for them to be hemmed in by crowds, the word of God was preached, not only in the churches, but at the crossroads, in the fields, and in the lanes. Everwhere faithful Catholics were strengthened in their faith and the lapsed learned the way back to the truth. Their achievements, indeed, were after the pattern of the apostles themselves; they ruled through consciences, taught through letters and worked miracles through their holiness. Preached by such men, the truth had full course, so that whole regions passed quickly over to their side.

The teachers of perverse doctrines lay low for a time, lamenting as wicked spirits do, when nations escape from their clutches and are lost to them. In the end, after prolonged consideration they ventured upon a contest. They came forth flaunting their wealth, in dazzling robes, surrounded by a crowd of flatterers. They preferred the risk of exposure to a silence that would put them to shame in the eyes of the people they had deceived, who would regard them as having condemned themselves if they had nothing to say.

And indeed there was assembled at the meeting-place a crowd of vast proportions, wives and children among them, drawn by the occasion. The people were present both as spectators and as jurymen. The two parties faced each other, ill matched and on unequal terms. On the one side was divine authority, on the other human presumption; on this side, faith, on that side, bad faith; those owned allegiance to Pelagius, these to Christ.

The holy bishops gave the privilege of opening the debate to their opponents, who took up the time of their hearers with empty words drawn out to great length but to little purpose. Then the revered prelates themselves poured out the floods of their eloquence, mingling them with the thunders of the apostle and the Gospels, for their own words were interwoven with the inspired writings and their strongest assertions were supported by the testimony of Scripture. Empty arguments were refuted, dishonest pleas were exposed; and their authors, as each point was made against them, confessed themselves in the wrong by their inability to reply. The jury of the people could hardly keep their hands off them and were not to be stopped from giving their verdict by their shouts.

15

Suddenly a man of high military rank, accompanied by his wife, stepped into the middle and put his ten-year-old daughter, who was blind, into the arms of the bishops. They told him to take her to their opponents. But the latter, stung by conscience and much alarmed, joined the parents in begging the bishops to cure the little girl. The bishops, seeing that the people were expectant and their opponents in a humbler frame of mind, offered a short prayer, after which Germanus, filled with the Holy Spirit and in the name of the Trinity, took from his neck the reliquary that always hung at his side and in full view of everybody put it to the eyes of the child.

Immediately it expelled their darkness and filled them with light and truth. The parents were filled with joy at the miracle and the onlookers with awe. From that day onward the false doctrine was so completely uprooted from men's minds that they looked to the bishops for teaching, with thirsty souls.

16

When this damnable heresy had been thus stamped out, its authors refuted, and the minds of all reestablished in the true faith, the bishops visited the shrine of blessed martyr Alban, to give thanks to God through him. As they were returning, a demon, lying in wait, contrived an accident that caused Germanus to fall and injure his foot. Little did it realize that this bodily misfortune, like those of blessed Job, would advance him in holiness.

The bishop was detained by his injury in one place for a considerable period, in the course of which a fire accidentally broke out close to where he was staying. It had burned several houses, which in those parts are roofed with reeds, and was being carried by the wind to the one in which he was himself lying. Everybody rushed to the prelate to carry him out of danger. But he rebuked them and, strong in his faith, refused to be moved. The crowd in desperation ran to meet the flames. But, the better to display the power of

God, everything the crowd tried to save was burned and what the injured man on his bed guarded was preserved. Shrinking from the house where he was a guest, the flames leaped over it and, although they raged on either side of it, there glittered unharmed amid the furnaces a tabernacle intact, preserved by the occupant within.

The people were overjoyed at the miracle and thankful that their intentions had been defeated by God's power. Day and night a countless throng lay around the poor man's hut, some wanting healing for their souls, others for their bodies. It would be impossible to record all that Christ did through His servant, who exercised these powers when impotent himself. But, although he would allow no one to bring remedies for his own infirmity, one night he saw before him a shining figure in snow-white garments, which stretched out its hand to him as he lay there and raised him up, telling him to stand firmly on his feet. From that moment the pain left him and he so completely recovered his soundness of limb that, when day returned, he resumed the toil of his journeyings without a qualm.

17

Meanwhile the Saxons and the Picts had joined forces to make war upon the Britons.[15] The latter had been compelled to withdraw their forces within their camp and, judging their resources to be utterly unequal to the contest, asked the help of the holy prelates. The latter sent back a promise to come, and hastened to follow it. Their coming brought such a sense of security that you might have thought that a great army had arrived; to have such apostles for leaders was to have Christ Himself fighting in the camp.

It was the season of Lent and the presence of the bishops made the sacred forty days still more sacred; so much so that the soldiers, who received instruction in daily sermons, flew eagerly to the grace of baptism; indeed, great numbers of this pious army sought the waters of salvation. A church was built of leafy branches in readiness for Easter Day, on the plan of a city church, though set in a camp on active service. The soldiers paraded still wet from baptism, faith was fervid, the aid of weapons was thought little of, and all looked for help from heaven.

15. Saxons can refer narrowly to the inhabitants of Saxony, northern Germany, or, in late antiquity, to almost any seaborne raiders. Picts were the inhabitants of modern Scotland. Britons were the largely Celtic inhabitants of what are now England and Wales.

Meanwhile the enemy had learned of the practices and appearance of the camp. They promised themselves an easy victory over practically disarmed troops and pressed on in haste. But their approach was discovered by scouts and, when the Easter solemnities had been celebrated, the army—the greater part of it fresh from the font—began to take up their weapons and prepare for battle and Germanus announced that he would be their general.[16] He chose some light-armed troops and made a tour of the outworks. In the direction from which the enemy were expected he saw a valley enclosed by steep mountains. Here he stationed an army on a new model, under his own command.

18

By now the savage host of the enemy was close at hand and Germanus rapidly circulated an order that all should repeat in unison the call he would give as a battle-cry. Then, while the enemy were still secure in the belief that their approach was unexpected, the bishops three times chanted the Alleluia. All, as one man, repeated it and the shout they raised rang through the air and was repeated many times in the confined space between the mountains.

The enemy were panic-stricken, thinking that the surrounding rocks and the very sky itself were falling on them. Such was their terror that no effort of their feet seemed enough to save them. They fled in every direction, throwing away their weapons and thankful if they could save at least their skins. Many threw themselves into the river which they had just crossed at their ease, and were drowned in it.

Thus the British army looked on at its revenge without striking a blow, idle spectators of the victory achieved. The booty strewn everywhere was collected; the pious soldiery obtained the spoils of a victory from heaven. The bishops were elated at the rout of the enemy without bloodshed and a victory gained by faith and not by force.

Thus this most wealthy island, with the defeat both of its spiritual and of its human foes, was rendered secure in every sense. And now, to the great grief of the whole country, those who had won the victories over both Pelagians and Saxons made preparations for their return. Their own merits and the interces-

---

16. The Latin is *dux proelii*, which means "leader for this battle." Remember that Germanus's public life had been spent as a military commander. The Roman army had been withdrawn from Britain between 407 and 410, which is why the locals were thrown back on their own defenses.

sion of Alban the Martyr[17] secured for them a calm voyage; and a good ship brought them back in peace to their expectant people.

19

All Gaul rejoiced at the return of the revered priests; the churches were gladdened, the demons trembled. The return of Germanus, in particular, had been prayed for by his diocese with a double intention, since he was looked to as its protector both in the court of heaven and in the tempests of this world.[18] A burden of taxes beyond the ordinary and countless other exactions had crushed the spirit of his people who, without him, had felt like orphaned children. So he took the destitute under his protection, inquired into complaints, condoled with the sorrowing. And, when he might have claimed quiet and repose after the dangers of the sea, he incurred the toil of a long journey by land, by undertaking to seek remedies for the distresses of his diocese. But, though about to travel right across Gaul, he contented himself with the smallest possible retinue and the poorest of mounts. Better than the amplest riches, he carried Christ in his breast.

20

I think it worthwhile putting on record that even the journey itself was notable for miracles. He was still in the territory of his own diocese, making his way without haste, and evening was coming on after a rainy day, when his retinue was suddenly increased by a very scantily equipped traveler, barefoot and without a hood, whose very nakedness moved Germanus to pity. Cunningly passing as one of the party, he shared its quarters in the inn and presently, night robber that he was, went off with the beast ridden by the bishop, while its unsuspecting guardians were occupied in watching God rather than the animals. When day returned, the loss of the animal was discovered and one of the clergy, in order that the bishop should have a mount, changed himself from a trooper into an infantryman.

17. Britain's first martyr. He died at Verulamium, today Saint Alban's, in one of Britain's known persecutions: 208–211, 251–259, or 303–305, probably the latter.

18. This passage shows well how, as Roman secular institutions were declining, Roman aristocrats, now in the guise of bishops, continued to exercise the kinds of patronage that members of their class had always exercised.

As they proceeded on their journey, those around him noticed in the man of blessings an unusual mirth that he was trying to conceal by covering his face: soon they had all seen it and one of them took it upon himself to inquire the reason for it.

"Let us halt for a little," replied the bishop, "for the plight of that unfortunate man is both laughable and pitiable. You will see him soon, all hot and bothered."

They stopped and dismounted and soon saw in the distance a man on foot leading the animal he had taken. Before long he had caught up with them, hurrying while they waited for him. At once he threw himself at the bishop's feet and confessed his crime. He described how all night long he had been held fast as it were in a trap. He could not go forward and had found that there was no other means of getting away except to restore the stolen animal. To this the man of blessings replied:

"If yesterday we had given you the clothing you lacked, you would not have been reduced to stealing. Now take this that you need, and restore what is ours."

Thus, for confessing his crime, the man received, instead of punishment, not only pardon but also a reward and a blessing.

21

This man so full of God always tried to keep his deeds secret and to be insignificant in men's eyes, but his miracles made him famous, verifying the words of the Gospel that a city set on a hill cannot be hidden. He denied himself the solace of the company of friends and avoided intercourse with strangers, but he shone with a majesty that could not be obscured. In all the places he passed through on his journey—villages, or towns, or cities—they flocked to meet him with their wives and children and, most of the time, formed a continuous procession, those who met him mingling with those who followed.

22

I would think it a sin to pass by in silence the miracle he worked while stopping at Alise.[19] There was a priest there named Senator, noble by birth and still

---

19. Modern-day Alise-Sainte-Reine (Dépt. Côte d'Or).

nobler by piety. He had a wife Nectariola, equally pious. The bishop for the sake of an old-time friendship sought them out when he passed through the town. They got the house ready for his visit, but the things that had to be provided were inversely proportionate to the importance of the visitor. The lady of the house, however, secretly put some straw under the bishop's pallet and he lay on it without knowing. He gave the night to prayer and psalms and when morning came resumed his journey.

The whole household were delighted to have had so illustrious a visitor and the good lady collected the remains of the straw and preserved it. Some days later a man of good position named Agrestius, with a household consisting of his wife, children, and parents, was entered by a demon, which took possession of him; and the absence of Germanus was as much lamented by the family as the obsession of the unhappy man himself.

But as there was no cure to be found, the revered lady Nectariola resorted to the power of faith. She brought out the straw she had put by and it was wrapped round the raving man. For a whole night he kept shrieking out the name of the bishop as if he were in a furnace, for though the bishop was absent his power was not. In the end the man was delivered from the demon by the divine aid, nor for the rest of his life did he run such a risk again.

23

On this journey to Arles[20] the bishop was carried down to Lyon on the River Saône. On his arrival the population, in eager excitement, came out together to meet him, regardless of age and sex. All begged his blessing and tried to touch him and those who could not touch him were proud even to have seen him. Maladies of all kinds were cured on all sides by his blessing and the city drew life from his preaching, for although he could only make a short stay he did not fail to refresh a thirsty people from the springs of truth.

But if I were to follow him through the whole of his journey, if I were to record everything, I would weary the reader with my prolixity. May God forgive me for omitting so much that I know!

So, then, the city of Arles received the man of blessings on his arrival with an exultant piety; they might have been receiving an apostle living in their

20. Probably in 335. Constantius *might* have seen Germanus.

own day. The bishop and luminary of the city was then Hilary,[21] a man bejeweled with every kind of virtue, a flame of faith, a torrent of sacred eloquence, and a tireless worker at the tasks of God. It was with the affection felt for a father as well as with the reverence due to an apostle that he received in honor the revered and holy Germanus.

24

Auxiliaris at that time governed Gaul from the very pinnacle of the prefecture.[22] He had two reasons for his joy at the bishop's coming. He wanted to make the acquaintance of a man so famous for his spiritual powers, and his own wife had for a long time suffered from a quartan ague. He advanced to meet him much earlier than etiquette required and was held motionless by wonder. The majesty of his bearing, his knowledge in discussion, the authority in his preaching, all filled Auxiliaris with awe and he realised that the bishop's fame did him less than justice; reality exceeded report. He offered him gifts, plied him with services, and asked as a favor of the man of blessings that he would condescend to accept what he had come to ask.

Then he spoke of his wife's illness. The bishop went to see her and the strength of the malady was so completely destroyed that the shaking that used to precede the attacks, and the fever that followed, both disappeared. Restored to her former health, the good lady partook also of a heavenly remedy that increased both the vigor of her body and the faith in her soul. Thus the bishop obtained boons from a willing Giver and brought back the desired relief to his diocese. But in the eyes of his flock the best remedy and the greatest joy that he brought back with him was his own return.

25

Meanwhile news came from Britain that a few promoters of the Pelagian heresy were once more spreading it; and again all the bishops joined in urging the man of blessings to defend the cause of God for which he had previously

21. 403–449, a monk of Lérins who became bishop of Arles sometime during 428 or 429. He wrote a life of his predecessor Honoratus, was involved in the Pelagian controversy, and quarreled with Pope Leo I (440–461).

22. He was Pretorian Prefect, the highest civilian official in all of Gaul. Because Gaul's Rhine frontiers were threatened, the safer Arles had been the administrative capital since the 390s.

won such a victory. He hastened to comply, since he delighted in toil and gladly spent himself for Christ. The malice of the demons, vanquished by the power of his holiness, had by this time ceased to trouble him; they dared not make an attempt against one they knew to be a friend of God. So, taking with him Severus,[23] a bishop of perfected sanctity, he embarked under Christ's leadership and the elements permitted a calm voyage; winds, waves, and atmosphere all helped the ship along.

26

Meanwhile evil spirits, flying over the whole island, made known through the involuntary prophecies of their victims the coming of Germanus, with the result that one of the leading men in the country, Elafius by name, came hurrying to meet the holy men without having had any news of them through any regular messenger. He brought with him his son who had been crippled in early youth by a most grievous malady. His sinews had withered and the tendons of the knee had contracted and his withered leg made it impossible for him to stand on his feet.

The whole province came along with Elafius. The bishops arrived and the crowds came upon them unexpectedly. At once blessings and the words of God were showered upon them. Germanus could see that the people as a whole had persevered in the faith in which he had left them and the bishops realized that the fallings-away had been the work only of a few. These were identified and formally condemned.

27

At this point Elafius approached to make obeisance to the bishops and presented to them his son, whose youth and helplessness made his need clear without words. Everyone felt acutely for him, the bishops most of all, and in their pity they had recourse to the mercy of God. The blessed Germanus at once made the boy sit down, then felt the bent knee and ran his healing hand over all the diseased parts. Health speedily followed the life-giving touch. What was withered became supple, the sinews resumed their proper work and, before the eyes of all, the son got back a sound body and the father got back a son.

23. Bishop of Trier, 426–476. This second visit to Britain took place in 444 or 445.

The crowds were overwhelmed by the miracle and the Catholic faith implanted in them was strengthened in all of them. There followed sermons to
the people to confute the heresy, the preachers of which were by common
consent banished from the island. They were brought to the bishops to be
conducted to the Continent, so that the country might be purged of them and
they of their errors. The effect of all this was so salutary that even now the
faith is persisting intact in those parts. And so, with everything settled, the
blessed bishops made a prosperous journey back to their own country.

28

He had hardly got home after his overseas expedition when a deputation from
Armorica came with a petition to the weary prelate. For Aetius the Magnifi-
cent,[24] who then governed the state, had been enraged by the insolence of that
proud region and, to punish it for daring to rebel, had given Goar, the savage
king of the Alans, permission to subdue it; and Goar, with a barbarian's greed,
was thirsting for its wealth.

So one old man was matched against a most warlike people and an idolatrous
king but, under the protection of Christ, he proved greater and stronger than
them all. He lost no time in setting out, for all the preparations for the
invasion had been made. The movement of the tribes had already begun and
their iron-armed cavalry were filling all the roads. Nevertheless our bishop
rode out toward them till he reached his meeting-place with the king, who
arrived soon after him.

Since the march was in progress when the meeting took place, the priest was
opposed to a warlord clad in armor and surrounded by his bodyguard. First he
made requests, through the medium of an interpreter. Then, as Goar disregarded them, he went on to rebuke him. Finally he stretched out his hand,
seized his bridle and halted him, and with him the whole army.

The wrath of the savage king at this was turned by God to marveling. He
was staggered by such firmness, awed by such dignity and shaken by the
strength of such insistent authority. The panoply of war and the rattle of arms
gave place to the courtesies of a peaceful interview. Laying aside his arrogance
the king dismounted and entered upon negotiations that ended by satisfying,

---

24. He was *Magister utriusque militiae*, that is, leader of both infantry and cavalry. For some
twenty years after 433 he was the most powerful man in the western empire. He attempted to
preserve Roman rule in Gaul by making alliances with various barbarian peoples, and by setting
one people off against another.

not the desires of the king, but the requests of the bishop. The king and his army camped peacefully where they were and he gave the most solemn assurances of peace on condition that the pardon which he himself had thus granted to the Armoricans was asked also of the emperor or Aetius. Meanwhile the mediation of the bishop, and his holiness, had restrained a king, recalled an army, and delivered a province from devastation.

29

From there Germanus set out for Italy;[25] it was enough for him that he should never be free from toil to enjoy a rest but, in the words of the prophet, should go on from strength to strength (see Ps 84.8). On the way he paid another visit for old times' sake to his friend Senator, the priest, who brought him a dumb girl, about twenty years old. First he blessed some oil and anointed her mouth and forehead and the rest of her face with it. Then he ordered spiced wine to be brought, in which he steeped three morsels of bread broken off with his own hands. He put one of them into the girl's mouth, telling her before she took it to ask him to bless it. This she did at once, before taking the bread, speaking quite distinctly; and the power of speech, thus miraculously acquired, remained for the rest of her life.

On his departure he embraced his friend with more than usual affection, kissing him on the mouth and forehead and eyes. As he clasped him to his breast, his last words were: "Farewell till eternity, my very dear brother; farewell, part of my very soul. God grant that at the Day of Judgment we may see each other without being put to confusion; in this world we shall not look upon each other again."

30

He made the journey alone, except for his retinue, but he was constantly thronged by the crowds that came out to meet him, so much so, that every eminence associated with his journey is to this day crowned by a chapel, a hermit's cell, or a cross erected where he prayed or taught. At Autun in

25. The imperial court was then at Ravenna, a swamp-surrounded city that was safe from barbarians. Germanus went there to seek from the emperor a pardon for the Armoricans who had revolted and incurred Aetius's Alan chastisement. Germanus's ties to Armorica went all the way back to his days as the region's military governor.

particular, as he passed through its territory, the people came out to meet him regardless of age or sex. Among them were two parents, who knelt in front of everybody and showed him their daughter, whose malady had in the course of time reduced her to a terrible condition. From birth the fingers of her right hand had been bent toward her palm by a contraction of the sinews, so that as her fingernails grew they pierced her tender flesh and every finger made a wound; and, had it not been that the bones of the palm to some extent checked the growing points, she would have had ulcers right through her hand.

The bishop took her hand and felt it and his healing touch brought a blessing. Then he took her fingers one by one and eased the tendons, restoring them to flexibility, and the hand which had caused its own destruction was thus made serviceable. Adding kindness to kindness, he himself with his own sacred hands cut the long nails on the straightened fingers down to the customary length.

31

So he passed through the cities of Gaul. To enter Italy he had to cross the Alps and he lightened the journey by conversation with some workmen who were returning to their own country after a spell of employment in Gaul. As these men, laden with excessively heavy packs, were climbing a pass that rose up into the clouds, they were held up by a mountain stream running through a steep and rocky gorge that gave firm foothold to neither man nor beast. One of these travelers was both lame and elderly and the man of blessings took his pack onto his own shoulders and carried it across amid the huge whirlpools. Then he crossed again to carry across on his back the man without his bundle. Moreover, in his humility he was most careful to let no one know who he was. When he came to Milan, however, he could no longer conceal his identity or his eminence.

32

He arrived on the solemn festival of its saints,[26] for which great numbers of bishops had assembled. While the sacred mysteries of the Mass were being celebrated at the altar, he entered, unknown and unexpected. Immediately, one

26. Probably this is a reference to the patron saints of Milan, Gervasius and Protasius. Thus the date would have been June 19. The year appears to have been 428.

of the congregation, who was possessed by a demon, shouted out in a tremendous voice:

"Germanus, why do you pursue us into Italy? Be content that you have driven us out of Gaul. Be content that your prayers have defeated both us and the ocean. Why do you scour the whole world? Take a rest and let us have a rest ourselves."

Amazement and terror filled the congregation. They looked at one another, asking which was Germanus; and, in spite of the poverty-stricken look of his clothes, he was recognized by the majesty of his face. when asked, he did not deny his position and episcopal rank. Thereupon all the bishops with fitting humility showed their reverence for this saint of God; and they asked him to treat the demoniac who had proclaimed his name. It was not from swaggering presumption but in a spirit of obedience that he had the man shown to him. He took him aside into the sacristy, speedily exorcised him, and sent him back into the congregation.

This was the first manifestation of miraculous powers given by Christ through this servant of His in Italy. Crowds came hurrying from all directions, coveting the blessing of a man of such proved sanctity; and when he followed up his miracles by sermons he healed souls as well as bodies.

33

On leaving that wealthy city, he pursued his journey gently and with much-appreciated pauses. Presently he encountered some beggars who asked for alms. He consulted his deacon as to how much there was in their purse. "Only three gold pieces," was the reply and at once he ordered them all to be bestowed upon the beggars.

"But what are we to live on today?" asked the deacon.

"God feeds His poor," replied the bishop; "give what you have to these who need it."

But the deacon kept one piece back as a precaution and gave away two.

Resuming their journey they noticed behind them some horsemen spurring after them. These soon caught up with them, jumped off their horses, and went down on their knees.

"Our master Leporius," they said, "a gentleman of rank, lives not far from here. He and his household are down with various illnesses, so that what with his own incapacitation and theirs he is quite prostrated. We have been sent to tell you of his troubles. Will you condescend to come and cure him? But if you are too much engaged to do as we ask, aid him with your prayers. Let him have the blessing you can obtain for him, even if he cannot have the privilege of seeing you."

This roused the compassion of the holy man and, even thought it meant leaving the road, he reckoned that the shortest way was the one that won the reward of a good deed. So, in spite of the protests of his party, he turned aside to pay the requested visit. "Nothing," said he, "should come before doing the Lord's will." Then the messengers in transports of joy presented to him two hundred gold pieces that had been entrusted to them for the purpose. Germanus turned to his deacon, saying:

"Take what they offer and remember that you have defrauded the poor; because if you had given those beggars all you had, our benefactor would have repaid you with *three* hundred gold pieces today."

The deacon was appalled at the thought that his guilt had been no secret from the bishop.

34

Meanwhile they had been hastening their pace and presently reached the house, where the holy man's arrival raised everybody's spirits as if health personified and entered it. He applied his usual remedies all round. He knelt in supplication to Christ, to win joy for others by his own tears. Then he visited the master and his family and the servants as well. Making no distinction he went the round of the cottages also, visiting every sickroom. Then he allowed a full day to pass and, so effective was the celestial medicine, that when he departed the next morning he left the whole household in the enjoyment of perfect health. The master of the house, whom he had found in bed when he arrived, conducted him on his way. Thus the holy man's reputation and praises preceded him and made all who heard of his coming eager to see him.

35

Rumor of it was, in fact, already circulating in Ravenna, where the populace, in their impatience to see him, found fault with him for the delays on his journey. But, after being long awaited, he could be welcomed at last. He had, indeed, planned to make a secret entry into the city by night, under cover of darkness, but his intentions were defeated, for sentinels stayed up to watch for him.

At that time the bishop of the city was Peter,[27] who ruled the church of Christ there in the tradition of the apostles. The Empress Placidia[28] reigned over the Roman Empire jointly with her son Valentinian, who was still a young man. They loved the Catholic faith so well that, though rulers of all, they obeyed with the deepest humility the servants of God. All these personages, for the love of God, vied with one another in the reception that they gave to the revered bishop. Princes courted him, nobles went out to meet him, the body of the faithful were in transports of joy. The revered empress sent to his lodgings a huge dish of silver laden with many kinds of delicious food, all prepared without meat. He accepted the gift, distributed the food to those who served him and kept the silver, sending back in its place a little wooden platter with a barley loaf on it. The empress treasured both, immensely delighted, both because her silver had passed through his hands to the poor and because she had received for herself the holy man's food on so humble a dish. Indeed, she afterwards had the wood set in gold and kept the bread to work many miracles of healing.

36

One day when crossing a wide square and hemmed in by crowds he passed in front of a jail crowded with prisoners awaiting torture or death. These got to know that he was passing and raised a tremendous clamor, shouting in unison. He inquired as to the reason and it was explained to him. So he sent for the guards but they kept out of his way, for all these wretched prisoners had been sentenced to that prison by one or another of the great officials of the palace the night before. His compassion saw no help anywhere.

At last he turned to his old resource and petitioned the divine majesty for the help so difficult to obtain from men. He walked up to the jail and threw himself on the ground in prayer. Then indeed did Our Lord show the crowd, standing by, with what favor He regarded His servant. The gates, secured by chains and bars, flew open; the iron bolts leapt back. God's kindness undid what man's cruelty had carefully contrived. They came thronging out from chains to liberty, displaying their futile loads of fetters and carrying in their hands the cords with which they had been bound. For once the jail was

27. Peter Chrysologus (c. 380–450), bishop of Ravenna, 431–450.

28. Galla Placidia, mother of the reigning emperor Valentinian III (r. 425–455). Constantius calls her "queen" (*regina*) not "empress." Neither title in fact existed in the Roman hierarchy, but Galla Placidia was, along with Aetius, the dominant figure in the Roman world for years.

harmless, because empty; and in triumphal procession to celebrate the victory of kindness the throng of unfortunates were restored to the bosom of a rejoicing church.

37

Each day men marveled at the pontiff more and spread his fame. The populace flocked to him, the sick were healed, and Christ continued to enlarge the favors that He granted. Six reverend bishops were continuously in devoted attendance on him and they marveled as much at the crucifixion he endured from his uninterrupted fasts as at his frequent miracles. Years afterward they were living to bear witness to his works.

38

A man named Volusianus, at that time first secretary to Sigisvult, the Patrician,[29] had a son who was suffering from a burning fever. The heat of his blood had so wasted the boy's bodily strength that his condition was openly despaired of. The doctors could do no more and gave no hope, and the parents resigned themselves to mourning. Then a belated hope sprang up; they thought of the man of blessings. They clung to his knees, their friends and neighbors with them, and the attendant bishops added their pleading. With them he hastened to the sickbed but they were met by a runner saying that the boy was dead and that it was useless for the holy man to tire himself.

But the prelates urged him on and the crowd begged him not to leave his work of mercy unfinished. They found the body lifeless, with the warmth of life departed, and already stiffening in the cold of death. With a prayer for his soul they were turning back, when suddenly the bystanders raised a cry of grief and the bishops clung to the hand of their elder to make him petition the Lord on behalf of the bereaved parents for the dead boy's return to life. For a long time he resisted them, full of embarrassment in his humility; but at last he yielded to pity and to the demands of charity. Girding himself with the weapons of faith, he sent the bystanders out and stretched himself out upon the corpse in prayer. He watered the ground with his tears, his deep groans went up to heaven, he

---

29. A purely honorific title occasionally bestowed by the imperial court as a mark of honor and to acknowledge particularly meritorious service.

called upon Christ with his sighs. Presently the dead moved and, little by little, the lifeless organs resumed their normal functions. The eyes opened to the light, the fingers twitched, at last the tongue uttered sounds.

Both rose, the one from prayer, the other from death. Germanus lifted the sleeper by the hand and he sat up, drew a breath, pulled himself together and looked about him. Little by little he regained strength, and full health returned. Thus a son was restored to his parents, mourning was turned into joy, and the power of God's majesty was acclaimed by the united voice of the people. And Christ continued to show His power through His servant and made him shine more than ever with the glory of miracles, since he was soon to be called to his rest.

39

A eunuch named Acolus, at that time supervisor of the imperial bedchamber had an adopted son to whom he had given an excellent education but who was now plagued by a demon. It was the kind that strikes down its victims every month at the new moon, by causing them to keep falling to the ground. The empress through her courtiers arranged for him to be taken to the holy man and put into his charge.

After a long examination of him, Germanus put off the exorcism to the next day, although he ordinarily expelled even the most rabid demons at the first laying on of hands. He did this because this demon had entered so deeply into the very inmost parts of the wretched youth that during the periods of possession it practically made his body its own. That night he arranged for the boy to occupy the same room as himself. Then, indeed, the demon burst out openly from its inner lair. As if in torture it revealed how it had first taken possession of its victim in the innocence of early childhood. Now at the bishop's order it went out of him, and the next day the youth was back in the palace, purged.

40

It had been the affairs of Armorica that had made this long journey necessary and Germanus would undoubtedly have had them settled as he wished, by obtaining for the Armoricans pardon and security for the future, if it had not been for the treachery of Tibatto, who persuaded that fickle and undisciplined people to rebel again. After that, not even the intercession of the bishop could

do anything for them, for common prudence made it impossible for the imperial government to trust them; and their many times perjured leader before
long paid the penalty of his reckless treason.

41

One day, when the night office had been recited and he was giving a spiritual
discourse to the bishops, he made a sorrowful announcement. "Dearest brethren," he said, "I commend my passing to your prayers. In my sleep last night I
saw myself as a traveler receiving his provision for the road from Our Lord
and, when I asked why I was setting out, He said to me: 'Do not be afraid. I am
not sending you on your travels again but to your fatherland, where you will
have quiet and eternal rest.' "

The bishops would have liked to give the dream another interpretation but,
more earnestly than ever, he commended his last moments to their prayers. "I
know quite well," said he, "what the fatherland is that God promises to His
servants."

42

An illness did in fact follow, a few days later. As it grew more serious, the
whole city was in consternation. But He who was calling him to glory hastened
his journey; the Lord was inviting the tired hero to receive the reward of his
laborious days.

The empress laid aside the haughtiness of royalty and went visiting the
pauper; she sought out the sick man and promised him anything he asked. But
he had only one request to make, and to this she consented most unwillingly,
that his dust should return to his native soil. Day and night the crowd of
visitors was as much as the house and the forecourt could hold. The chanting
of the psalms was kept up continuously; and the seventh day of the illness saw
the passing of his faithful and blessed soul to heaven.

43

Then came the division of what he had left behind him. The empire and the
church each claimed a share; and over his scanty possessions there arose a
dispute such as we associate with great riches—there was so little for them to

seize, poor heirs of a mere benediction! The empress took the reliquary;[30] Bishop Peter annexed the cloak with the hair-shirt inside it. The six prelates, to make sure of having something associated with the saint, were glad to tear to pieces what remained. One had his pallium,[31] the second his girdle, two divided his tunic, and two his soldier's cape.

44

Next came an eager rivalry over his funeral, everyone insisting that no expense should be spared. Acolius had the body embalmed in spices; the empress saw to its vestments. When all this was duly accomplished, the emperor provided the bier and the equipage for the journey and a large body of his own servants to attend them. The clergy were in charge of the chanting of the liturgy, at each stage arranging for it to be carried on by those of the next town—there was one long procession all the way to Gaul.

45

The body[32] reached Piacenza on its journey when it was quite dark. It was placed in the church, and, while the liturgical prayers were being recited, a lady of the town who was so badly paralyzed that she could use none of her limbs asked as a favor to be placed under the bier. There she remained stretched out till dawn. When, early in the morning, the corpse was taken up again, the woman rose too and astonished everybody by following in the procession on her own feet.

46

Even greater was the devotion manifested in Gaul to its own protector, for there was personal affection as well as reverence. Every kind of person has-

---

30. A vessel of almost any kind designed to hold or to display relics, physical remains of saints.

31. A narrow stole of white lambs' wool worn by the pope and conferred by him on archbishops and sometimes bishops. It initially symbolized the bond that yoked a pastor to his flock, and later was interpreted as a mark of the yoke of obedience that tied all members of the ecclesiastical hierarchy to the pope.

32. The reader meets here for the first time a later convention of hagiography: an account of miracles performed after the saint's death by, or in the immediate vicinity of, his or her body.

tened to perform every kind of service. Some smoothed the roads by clearing away stones, others linked them by restoring bridges. Some contributed to the expenses, others chanted the psalms, others again took the bier onto their shoulders. The profusion of torches ousted the sun's rays and provided light for the day. Such were the services of love with which he was brought back to his own see, where his body is buried but he himself lives on in his daily miracles and his glory.

Of you, my reader, I must ask pardon twice over, first for the solecisms and the rustic idiom with which I have offended your ears, then for a prolixity that must have been wearisome. But we ought not to find it too tedious to read through what Christ did not find it too tedious to do for us—Christ, who when He gives glory to His saints is giving an invitation to us. I call God to witness, who knows all secrets, that the known and attested miracles of my lord Bishop Germanus that I have passed over in silence are more numerous than those I have recorded;[33] and I have to own myself guilty of suppressing marvels that the power of God wrought for the benefit of all. I think that I have written too summarily rather than too much.

33. The idea that much more could be related is a hagiographical convention based on Jn 21.25.

Willibald

THE LIFE OF SAINT BONIFACE

Translated by C. H. Talbot

Willibald is an extremely obscure figure. He was an Anglo-Saxon priest who came to the Continent sometime after the death of Boniface in 754. He was, it seems, a canon—a member of the cathedral clergy—of Mainz, the see of Boniface himself. The dates of his birth and death are unknown. There is no record of his involvement in major public affairs and other texts by him are unrecorded.

Both Lull, Boniface's successor as bishop of Mainz, and Megingoz, the bishop of Würzburg, received numerous requests for a life of the famous Anglo-Saxon missionary and ecclesiastical founder, Boniface. Before 768, perhaps between 763 and 765, they turned to Willibald to prepare that life. Oral traditions at Mainz and Boniface's own letters served Willibald as his primary evidence.

As the *Life* itself is richly detailed, only a few points need to be made here by way of introduction. Boniface—or Winfrid, his English name—was born in Wessex in 680 and died in Frisia in 754. After a monastic upbringing, he

decided to become a missionary on the Continent, in lands where his countrymen had preceded him. Though he spent time in Frisia (roughly Holland) and
Bavaria, he concentrated his efforts in central Germany, in Hesse and
Thuringia. He visited Rome three times and always worked very closely with
the papacy. He was usually assisted by the rulers of the Franks.

With this text we move sharply out of the world of late antique literary
culture. Although Willibald's Latin is for the most part correct, it lacks the
polish and elegance of that of Sulpicius and Constantius. It is important to
remember that for Willibald Latin was a foreign language that he had learned
in school. It was not even, as it had been for Possidius, the common tongue of
street and market. The key influence on Willibald's style was Aldhelm (639–
709), an immensely learned Anglo-Saxon scholar who had studied in Ireland
and who wrote in an astonishingly complicated style, marked by odd syntax,
neologisms, and prolixity. Willibald evinces familiarity with a small number of
Christian authors and with no classical authors.

Like Possidius and Constantius, Willibald focuses on Boniface's ecclesiastical
career. This means that many key events in Boniface's life, especially his
complex political maneuverings, are slighted. Like Possidius too, but unlike
Sulpicius and Constantius, Willibald leaves out the miraculous element in his
Life. This was the first saint's life written in Germany and it is interesting to
see how it pulled together several traditions in hagiography.

Texts and References

The standard Latin text remains *Vita Bonifatii auctore Willibaldo,* ed. Wil-
helm Levison, Monumenta Germaniae Historica, Scriptores Rerum Ger-
manicarum in Usum Scholarum (Hannover, 1905). Little has been written on
Willibald. See L. Kurrai, "Willibald of Mainz," *New Catholic Encyclopedia*
(New York, 1967), 14:945; Ph. A. Brück, "Willibald von Mainz," *Lexikon für
Theologie und Kirche* (Freiburg, 1965), 10:cols. 1165–66; Max Manitius,
Geschichte der lateinischen Literatur des Mittelalters, 3 vols. (Munich, 1911–
31), 1:637–38; Franz Brunhölzl, *Geschichte der lateinischen Literatur des
Mittelalters,* 2 vols. (Munich, 1975), 1:239. The fundamental book on
Boniface remains Theodor Schieffer, *Winfrid-Bonifatius und die christliche
Grundlegung Europas* (originally published 1954: repr. Darmstadt, 1980).
Uneven in quality but helpful are the essays in *The Greatest Englishman:
Essays on St. Boniface and the Church at Crediton,* ed. Timothy Reuter
(Exeter, 1980).

✤ ✤ ✤

1[1]

To my holy and dear lords in Christ, Bishops Lull[2] and Megingoz,[3] Willibald, an unworthy priest in the Lord.

I have with goodwill yielded to the order, or perhaps simply desire, enjoined by your devoted fatherly care, not confident in my own literary craft, but owing deference and obedience to your holiness. With my feeble talents I have begun the arduous task that you enjoined on me and carried it through to completion. But, if the result should fall short of your expectations, I beg that with measured spirit you compare my lack of skill to the difficulty of the charge, since the greatest mark of my reverence for you is the fact that, in obedience to your sublime command, I did not shirk this task. But if I produce something worthy of our contemporaries and future generations, then ascribe it to divine aid and to your personal intervention and desire, for your earnest entreaties may be compared to the hand that controls the winepress, which by its strength squeezes out some small amount of the sweet juice of knowledge and hands it around to refresh the thirsty. Your holiness has seen fit to equate—or even to prefer—me, although I am foolish and less than capable, to the wise and the prudent. You have chosen to keep this work away from scholarly discourse and to impose it on me, although I am unlettered. But I beg you, since you have brought pressure to bear on me, that you support me with your prayers. May the power of your love and entreaties rouse my mind, weighed down by dark sloth, from sleep, so that those things which you have called on me to write might be rendered into a clear and vigorous narrative.

You have urged me so at the request of religious-minded and orthodox men who have heard—in the region of Tuscany, or in the marches of Gaul, or at the portals of Germany, or even in the furthest reaches of Britain—the reputation and the many miracles of Saint Boniface the martyr. You have suggested that I write, following the model of those whose chaste lives and saintly manners have been turned into elegant words and put down on parchment by the holy fathers. Just so I will put down in writing an account of Boniface's life from the beginning through its midst up to its very end, as much as I know through investigation. I have learned my information from disciples who spent much time with him and from your own references. Just as, after the agreement of the first false oath was

---

1. The prologue (chapter 1, pages 109–10) has been wholly retranslated by T. Head.
2. Bishop of Mainz, 754–785.
3. Archbishop of Wurzburg, 753–785.

undone and the rays of the true light dawned, Hegesippus[4] (who is said to have
come to Rome in the reign of Anacletus)[5] was persuaded to produce five books of
ecclesiastical history for the edification of his readers; and as Eusebius of Caesarea[6] (the best-known writer of history) produced, with his assistant Pamphilus[7]
the martyr, many volumes that recorded in eloquent writing the histories of their
own and preceding times; and as Gregory[8] of blessed memory (who was a most
learned man in the study of literature and presided from the glorious heights of
the Apostolic See) composed the life of the blessed confessors,[9] in the process dem-
onstrating in his wonderful style his mastery of the arts of expression, in four
books that to this day are found in the libraries of churches and furnish to posterity the hard-won dignity of knowledge; in that same manner you order me to
unfold before my contemporaries and for later generations the life, the excellent
virtues, the practical piety, and the ascetic habits of this blessed man. I realize that
my talents are slender and my powers small for the telling of such a tale. Nevertheless I will attempt that work that you, in the power of your benevolence, have
demanded of me, not presuming on my own powers, but rather putting my trust
in the kindly help of my fellow Catholics. I shall not try to increase my own stature with this publication in the manner of the games, but only to furnish future
readers with an example from the narration of these matters, so that they may be
instructed by Boniface's model and led to better things by his perfection.

Here Begins the Life of Saint Boniface

How, in childhood, he began to serve God

What I am attempting to do here is to describe the blessed life and character of
Saint Boniface, the archbishop, insofar as I have learned the facts from holy

4. We do not know much more about this figure than Willibald did. He seems to have drawn
up the first authoritative list of the bishops of Rome.

5. He means Anicetus, bishop of Rome (i.e., Pope), c. 155–c. 166. Anacletus was bishop from
c. 79 to c. 91.

6. C. 260–c. 340; bishop of Caesarea in Palestine from about 315, he was the originator of
church history as a literary genre. Although he wrote in Greek, Latin translations and abridg-
ments of his works were widely influential in the West.

7. C. 260–309. He was a noted theological teacher at Caesarea.

8. Gregory I "the Great," pope, 590–604, was especially dear to the Anglo-Saxons and,
perhaps through their mediation, to the Franks as well.

9. Willibald is referring to Gregory's *Dialogues*, a work in four books that was intended, among
other things, to show that Italy was no less richly endowed with saints than other areas. Book 2 was
devoted to Saint Benedict and helped to spread the reputation of the famous founder of Monte Cassino.

men who lived in daily contact with him and who, therefore, knew his manner of life and were in a position to recall those details that they have heard or witnessed. Though I labor under the disadvantage of having had only an indirect acquaintance with him, my design is to weave into the texture of my narrative and to present in as brief a form as possible all the facts ascertainable by a thorough investigation into his holinesss and divine contemplation.

In his very early childhood, after he had been weaned and reared with a mother's usual anxious care, his father lavished upon him more affection than upon the rest of his brothers. When he reached the age of about four or five he conceived a desire to enter the service of God and began to think deeply on the advantages of the monastic life. Even at this early age he had subdued the flesh to the spirit and meditated on the things that are eternal rather than on those that are temporal.

When priests or clerics, traveling abroad, as is the custom in those parts, to preach to the people, came to the town and the house where his father dwelt the child would converse with them on spiritual matters and, as far as the capacity of his tender years permitted, would ask them to advise him on the best means of overcoming the frailties of his nature. After some time, when he had given long consideration to the things of God and his whole nature craved for a future life, he revealed his desires to his father and begged him to take his confidences in good part. His father, taken aback at the views he expressed, rebuked him with violence and, while forbidding him to leave his side, enticed him with promises of worldly success, hoping by this means to retain the boy as guardian, or rather heir of his worldly possessions. Employing all the subtle craft of human wisdom, he endeavored by long discussions to dissuade the boy from carrying out his purpose, and mingled promises with flattery in the hope of persuading him that life in the world would be more congenial for one of his age than the austere regime of the monastic and contemplative life. In order to turn the boy aside from pursuing his purpose he paraded before him all the inducements of pleasure and luxury. But the saint, even at that early age, was filled with the spirit of God. The more his father attempted to hold him back, the more stoutly and doggedly he determined to pursue the heavenly ideal and to devote himself to the study of sacred letters. And in accordance with the workings of divine mercy it fell out in a remarkable way that divine providence not only confirmed him in his undertaking but also changed the obstinate mood of his father, for at one and the same instant his father was struck down by a sudden and fatal sickness, while the boy's intentions, long frustrated, grew in strength and were, by help of God, brought to their fulfilment.

When, by the inscrutable judgment and dispensation of God, the saint's father fell sick, he suddenly changed his previous obstinate attitude and, after calling together all the members of his family, sent the boy under the care of trustworthy messengers to the monastery of Examchester,[10] which was ruled at that time by Abbot Wulfhard. There, surrounded by his friends, he made known to the abbot his desire to enter the monastic life and, in a manner mature for his years, presented his petition according to the instructions previously given to him by his parents. The father of the monastery thereupon took counsel with the rest of the brethren and, after receiving their blessing as is prescribed by the monastic rule,[11] gave his consent. In this way the man of God was bereaved of his earthly father and embraced the adoptive Father of our redemption. He thus renounced all worldly and transitory possessions for the sake of acquiring the eternal inheritance in order that, to quote the words of the Gospel, by forsaking father and mother and lands and the other things of this world he might receive a hundredfold hereafter and possess everlasting life.

2

How in the beginning he overcame the passions of youth and kept to all that was good.

The first part of our narrative, though briefly expressed, is now completed. We shall now describe the virtuous habits in which the saint trained himself at the beginning of his monastic life. Then, after we have established our work on a firm basis, we can raise the structure little by little to its crowning point.

After he had increased in age and strength and knowledge and, completing the seven years of childhood, had reached the bloom of youth, the grace of God, as later events in this book will show, endowed him with wonderful intellectual qualities. He was conspicuous for the purity of his many virtues learned from the example of earlier holy men, but also for submitting publicly and humbly to the customs of the venerable fathers [of his own monastery]. Moreover, he was endowed with a spark of divine genius and so assiduously fostered it by study that every hour and moment of his long and active life only served to increase the divine gifts that had been showered upon him. The longer he continued in the service of the priesthood, the more, as we are told by his trusted and intimate friends, did his continual studies and his protracted endeavors in the literary field stimulate him in his search for eternal bliss. This was a marvelous protection against the enticements and diabolical suggestions that beset young men in

10. Near Exeter.
11. It is not clear just what rule is implied.

the flower of their youth and that cloud their minds with a kind of darkness. As a result, the fiery passions of youth and the fleshly lusts that at first made violent assaults upon him lost their power through his ceaseless vigilance and his assiduous inquiries into the meaning of sacred Scripture. His studies, pursued with increasing ardor, led him inevitably to undertake the task of teaching others, a labor that after a short time and in accordance with episcopal and ecclesiastical ordinances he duly carried out. He spurned the fleeting successes of this world and continued under the able guidance of Abbot Wulfhard to follow faithfully and conscientiously the true pattern of monastic observance. When he had outgrown his boyhood and youth his enthusiasm for study and the lack of suitable teachers moved him to seek permission from the abbot and community to pass over to a neighboring monastery. He prayed constantly and perseveringly for the approval of God on his undertaking, and finally, under the inspiration of divine grace, he went to the monastery that to this day is called Nursling.[12] There, attracted by the desire for learning, he became a disciple of the venerable abbot Winbert,[13] of blessed memory, and joined the community of the brethren who dwelt there with him in the Lord. Thus united to the servants of God, he showed great zeal for meditation, devotion to the service of God, perseverance in watching and assiduity in the study of the Scriptures. In this way he became proficient not only in grammar and rhetoric and the writing of verses but also in the literal and spiritual exposition of the Bible.[14] In the end he became so renowned for his profound understanding of the Scriptures and for his skill in imparting his knowledge to others that he was accepted as a trustworthy guide in traditional doctrine. As a teacher he was a model, because he did not refuse to learn from his pupils, for it is a principle in monastic houses that no one should presume to rule others unless he has previously learned to submit. No man who has failed to render obedience to the superiors set over him by God can rightly exact obedience from his inferiors. Such obedience as befits a monk was given by the saint to all the members of the community, and particularly to the abbot, and he applied himself assiduously, according to blessed Father Benedict's

12. A few miles southwest of Winchester.

13. An obscure figure whose connections with the royal court at Winchester may have fostered the growth of Nursling into an attractive intellectual center.

14. Augustine, in his *On Christian Learning*, and Cassiodorus (c. 490–585), in his *Institutes of Divine and Human Readings*, sketched an educational program that was Christian and utilitarian. That is, the purpose of education was to read and understand the Scriptures and, through them, to gain salvation. To secure the education necessary to read the Scriptures and their most authoritative commentaries, the traditional literary disciplines of antique education had still to be acquired: grammar, the study of the Latin language; rhetoric, the study of forms of speech (formerly to produce skilled speakers but now to produce careful readers); and dialectic, the science of right reasoning. It will be seen that monasticism had brought this system of education to far-off Britain.

prescribed form of proper arrangement[15] to the daily manual labor and the regular performance of his duties. In this way he was an example to all both in word, deed, faith, and purity. All could profit by his good deeds, while he on his side shared in their common eternal reward. But God alone, from whom nothing is concealed, knew the hidden depths of his heart and the extent of his humility and charity that had won for him an ascendancy over all his brethren. They looked upon him with love mingled with fear; and though he was their companion in the pursuit of divine love, they considered him, in the words of the apostle (see Rom 12.10) as their father. His kindliness toward the brethren and the extent of his learning increased to such a degree that his fame as a teacher spread far and wide among monasteries both of men and women. Of their inmates great numbers of men, attracted by a desire for learning, flocked to hear him and under his guidance studied the whole extent of the Scriptures; but the nuns, who were unable continually to come to his lectures, stimulated by his vast wisdom and his spirit of divine love, applied themselves with diligence to the study of the sacred texts, scanning page after page as they meditated on the sacred and hidden mysteries.

Guided and sustained as he was by supernatural grace, he followed both the example and the teaching of the Apostle of the Gentiles: "Follow the pattern of the sound words which you have heard from me in the faith and love which are in Christ Jesus. . . . Do your best to present yourself to God as one approved, a workman who has no need to be ashamed, rightly handling the word of truth" (2 Tm 1.13, 2.15).

3

How he gave instruction to all and assumed the office of teacher, not at his own whim but on the attainment of the proper age

We will now turn our attention for a moment to the general tenor of the saint's daily contemplation and to his perseverance in fasting and abstinence. In this way, making gradual progress, we shall relate with conciseness and brevity his

---

15. This passage provides a good example of how difficult it is to determine exactly what monastic rule was in force. The Latin has "secundum praefinitam beati patris Benedicti rectae constitutionis formam," a remarkable circumlocution that probably means that Boniface particularly liked some aspects of Benedict's Rule, not that he actually lived in a monastery uniquely governed by that Rule.

wonderful deeds, follow his life to its close, and examine it in greater detail. By balancing one aspect of his life against another we shall show that the venerable and holy Boniface was an example for us of eternal life in his evenly balanced moderation and that he laid before us the precepts of apostolic learning. Following the example of the saints, he climbed the steep path that leads to knowledge of heavenly things and went before his people as a leader who opens the gates of paradise through which only the upright shall enter.

From the early days of his childhood even to infirm old age he imitated in particular the practice of the ancient fathers in daily committing to memory the writings of the prophets and apostles, the narratives of the passion of the martyrs and the Gospel teaching of Our Lord. To quote the words of the apostle: whether he ate or drank or whatsoever else he did, he always praised and thanked God both in heart and word; as the psalmist says, "I will bless the Lord at all times; his praise shall continually be in my mouth" (Ps 34.1). To such a degree was he inflamed with a love of the Scriptures that he applied all his energies to learning and practicing their counsels, and those matters that were written for the instruction of the people he paraphrased and explained to them with striking eloquence, shrewdly spicing it with parables. His discretion was such that his rebukes, though sharp, were never lacking in gentleness, while his teaching, though mild, was never lacking in force. Zeal and vigor made him forceful, but gentleness and love made him mild. Accordingly he exhorted and reproved with equal impartiality the rich and powerful, the freedmen and the slaves, neither flattering and fawning upon the rich nor oppressing and browbeating the freedmen and slaves but, in the words of the apostle, he had "become all things to all men that [he] might by all means save some" (1 Cor 9.22).

He did not take upon himself the office of preacher either as an expression of his caprice or before the appointed time, nor did he seek the position through contumacy and greed. But he waited, as was in keeping with his humble character, until he had reached the age of thirty or more, when, by the recommendation and choice of his superior and brethren, he was ordained in accordance with the rules laid down by the ecclesiastical decrees. As a priest he received diverse gifts and presents, and as far as he was allowed by the severity of the regular and the monastic life he gave himself up to almsgiving and works of mercy. He always rose before the hours of vigils and occupied himself in the laborious exercise of prayer. Anger could not undermine his patience, rage did not shake his forbearance. Lust was impotent in the presence of his chastity, and gluttony was unable to break down his abstemiousness. He subdued himself by fasting and abstinence to such a degree that he drank neither wine nor beer and in this imitated the great figures of the Old and New Testament. With the Apostle of the Gentiles he could say: "I pommel my body and subdue it, lest after preaching to others I myself should be disqualified" (1 Cor 9.27).

4

How he was sent to Kent by all the nobles, and how afterward he went to Frisia

In the previous chapter we collected together some isolated examples of Saint Boniface's admirable virtues. We consider that the others that follow, which have been elicited from trustworthy witnesses and that we shall attempt to recount, should not be passed over in silence. These are concerned with his constancy in the projects he had undertaken and his zeal in bringing others to their desired end. When he had trained himself over a long period in the virtues already mentioned and had given proof during his priesthood of many outstanding qualities, there arose a sudden crisis during the reign of Ine, king of the West Saxons,[16] occasioned by the outbreak of a rebellion. On the advice of the king the heads of the churches immediately summoned a council of the servants of God, and as soon as they were all assembled a discussion, satisfactory from every point of view, took place among the priests. They adopted the prudent measure of sending trustworthy legates to Bertwald, the archbishop of Canterbury,[17] fearing that if they made any decision without the advice of the archbishop they would be accused of presumption and temerity. At the conclusion of the discussion, when the entire gathering had reached an agreement, the king addressed all the servants of Christ, asking them whom they would choose to deliver their message. Without hesitation Winbert, the senior abbot present, who ruled over the monastery of Nursling; Wintra, the abbot of Tisbury; Beorwald, the abbot of Glastonbury, and many others who professed the monastic life summoned the saint and led him into the presence of the king. The king entrusted the message and the principal responsibilities of the embassy to him and, after giving him companions, sent him on his way in peace. In accordance with the commands of his superiors he set out with the message and, after a prosperous journey, came to Kent, where he skillfully made known to the archbishop all the matters, from first to last, that the king had told him. On receiving an immediate reply, he returned home after a few days and delivered the archbishop's

16. That is, king of Wessex, 688–725.
17. From 692–693 to 731.

answer to the king as he sat with the servants of God, bringing great joy to them all. Thus by the wonderful dispensation of God his good name was made known on all sides, and his reputation was high both among the lay nobility and the clergy. From that moment his influence increased by leaps and bounds, so that he became a regular member of their synodal assemblies.

But because a mind intent on God is not elated nor dependent upon the praise and approbation of man, he began carefully and cautiously to turn his mind to other things, to shun the company of his relatives and acquaintances, and to set his heart not on remaining in his native land but on traveling abroad. After long deliberation on the question of forsaking his country and his relatives, he took counsel of Abbot Winbert, of blessed memory, and frankly disclosed to him the plans that up to that moment he had carefully concealed. He importuned the holy man with loud and urgent requests to give his consent to the project, but Winbert, astounded, at first refused to grant his permission, thinking that delay might turn him away from carrying out his proposals. At last, however, the providence of God prevailed and Boniface's petition was granted.

So great was the affection of the abbot and brethren, with whom he had lived under the monastic discipline, that they willingly provided the money for his needs and continued long afterward to pray to God on his behalf: and so he set out upon his journey and, with God's help, safely completed it.

Much strengthened by their spiritual support and liberally supplied with earthly goods, the saint lacked nothing necessary for soul and body. Accompanied by two or three of the brethren on whose bodily and spiritual comfort he depended, he set out on his journey; and after traveling wide stretches of countryside, happy in the companionship of his brethren, he came to a place where there was a market for the buying and selling of merchandise. This place is called Lundenwich[18] by the Anglo-Saxons even to this day. After a few days, when the sailors were about to embark on their return home, Boniface asked permission of the shipmaster to go on board, and after paying his fare he set sail and came with a favorable winds to Dorestad,[19] where he tarried for a while and gave thanks to God night and day.

But a fierce quarrel that broke out between Charles,[20] the prince and noble

18. London.

19. Now Wijk bij Duurstede, twelve miles south of Utrecht. It was a major trading center before the Vikings destroyed it in 834. Boniface arrived in 716.

20. Charles Martel, who struggled between 714 and 719 to become mayor of the palace (chief administrative officer to the Merovingian dynasty of Frankish kings) and then held that office until his death in 741. His family, called Carolingian after Charlemagne, its most famous member, assisted Boniface.

leader of the Franks, and Radbod,[21] the king of the Frisians, as a result of a hostile incursion by the pagans, caused great disturbances among the population of both sides, and through the dispersion of the priests and the persecution of Radbod the greater part of the Christian churches, which previously had been subject to Frankish control, were laid waste and brought to ruin. Moreover, the pagan shrines were rebuilt and, what is worse, the worship of idols was restored. When the man of God perceived the wicked perversity of Radbod he came to Utrecht and, after waiting for a few days, spoke with the king, who had also gone there. And having traveled about the country and examined many parts of it to discover what possibility there might be of preaching the Gospel in future, he decided that if at any time he could see his way to approach the people he would minister to them the Word of God. On this purpose of his, his glorious martyrdom many years later set its seal.

A strange thing in the sanctity of the saints is that when they perceive that their labors are frustrated for a time and bear no spiritual fruit they betake themselves to other places where the results are more palpable, for there is nothing to be gained if one stays in a place without reaping a harvest of souls. With this in mind, when the saint had spent the whole of the summer in the country of the Frisians to no purpose and the autumn was nearing its end, he forsook the pastures that lay parched through lack of heavenly and fruitful dew, and, taking several companions with him for the journey, he departed to his native land. There in the seclusion of his monastery he spent two winters and one summer[22] with the brethren, who received him with open arms. In this manner he fulfilled that passage in the writings of the Apostle of the Gentiles, where it says: "For I have decided to spend the winter there" (Ti 3:12).

5

How after the death of his abbot he tarried a short time with the brethren and then went to Rome

Having now touched briefly on the virtues of the saint, we shall make known the subsequent events of his life as we have ascertained them from reliable wit-

21. He was more the leader of a rebellious gang of Frisians who objected to Frankish overlordship than a true king. The pagans referred to here are, in fact, the Frisians themselves. An Anglo-Saxon missionary, Willibrord (whose life by Alcuin is in this book), had preceded Boniface in the area of Utrecht.
22. From the autumn of 716 to the spring of 718.

nesses, that his life and character may be made more clearly manifest to those who wish to model themselves on the example of his holy manner of life.

After accomplishing his dangerous journey and escaping unharmed from the perils of the sea, he returned to his native soil and rejoined once more the fellowship of his brethren. But when he had enjoyed their company for many days a deep sorrow began to gnaw at his heart and grief weighed heavily on his soul, for as the days went by he noticed that the aging limbs of his master were growing weaker and weaker, and as a violent sickness shook and troubled his body he saw the day of his master's death approaching. At length Winbert laid aside of the prison of his body and breathed his last sigh while the monks looked sadly on. Often in the hearts of the saints the feeling of compassion for those who are overtaken by trouble wells up with particular force. For a time they themselves may be sad at heart, but through putting their trust in the words of the apostle they receive everlasting consolation in the Lord.

On this occasion the saint addressed the brethren with words of comfort and, ever mindful of the tradition of the fathers, exhorted them in a spiritual discourse always to preserve down to their smallest detail both the form of regular organization and the norm of ecclesiastical prescription. He counseled them also to choose someone as their spiritual father. Then all of one accord and with one voice earnestly implored the holy man, who at that time was called Winfrith, to take upon himself the abbatial office. But since he had already forsaken the comfort of his native land and put aside all idea of ruling others, particularly as he was now eagerly preparing to put his own plans into execution, he tactfully declined.

Now when the winter season was over and the summer was well advanced he called to mind his intention of the previous year and carefully set about preparing the journey that had been deferred. Provided with letters of introduction from Bishop Daniel,[23] of blessed memory, he tried to set out on his way to the tombs of the apostles. But for a long time he was detained by the needs of the brethren, who, now bereft of a superior, opposed his departure. Faced with their tears and wailings, he was restrained from leaving them through his feelings of affection and compassion; but so great a mental anguish oppressed him that he knew not which way to turn, for he was afraid that if he forsook the flock that had been committed to his master's care and that was now without a watchful guardian it might be exposed to ravening wolves, but on the other hand he was anxious not to miss the opportunity of going abroad in the autumn season. And when Almighty God, not unmindful of his paternal love, desired to deliver His

23. Bishop of Winchester, 704–745.

servant from his perplexity, anxiety, and grief, and to provide a suitable superior for the community, Bishop Daniel busied himself with the brethren's needs and set over the monastery a man of sterling character named Stephen. Thereupon he sped the holy man safely on his pilgrim way.

Bidding farewell to the brethren, he departed, and after traveling a considerable distance he came at length, in fulfillment of his desire, to the town that, as we have said, is called Lundenwich. He embarked immediately on a small swift ship and began to cross the pathless expanse of the sea. The sailors were in good spirits, the huge sails bellied in the northwest wind, and, helped along by a stiff following breeze, they soon came after an uneventful crossing in sight of the mouth of the river called Cuent. Here, safe from shipwreck, they set foot on dry land. At Cuentwick[24] they pitched their camp and waited until the remainder of the party came together.

When they had all met they set out straightway on their journey, for with the passing of the days the threat of winter hung over them. Many a church they visited on their way to pray that by the help of Almighty God they might cross in safety the snowy peaks of the Alps, find greater kindness at the hands of the Lombards,[25] and escape with impunity from the savage ferocity of the undisciplined soldiery.[26] And when at last, through the prayers of the saints and the providence of God, the saint and his whole retinue had reached the tomb of Saint Peter the Apostle unharmed, they immediately gave thanks to Christ for their safe journey. Afterward they went with deep joy to the Church of Saint Peter, chief of the apostles, and many of them offered up gifts, begging absolution of their sins. Now after several days had passed, the holy man spoke with the venerable man who occupied the Apostolic See, Pope Gregory of blessed memory.[27] He was the second pope of that name, predecessor of the more recent Gregory [Gregory III, 731–741], and was known as "the Younger" in the vernacular tongue of the Romans. He described the work that was closest to his heart and for which he had labored so anxiously and so long. The saintly pope, suddenly turning his gaze upon him, inquired with cheerful countenance and smiling eyes whether he carried any letters of recommendation from his bishop.

24. More commonly Quentovic, a "vic" or port (from Latin, *vicus*) on the mouth of the Canche (Cuent) in what is now Normandy. The town no longer exists. Here as elsewhere, Willibald gives Continental names in their Old English forms.

25. Germanic people who took over northern Italy in 568–569, long tried to dominate central and southern Italy, and were finally conquered by Charlemagne in 774.

26. Probably a reference to the Byzantine troops around Ravenna who, though often powerless, were technically the masters of Italy.

27. Gregory II, pope, 715–731.

Boniface, coming to himself, drew back his cloak and produced both a parchment folded in the customary fashion and other letters, which he gave to that admirable man of holy memory. As soon as Gregory had taken the letters, he signaled for Boniface to withdraw. After the pope had read the letters of recommendation and examined the writing on the parchment, he thereafter met with Boniface on a daily basis and discussed his plans assiduously, until the approach of the summer season, when it was necessary for Boniface to set out on his return journey.[28] When the end of the month of Nisan, that is April, had been reached, then Boniface, having sought and received both a blessing and letters from the Apostolic See, was sent by the blessed pope to make a report on the savage peoples of Germany. The purpose of this was to discover whether their untutored hearts and minds were ready to receive the seed of the divine Word.

And so, collecting a number of relics of the saints, he retraced his steps in the company of his fellows and reached the frontiers of Italy, where he met Liudprand, king of the Lombards,[29] to whom he gave gifts and tokens of peace. He was honorably received by the king and rested awhile after the weary labors of the journey. After receiving many presents in return, he crossed the hills and the plains and scaled the steep mountain passes of the Alps.

He then traversed the territories of the Bavarians and their German neighbors, unknown to him till then, and, in accordance with the injunction of the Apostolic See, proceeded on his journey of inspection into Thuringia.[30] Thus like the busy bee which, borne along by its softly buzzing wings, flits over fields and meadows and picks its way among a thousand different sweet-smelling flowers, testing with its discriminating tongue the secret hoards of honey-

28. These remarks make two interesting points. First, clerics were not supposed to wander about aimlessly. If they were traveling they needed official documents. Second, those official documents took the form of an *epistola formata*. Official letters might be folded in distinctive ways but, even more important, they were authenticated by means of an elaborate numerical code first laid down at the Council of Nicaea in 325. The code is based on the fact that the letters of the Greek alphabet all had numerical values. A ninth-century monk of Saint Gall, Notker the Stammerer, explained the matter this way to his bishop: "Let the addition [the authenticating number] include the Greek first letters of [the names of] the Father, the Son, and the Holy Spirit, which are Π, Υ, and Α, representing the numbers 80, 400, and 1. To this should be added the first letter of [the name of] the apostle Peter, Π, representing 80; the first letter of the writer of the *epistola* [letter]; the second letter of the addressee; the third letter of the bearer; the fourth of the city in which it was written; and the number of the current indiction. And so when all these Greek letters, which, as we have said, represent numbers, have been added, the sum should be recorded on the letter. The recipient should examine it with great care." Trans. Bernice Kaczynski, *Greek in the Carolingian Age: The St. Gall Manuscripts* (Cambridge, Mass., 1988), 34.

29. 712–744.

30. Territory in central Germany where Boniface later did most of his missionary work. See map.

bearing nectar and completely ignoring all bitter and poisonous juices, and then comes back with nectar to its hive and, to use an illustration from the words of the apostle, "test all things and hold on to what is good" (1 Thes 5.21). In Thuringia the holy man followed the mandate given him by the Apostolic See. He spoke to the senators of each tribe and the princes of the whole people with words of spiritual exhortation, recalling them to the true way of knowledge and the light of understanding that for the greater part they had lost through the perversity of their teachers. By preaching the Gospel and turning their minds away from evil toward a life of virtue and the observance of canonical decrees he reproved, admonished, and instructed to the best of his ability the priests and the elders, some of whom devoted themselves to the true worship of Almighty God, while others, contaminated and polluted by unchastity, had forsaken the life of continence to which, as ministers of the altar, they were vowed.[31]

Afterward, accompanied by his brethren, he went into Francia, and, on learning of the death of Radbod, king of the Frisians, being desirous that Frisia also should hear the Word of God, he joyfully took ship and sailed up the river. In this way he reached districts that had hitherto been left untouched by the preaching of the Gospel. The ending of the persecution raised by the savage King Radbod permitted him to scatter abroad the seed of Christian teaching to feed with wholesome doctrine those who had been famished by pagan superstition. The results of this work, so close to his heart, were swift and spontaneous. The divine light illumined their hearts, the authority of the glorious leader Charles over the Frisians was strengthened, the word of truth was blazened abroad, the voice of preachers filled the land, and the venerable Willibrord with his fellow missioners propagated the Gospel.

When he saw that the harvest was abundant and the laborers were few the holy servant of God offered his services for three years[32] to Archbishop Willibrord and labored indefatigably. He destroyed pagan temples and shrines, built churches and chapels, and with the help of Willibrord gained numerous converts to the church. When Willibrord grew old and was becoming infirm he decided on the suggestion of his disciples to appoint an assistant to relieve him of the burden of the ministry in his declining years and to choose from his small flock some man of faith who would be able to govern so numerous a people. He summoned to him the servant of God and urged him with salutary

31. The point is that Christianity had indeed already entered Germany along many paths but it was unorganized and undisciplined. How to deal with this complex situation is probably what Boniface and the pope discussed at such length in Rome.

32. 719–722.

words of advice to accept the responsibility and dignity of the episcopal office and to assist him in governing the people of God. Boniface in his humility hastily declined, answering that he was unworthy of the episcopal office, that so great a responsibility ought not to be imposed upon him at so young an age and that he had not yet reached the age of fifty required by canon law. All these excuses he put forward to avoid being raised to this exalted position. Archbishop Willibrord therefore sternly reproved him and urged him to accept the work offered him, adducing, as a final argument, the extreme need of the people over whom he ruled. When not even Willibrord's reproof could bring the saint to acquiesce and every kind of argument had been employed, they amicably agreed to differ. The saint on the one hand, held back by the feeling of humility, declined so high a position of honor; Willibrord on the other, intent on spiritual gain, thought only of the salvation of souls. Accordingly, after they had expressed their personal views, the servant of God, as if taking part in a kind of spiritual contest, at last brought forward an unanswerable argument. He said: "Most holy Bishop, you, as spiritual leader here, know full well that I came to Germany at the express command of Pope Gregory, of holy memory. As the envoy of the Apostolic See sent to the barbarian countries of the west, I freely gave my services to you and to your diocese without the knowledge of my master, to whose service I am bound by vow even to this day. Therefore without the counsel and permission of the Apostolic See and without its express command I dare not accept so exalted and sublime an office." To this rejoinder he added a reasonable request in these words: "I beseech you, therefore, to send me, bound as I am by the ties of my own promise, to those lands to which originally I was dispatched by the Apostolic See."

As soon as Willibrord had learned the reason of the saint's solemn promise, he gave him his blessing and granted him permission to depart. Thereupon the saint set out and reached the place called Amanburch,[33] "nourished," according to the apostle, "on the words of the faith and of the good doctrine which you have followed" (1 Tm 4.6).

6

We have given, step by step, proofs of this holy man's virtue and of his perseverance in the work of the Lord in order that we may recall to memory, both in general and in detail, the subsequent examples of his good deeds.

33. Amoeneburg in Hesse.

When he had converted to the Lord a vast number of people among the Frisians and many had come through his instruction to the knowledge of the truth, he then traveled, under the protection of God, to other parts of Germany to preach there and in this way came, with the help of God, to the place already mentioned, called Amanburch. Here the rulers were two twin brothers named Dettic and Devrulf, whom he converted from the sacrilegious worship of idols which was practiced under the cloak of Christianity.[34] He turned away also from the superstitions of paganism a great multitude of people by revealing to them the path of right understanding, and induced them to forsake their horrible and erroneous beliefs. When he had gathered together a sufficient number of believers he built a small chapel. Similarly he delivered the people of Hesse, who up to that time had practiced pagan ritual, from the captivity of the devil by preaching the Gospel as far as the borders of Saxony.

Having converted many thousands of people from their long-standing pagan practices and baptized them, he sent to Rome an experienced and trustworthy messenger, Bynnan by name, with a letter in which he made known to the venerable father and bishop of the Apostolic See all the matters that by God's grace had been accomplished, and the number of people who, through the operation of the Holy Spirit, had received the sacrament of baptism. In addition he asked for guidance on certain questions concerning the day-to-day needs of the church and the progress of the people, for he wished to have the advice of the Apostolic See. When the aforesaid messenger had tarried in Rome for some days and the time for his return journey drew near, the bishop of the Apostolic See gave him a letter in reply to the message he had brought on his embassy. Returning immediately, he quickly brought to his master the letter dictated by the pope.

On reading the missive brought to him by the messenger, he learned that he was summoned to Rome, and with all haste he prepared to carry out this injunction in a spirit of complete obedience. Without delay he set out on his journey accompanied by a large retinue and a number of his brethren. Passing through the lands of the Franks and Burgundians, he crossed the Alps and descended through the marches of Italy and the territory held by the soldiers. Eventually he came in sight of the walls of Rome and, giving praise and thanks to God on high, went quickly to the Church of Saint Peter, where he fortified himself in long and earnest prayer. After he had rested his weary limbs for a brief space of time a message was sent to blessed Gregory, bishop of the

34. Here, and more fully in Boniface's letters, we get a glimpse of Christianity existing alongside vestigial paganism in the absence of a resident, trained clergy.

Apostolic See, saying that the servant of God had arrived; he was then welcomed with great kindness and conducted to the pilgrim's lodge.

A convenient day was fixed for a meeting, and at the appointed time the pontiff came down to the Basilica of Saint Peter the Apostle, and the servant of God was summoned to his presence. After they had exchanged a few words of greeting, the bishop of the Apostolic See interrogated him on his teaching, on the creed and on the tradition and beliefs of his church. To this the man of God gave an immediate and humble reply, saying: "My Lord Pope, as a stranger I am conscious that I lack the skill in the use of the tongue[35] with which you are familiar, but grant me leisure and time, I beseech you, to write down my confession of faith, so that my words and not my tongue may make a reasonable presentation of the truths I believe." To this Gregory agreed at once and commanded him to bring his written statement as quickly as possible. Within a short time he presented his written confession of faith, expressed in polished, eloquent, and learned phrases, and delivered it to the aforesaid pope. He then waited patiently for some days.

At length he was invited once more and was conducted within the Lateran Palace,[36] where he cast himself prostrate upon his face at the feet of the apostolic pontiff and begged for his blessing. Gregory quickly raised him from the ground, and, after giving into the hands of the servant of God the document in which the pure and uncontaminated truth of the faith was clearly expressed, he invited him to sit at his side. With wise counsel and wholesome doctrine he admonished him to preserve at all times the deposit of the faith and to the best of his ability to preach it vigorously to others. They discussed and debated many other matters relating to holy religion and the true faith, and in his exchange of views they spent almost the whole day. At last the pope inquired how the people who previously had been steeped in error and wickedness received his preaching of the true faith. On learning that a vast number had been converted from the sacrilegious worship of idols and admitted to the communion of the church, the pope told him that he intended to raise him to the episcopal dignity and set him over peoples who up to that time had been without a leader to guide them and who, in the words of our Lord, "languished as sheep without a shepherd." The holy man, because he dared not contradict so great a bishop of the Apostolic See,

35. Boniface's native language was Old English. He had learned to read and write Latin in school but probably could not pronounce it the way people in Rome did. He was concerned about being misunderstood.

36. The palace attached to the Basilica of Saint John Lateran, the pope's cathedral church. Popes often met visiting dignitaries at Saint Peter's, which was then outside the city.

consented, that is, obeyed. And so the highest bishop, he of holy authority, set a day for the ordination: November 13.

When the holy day for the sacred solemnity dawned, which was both the feast day of Saint Andrew and the day set aside for his consecration, the holy pontiff of the Apostolic See conferred upon him the dignity of the episcopate and gave him the name of Boniface.[37] He put into his hands the book in which the most sacred laws and canons of the church and the decrees of episcopal synods have been inscribed or compiled, commanding him that henceforth this norm of church conduct and belief should be kept inviolate and that the people under his jurisdiction should be taught on these lines. He also offered to him and to all his subjects the friendship of the holy Apostolic See thenceforth and for ever. By means of his most sacred letters, the pope placed the holy man, now strengthened by episcopal rank, under the protection and devotion of the glorious leader Charles.

After Boniface had passed by devious ways through the densely populated territories of the Franks he came at last into the presence of the aforesaid prince and was received by him with marks of reverence. He delivered to him the letters of the bishop of Rome and of the Apostolic See, and after acknowledging the prince as his lord and patron, returned with the leader's permission to the land of the Hessians in which he had previously settled.

Now many of the Hessians who at that time had acknowledged the Catholic faith were confirmed by the grace of the Holy Spirit and received the laying-on of hands. But others, not yet strong in the spirit, refused to accept the pure teachings of the church in their entirety. Moreover, some continued secretly, others openly, to offer sacrifices to trees and springs, to inspect the entrails of victims; some practiced divination, legerdemain, and incantations; some turned their attention to auguries, auspices, and other sacrificial rites; while others, of a more reasonable character, forsook all the profane practices of the Gentiles [i.e., pagans] and committed none of these crimes. With the counsel and advice of the latter persons, Boniface in their presence attempted to cut down, at a place called Gaesmere,[38] a certain oak of extraordinary size called in the old tongue of the pagans the Oak of Jupiter. Taking his courage in his hands (for a great crowd of pagans stood by watching and bitterly cursing in their hearts the enemy of the gods), he cut the first notch. But when he had

37. Literally the "doer of good deeds." His consecration took place in either 722 or 723, probably the latter. At this stage Boniface was made bishop without a fixed see, an unusual situation.

38. It is not known where this place, Geismar in German, was located.

made a superficial cut, suddenly the oak's vast bulk, shaken by a mighty blast of wind from above, crashed to the ground shivering its topmost branches into fragments in its fall. As if by the express will of God (for the brethren present had done nothing to cause it) the oak burst asunder into four parts, each part having a trunk of equal length. At the sight of this extraordinary spectacle the heathens who had been cursing ceased to revile and began, on the contrary, to believe and bless the Lord. Thereupon the holy bishop took counsel with the brethren, built an oratory from the timber of the oak and dedicated it to Saint Peter the Apostle. He then set out on a journey to Thuringia, having accomplished by the help of God all the things we have already mentioned. Arrived there, he addressed the elders and the chiefs of the people, calling on them to put aside their blind ignorance and to return to the Christian religion that they had formerly embraced. For, after the authority of their kings came to an end, Theobald and Heden had seized the reins of government. Under their disastrous sway, which was founded more upon tyranny and slaughter than upon the loyalty of the people, many of the counts had been put to death or seized and carried off into captivity, while the remainder of the population, overwhelmed by all kinds of misfortunes, had submitted to the domination of the Saxons. Thus when the power of the leaders, who had protected religion, was destroyed, the devotion of the people to Christianity and religion died out also, and false brethren were brought in to pervert the minds of the people and to introduce among them under the guise of religion dangerous heretical sects. Of these men the chief were Torchtwine, Zeretheve, Eaubercht, and Hunraed, men living in fornication and adultery, whom, according to the apostle, God had already judged (see Heb 13.4). These individuals stirred up a violent conflict against the man of God; but when they had been unmasked and shown to be in opposition to the truth, they received a just penalty for their crimes.[39]

When the light of faith had illumined the minds of the people and the population had been loosed from its bonds of error, when also the devil's disciples and the insidious seducers of the people, whom we have already mentioned, had been banished, Boniface, assisted by a few helpers, gathered in an abundant harvest. At first he suffered from extreme want and lacked even the necessaries of life, but, though in straitened circumstances and in deep distress, he continued to preach the Word of God. Little by little the number of

39. This impenetrable account hints at the political struggles in central Germany as Charles Martel attempted to reestablish Frankish control after a lapse of nearly a century. Boniface was both aided by Charles and impeded by social and political forces over which he had no control. Heden, for instance, who comes off badly here, had made donations to Willibrord in 704 and 717.

believers increased, the preachers grew more numerous, church buildings were restored and the Word of God was published far and wide. At the same time the servants of God, monks of genuinely ascetic habits, were grouped together in one body and they constructed a monastery in a place called Orthorpf.[40] In the manner of the apostles (see 1 Cor 4.12), they procured food and clothing with their own hands and contented themselves with constant labor.

By this means the report of his preaching reached far-off lands so that within a short space of time his fame resounded throughout the greater part of Europe. From Britain an exceedingly large number of holy men came to his aid, among them readers, writers, and learned men trained in the other arts. Of these a considerable number put themselves under his rule and guidance, and by their help the population in many places was recalled from the errors and profane rites of their heathen gods. While some were in the province of Hesse and others scattered widely among the people of Thuringia, they preached the word of God in the countryside and in the villages. The number of both peoples who received the sacraments of the faith was enormous and many thousands of them were baptized. On the death of Gregory the Second, of blessed memory, ruler of the Apostolic See, the renowned Gregory the Younger[41] ascended the papal throne. Once more Boniface's messengers journeyed to Rome and spoke with the holy pontiff of the Apostolic See, presenting to him the pledge of friendship that his predecessor had previously bestowed upon Saint Boniface and his people. They assured the pope of Boniface's devoted and humble submission to the Apostolic See both in the past and for the future, and begged the pontiff, in accordance with the instructions they had received, to allow his loyal subject to remain in the brotherhood and communion of the pope and Apostolic See. To this the pontiff gave an immediate reply and granted to Saint Boniface and to all those under his care fraternal and friendly communion both with himself and the Apostolic See. Furthermore, he gave the archiepiscopal pallium[42] to the envoys, loaded them with gifts and the relics of numerous saints, and dispatched them homewards.

When his envoys returned bearing the immediate responses of the pope, Boniface, rejoicing greatly, was deeply comforted by the support of the Apostolic See and inspired by the abundance of divine mercy. Thus he built two churches. One was in Frideslare,[43] which he dedicated to Saint Peter, prince of

40. Ohrdruf near Gotha.
41. Gregory III, pope, 731–741.
42. On the pallium, see above, page 105, note 31. Again, Boniface had no fixed see.
43. Fritzlar.

the apostles. The other was in Amanburch, which he dedicated to Saint Michael the Archangel. He attached two small monasteries to these two churches and invited a large number of monks to serve God there, with the result that even to this day praise and blessing and thanksgiving are offered to the Lord our God.

When all these arrangements had received their final completion he set out on a journey to Bavaria where Hugobert was then duke. Here he continued to preach and to make visitations of all the churches. So great was his zeal and spiritual courage that he condemned and expelled in accordance with canonical decrees a certain schismatic named Eremwulf, who was imbued with heretical opinions. Boniface then converted the people of this misguided sect from their worship of idols. After this he departed from them and returned to the people of his own diocese, being moved by a desire, as the apostle puts it, to come to his own brethren (see Rom 15.23).

7

How he expelled the heretics from the provinces of Bavaria and divided it into four dioceses

We have spent no little time in recounting some of the merits of Boniface in order that we may describe, though not in detail, the powerful religious sense that guided him throughout the whole of his life. For, as history shows, it is a characteristic of the saints that, setting the example of others before their own eyes, they arouse in themselves the desire for better things, and as their life draws to its close they increase the love of God in their hearts.

When a considerable number of churches had been built in Hesse and Thuringia and a superior had been appointed over each church he set out on a journey to Rome for the third time,[44] accompanied as usual by a group of disciples. His intention was to have further discussions with the apostolic father and to commend himself in his declining years to the prayers of the saints. When at the end of his long and painful journey he was brought into the presence of the apostolic lord Gregory, the second pope to be called "the Younger," he was received with great kindness and was held in such veneration by everyone, as well Romans and strangers, that many flocked together to listen to his preaching. A multitude of Franks and Bavarians, as well as of

44. 737–738.

Saxons arriving from Britain and other provinces, followed his teaching with the closest attention.

When he had spent the better part of a year in these parts, visiting and praying at the shrines of the saints, he took his leave of the venerable bishop of the Apostolic See and returned home, carrying with him many gifts and sacred relics of the saints. After traversing Italy, he came to the walls of the city of Picena, and, as his limbs were weary with old age, he rested awhile with Liudprand, king of the Lombards.

On his departure from Italy he made a visit to the Bavarians, not only because Duke Odilo had sent him an invitation but also because he himself was desirous of seeing them. He remained among them[45] for some time preaching the Word of God, restored the sacraments of the faith to their primitive purity, and banned those men who destroyed the churches and perverted the people. Some of these had arrogated to themselves the dignity of bishops, others the office of priests, while others, by these and by a thousand other lying pretexts, had led the greater part of the populace into error. The saint, who had dedicated himself to God's service from his earliest childhood and was therefore ill able to brook the insult offered to his Lord, compelled Duke Odilo and his subjects to forsake their evil, false, and heretical doctrines and put them on their guard against the deceitfulness of immoral priests. With the consent of Duke Odilo he divided the province of Bavaria into four dioceses and appointed over them four bishops, whom he consecrated for this purpose. Of these, the first, John by name, was appointed to the see in the town that is called Salzburg. The second was Erembert, who took upon himself the obligation of governing the church in the city of Regensburg.[46] When everything was set in order in Bavaria, a Christian form of life established and the prescriptions of canon law enforced, Boniface returned home to his own diocese. He governed the people committed to his care, diligently provided for the needs of his flock, and appointed priests to defend the faithful and deliver them from the attacks of ravening wolves.

The temporal rule of the glorious leader Charles eventually came to an end[47] and the reins of power passed into the strong hands of his two sons Carloman and Pepin. Then by the help of God and at the suggestion of the archbishop Saint Boniface the establishment of the Christian religion was confirmed, the

45. 739–740.

46. Bavaria's other dioceses were Freising and Passau. Boniface was here forwarding plans initiated by Pope Gregory II in 719. Note well Boniface's continual stress on preaching the Gospel, eradicating heresy, and building solid structures.

47. 741.

convening of synods by orthodox bishops was instituted among the Franks and all abuses were redressed and corrected in accordance with canonical authority. On the saint's advice the unlawful practice of concubinage among the layfolk was suppressed while the sacrilegious marriages of the clergy were annulled and the sinful parties separated. So great was the religious fervor kindled by the teaching of Saint Boniface that Carloman and Pepin freed the faithful to a large extent from the evil practices in which through long neglect they had become deeply rooted and through which, partly by giving rein to their own passions, partly by being misled by the insidious doctrines of heretics, they had forfeited their right to eternal bliss. For so thoroughly had the heretics quenched the light of religious teaching among the people that a dark impenetrable gloom of error had settled down over a large section of the church. Two of the heretics, for example, named Adalbert and Clement, led astray by this greed for filthy lucre, strove with all their might to turn away the people from the truth. But when the holy archbishop Boniface with the cooperation of the leaders Carloman and Pepin forcibly ejected them from the communion of the church they were delivered, according to the apostle, "to Satan for the destruction of the flesh, that his spirit may be saved in the day of the Lord Jesus" (1 Cor 5.5).

8

How throughout his whole life he preached with zeal and how he departed from this world

During the rule of Carloman all the bishops, priests, deacons, and clerics and everyone of ecclesiastical rank gathered together at the ruler's instance and held four synodal councils. At these Archbishop Boniface presided, with the consent and support of Carloman and of the metropolitan of the see and city of Mainz. And being a legate of the Roman Church and the Apostolic See, sent as he was by the saintly and venerable Gregory II and later by Gregory III, he urged that the numerous canons and ordinances decreed by these four important and early councils should be preserved in order to ensure the healthy development of Christian doctrine. For as at the Council of Nicaea, held under Constantine Augustus, the errors and blasphemies of Arius were rejected; as under Theodosius the Elder an assembly of one hundred and fifty bishops condemned Macedonius, who denied the divinity of the Holy Spirit; as in the city of Ephesus under Theodosius [II] two hundred bishops excommunicated Nestorius for declaring that there are two Persons in Christ; and as at the Council of Chalcedon an assembly of six hundred and thirty bishops, basing their decision on an earlier one of the fathers, pronounced an anathema against Eutyches, an abbot of Constantinople, and Dioscorus, who defended him, for attacking the foundations of the Catholic faith[48]—so in the Frankish territories, after the eradication of heresy and the destruction of wicked conspirators, he urged that later developments of Christian doctrine and the decrees of the general councils should be received. With this in view there should be a meeting of the bishops in synod each year in accordance with the decree of the aforesaid council of bishops. This holding of synods had fallen into desuetude through the constant fear of war and the hostility and attacks of the surrounding barbarian tribes and through the attempts of hostile enemies to destroy the Frankish realm by violence. They had been forgotten so completely that no one could recall such an assembly's having taken place within living memory. For it is in the nature of the world to fall into ruin even though it is daily restored, while if no attempt is made to reform it it quickly disintegrates and rushes headlong to its predestined doom. Therefore if in the course of this mortal life means have been discovered to remedy such evils they should be preserved and strongly defended by Catholics and fixed indelibly in the mind. Otherwise human forgetfulness and the enticement of pleasure, both of them instigated by the devil, will prove a stumbling block. For this reason the holy bishop, in his anxiety to deliver his people from the baleful influence of the devil, repeatedly urged Carloman to summon the episcopal synods already mentioned in order that both present and later generations should learn spiritual wisdom and should make the knowledge of Christianity available to all. Only in this way could unsuspecting souls escape being ensnared.

After he had set before all ranks of society the accepted norm of the Christian life and made known to them the way of truth, Boniface, now weak and decrepit, showed great foresight both as regards himself and his people by appointing a successor to his see, as ecclesiastical law demands. So, whether he lived or whether he died, the people would not be left without pastors and their ministration. He promoted two men of good repute to the episcopate, Willibald[49] and Burchard, dividing between them the churches that were under

48. Willibald here condenses the account of these councils that he found in Isidore of Seville (*Etymologies*, 6.16.5). The councils met in the following years: Nicaea, 325; Constantinople, 381; Ephesus, 431; Chalcedon, 451.

49. This is the Willibald whose life by Huneberc is in this volume, not the Willibald who wrote the present text.

his jurisdiction in the land of eastern Franks and on the Bavarian marches. To Willibald he entrusted the diocese of Eichstätt, to Burchard that of Würzburg, putting under his care all the churches within the borders of the Franks, Saxons, and Slavs. Nevertheless, even to the day of his death he did not fail to instruct the people in the way of life.

Then Pepin, with the help of the Lord, took over the rule of the kingdom of the Franks as the happy successor to his above-mentioned brother [Carloman].[50] When disorders among the people had subsided, he was elevated to the kingship. From the outset he conscientiously carried out the vows he had sworn to the Lord, to put into effect without delay the synodal decrees, and he renewed the canonical institutions which his brother, following the advice of the holy archbishop Boniface, had so dutifully set on foot. He showed the saint every mark of veneration and friendship and obeyed his spiritual precepts. But because the holy man, owing to his physical infirmities, was not able to attend the synodal assemblies, he decided, with the king's approval and advice, to appoint a suitable person to minister to his flock. To his purpose he appointed Lull, a disciple of outstanding ability, whose duty it would be to continue his instruction to the people.[51] He consecrated him bishop, and committed to his care the inheritance that he had won for Christ by his zealous efforts. Lull was the man who had been his trusted companion on his journeys and who had been closely connected with him both in his sufferings and his consolations.

When the Lord willed to deliver his servant from the trials of this world and to set him free from the vicissitudes of this mortal life, it was decided, under God's providence, that he should travel in the company of his disciples to Frisia, from which he had departed in body though not in spirit. And this was done so that in dying there he might receive the divine recompense in the place where he had begun his preaching.

To Bishop Lull he foretold in an astonishing prophecy the approaching day of his death and made known to him the manner in which he would meet his end. Then he drew up plans for the construction of further churches and for the evangelization of the people. "My wish," he said, "is to complete the journey on which I have set my heart, and nothing can prevent me from doing so. The day of my departure from this life draws near and the time of my death is approaching. In a short time I shall lay aside the burden of my body

---

50. Carloman abdicated as mayor of the palace in 747, went to Rome, became a monk, and finally retired to Monte Cassino. Pepin became king of the Franks in 751.

51. Boniface's see had been fixed at Mainz in 747. Mainz was assigned to Lull between 751 and 753.

and receive the prize of eternal bliss. But you, my dear son, must bring to completion the building of the churches that I began in Thuringia. Earnestly recall the people from the paths of error, finish the construction of the basilica at Fulda, which is now in the process of building, and bring thither this body of mine now wasted by the toil of years." When he had ended his instructions he added the following words, or words to this effect: "Carefully provide everything that we shall need on our journey, not forgetting to place in the chest, where my books are kept, a linen sheet in which my aged body may be wrapped."

At these sad words Bishop Lull could not restrain his tears and gave vent to his profound sorrow; but Boniface, having expressed his last wishes, went about his business unconcerned. After the lapse of a few days, he still persevered in his decision to set out on the journey, and so, taking with him a few companions, he went on board a ship and sailed down the Rhine. Eventually he reached the marshy country of Frisia, crossed safely over the stretch of water, which in their tongue is called Aelmere,[52] and made a survey of the lands round about, which up till then had borne no fruit. After bravely hazarding the perils of the river, the sea and the wide expanse of the ocean, he passed through dangerous places without fear of danger, and visited the pagan Frisians, whose land is divided into many territories and districts by intersecting canals. These territories, though bearing different names, are, nevertheless, the property of one nation. But since it would prove tedious to give a list of these districts one after the other, we will merely mention one or two of them by name to prove the veracity and add to the continuity of our narrative. In this way the place and its name will bear witness to the activities of the saint as we relate them and show the kind of death that took him from this world.

This, then, is how he traversed the whole of Frisia, destroying pagan worship and turning away the people from their pagan errors by his preaching of the Gospel. The pagan temples and gods were overthrown and churches were built in their stead. Many thousands of men, women, and children were baptized by him, assisted by his fellow missionary and suffragan bishop Eoban, who, after being consecrated bishop in the city which is called Trecht [Utrecht], was summoned to Frisia to help Boniface in his old age. He was also assisted in his labors by a number of priests and deacons whose names are subjoined: Wintrung, Walthere, Ethelhere, priests; Hamrind, Scirbald, and Bosa, deacons; Wachar, Gundaecer, Illehere and Hathowulf, monks. These in company with Saint Boniface preached the Word of God far and wide with

52. Zuider Zee.

great success and were so united in spirit that, in accordance with the teaching of apostolic practice, they were "of one heart and soul" (Acts 4.32). Thus they deserved to share in the same crown of martyrdom and the same final and eternal reward.

When, as we have already said, the faith had been planted strongly in Frisia and the glorious end of the saint's life drew near, he took with him a picked number of his personal followers and pitched a camp on the banks of the river Bordne,[53] which flows through the territories called Ostor and Westeraeche and divides them. Here he fixed a day on which he would confirm by the laying-on of hands all the neophytes and those who had recently been baptized; and because the people were scattered far and wide over the countryside, they all returned to their homes, so that, in accordance with the instructions laid down by the holy bishop, they could meet together again on the day appointed for their confirmation.

But events turned out otherwise than expected. When the appointed day arrived and the morning light was breaking through the clouds after sunrise, enemies came instead of friends, new executioners in place of new worshipers of the faith. A vast number of foes armed with spears and shields rushed into the camp brandishing their weapons. In the twinkling of an eye the attendants sprang from the camp to meet them and snatched up arms here and there to defend the holy band of martyrs (for that is what they were to be) against the insensate fury of the mob. But the man of God, hearing the shouts and the onrush of the rabble, straightway called the clergy to his side, and, collecting together the relics of the saints, which he always carried with him, came out of his tent. At once he reproved the attendants and forbade them to continue the conflict, saying: "Sons, cease fighting. Lay down your arms, for we are told in Scripture not to render evil for good but to overcome evil by good. The hour to which we have long looked forward is near and the day of our release is at hand. Take comfort in the Lord and endure with gladness the suffering He has mercifully ordained. Put your trust in Him and He will grant deliverance to your souls." And addressing himself like a loving father to the priests, deacons, and other clerics, all trained to the service of God, who stood about him, he gave them courage, saying: "Brethren, be of stout heart, fear not them who kill the body, for they cannot slay the soul, which continues to live for ever. Rejoice in the Lord; anchor your hope in God, for without delay He will render to you the reward of eternal bliss and grant you an abode with the angels in His heaven above. Be not slaves to the transitory pleasures of this world. Be not seduced by

53. Boorne.

the vain flattery of the heathen, but endure with steadfast mind the sudden onslaught of death, that you may be able to reign evermore with Christ."

Whilst with these words he was encouraging his disciples to accept the crown of martyrdom, the frenzied mob of pagans rushed suddenly upon them with swords and every kind of warlike weapon, staining their bodies with their precious blood.

Suddenly, after the mortal remains of the just had been mutilated, the pagan mob seized with exultation upon the spoils of their victory (in reality the cause of their damnation) and, after laying waste the camp, carried off and shared the booty; they stole the chests in which the books and relics were preserved and, thinking that they had acquired a hoard of gold and silver, carried them off, still locked, to the ships. Now the ships were stocked with provisions for the feeding of the clerics and attendants and a great deal of wine still remained. Finding this goodly liquor, the pagans immediately began to slake their sottish appetites and to get drunk. After some time, by the wonderful dispensation of God, they began to argue among themselves about the booty they had taken and discussed how they were to share the gold and silver they had not even seen. During the long and wordy discussion about the treasure, which they imagined to be considerable, frequent quarrels broke out among them until, in the end, there arose such enmity and discord that they were divided into two angry and frenzied factions. It was not long before the weapons that had earlier murdered the holy martyrs were turned against each other in bitter strife. After the greater part of the mad freebooters had been slain, the survivors, surrounded by the corpses of their rivals for the booty, swooped down upon the treasure that had been obtained by so much loss of life. They broke open the chests containing the books and found, to their dismay, that they held manuscripts instead of gold vessels, pages of sacred texts instead of silver plate. Disappointed in their hope of gold and silver, they littered the fields with the books they found, throwing some of them into reedy marshes, hiding away others in widely different places. But by the grace of God and through the prayers of the archbishop and martyr Saint Boniface the manuscripts were discovered, a long time afterward, unharmed and intact, and they were returned by those who found them to the monastery,[54] in which they are used with great advantage to the salvation of souls even at the present day.

54. Fulda, three of whose medieval manuscripts are believed to be the very books mentioned here. One of these has been hacked nearly in half. Legend says Boniface defended himself with this book.

Disillusioned by the loss of the treasure on which they had reckoned, the murderers returned to their dwellings. But after a lapse of three days they were visited with a just retribution for their crimes, losing not only all their worldly possessions but their lives also. For it was the will of the omnipotent Creator and Savior of the world that He should be avenged of His enemies; and in His mercy and compassion He demanded a penalty for the sacred blood shed on His behalf. Deeply moved by the recent act of wicked savagery, He deigned to show the wrath He had concealed so long against the worshipers of idols. As the unhappy tidings of the martyr's death spread rapidly from village to village throughout the whole province and the Christians learned of their fate, a large avenging force, composed of warriors ready to take speedy retribution, was gathered together and rushed swiftly to their neighbors' frontiers. The pagans, unable to withstand the onslaught of the Christians, immediately took to flight and were slaughtered in great numbers. In their flight they lost their lives, their household goods, and their children. So the Christians, after taking as their spoil the wives and children, men and maidservants of the pagan worshipers, returned to their homes. As a result, the pagans round about, dismayed at their recent misfortune and seeking to avoid everlasting punishment, opened their minds and hearts to the glory of the faith. Struck with terror at the visitation of God's vengeance, they embraced after Boniface's death the teaching they had rejected while he still lived.

The bodies of the holy bishop and of the other martyrs were brought by boat across the water called Aelmere, an uneventful voyage of some days, to the above-mentioned city that is called Trecht. There the bodies were deposited and interred until some religious and trustworthy men of God arrived from Mainz. From there they had been sent in a ship by Bishop Lull, the successor of our holy bishop and martyr, to bring the body of the saint to the monastery built by him during his lifetime on the banks of the river Fulda. Of these men there was one named Hadda, remarkable for his continence and chastity, who planned the journey and organized the party. On him particularly and on all the brethren who accompanied him Lull imposed the obligation of setting out on the journey and of bringing back the sacred body in order that greater honor and reverence might be paid to the holy man and greater credence might be given to all the facts they saw and heard.

The venerable and holy company came to the above-mentioned city [Utrecht] and was met by a small throng of people. But the count of the city declared in the hearing of all that an edict had been issued by King Pepin forbidding anyone to remove the body of Bishop Boniface from that place.[55] As, however, the power of Almighty God is greater than the strength of men, suddenly in their presence a marvelous miracle took place, wrought through angelic rather than human intervention. The bell of the church, untouched by human hands, began to ring, as if the body of the saint was issuing a warning; and every person present, smitten by a sudden feeling of awe, was struck with terror and cried out that the body of this holy man should be given up. The body, consequently, was handed over at once and was taken away in great honor by the brethren already mentioned. And so, to the accompaniment of psalms and hymns, without having to row against the current of the stream, the body was brought, thirty days after the saint's decease, to the city of Mainz. It fell out by the wonderful providence of God that on one and the same day, although no fixed arrangement had been made, there assembled together for the interment of this great man not only the envoys who had brought the sacred body but also many men and women of the faith from distant and widely scattered districts, just as if they had been forewarned of the event. Moreover, Lull, the saint's successor, who at that time was engaged at the royal palace and was not informed of the arrival of the sacred body and was quite ignorant of what was afoot, came to Mainz almost at the same hour and moment. And though all strangers and citizens alike were weighed down with sorrow and grief, yet they experienced a great joy. For while they were struck with grief when they considered the circumstances of his death, they felt, on the other hand, that he would protect them and their heirs for all time to come. Therefore the people with the priests, deacons, and all ranks of the clergy carried the sacred body, with hearts torn by conflicting emotions, to the spot that he had decided upon during his lifetime. A new sarcophagus was made in the church and the body was laid in it with all the customary rites of burial. When the ceremony was over they all returned to their homes, strengthened and comforted in the faith.

From that moment the spot in which the sacred body was interred became the scene of many divine blessings through the prayers of the saint; many of those who came there, troubled by various sicknesses and diseases, were healed in soul and body. Some who were at death's door and practically lifeless, deprived of everything except their last breath, were restored to vigorous

---

55. It was not unusual for both persons and religious communities to become fierce rivals for possession of the bodies of famous saints. The next paragraph, telling of miracles at Boniface's tomb, makes clear that a flow of pilgrims and worshipers could enhance the prestige, and the economic standing, of a church.

health. Others, whose eyes were dim with blindness, received their sight; others, bound fast by the snares of the devil, unbalanced in mind and out of their sense, regained their peace of mind and after their cure gave praise and thanks to God. God deigned to honor and enrich His servant, who possessed this great gift, and glorified him in the eyes of present and future ages, forty years after his pilgrimage was over, i.e., 716, which year is reckoned as the year of the Incarnation of our Lord seven hundred and fifty-five, the eighth indiction.[56] He occupied the episcopal thirty-six years, six months, and six days. Thus, in the manner described above, on the fifth day of June, crowned with the palm of martyrdom, he departed to the Lord, to whom be honor and glory for ever and ever. Amen.

9

How in the place where the blood of the martyrs was shed a living fountain appeared to those who were surveying the site for a church

Now that we have narrated the outstanding events in the saint's childhood, boyhood, youth, middle life, old age, let us return to the marvelous happenings that were wrought by the help of God after his life's work was over, and make known to men the sanctity of his life.

Let us recall to memory a miracle that people still remember and recount. This story was told to us by the venerable Bishop Lull, who learned it from King Pepin, who in turn heard it from eyewitnesses. The story as related by Lull goes as follows: A plan was drawn up with the advice of the ecclesiastical authorities and the majority of the Frisian people to raise an enormous mound of earth on the spot where some years before the precious blood of the holy martyr had been spilled. This was because the violent neap and spring tides at different times of the year affect the ocean swell and cause disturbances in the incoming and outgoing floods of water. On the mound they proposed to build a church (as was done later) and to construct on the same spot a monastery for the servants of God. But when the mound had been raised and the work of building it up had been completed, the residents and inhabitants of the district began to discuss on their return home the difficulty of obtaining fresh water, for throughout almost all Frisia this is a great problem both for man and beast.

---

56. Indictions were fifteen-year-long Roman tax cycles. This official form of Roman dating persisted in some places into the early Middle Ages.

At last a certain man named Abba, who was an administrator under King Pepin and director of the work in question, taking some attendants with him, mounted his horse, rode over the hill, and inspected the mound. Suddenly and unexpectedly the horse of one of the attendants, which had barely trod upon the ground, felt it sinking and giving way altogether. With its forelegs held firmly in the soil, the horse rolled helplessly about until those who were more active and experienced hurriedly dismounted from their horses and extricated it as it lay fast in the earth. At once an astonishing miracle happened, worthy to be remembered by all those who were present and saw it. A fountain of water much clearer than any found in that country, extraordinarily sweet and pleasant to the taste, came bubbling up and flowed out through innumerable channels until it formed a considerable stream. Astounded at this miracle, they returned to their homes in joy and gladness, spreading the news in the churches of what they had seen.

Huneberc of Heidenheim

THE HODOEPORICON
OF SAINT WILLIBALD

Translated by C. H. Talbot

This strangely titled work—*hodoeporicon* means "relation of a voyage"—is remarkable in two respects. Much of it is less a life of Willibald than an account of his journey to the Holy Land undertaken between 722 and 729. As such, it fits into the group of such pilgrims' accounts whose other representatives are Arculf's of the seventh century and Bernard's of the ninth. More striking, however, is the fact that its author is a woman.

The identity of Huneberc (sometimes Hugeberc) was only discovered in 1931 when Bernhard Bischoff deciphered a cryptogram in a Munich manuscript of the present text. She wrote this work as well as a life of Willibald's brother Wynnebald. No other writings by Huneberc are known, however, so all that can be said about her must be deduced from these documents. She appears to have been the only woman author of a saint's life from the Carolingian period.

Huneberc left England in or just after 761 to join her relative Walburga, the abbess of Heidenheim (in Alamannia, just north of the Danube). Heidenheim had been founded in 752 by Wynnebald, with the support of his brother Willibald, the bishop of Eichstätt. The community was a double monastery, meaning that it had both monks and nuns. When Wynnebald died his sister Walburga became abbess and ruled the monastery. Such double houses were common in early Anglo-Saxon England and also on the Continent where English influences were strong.

Under circumstances about which we are totally uninformed, Huneberc acquired a good basic education. She also knew the forms of hagiography that had become classic by her time. Like Willibald—Boniface's biographer, that is, not Huneberc's subject—she was deeply influenced by Aldhelm and his intricate Latin style. Critics agree that it is interesting that a woman should have tried to imitate Aldhelmian Latin, but revealing that her education—again like Willibald's—was insufficient to permit her to achieve her goal with complete success.

Recent students of this text have, however, been more positive in their assessment of Huneberc's overall achievement. She herself tells us that she got most of her information directly from Willibald himself. For many readers this has been taken to mean that Huneberc's text was more stenography that literary composition. That opinion is now changing. Huneberc is today seen to have been an author of vision and imagination who consciously shaped her own material despite adopting the conceit of attributing everything to Willibald. In all probability, she was using the modesty topos so common to the hagiographic genre. This work was written before 786. It was not widely circulated and survives in few manuscripts.

The *Life* provides essential details concerning Willibald. By way of introduction it may be said that he was born in 700 and died in 786. In 722 he set out from England on a pilgrimage to Rome and, on arriving in the city, decided on a trip to the eastern Mediterranean and the Holy Land. After this venture, he spent ten years at Monte Cassino. He shared the wanderlust common to Willibrord, Boniface, Huneberc herself, and so many other Anglo-Saxons. In 742 Boniface, his kinsman, consecrated him bishop of Eichstätt. Few details are known about Willibald's ecclesiastical career.

Texts and References

The standard Latin text is *Vita Willibaldi episcopi Eischstetensis et vita Wynnebaldi abbatis Heidenheimensis auctore sanctimoniale Heidenheimensis*, ed. O. Holder-Egger, Monumenta Germainiae Historica, Scriptores, vol. 15, part 1, pp. 80–117. There is only one significant study of Huneberc and it focuses almost exclusively on her Latinity: Eva Gottschaller, *Hugeberc von Heidenheim: Philologische Untersuchungen zu den heiligen Biographen einer Nonne des 8. Jahrhunderts*, Münchener Beiträge zur Mediävistik and Renaissance-Forschung 12 (Munich, 1973). For brief but valuable accounts see Thomas Head, "Hugeberc of Heidenheim," in *An Encyclopedia of Continental Women Writers*, ed. Katharina M. Wilson, 2 vols. (New York, 1991), 1:575–76; Peter Dronke, *Women Writers of the Middle Ages* (Cambridge, 1984), 33–35; Claudio Leonardi, "Una scheda per Ugeburga," in *Tradition und Wertung: Festschrift für Franz Brunhölzl zum 65. Geburtstag*, ed. Günter Bernt, Fidel Rädle, and Gabriel Silagi (Sigmaringen, 1989), 23–26.

Prologue

Here begins the life of the brothers Willibald and Wynnebald,[1] addressed to all priests, deacons, and princes of the ecclesiastical order. To all those reverend and most beloved in Christ clerics known under the honorable title of priest, and deacons of excellent nature, and abbots, as well as all princes of the secular order: our pious bishop [Willibald] by virtue of his pastoral care appointed you, some as priests in the holy order, others as deacons chosen for sobriety and chasteness, others as monks of the cenobitical army, still others—chosen for their skillful study of texts—into the garb of scholars in order to study, to teach, and thus to inculcate a better standard of government in the realm. Throughout his diocese the bishop used to nourish you diligently with his care, not simply as foster sons, but as his own children.

For all such people who live in this region under the guidance of sacred law, although I am an unworthy Saxon woman,[2] and but a novice—not only in years, but also in experience—among those of that race who have come to this place, and but a weakly woman in comparison to my fellow countrymen, I have nonetheless made up my mind to touch briefly on the early life of that venerable man Willibald for the sake of you religious and orthodox men and you preachers of the heavenly books, compressing [the narrative] into a few

---

1. This volume provides only the *Life of Willibald*. The preface has been retranslated by Thomas Head.

2. Huneberc makes full use of the humility topos we have already met. It is that she is rhetorically adroit, not that she is a woman, that is important here.

words so that they may be easily remembered. I am but womanly, stained by the frailty and weakness of my sex, and supported neither by pretense to wisdom nor by exalted aspiration to great power, but freely prompted by my own willful impetuosity, like some ignorant child who at her heart's discretion plucks a few small things from trees rich in foliage and fruit. Nonetheless I would be pleased to pluck, collect, and display, with however small an art, a few tokens from the lowest branches for you to keep in your memory. But presently I will retrace my speech and say once again that I dare to undertake such a task neither on the prompting of my own presumption nor on some sudden rash insolence.

Inspired first by the grace of God, then by the breadth of the experience of that venerable man Willibald, then by your excellent authority, and not least by your willing help and strong support, I thought myself capable of describing the places where there occurred those celestial wonders, miracles, and signs of virtue which the Lord—when He humiliated Himself for the salvation of humanity and descended to take on a human body—deigned to execute and perform in this world, as he was strengthened by divine power. It is these things we will undertake to narrate, which the reverend man Willibald saw with his own eyes and over which he trod with his own feet. And he saw not only those marvels that have been demonstrated to us to be true by the grace of the four Gospels, but also the very places where our Lord was born, where He suffered, and where, having risen from the dead, He appeared to us. And Willibald also saw the traces of other prodigies the Lord deigned to perform and virtues he deigned to divulge in those lands. Strengthened by faith, fortunate in his fate, a bold traveler, this perfect teacher [Willibald] has transmitted all that he saw and learned while visiting these places to us.

At the present time, if I may say so, it seemed to me surely shameful that a human voice should, in mute tenacity and with sealed lips, keep silent about those things our Lord deemed worthy to reveal, in order to make them known in our times, to his servant Willibald through the exertions of his body and the vision of his eyes. We know these things because they were related to us, not by means of the meandering turnings of apocryphal stories, but because, having encountered Willibald himself, we resolved to hear them as told to us in dictation from his own mouth and so to write them down—with two deacons as witnesses who heard them with me—on Tuesday the twenty-third of June [778?], the day before the summer solstice. Being an unlearned woman, I do not undertake to examine these matters in a literary form because I underestimate the talents of your wisdom or because I do not well know that there are many of you whom our Lord God has deigned to place as bishops above me, who are more outstanding not only in being of the male sex, but also in the divinely bestowed dignity of the priesthood, and who would be able to lay out and explain these matters much better than I because of their knowledge of divine law, not to mention their cleverness at investigation. But, although I am an unworthy woman, I know that I have flowered from the same genealogical root as these men [of whom I shall write], albeit from the lowest stalks of its branches, and therefore I have felt disposed to place in the hands of readers something worthy of remembrance concerning such great and venerable men and concerning the ways in which their lives were blessed, not only in their deeds, but in the various journeys they undertook and the great miracles they performed.

The first of these men was a bishop raised to the highest degree of priestly rank and of pastoral care, that renowned lover of the cross and master of many men, Willibald. And the other was a man who uprightly followed the path of virtue, making the crooked path straight, the uneven and rough places a plain (see Is 40.4), and the wild regions tame. By constant effort he did away with all the thickly sown vices of the worldly and the shameless sins of the idolators, [acting] not with the idle languor of a wavering mind, but happily and boldly with a rash audacity, strengthened from above with a zealous wisdom. Numbered as a prelate because of his priestly honors and pastoral duties, this man was an abbot, that renowned lover of the cross, Wynnebald.

All these writings, which are but black tracks ploughed by a pen in a furrowed path on the white plains of these fields [of parchment], are presented to your knowledgeable and loving care. We commend them to the protection of the grace of God and of your shield against all the calumnies of the envious; we also commend them to your acceptance with pleasure, so that in all matters we may joyfully praise our liberal Lord, the giver of gifts.

1

First of all, I will tell of the early life of the venerable high priest of God, Willibald: how he submitted to the discipline of sacred law, how he followed the examples of the saints, and how he imitated and observed their way of life. Then I will speak of his early manhood, the time of his maturity and of his old age, even till he became decrepit, combining and putting into order the few facts that there are and weaving them into a continuous narrative.

When he was a baby in the cradle, a lovable little creature, he was cher-

ished fondly by those who nursed him, especially by his parents, who lavished their affection on him and brought him up with great solicitude until
he reached the age of three. At that age, when his limbs were still weak and
delicate, he was suddenly attacked by a severe illness: the contraction of his
limbs made it impossible for him to breathe and threatened to end his life.
When his father and mother saw that he was at the doors of death they were
full of fear and grief, and their suspense grew as they saw him, gripped by
the disease, hovering between life and death. It seemed that the child, whom
they had hoped would be their survivor and heir, would soon be carried to an
untimely grave. But God Almighty, Creator of heaven and earth, did not
intend that His servant should be released from the prison of his body and
depart unknown to the rest of the world, for he was destined to preach the
Gospel to the ends of the earth and to bring a multitude of neophytes to the
faith of Christ,

But let us return to the early infancy of the blessed man. When his parents,
in great anxiety of mind, were still uncertain about the fate of their son, they
took him and offered him up before the holy cross of our Lord and Savior. And
this they did, not in a church but at the foot of a cross, such as it is the custom
for nobles and the wealthier men of the Saxon people to have erected on some
prominent spot in their estates, dedicated to our Lord and held in great reverence for the convenience of those who wish to pray daily before it. There
before the cross they laid him. Then they began earnestly to implore God, the
Maker of all things, to bring them consolation and to save their son's life. And
in their prayers they made a solemn promise that in return for the health of
their child they would at once have him tonsured as the first step to holy
orders and would dedicate him to the service of Christ under the discipline of
monastic life.

No sooner had they made these vows than they put their words into deeds.
They enlisted their son in the service of the heavenly King; their favor was
granted by the Lord, and the former health of the child was restored.

2

When this remarkable boy had reached the age of five he began to show the
first signs of spiritual understanding. His parents hastened to carry out the
promises they had made, and as soon as they had taken council with their
noble friends and kinsfolk they lost no time in instructing him in the sacred
obligations of monastic life. Without delay they entrusted him to the care of

Theodred, a man both venerable and trustworthy, and begged him to be responsible for taking the child to the monastery, where he should make suitable arrangements and dispositions on his behalf. So they set out and took him to the monastery which is called Waldheim [Bishops Waltham].[3] There they handed him over to the venerable Abbot Egwald, offering him as a novice, because of his age, to be obedient in all things. In accordance with the rules of monastic life the abbot immediately laid the case before the community and asked them if they would advise and allow this to be done. The response of the monks was immediate, and by their unanimous consent he was accepted and received by them into the community to share in their life.

Afterward this boy of unassuming manners was initiated and perfectly trained in sacred studies. He gave careful and assiduous attention to the learning of the psalms and applied his mind to the examination of the other books of Sacred Scripture. Young though he was in age, he was advanced in wisdom, so that in him through the divine mercy the words of the prophet were fulfilled: "By the mouth of babes and infants, thou hast founded a bulwark" (Ps 8.2). Then, as his age increased and his mental powers developed, and more so as the growth of divine grace kept pace with his increasing strength and stature, he devoted his energies to the pursuit of divine love. Long and earnest meditation filled his days. Night and day he pondered anxiously on the means of monastic perfection and the importance of community life, wondering how he might become a member of that chaste fellowship and share in the joys of their common discipline.

Next he began to inquire how he could put these ideas into effect so that he could despise and renounce the fleeting pleasures of this world and forsake not merely the temporal riches of his earthly inheritance but also his country, parents, and relatives. He began also to devise means of setting out on pilgrimage and traveling to foreign countries that were unknown to him. After some time had elapsed, when he had outgrown the foolish pranks of childhood, the unsteadiness of youth, and the disturbing period of adolescence, through the ineffable dispensation of divine grace he came to manhood. By that time he was greatly beloved by the community because of his obedience and his meekness. All held him in the deepest affection and respect. By assiduous application to his daily duties and continual attention to his studies he disciplined his mind with such vigor and firmness that he made unbroken progress in the way of monastic perfection.

3. In Hampshire.

3

The young servant of Christ, as we have already mentioned, was eager to go on pilgrimage and travel to distant foreign lands and find out all about them. When he had decided to brave the perils of the pathless sea he went immediately to his father and opened his heart to him, telling him the secrets he had concealed from others. He begged him earnestly to advise him on the project and to give his permission; but not content with that, he asked his father to go with him. He invited him to share in this hazardous enterprise and to undertake this difficult mode of life, eager to detach him from the pleasures of the world, from the delights of earth, and from the false prosperity of wealth.[4] He asked him to enter, with the help of God, into the divine service and to enroll in the heavenly army, to abandon his native country and to accompany him as a pilgrim to foreign parts. Using all his powers of persuasion, he coaxed him to join his sons on a visit to the sacred shrine of Saint Peter, prince of the apostles. At first his father declined, excusing himself from the journey on the plea that he could not leave his wife and small children. It would be cruel, and unchristian, he said, to deprive them of his protection and to leave them at the mercy of others. Then the soldier of Christ repeated his solemn exhortations and his long and urgent entreaties, beseeching him, now with fearful threats of damnation, now with bland promises of eternal life, to consent, softening his heart by describing the beauty of paradise and the sweetness of the love of Christ. In this way, employing every means of persuasion and speaking to him heart to heart, he strove to extort from him his agreement to the plan. At last, by the help of Almighty God, his insistence prevailed. His father and his brother Wynnebald gave their promise that they would embark on the enterprise he had in mind and in which he had persuaded them to join.

Following this discussion, a certain time elapsed. At the change of the seasons, toward the end of summer, his father and unmarried brother set out on the journey to which they had agreed. At a suitable time in the summer they were ready and prepared. Taking with them the necessary money for the journey and accompanied by a band of friends, they came to a place that was known by the ancient name of Hamblemouth, near the port of Hamwih.[5]

4. Two interesting points emerge here. First, Willibald's family was wealthy. This made possible his entry into a monastery at so early an age—financial provision would have been made for him. Second, entry into monastic life did not necessarily cut a person off from intercourse with family and associates.

5. On the southern coast of England.

Shortly afterward they embarked on a ship. When the captain of the swift-sailing ship had taken their fares, they sailed, with the west wind blowing and a high sea running, amid the shouting of sailors and the creaking of oars. When they had braved the dangers at sea and the perils of the mountainous waves, a swift course brought them with full sails and following winds safely to dry land. At once they gave thanks and disembarked, and, pitching their tents on the banks of the river Seine, they encamped near the city that is called Rouen, where there is a market.

For some days they rested there and then continued their journey, visiting the shrines of the saints that were on their way and praying there. And so going by degrees from place to place they came to Gorthonicum.[6] Pursuing their journey, they came to Lucca. Hitherto Willibald and Wynnebald had taken their father along with them on their journey. But at Lucca he was struck down almost at once by a severe bodily sickness and after a few days it seemed that his end was near. As the sickness increased, his weary limbs grew cold and stiff, and in this way he breathed his last. As soon as the two brothers saw that their father was dead they wrapped his body in a fine shroud and with filial piety buried it in the Church of Saint Prician [Frigidian] in the city of Lucca, where it still rests. Immediately afterward they set out on their way, going steadily on foot through the vast land of Italy, through the deep valleys, over the craggy mountains, across the level plains, climbing upward toward the peaks of the Apennines. And after they had gazed on the peaks covered with snow and wreathed in banks of cloud, with the help of God and the support of His saints they passed safely through the ambushes of the fierce and arrogant soldiery and came with all their relatives and company to the shrine of Saint Peter, prince of the apostles. There they besought his protection and gave many thanks to God, because they had escaped unscathed from the grievous perils of the sea and the manifold difficulties of travel in a foreign land, and been accounted worthy to climb the Scala Santa[7] and reach the famous Basilica of Saint Peter.

The two brothers remained there from the feast of Saint Martin until Easter of the following year.[8] During that time, while the cold and bare

6. Probably Cortina in northwestern Italy. given that Willibald and company had landed on the coast of what later became Normandy and then camped at Rouen about twenty miles from the sea, Huneberc has left out—or did not know—a great deal in picking up the story in Italy.

7. Steps near the Lateran basilica, not Saint Peter's. According to legend they were the twenty-eight steps down which Jesus descended after his condemnation by Pilate. Helena, mother of the emperor Constantine, is supposed to have brought them to Rome in the early fourth century.

8. From 11 November 721 to 28 March 722.

winter was passing and spring with its flowers was beginning to appear and Eastertide was shedding its sunny radiance over the whole earth, the two brothers had been leading a life of monastic discipline under the prescriptions of sacred law. Then with the passing of the days and the increasing heat of the summer, which is usually a sign of future fever, they were struck down with sickness. They found it difficult to breathe, fever set in, and at one moment they were shivering with cold, the next burning with heat. They had caught the black plague. So great a hold had it got on them that, scarcely able to move, worn out with fever and almost at the point of death, the breath of life had practically left their bodies. But God in His never-failing providence and fatherly love deigned to listen to their prayers and come to their aid, so that each of them rested in turn for one week while they attended to each other's needs. In spite of this, they never failed to observe the normal monastic observance as far as their bodily weakness would allow; they persevered all the more zealously in their study and sacred reading, following the words of Truth, who said: "But he who endures to the end will be saved" (Mt 10.22).

4

After this celebrated bearer of Christ's Cross had continued to pursue the life of perfection with great steadfastness of mind and inward contemplation, he grew eager to follow a stricter mode of life. A more austere and rigorous observance of the monastic way of life, not an easier one, was what he most desired. He longed to go on pilgrimage to a more remote and less well known place than the one in which he was now staying. So, energetic as ever, he sought the advice of his friends and asked permission from his kinsmen to go. He begged them to follow him on his wanderings with their prayers, so that throughout the course of his journey their prayers would keep him from harm and enable him to reach the city of Jerusalem and gaze upon its pleasant and hallowed walls.

So after the solemnities of Easter Sunday were over this restless battler set off on his journey with two companions. On their way they came to a town east of Terracina [Fondi] and stayed there two days. Then, leaving it behind, they reached Gaeta, which stands at the edge of the sea. At this point they went on board a ship and crossed over the sea to Naples, where they left the ship in which they had sailed and stayed for two weeks. These cities belong to the Romans: they are in the territory of Benevento, but owe allegiance to the

Romans.[9] And at once, as is usual when the mercy of God is at work, their fondest hopes were fulfilled, for they chanced upon a ship that had come from Egypt, so they embarked on it and set sail for a town called Reggio in Calabria. At this place they stayed two days; then they departed and betook themselves to the island of Sicily, that is to say, to Catania, where the body of Saint Agatha, the virgin, rests. Mount Etna is there. Whenever the volcanic fire erupts there and begins to spread and threaten the whole region the people of the city take the body of Saint Agatha and place it in front of the oncoming flames and they stop immediately. They stayed there three weeks. Thence they sailed for Syracuse, a city in the same country. Sailing from Syracuse, they crossed the Adriatic and reached the city of Monembasia, in the land of Slavinia, and from there they sailed to Chios, leaving Corinth on the port side. Sailing on from there, they passed Samos and sped on toward Asia, to the city of Ephesus, which stands about a mile from the sea. Then they went on foot to the spot where the Seven Sleepers lie at rest.[10] From there they walked to the tomb of Saint John, the Evangelist, which is situated in a beautiful spot near Ephesus, and thence two miles farther on along the seacoast to a great city called Phygela, where they stayed a day. At this place they begged some bread and went to a fountain in the middle of the city, and, sitting on the edge of it, they dipped their bread in the water and so ate. They pursued their journey on foot along the seashore to the town of Hierapolis, which stands on a high mountain; and thence they went to a place called Patara, where they remained until the bitter and icy winter had passed. Afterward they sailed from there and reached a city called Miletus, which was formerly threatened with destruction from the waters. At this place there were two solitaries living on a "style," that is a column built up and strengthened by a great stone wall of immense height, to protect them from the water.[11] Thence they crossed over by sea to Mount Chelidonium and traversed the whole of it. At this point they suffered very much from hunger, because the country was wild and desolate, and they grew so weak through lack of food that they feared their last day had come. But the Almighty Shepherd of His people deigned to provide food for His poor servants.

Sailing from there, they reached the island of Cyprus, which lies between the Greeks and the Saracens, and went to the city of Pamphos, where they

9. That is, the Byzantines.

10. The Seven Sleepers were famous martyrs who were shut up in a cave and starved to death under Emperor Decius in about 250. After "sleeping" for a while, the reemerged alive.

11. Ever since Saint Simeon Stylites (c. 390–459) had ascended a column in a ruined temple, there had been numerous "pillar saints" in the Christian East.

stayed three weeks. It was then Eastertime, a year after their setting out. Thence they went to Constantia, where the body of Saint Epiphanius rests, and they remained there until after the feast of Saint John the Baptist.[12]

Once more they set sail and reached the town of Antarados, which lies near the sea in the territory of the Saracens. Then they went on foot for about nine or twelve miles to a fort called Arche, where they had a Greek bishop. There they sang a litany according to the Greek rite. Leaving this place, they set out on foot for the town named Emesa, about twelve miles distant, where there is a large church built by Saint Helena in honor of Saint John the Baptist and where his head was for a long time preserved. This is in Syria now.

At that time there were seven companions with Willibald and he made the eighth. Almost at once they were arrested by the pagan Saracens,[13] and because they were strangers and came without credentials they were taken prisoner and held as captives. They knew not to which nation they belonged, and, thinking they were spies, they took them bound to a certain rich old man to find out where they came from. The old man put questions to them asking where they were from and on what errand they were employed. Then they told him everything from the beginning and acquainted him with the reason for their journey. And the old man said: "I have often seen men coming from those parts of the world, fellow countrymen of theirs; they cause no mischief and are merely anxious to fulfill their law." Then they left him and went to the court, to ask permission to pass over to Jerusalem. But when they arrived there, the governor said at once that they were spies and ordered them to be thrust into prison until such time as he should hear from the king what was to be done with them. While they were in prison they had an unexpected experience of the wonderful dispensation of Almighty God, who mercifully deigns to protect his servants everywhere, amid weapons of war and tortures, barbarians, and soldiers, prisons and bands of aggressors, preserving and shielding them from all harm. A man was there, a merchant, who wished to redeem them and release them from captivity, so that they should be free to continue their journey as they wished. He did this by way of alms and for the salvation of his own soul. But he was unable to release them. Every day, therefore, he sent them dinner and supper, and on Wednesday and Saturday he sent his son to the prison and took them out for a bath and then took them back again. Every Sunday he took them to church through the marketplace, so that if they

12. 24 June 724.
13. That is, by Muslims who were not pagans despite routinely being so characterized by western Christian writers.

saw anything on sale for which they had a mind he could buy it for them and so give them pleasure. The citizens of the town, who are inquisitive people, used to come regularly to look at them, because they were young and handsome and clothed in beautiful garments. Then while they were still languishing in prison a man from Spain came and spoke with them inside the prison itself and made careful inquiries about their nationality and homeland. And they told him everything about their journey from first to last. This Spaniard had a brother at the king's court, who was the chamberlain of the king of the Saracens. And when the governor who had sent them to prison came to court, both the Spaniard who had spoken to them in prison and the captain of the ship in which they had sailed from Cyprus came together in the presence of the Saracens' king, whose name was Murmumnus (Emir-al-Mummenin). And when the conversation turned on their case, the Spaniard told his brother all that he had learned about them while speaking to them in the prison, and he asked his brother to pass this information on to the king and to help them. So when, afterward, all these three came to the king and mentioned their case, telling him all the details from first to last, the king asked whence they came; and they answered: "These men come from the West where the sun sets; we know nothing of their country except that beyond it lies nothing but water." Then the king asked them, saying: "Why should we punish them? They have done us no harm. Allow them to depart and go on their way." The other prisoners who were in captivity had to pay a fine of three measures of corn, but they were let off scot-free.

With this permission they at once set out and traveled a hundred miles to Damascus, in Syria, where the body of Saint Ananias rests. They stayed there a week. About two miles distant stands a church on the spot where Saint Paul was first converted and where our Lord said to him: "Saul, Saul, why do you persecute me?" (Acts 22.7). After praying in the church, they went on foot to Galilee, to the place where Gabriel first came to our Lady and said: "Hail Mary" (Lk 1.28). There is a church there now, and the village where the church is is called Nazareth. The Christians have often had to come to terms with the pagan Saracens about this church, because they wished to destroy it. After commending themselves to the Lord there, they set out on foot and came to the town of Chanaan (Cana), where our Lord changed water into wine. A vast church stands there, and in the church one of the altars has on it one of the six waterpots that our Lord ordered to be filled with water and then changed into wine; from it they drank some wine. They stayed for one day there. Departing thence, they reached Mount Thabor, where our Lord was transfigured. At the moment there is a monastery of monks there, and the church is dedicated to our Lord, Moses and Elias, and the place is called by those who live there Holy Mount. There they prayed.

Then they made for the town called Tiberias. It stands at the edge of the sea on which our Lord walked dry-shod and where Peter sank when walking on the waters toward Him. Many churches and synagogues of the Jews are built there, and great honor is paid to our Lord. They remained there for several days. At that point the Jordan flows into the lake. Thence they set off round the lake and went to the village of Magdalene and came to the village of Capharnaum, where our Lord raised to life the ruler's daughter. Here there was a house and a great wall, and the people said that Zebedee used to live there with his sons John and James. Then they went to Bethsaida, the native place of Peter and Andrew. A church now occupies the site where their home once stood. They passed the night there, and on the following morning set off for Corazain, where our Lord cured the man possessed of the devil and drove the demons into a herd of swine. A church stands there now.

After praying there, they departed and came to the spot where two fountains, Jor and Dan, spring from the earth and then pour down the mountainside to form the river Jordan. There, between the two fountains, they passed the night and the shepherds gave us[14] sour milk to drink. At this spot there are wonderful herds of cattle, long in the back and short in the leg, bearing enormous horns; they are all of one color, dark red. Deep marshes lie there, and in the summertime, when the great heat of the sun scorches the earth, the herds betake themselves to the marshes and, plunging themselves up to their necks in the water, leave only their heads showing.

Departing thence, they came to Caesarea, where there was a church and a great number of Christians. They rested there for a short time and set out for the monastery of Saint John the Baptist, where about twenty monks were living. They stayed the night and then went forward about a mile to the Jordan, where our Lord was baptized. At this spot there is now a church built high up on columns of stone; beneath the church, however, the ground is dry. On the very place where Christ was baptized and where they now baptize there stands a little wooden cross: a little stream of water is led off and a rope is stretched over the Jordan and tied at each end. Then on the feast of the Epiphany the sick and infirm come there and, holding onto the rope, plunge themselves in the water. Barren women also come there. Our Bishop Willibald bathed himself there in the Jordan. They passed the day there and then departed.

---

14. The "us" implies that Huneberc is reporting Willibald's own words, not that she herself was present.

Thence they came to Galgala, which is about five miles away. In the church there, which is small and made of wood, there are twelve stones. These are the twelve stones that the children of Israel took from the Jordan and carried more than five miles to Galgala and set up as witnesses of their passage. After saying prayers there, they went on toward Jericho, which is more than seven miles distant from the Jordan. The fountain that bubbled up there on the brow of the hill was barren and quite useless to man before the prophet Eliseus came and blessed it and made it flow. Afterward the people of the city drew it off into their fields and gardens and other places that needed it, and now wherever this fountain flows, the crops increase and promote health, all by reason of the blessing given by Eliseus the prophet. They went on from there to the monastery of Saint Eustochium, which stands in the middle of the plain between Jericho and Jerusalem.

Then they came to Jerusalem, to the very spot where the holy cross of our Lord was found. On the site of the place called Calvary now stands a church. Formerly this was outside Jerusalem, but when Helena discovered the cross she placed the spot within the walls of Jerusalem. There now stand three crosses outside the church near the wall of the eastern end, as a memorial to the cross of our Lord and those who were crucified with Him. At present they are not inside the church, but outside beneath a pent roof. Nearby is the garden in which the tomb of our Savior was placed. This tomb was cut from the rock and the rock stands above ground: it is squared at the bottom and tapers toward a point at the top. On the highest point of it stands a cross, and a wonderful house has been constructed over it. At the eastern end a door has been cut in the rock of the sepulcher, through which people can enter into the tomb to pray. Inside there is the slab on which the body of our Lord lay, and on this slab fifteen lamps of gold burn day and night; it is situated on the north side of the interior of the tomb and lies at one's right hand as one enters the tomb to pray. In front of the door of the sepulcher lies a great square stone, a replica of that first stone that the angel rolled away from the mouth of the sepulcher.

On the feast of Saint Martin[15] our bishop came there, and as soon as he reached the spot he began to feel sick and was confined to his bed until a week before Christmas. Then when he recovered and began to feel a little better he got up and went to the church called Holy Sion, which stands in the center of Jerusalem. He prayed there and then went to Solomon's Porch, where there is a pool at which the sick used to lie waiting for the angel to move the waters,

15. 11 November 724.

after which the first who went down into them was cured: this is where our Lord said to the paralytic: "Rise, take up your pallet, and walk" (Jn 5.8).

Willibald himself said that in front of the gate of the city stood a tall pillar, on top of which rose a cross, as a sign and memorial of the place where the Jews attempted to take away the body of our Lady. For when the eleven Apostles were bearing the body of holy Mary away from Jerusalem the Jews tried to snatch it away as soon as they reached the gate of the city. But as soon as they stretched out their hands toward the bier and endeavored to take her their arms became fixed, stuck as it were to the bier, and they were unable to move until, by the grace of God and the prayers of the apostles, they were released, and then they let them go. Our Lady passed from this world in that very spot in the center of Jerusalem that is called Holy Sion. And then the eleven apostles bore her, as I have already said, and finally the angels came and took her away from the hands of the apostles and carried her to paradise.

Bishop Willibald came down from the mount and went to the valley of Josaphat: it is situated to the east of the city of Jerusalem. In the valley there is a church of Our Lady and in the church is her tomb (not that her body lies at rest there, but as a memorial to her). After praying there, he climbed Mount Olivet, which is near to the valley at its eastern end—the valley lies between Jerusalem amd Mount Olivet. On Mount Olivet there is now a church on the spot where our Lord prayed before His passion and said to his disciples: "Watch and pray that you may not enter into temptation" (Mt 26.41). Then he came to the very hill whence our Lord ascended into heaven. In the center of the church is a beautiful candlestick sculptured in bronze: it is square and stands in the middle of the church where our Lord ascended into heaven. In the middle of the bronze candlestick is a square vessel of glass, and in the glass is a small lamp, and round about the lamp, closed on all sides, is the glass. The reason why it is closed on all sides is that the lamp may burn both in good weather and bad. The church has no roof and is open to the sky, and two pillars stand there inside the church, one against the northern wall, the other against the southern wall. They are placed there in remembrance of the two men who said: "Men of Galilee why do you stand looking into heaven?" (Acts 1.11). Any man who can squeeze his body between the pillars and the wall is freed from his sins.

Then he came to the place where the angel appeared to the shepherds and said: "I bring you news of a great joy" (Lk 2.10). Thence he came to Bethlehem, where our Lord was born, about six miles distant from Jerusalem. The place where our Lord was born was formerly a cave underneath the ground and is now a square chamber cut out of the rock; the earth has been dug away on

all sides and thrown aside, and now the church has been built above it. There
our Lord was born. An altar has been raised above it also, but another small
altar has been made, so that when they wish to celebrate Mass within the cave
they can take up the small altar while Mass is being said and afterward can take
it out again. The church that stands over the spot where our Lord was born is
built in the form of a cross, a house of great beauty.

After praying there, they departed and came to a large town called Thecua:
this is the place where the Holy Innocents were slaughtered by Herod. A
church stands there now. In it rests the body of one of the prophets. Then they
came to the Laura[16] in the valley: it is a great monastery and there resides the
abbot and the doorkeeper who keeps the keys of the church. Many are the
monks who belong to that monastery, and they dwell scattered round the
valley on the summits of the hills where they have little cells cut out for them
from the stony rock of the hills. The mountain surrounds the valley in which
the monastery is built: there lies the body of Saint Saba.

Thence they came to the spot where Philip baptized the eunuch. A small
church stands there in the wide valley between Bethlehem and Gaza. From
there they made toward Gaza, where there is a holy place, and after praying
there they went to Saint Mathias, where there is a large temple of the Lord.
And while Solemn High Mass was being celebrated there, our Bishop Willibald, standing and listening, lost his sight and was blind for two months.
Thence they went to Saint Zacharias, the prophet, not the father of Saint John
the Baptist, but the other prophet. Thence they went to the town of Hebron,
where lie the bodies of the three patriarchs Abraham, Isaac, and Jacob with
their wives.

Then he returned to Jerusalem, and, going into the church where the holy
cross of Christ was found, his eyes were opened and he received his sight. He
stayed there for a little while and then set out for a place called Lydda, to the
Church of Saint George, which lies about ten miles distant from Jerusalem.
Thence he came to another village [Joppa], where stands a church to Saint
Peter the Apostle: this was where Saint Peter raised up the widow Dorcas to
life. He prayed there and set out once more and came to the Adriatic Sea at a
great distance from Jerusalem, to the cities of Tyre and Sidon. These two cities
are six miles apart and stand on the edge of the sea. Thence he went to Tripoli
on the seashore, and crossed over Mount Libanus to Damascus. From there he

---

16. A Laura (or Lavra) was a characteristic type of monastery in the eastern Christian world in
which monks, though residing within a single enclosure, lived in individual cells and had very
little to do with one another.

went to Caesarea and back once more, for the third time, to Jerusalem, where he spent the whole winter.

He then traveled more than three hundred miles to the town of Emesa in Syria, and thence he came to Salamias, which is on the farther borders of Syria. He spent the whole season of Lent there because he was ill and unable to travel. His compaions, who were in his party, went forward to the king of the Saracens, named Murmumnus, to ask him to give them a letter of safe conduct, but they could not meet him because he himself had withdrawn from that region on account of the sickness and pestilence that infested the country. And when they could not find the king they returned and stayed together in Salamias until a week before Easter. Then they came again to Emesa and asked the governor there to give them a letter of safe conduct, and he gave them a letter for every two persons. They could not travel there in company but only two by two, because in this way it was easier for them to provide food for themselves. Then they came to Damascus.

From Damascus they came for the fourth time to Jerusalem, and after spending some time there they went to the town of Sebaste, which was formerly called Samaria; but after it was destroyed they built another town there and called it Sebaste. At the present time the bodies of Saint John the Baptist, Abdias, and Eliseus the prophet rest there. Near the town is the well where our Lord asked the Samaritan woman to give Him water to drink. Over that well there now stands a church, and there is the mount on which the Samaritans worshiped and of which the woman said to our Lord: "Our fathers worshiped on this mountain; and you say that in Jerusalem is the place where men ought to worship" (Jn 4.10). Then, after praying there, they passed through the country of the Samaritans to a large town on the far borders of their land and spent one night there.

Then they traveled across a wide plain covered with olive trees, and with them traveled an Ethiopian and his two camels, who led a woman on a mule through the woods. And as they went on their way, a lion with gaping jaws came out upon them, growling and roaring, ready to seize and devour them; it terrified them greatly. But the Ethiopian said: "Have no fear—let us go forward." So without hesitation they proceeded on their way and as they approached the lion it turned aside and, through the help of Almighty God, left the way open for them to continue their journey. And they said that a short time after they had left that place they heard the same lion roaring, as if in his fury he would devour many of the men who went there to gather olives. When they came to the town that is called Ptolomaeis, which stands by the edge of the sea, they continued their journey and reached the summit of Libanus, where that mountain juts out into the sea and forms a promontory.

There stands the tower of Libanus. Anyone who lands there without having a safe conduct cannot pass through the place because it is guarded and closed; and if anyone comes without a pass the citizens arrest him immediately and send him back to Tyre. The mount is between Tyre and Ptolomaeis. Then the bishop came to Tyre for the second time.

When Bishop Willibald was in Jerusalem on the previous occasion he bought himself some balsam and filled a calabash[17] with it; then he took a hollow reed that had a bottom to it and filled it with mineral oil and put it inside the calabash. Afterward he cut the reed equal in length to the calabash so that the surfaces of both were even and then closed the mouth of the calabash. When they reached the city of Tyre the citizens arrested them, put them in chains, and examined all their baggage to find out if they had hidden any contraband. If they had found anything they would certainly have punished them and put them to death. But when they had thoroughly scrutinized everything and could find nothing but one calabash that Willibald had, they opened it and sniffed at it to find out what was inside. And when they smelt mineral oil, which was inside the reed at the top, they did not find the balsam that was inside the calabash underneath the mineral oil, and so let them go.

They were there for a long time waiting for a ship to get ready. Afterward they sailed during the whole of the winter, from the feast of Saint Andrew[18] until a week before Easter. Then they landed at the city of Constantinople, where the bodies of three saints, Andrew, Timothy, and Luke the Evangelist, lie beneath one altar, while the body of Saint John Chrysostom lies before another. His tomb is there where, as a priest, he stood to celebrate Mass. Our bishop stayed there for two years and had an alcove in the church so that every day he could sit and gaze upon the place where the saints lay at rest. Thence he went to Nicaea, where formerly the Emperor Constantine held a council at which three hundred and eighteen bishops were present, all taking an active part. The church there resembles the one at Mount Olivet, where our Lord ascended into heaven; and in the church are all the portraits of the bishops who took part in the council. Willibald went there from Constantinople to see how the church was built, and then returned by water to Constantinople.

After two years they set sail from there with the envoys of the pope and the emperor[19] and went to the city of Syracuse in the island of Sicily. Thence they

17. A dried gourd used as a container.
18. 30 November 727.
19. Pope Gregory II and Emperor Leo III were in the midst of a heated controversy occasioned by the latter's prohibition of sacred images—the beginning of the so-called Iconoclastic Controversy that agitated the Byzantine world and poisoned Byzantine-Western relations from 726 to 787.

came to Catania and then to Reggio, a city of Calabria. They embarked again for Volcano, where the inferno of Theodoric is.[20] When they arrived there they disembarked to see what this inferno was like. Willibald, who was inquisitive and eager to see without delay what this inferno was like inside, wanted to climb to the top of the mountain underneath which the crater lay: but he was unable to do so because the ashes of black tartar that had risen to the edge of the crater, lay there in heaps: and like the snow that, when it drops from heaven with its falling masses of flakes, heaps them up into mounds, the ashes lay piled in heaps on the top of the mountain and prevented Willibald from going any farther. All the same, he saw the black and terrible and fearful belching forth from the crater with a noise like rolling thunder: he gazed with awe on the enormous flames, and the mountainous clouds of smoke rising from below into the sky. And that pumice stone that writers speak of he saw issuing from the crater, thrown out with flames and cast into the sea, then washed up again on the seashore by the tide, where men were collecting it and carting it away. After they had satisfied their curiosity with the sight of the fearsome and terrible burning fire, its fumes, its stinking smoke, and its shooting flames, they weighed anchor and sailed to the church of Saint Bartholomew the Apostle [at Lipari], which stands on the seashore, and they came to the mountains that are called Didyme, and after praying there they spent one night. Embarking once more, they came to a city called Naples and remained there several days. It is the seat of an archbishop whose dignity is great there. Not far away is the small town of Lucullanum, where the body of Saint Severinus is preserved. Then he came to the city of Capua, and the archbishop there sent him to the bishop of another town; that bishop sent him to the bishop of Teano, and he in turn sent him to the monastery of Saint Benedict (Monte Cassino). It was autumn when he reached Monte Cassino, and it was seven years since he first began his journey from Rome and ten years in all since he had left his native country.

5

And when the venerable man Willibald and Tidbercht, who had traveled everywhere with him, came to the monastery of Saint Benedict they found only a few monks there under Abbot Petronax. Without delay he joined the commu-

---

20. A small volcanic island off the coast of Sicily. In legend the Ostrogothic king Theodoric (r. 493–526) was cast into hell here for having killed Pope John V.

nity, for which he was so well fitted both by his great self-discipline and his natural aptitude for obedience. He learned much from their careful teaching, but he in turn taught them more by his outward bearing; he showed them not so much by words as by the beauty of his character what was the real spirit of their institute; and by proving himself to be a model of monastic virtue he compelled the admiration, love, and respect of all.

In the first year that he spent there he was sacristan of the church, in the second a dean of the monastery, and for eight years afterward he was porter in two monasteries, four years as porter in the monastery that is perched on a very high hill, and four years more in the other monastery, which stands lower down near the river Rapido, about two miles away. So for ten years[21] the venerable man Willibald tried to observe, as far as possible, every detail of the monastic observance as laid down by the Rule of Saint Benedict. And he not only observed it himself but led the others, whom he had brought over long distances by foot and by sea, to follow him in the traditional path of monastic life.

After this, a priest who came from Spain to the monastery of Saint Benedict and stayed there asked permission of Abbot Petronax to go to Rome. When the permission was asked, Petronax without heistation begged Willibald to accompany him and take him to the shrine of Saint Peter. He gave his consent at once and promised to fulfill the mission. So they set out, and when they came to Rome and entered the Basilica of Saint Peter they asked the protection of the heavenly keeper of the keys and commended themselves to his kindly patronage. Then the sacred pontiff of the Apostolic See, Gregory III, hearing that the venerable man Willibald was there, sent for him to come into his presence. And when he came to the supreme pontiff he fell down at once on his face to the ground and greeted him. And immediately that pious shepherd of the people began to question Willibald about the details of his journey and asked him earnestly how he spent seven years traveling to the ends of the earth and how he had contrived to escape for so long a time the wickedness of the pagans.

Then the servant of Christ humbly recounted to the glorious governor of the tribes all the details of his travels as they occurred. He told him how he had passed from place to place, how he had visited Bethlehem and prayed in the birthplace of his heavenly Creator, how he had seen where Christ was baptized in the river Jordan and had himself bathed there. He described his four visits to Jerusalem and Holy Sion, where Our Holy Savior had hung on the cross, was killed and buried and then ascended into heaven from Mount Olivet. All these things he told him and described.

21. 730–740.

After they had discussed these matters during a pleasant and intimate conversation, the sacred and holy pontiff intimated to Willibald in a serious and unmistakable tone that Saint Boniface had asked him to arrange for Willibald to leave the monastery of Saint Benedict and come to him without delay to the Frankish people. And after the apostolic lord, Pope Gregory III, had made known to him the desires of Saint Boniface, he tried to persuade him, now with peaceable words of exhortation, now pleading, now commanding, to go to Saint Boniface. Then the illustrious athlete of God, Willibald, promised that he would carry into immediate effect the request and command of the pontiff provided he could ask permission, according to the prescriptions of the Rule, from his abbot. The supreme pontiff, in whom is vested the highest authority, at once replied that his command was sufficient permission, and he ordered him to set out obediently without any qualm of conscience, saying: "If I am free to transfer the abbot Petronax himself to any other place, then certainly he has no permission or power to oppose my wishes." And so Willibald replied on the spot that he would willingly carry out his wishes and commands, not only there but anywhere in the world, wherever he had a mind to send him. He then pledged himself to go in accordance with his wishes without any further delay. After this, the discussion being ended, Willibald departed at Eastertime, reaching his journey's end on the feast of Saint Andrew. Tidbercht, however, remained behind at the monastery of Saint Benedict.

He went to Lucca, where his father was buried, and thence to the city of Pavia, from there to Brescia and thence to a place that is called Garda. Then Willibald came to Duke Odilo and stayed a week with him, and thence to Suitgar, with whom he also stayed a week. Suitgar and Willibald left there for Linthard, where Saint Boniface was, and Saint Boniface sent them to Eischstätt to see how they liked the place. Suitgar handed over the territory there to Saint Boniface for the redemption of his soul, and Saint Boniface passed it on to our bishop Willibald. At that time it was all wasteland—there was not a single house there and the only building was the church of Saint Mary, which still stands, smaller than the other church that Willibald afterward built on the site.

When Willibald and Suitgar had remained together at Eichstätt for some little time, they explored and surveyed the ground and eventually chose a site suitable for a house. After that they went to Saint Boniface at Freising and stayed with him until all of them returned once more to Eichstätt. There Saint Boniface ordained Willibald to the priestly dignity.[22] The day on which Willi-

22. In 740.

bald was ordained was 22 July, the feast of Saint Apollinaris and Saint Mary Magdalen.

After a whole year had passed, Saint Boniface commanded him to come to him at once in Thuringia. And the venerable man of God, Willibald, set off at once for Thuringia and dwelt as a guest in the house of his brother Saint Wynnebald, who had not seen him for the past eight and a half years since he had parted from him in Rome. And they were glad to see each other and congratulated each other on their meeting. It was then the season of autumn when Willibald came to Thuringia.

Soon after he came there, the archbishop Saint Boniface, Burchard, and Wizo consecrated him and vested him with the sacred authority of the episcopate. [23] He remained there for a week after he was consecrated bishop and then returned once more to the place that had been allotted him. At the time of his consecration Willibald was forty-one years old; he was consecrated at Salzburg in the autumn, about three weeks before the feast of Saint Martin.

6

The long course of Willibald's travels and sightseeing on which he had spent seven long years was now over and gone. We have tried to set down and make known all the facts that have been ascertained and thoroughly investigated. These facts were not learned from anyone else but heard from Willibald himself; and having received them from his own lips, we have taken them down and written them in the monastery of Heidenheim, as his deacons and other subordinates can testify. I say this so that no one may afterward say that it was an idle tale.

At the time that he came to the province from Rome with three of his fellow countrymen he was forty-one years old, already mature and middle-aged; then he was consecrated bishop. Afterward he began to build a monastery in the place called Eichstätt, and shortly afterward practiced the monastic life there according to the observance he had seen at the monastery of Saint Benedict (at Monte Cassino), and not merely there, but also in many other monastic houses that he had examined with his experienced eye as he traveled through various lands. This observance he taught to others by the example of his own life. With a few fellow laborers he tilled the wide and spacious fields for the divine seed, sowing and cultivating them until harvest-time. And so

23. In 741 he became the first bishop of Eichstätt.

like a busy bee that flits through the meadows, purple with violets, aromatic with scented herbs and through the tree branches yellow with blossom, drinking the sweet nectar but avoiding bitter poison, and returns to the hive bearing honey on its thighs and body, so the blessed man chose out the best from all that he had seen abroad with his own eyes, adopted it, and, having adopted it, submitted it to his disciples for acceptance, showing them good example by word and deed, in zeal for observance, avoidance of evil, piety, forbearance, and temperance.

Soon after the energetic champion of our good God had begun to dwell in the monastery men flocked to him from all sides, not only from the neighboring provinces but even from distant countries, to hear his salutary teaching and wisdom. Willibald and Mother Church, like a hen that cherishes her offspring beneath her wings, won over many adoptive sons to the Lord, protecting them continually with the shield of his kindliness. These he trained with gentleness and sympathy, detaching them from their imperfections until they reached perfect maturity. These, having followed in the steps of their master and absorbed his teaching, have now become famous for the training they give to others.

This, then, was Willibald, who at first began to practice a holy life with the support of but a few helpers, but who at last, after struggling in many ways against the opposition of numerous chieftains and courtiers, gained possession of a people worthy of the Lord. Far and wide through the vast province of Bavaria he drove his plow, sowing the seed and reaping the harvest with the help of many fellow laborers. And all though the land of Bavaria, now dotted about with churches, priests' houses, and the relics of the saints, he amassed treasures worthy of our Lord. From these places antiphons now resound, sacred lessons are chanted, a noble throng of believers shout aloud the miracles of Christ, and with joyful hearts echo from mouth to mouth triumphant praises of their Creator.

What shall I now say of Willibald, my master and your devoted brother? Who was more outstanding than he in piety, more perfect in humility? Who more forbearing in patience, more strict in temperance, greater in meekness? When was he ever backward in consoling the downcast? Who was more eager to assist the poor or more anxious to clothe the naked? These things are said not for the sake of boasting but for the sake of recounting what I have seen and heard, things done not by the power of man but by the grace of God, in order that, according to the words of the apostle: "Let him who boasts, boast of the Lord" (1 Cor 1.31). Amen.

Eigil

THE LIFE OF SAINT STURM

Translated by C. H. Talbot

With Eigil (c. 750–822) we return to the circle of Boniface. But in this life, written about 794, we can discern some of the sharp tensions that had arisen among the followers of the great missionary.

About Eigil not too much is known. He was a Bavarian aristocrat from the area of Noricum. He entered the monastery of Fulda as a child and was educated there by his kinsman Sturm, who had been entrusted by Boniface with the foundation of the house in 744. He spent twenty years under Sturm and must have come to know him well. As the present text shows only too clearly, however, Eigil also acquired considerable familiarity with the struggles that surrounded Fulda, the politics of its abbots, the monastery's properties, and technical questions of ecclesiastical jurisdiction. The present *Life*, therefore, opens up another use to which hagiography was put: deploying the memory of a saint as a weapon in contemporary battles.

Here we have a dedicatory letter to the virgin Angildruth—otherwise unknown—and the *Life of Sturm*. Eigil's epitaph also survives, but otherwise we have no words from his pen. His own life was written, in both prose and verse forms, in the mid-ninth century by Candidus, a monk of Fulda. That text, then, supplies few details that are of any help in understanding Eigil as a writer. His Latin is adequate but lacks the polish of that of later writers who were much more heavily influenced by the cultural efflorescence that scholars call the "Carolingian Renaissance." One critic says that Eigil's performance in the *Life of Sturm* is "above average." The reader will see that the text adheres faithfully to the conventions of hagiography.

Sturm, Eigil's subject, lived from 715 to 779. From 744 he was abbot of Fulda, although he was away from his monastery several times, notably during his exile to Jumièges from 763 to 765. Sturm, as will be seen, was neither a wonder-worker nor a missionary nor a scholar. He was, however, deeply involved in the ecclesiastical politics of his day.

Texts and References

No improvements have been made on the Latin text of G. H. Pertz, *Vita Sturmi*, Monumenta Germaniae Historica, Scriptores, 2:365–77. Very little has been written on Eigil. For a start, see Ralph Whitney Mathisen, "Eigil," *Dictionary of the Middle Ages* (New York, 1982), 4:408; Franz Brunhölzl, *Geschichte der lateinischen Literatur des Mittelalters*, 2 vols. (Munich, 1975) 1:324–25.

The reader will note two chapters enumerated 15. For some reason the MGH editor labeled two consecutive chapters "15." Instead of turning the second of these into a 16 and carrying on from there, we elected to mark them 15a and 15b so that all of the rest of the chapters could retain their original numbering.

Prologue

1

I have always known, O Angildruth, that you were fired with divine love and filled with a desire for better things. And for this reason I comply with your request. For you ask me to recount the life of the holy and venerable Abbot Sturm and to put into writing the early beginnings of the monastery of the Holy Savior that he founded and that is known by the name of Fulda. You also ask me to describe the events connected with the monastery as I have heard or seen them. As far as my capabilities allow, I have carried out your request and I have compressed into this little book both the early days and life of Sturm as reliable witnesses have recounted them to me, and the foundation of the aforesaid monastery. I have also added some details about the changes effected in the course of time, such as I have heard from others or seen with my own two eyes. For I, Eigil, was his disciple for more than twenty years,[1] and I was brought up and trained in the observance of his monastery from childhood. Some of the events, therefore, that I describe can be vouched for from my own experience.

So here you have what you asked for, a slip of parchment inscribed with your name to be kept or laid aside as you choose. It rests with you to answer for me to the criticisms of my enemies: defend me as one moved more by goodwill than presumption, and sustain me by your holy prayers with Christ as your true Spouse.

2

At the time the venerable Archbishop Boniface set foot in Noricum,[2] imparting the faith to the priests and people of the church, suppressing there the errors of the heretics and curbing with the true doctrine of Chirst those people who, although already Christians, were infected with the evil teaching of the pagans, certain nobles came to him vying with each other to offer their sons to be brought up in the service of God. Among those whom he accepted at the instance of his parents was Sturm, a native of Noricum and a member of a noble Christian family. Leaving behind all his relatives and following the Father of our redemption, he set out joyfully on a journey with the bishop who had accepted him, much to the grief of his father and mother. After they had traversed several provinces they reached Fritzlar in the land of the Hessians, where the bishop entrusted him to the care of a certain priest named Wigbert. This holy priest took great pains to instruct the boy Sturm in the service of God.

After he had learned the psalms by heart[3] and mastered many books by repeatedly going over them in his mind, the boy began to understand the spiritual meaning of the Scriptures and set himself to learn the hidden secrets

1. Sturm lived c. 715–779. Eigil says he was a disciple of Sturm for more than twenty years so he must have entered Fulda as a young boy before 759.

2. C. 734.

3. The Psalter formed the basis of the divine office—seven daily rounds of prayer—celebrated by members of monastic communities. The point of this remark is to show that Sturm was equipped to be a monk, not that he was intellectually precocious.

of the four Gospels of Christ, and, as far as he was able, to fix in his mind by continual reading the Old and New Testaments. His meditation was upon the law of God, as Scripture says, night and day. His understanding was profound, his thoughts full of wisdom, his words of prudence. Pleasant in countenance, modest in bearing, good-mannered, irreproachable in his conduct, charitable, humble, mild, ready to perform any service, he drew to himself everyone's affection.

3

After a certain length of time he was, with common consent, ordained priest,[4] and as opportunity presented itself he began to explain to the people the hidden words of Christ. Through the power of the Holy Spirit many miracles were wrought by him. Many times he drove out evil spirits by his prayers from sinful Christians. Many times he cured souls that had been infected with the poisonous doctrines of error. Those who were at enmity with one another were ordered by him to become reconciled before the setting of the sun; and to all he taught patience, mildness, humility, longanimity, faith, hope, and charity.

4

When he had spent almost three years of his priesthood preaching and baptizing he was divinely inspired to undertake the rigorous life of a hermit. This idea haunted him at every moment of the day, until on a divine impulse he opened his heart to his spiritual master, the archbishop Boniface. On learning of his intention, the holy man quickly saw that the Lord had deigned to move him by His grace, and, seeing that the inspiration came from God, he encouraged him and became the chief supporter in his design. He therefore gave him two companions, carefully instructed them and, after praying and giving them his blessing, said: "Go to the solitude that is called Bochonia and see if the place is fit for servants of God to dwell in, for even in the desert God is able to prepare a place for His followers."

So the three of them set out to find a place for a hermitage; and when they reached a wild and uninhabited spot and could see nothing except earth and sky

---

4. Sturm's ordination in about 740 may have been deemed worthy of mention because it was not common for monks to be priests in the eighth century, although this did become common in the ninth and later centuries.

and enormous trees they devoutly prayed to God to guide their footsteps in the way of peace. After three days they came to a place that is nowadays called Hersfeld,[5] and when they had explored all the district round about they asked Christ to bless it and make it fit for them to dwell in. This is the spot on which the monastery now stands. There they made small huts roofed over with the bark of trees, and there they stayed for a long time serving God in fasts, watching, and prayer.

5

Some time later, when Sturm had settled down to the eremitical life, he left the solitude and went to the holy archbishop Boniface, to whom he described in detail the situation, the quality of the soil, the running water, the foundations and valleys, and everything else connected with his foundation. Boniface listened intently to all he had to say, and after turning it over in his mind ordered him to remain at his side for a time. They discussed together, among other things, the abundant consolation to be found in Holy Scripture, and then the archbishop said: "You have indeed found a place to live in, but I am afraid to leave you there on account of the savage people who are close by, for, as you are aware, there are Saxons not far from that place and they are a ferocious race. Look for a spot farther away, deeper in the woods, where you can serve God without danger to yourselves."

Thereupon blessed Sturm meekly accepted the suggestion of the archbishop and, being anxious to discover another site, set out eagerly for the hermitage. When he reached his companions he found them in their huts anxiously awaiting his return. As soon as he saw them he gave them greetings from the archbishop and brought them comfort by telling them all about his journey, about the archbishop, and described in detail all that the archbishop had said to him. Then he took the two brothers with him and set off upstream in a boat. As they glided along the river Fulda they kept a sharp lookout for streams and fountains. They then disembarked and traversed the country on all sides, looking at the soil, the mountains, the hills, the heights, and the valleys to see if the Lord would show them a place in the wilderness fit for them to live in.

At last, on the third day, they came to a spot where the river Luodera flows into the Fulda. But finding nothing that suited their purpose, they turned downstream from there and began to row back to their own hermitage, stop-

5. About fifty miles south of Fritzlar. Later the site of an important monastery.

ping for a short time on the way at a place called Ruohenbach, where it seemed possible that servants of God might be able to live. On the whole they thought that the archbishop might not approve of it. Then, sailing back along the same river, after a short time they arrived at their own poor huts. There they continued to pray to God to find them a suitable site for a hermitage where they might be able to serve Him in accordance with the requirements of the archbishop Boniface. Day and night they persevered in fasting, watching and prayer, always keeping the memory of God before their eyes and saying in their hearts: "I keep the Lord always before me; because he is at my right hand, I shall not be moved" (Ps 16.8). The praise of God was also ever on their lips and in their hearts, and they fulfilled the saying of the psalmist: "I will bless God at all times, his praise shall continually be in my mouth" (Ps 24.1).

6

Then the holy bishop Boniface, mindful of his hermit Sturm and pleased at what he had done to find another site, sent for him and asked him to come quickly to his presence. The messenger lost no time in coming and found him dwelling in the above-mentioned huts and greeted him, saying: "Our revered bishop has great desire to see you. You should come because he has many matters to discuss." At these words the holy man Sturm gave this humble reply: "I give thanks to God that so great a bishop should be mindful of my lowly self and should deign to send his messenger to me in this wilderness." Then calling his brethren to him, he commanded them to show all kindness to the messenger. Carefully carrying out his behest, they set a table before him and offered him such food as they had; and when he had eaten, the brethren asked his leave to withdraw. Then the man of God summoned the messenger, thanked him for his labor and said: "Greet the holy bishop Boniface in the name of his servants and say that I will hasten to him as quickly as I can." Then he blessed him and allowed him to return.

On the following day the man of God asked the blessing of his brethren and set out at once and, taking the road to Seleheim (near Amoeneburg), hastened to meet the bishop. On the second day after he had set out he met him in the place we have already mentioned, called Fritzlar. When it was told the bishop that the hermit Sturm had arrived he gave orders that he should be brought into his presence. When this had been done Sturm fell prostrate at his feet and, greeting the bishop, asked for his blessing. The bishop returned his greetings, blessed him, and ordered him to approach and, after kissing him,

commanded him to sit at his side. He rejoiced at his coming and asked him for
the sake of the love he bore to relax somewhat his usual fast. The man of God,
acting with great discretion and out of reverence for his master the bishop,
complied. "Anything that you may command," said he, "I believe to be holy."

Presently the table was set in the presence of the bishop, and Sturm ate the
food that he had commanded him to take. When he had eaten and the table
was removed the bishop rose, took him aside into a quiet place where they
could be alone, and there they talked for a long time about spiritual matters
and about the Christian life. For, as afterward appeared, the bishop was very
eager to establish monastic life in the wilderness, and for this reason he
inquired, among other things, what had transpired in the hermit's search for a
site. Sturm answered: "We traveled upstream along the river Fulda for several
days, but we found no place that we could recommend to you." The holy
bishop understood from this that the place predestined by God had not yet
been revealed, and an interior prophetic voice told him: "A place has indeed
been prepared in the wilderness, and when Christ wills He will show it to His
servants. For this reason continue the search, knowing and believing that you
will certainly find it." And so, assuring Sturm that a site would eventually be
found, and, encouraging him in his love of monastic life and fortifying him
against the attacks of the devil, he allowed him to return to his hermitage.
Coming to his cell, which had been built at Hersfeld, already mentioned, he
greeted his brethren and related to them the commands and the promise of the
bishop.

7

When he had rested with them for a short time and recovered from his fatigue
he saddled his ass and, taking provisions, set out alone, commending his
journey to Christ, who is the Way, the Truth, and the Life (see Jn 14.6). Alone
on his ass, he began his wanderings through the pathless wilderness.

Then the insatiable explorer, scrutinizing with his experienced gaze the
hills and the plains, the mountains and valleys, the fountains and streams
and rivers, went on his way. Singing psalms with his mouth, he raised his
mind to God in prayer, staying in no place except where night compelled him
to stop. And wherever he spent the night he cut down trees with a tool that
he carried in his hand and made a circular fence for the protection of his ass,
so that it would not be devoured by the wild beasts that were numerous
there. He himself, making a sign of the cross on his forehead, lay down to

rest without fear. And thus the man of God, accoutred with weapons of the spirit, covering his body with the breastplate of justice, guarding his breast with the shield of faith, protecting his head with the helmet of salvation, girded with the sword of the Word of God, went forth to the fray against the devil. One day, while he was ambling along, he came to a road leading from Thuringia to Mainz which the merchants use, and in the street that goes over the river Fulda he came upon a great number of Slavs swimming in the river and washing themselves. When the ass on which he was riding saw their naked bodies he began to quiver with fear, and even the man of God could not bear the stench of them. They, on their side, like all pagans, began to jeer at him, and when they tried to do him harm they were held back by divine power and prevented from carrying out their intention. One of them, who acted as their interpreter, asked him where he was going. He replied that he was on his way to a hermitage higher up.

8

So the man of God continued his journey through the frightful wilderness, seeing nothing but wild beasts, of which there was a great number, birds flying, enormous trees, and the rough thickets of the forests, until on the fourth day he passed the spot where the monastery now stands, and, climbing up a hill, reached the confluence where the river Gysilaha flows into the Fulda. Continuing a little farther, he came at sunset to the path that was called by the old name Ortessveca. There he passed the night after providing protection for his ass against attacks. While he was busy there putting up the fence he heard afar off the sound of water trickling, but he could not make up his mind whether the noise was caused by man or beast. He stood stock-still listening intently, and again he heard the trickle of water. Then because the man of God did not wish to shout, and knowing instinctively that a man was astir, he struck a hollow tree with the weapon he was carrying in his hand. The other, hearing the sound of the beaten tree trunk, came running toward him, crying out. When he came near they saw and greeted each other. The man of God asked him who he was and where he came from. The other replied that he was on his way from Wetteran and that the horse he was leading by the halter belonged to his lord Ortis. And so, talking, they passed the night together in that place, for the other man knew the district very well; and when the man of God told him what he had in mind and what he wished to do the other gave him the names of the various places and explained where the streams and fountains were to be found. The place in which they were resting was called Eihloh. The next morning when they rose they blessed each other and immediately the layman set out on his journey to Grapfelt.

9

But Sturm, the servant of God, taking another direction and placing his trust in God, began to pick his way through the wilderness alone. After he had made a circuit of Eihloh and found it unsuitable for his purpose he went toward the torrent that even now is called Grezzibach and spent some time there examining the site and the quality of the soil. Then he turned back a short distance and came to the blessed spot foreordained by God on which the present monastery is built. At the sight of it Sturm was filled with great joy and continued his journey in high spirits, for he was convinced that through the merits and prayers of Saint Boniface the place had been revealed to him by God. As he walked over the ground and saw all the advantages the place possessed, he gave thanks to God; and the more he looked at it from every angle, the more pleased with it he became. So charmed was he with the beauty of the spot that he spent practically a whole day wandering over it, exploring its possibilities. Finally, he blessed it and turned his face toward home.

10

After two days' journey the man of God arrived at Hersfeld, where he found his brethren engaged in prayer. He told them of the new site and ordered them to set out with him at once. Without further delay he asked the prayers of the brethren for himself and set off to see the bishop. The journey took several days, but when he came into his presence and was kindly received by him he began to describe the place he found and to enlarge upon its advantages. "I think," he said, "that I have found a site of which you will approve," and when he had acquainted him with the lay of the land, the fertility of the soil, and of the supply of running water, which satisfies the needs of the monastery even at the present time, the bishop was filled with enthusiasm. Both of them congratulated each other and gave thanks to God: and then they embarked upon a long discussion on the monastic life and its observances.

11

For a few days the bishop entertained the hermit in his house, and after some pleasant talks together he took pains to speak to him on spiritual matters, stimulating him to a love of the monastic life by examples taken from Sacred Scriptures. And so, instructed and confirmed by sound doctrine and the teaching of Holy Writ, Sturm was allowed by the bishop to return to his cell. Boniface on his part set out for the king's court to seek confirmation for the appropriation of the land for the monastery. Eventually Sturm returned to his brethren, who were dwelling in the hermitage. But when he was on the point of taking them with him to the place he had discovered, which was nine years[6] after he first began to live the solitary life, and of returning from Hersfeld, the devil, who is envious of good designs, fearing the effect of their good lives in the wilderness, stirred up the passions of wicked men to prevent the servants of God from taking possession of the site. Being unable to withstand their stubborn opposition, the servants of God withdrew and settled in another place called Dryhlar.

12

Saint Boniface, as we have mentioned, went to Carloman,[7] the king of the Franks, and addressed him with these wise and humble words: "I believe that it would redound to your everlasting reward if, God willing, and with your help, monastic life could be established and a monastery could be founded in the eastern part of your kingdom, a thing that has not been attempted before our time. For this reason I beg your kind help in this project, so that in future and for ever a never-fading reward may be laid up for you before Christ, the High King. We have found a site suitable for monastic life in the wilderness that is called Bochon, near the river of Fulda, but this property belongs to you. I now beg Your Highness to give us this place, so that under your protection we may serve Christ there."

On hearing these words the king was glad and called together the nobles of his court. He spoke to them with approbation of the bishop's request and in their presence handed over to him the property for which he had asked. "The

---

6. Fulda was founded in 744. Sturm had not then been a solitary for nine years, although he had been a monk for about that long.

7. He was not king but mayor of the palace (741–747) in the eastern reaches of the Frankish kingdom.

place you seek and which, as you say, is called Eihloh on the banks of the river Fulda, and any other property I am supposed to possess there at this date, is granted whole and entire to God, and all the land that lies north, south, east, and west of that point for a distance of four miles shall be included." A charter of this gift was ordered to be drawn up, signed by the king's own hand, and all the nobles in the vicinity of Grapfelt were summoned by messengers and asked to follow the king's example, if by any chance they possessed any property in that quarter. On the day appointed, when they had gathered together, the messengers of the king addressed them. "All of you," they said, "have come here in obedience to the king's command; He asks, or, more correctly, he requires each one of you who has any claim to land in the place called Eihloh to give it to the servants of God for the use of their monastery." On hearing this, they eagerly abandoned in favor of Sturm whatever rights to property they had in that place, and thus was God's will fulfilled.

13

The donation was accordingly confirmed by all and passed from the possession of men into the possession of God. Blessed Sturm departed to his brethren at Dryhlar and after a few days took seven of the brethren with him to the spot where the monastery now stands. On the twelfth day of January in the year of the Incarnation seven hundred and forty-four, during the reign of the two brothers Carloman and Pepin,[8] the twelfth indiction, the brethren set foot for the first time on this holy spot preordained for this purpose by God. They prayed to the Lord to watch over and protect it at all times by His invincible power, and then, serving Him day and night in fasting, watching, and prayer, they set to work, as far as they were able, to cut down the trees and to clear the site with their own hands.

At the end of two months, the venerable archbishop Boniface, accompanied by a great throng of men, came to see them, and after inspecting all the ground and being made aware of all its advantages and usefulness, he rejoiced in the Holy Spirit and gave thanks to God for having granted to His servants so suitable a place to dwell in. The bishop and the monks then agreed that a church should be built, and so he ordered all the men who had accompanied him to the spot to cut down the woods and clear the undergrowth, while he

---

8. He was mayor of the palace (741–751) in the western regions of the Frankish kingdom and then king of the Franks (751–768).

himself climbed the brow of a hill, which is now called Bishop's Mount, and spent his time praying to God and meditating on Sacred Scripture. This is the reason the hill bears its name.

After a week of felling trees and clearing away the brushwood the turf was piled up ready to make lime: then the bishop gave the brethren his blessing, commended the place to God and returned home with the workmen he had brought with him. The following year the bishop came again to visit his new monastery, which by that time was called Fulda, taking its name from the river that flowed close by; and after greeting them remained with them for several days, during which time he gave the newly recruited monks instruction and he did not cease to inculcate among them the discipline of a regular monastic life led according to Sacred Scripture. And when he was expounding the Sacred Scriptures for his brothers, he read that wine was in no way meant for monks, and so they decided by common consent not to take any strong drink that might lead to drunkenness but only to drink weak beer. Much later this rule was relaxed at a council held in the time of King Pepin, when, owing to the increasing numbers in the community, there were many sick and ailing among them. Only a handful of the brethren abstained from wine and strong drink until the end of their lives.

Shortly afterward the bishop had a confidential talk with Sturm and gave him advice about the way to govern others, and then, after addressing the brethren on the need for obedience and submission, he commended them to Christ, bade them farewell and departed. Every year he came to visit them in this way, and whenever he was free from his episcopal duties, which were exacting, he came to stay with them and worked with his own hands. And often he spent long hours on his beloved hill, of which we have already spoken, mediating on the hidden truths of the Scriptures.

14

When the brethren had conceived a burning desire to follow the rule of the holy father Saint Benedict, and had striven to conform their ideas and actions to the discipline of the monastic life, they formed a plan of sending some of their members to well-established monasteries in other places so that they could become perfectly acquainted with the customs and observances of the brethren. When this prudent plan was submitted to the bishop he heartily approved of it and commanded Sturm to undertake the experiment himself. All necessary preparations were made for the journey, two other brethren were chosen to accompany him, and so, four years after the foundation of the monastery, he set out for Rome.[9] There he visited all the monasteries and spent a whole year inquiring into the customs, observances, and traditions of the brethren who lived in them. In the following year, much edified by the holiness he had met, he returned home. When he reached his own country he was seized with sickness, and by divine providence was compelled to remain in bed for four weeks at the monastery of Kitzingen.[10] But he recovered from his illness and set out to visit Bishop Boniface, who at that time was in Thuringia. On seeing him, the bishop was greatly pleased, and, giving thanks to God for his safe return, asked him many questions about the places he had seen. And when he noticed how shrewdly Sturm had observed the manners of the people and the observance of the monks there, he said: "Go back to the newly founded monastery at Fulda and as far as you are able establish monastic discipline on the pattern of the monks you have seen there." Blessed Sturm begged the bishop's blessing, and, setting off at once to his solitude, reached it after four days, full of joy at seeing his brethren once again. To them he described what he had seen in Italy and the things he had learned from the fathers of the monasteries in Tuscany, and by wise remarks and his personal example stimulated them to follow in his footsteps. For whenever he suggested the adoption of some point of monastic discipline he always took pains to do it first himself so that no one should say: "Why are your words not confirmed by deeds?"

At that time there was a great desire in the community to adapt their mode of life to the observances either described or shown to them or exemplified in the lives of the saints, and they carried out in every detail the Rule of Saint Benedict that they had vowed to follow. So for many years they lived in fervor and holiness. Through the coming of recruits the monastery increased, since many came to serve God there and offered both themselves and their possessions. With this growth in the community and the enlarging of their estates the reputation of Fulda spread throughout the countryside, so that its good name reached the ears of brethren in monasteries situated at great distances from it. And since a great number of monks led there a strict life under the discipline of the holy Rule, the bishop was eager to visit them often; and as he was moved to pity at the sight of their poverty, he gave them small properties in order to provide them with necessary food.

9. Sturm's journey to Rome and Monte Cassino took place in 747–748. See below, page 265, in Rudolf's *Life of Leoba*, where it is explicitly stated that Boniface sent Sturm to Monte Cassino.

10. About sixty miles southeast of Fulda.

15A

Ten years after his first visit to the holy place the archbishop Boniface took counsel with the king and the other Christians and went into the distant parts of Frisia, which were steeped in paganism. There by teaching and baptizing he gained a great number of people to the faith of Christ. Some years later he departed from them and returned unharmed to the church in Germany. But the following year he went once more to the swampy homesteads of the Frisians, hoping to complete the missionary work he had begun. On a certain day after his arrival, when he had called the people together to listen to his teaching, they came, not humbly to hear the Word of God, but stirred by an evil spirit. They rushed in during the sermon brandishing weapons, slew the holy Christian bishop with the sword and slaughtered all his companions. After the martyrdom of the bishop and of many who were with him the brethren from the monastery of Trech in upper Frisia came and took the bodies of the martyrs, placing some in tombs, bringing others with them, among them being the bodies of Bishop Boniface, the deacons and priests who suffered with him, and a certain bishop named Eoban, whose head, which was cut off by the attackers, could not be found. When they came [to Trech] they placed the body of Saint Boniface together with the bier, on which it had been brought by boat, in a small church, which was near by. The rest of the martyrs' remains they buried. Then all the inhabitants of that place decided that the remains of Saint Boniface should always rest among them, for they thought that it would be a great help to them to remain under the protection of so great a martyr.[11] Fasting and prayer was enjoined and they prayed to God that the holy martyr would deign to remain in their midst. But the holy martyr wished his body to be taken to the place of solitude that by the will of God he had chosen for himself. This soon became clear, for, while they were trying to bear him to the other church and place him in a tomb there, they put their hands to the bier but were unable to move it. Many others joined forces with them, but even so they were unable to raise the bier on which the holy body lay.

15B

They understood, therefore, that he did not wish to stay in that place, so they said that he should be taken to the city of Mainz. Straightway they raised it

---

11. Compare this account with Willibald's (above, pages 138–40) treatment of the fate of Boniface's remains.

without difficulty, and, taking it to the river and placing it on board a boat, they began to draw the boat along the Rhine and make upstream. When Sturm heard of this he made haste from his abbey of Fulda in the wilderness to meet them and went along with them until they came after a quiet and uneventful journey to Mainz. Forthwith the priests, clergy, and people with one voice declared that it was not right to remove the holy martyr of God to another place but that his body should rest where during his life he had held his episcopal see. A messenger also came from the king's court bringing orders that the martyr's body should remain in the city if he so wished.

But Sturm and those who had gathered together from the monastery repeatedly declared that on many occasions while the bishop was staying with them he had pointed out the place where they should lay his body to rest and they had no doubts that he would wish to remain at the monastery. But while they were arguing in this way, and Lull, the bishop of the city, strongly forbade the body to be taken to the solitude, the holy bishop appeared one night in a dream to a certain deacon and said: "Why do you delay to take me to my place at Fulda? Arise and bear me into the wilderness where God has foreordained a place for me." And the deacon rose and recounted what had been told him in the dream, first to Sturm and then to all the nobles. At this all were struck with fear and did not dare to oppose any further the removal of the holy martyr from that place. Lull, however, who was bishop there, did not wish to believe in the revelation until the man who had seen the vision had placed his hand upon the altar and taken an oath on the veracity of what he had seen. Then, according to the power of God, whose will cannot be withstood, the body of the blessed martyr was raised with great honor, borne to the river to the accompaniment of hymns, placed on board a ship and rowed as far as Hohleim, a village standing on the banks of the Moyn. From there, after a few days—that is, thirty days after his death—the sacred remains of the bishop were carried to the abbey of Fulda and placed in a new tomb. On the following day Bishop Lull departed together with the clerics and the throng of people who had come with him. Then the venerable abbot Sturm and his brethren gave thanks to God because they had been granted the presence of so powerful a patron as the holy martyr Saint Boniface in their midst.

After the coming of the martyr the spot chosen by God began to increase, its reputation was enhanced and the monastery grew in numbers, because many nobles vied with each other in going there and offered themselves and their goods to the Lord. So, day by day, the number of monks grew apace, and under the protection of the Lord the brethren who served God there preserved the strict observance of their holy life with unabated and unflagging fervor. How

many miracles were performed there and are still performed to this day I leave
to writers better than myself to describe.

16

But Sturm, who was beloved by all the community and revered by all the people,
dutifully fulfilled his ministry, setting himself as an example to the others, for
he exhibited in his conduct what he taught by his words. Lull, however, who was
bishop there, grew envious of his good reputation and allowed his jealousy to
influence his conduct toward him. Since Sturm preached the Word of God
everywhere and at all times and was listened to by all with rapt attention, the
bitter enemy of the human race, not enduring so great usefulness to remain
among the people, began to sow discord among the brethren and stirred up three
false brethren to make false accusations against Sturm in the presence of the
king, Pepin. These men, led astray by the persuasion of the devil, entered into a
conspiracy and, relying on the support of Bishop Lull, went to the king and
accused the blessed man of a trumped-up crime, saying that he was an enemy of
the king. And when the man of God presented himself at the court he patiently
bore their untruths and made no attempt to exculpate himself. "My witness,"
he said, " 'Behold my witness is in heaven, and he that vouches for me is on
high' (Jb 16.19) and therefore I am not put into confusion."

The will of the wicked, however, prevailed, and King Pepin ordered the
blessed man to be taken away and sent with some of his monks and clerics into
exile at the great abbey of Jumièges, where he was welcomed with kindness
and honor by the abbot who governed that monastery.[12] For two years he lived
in exile there, beloved by all. When the monks at the Abbey of Fulda heard
this and it was told them that their abbot had been taken away from them they
were greatly troubled and grieved more than one can say. Then there arose a
great disturbance in the house of God: some wished to leave the monastery,
others to go to court, others implored God with fasting and prayer to show His
mercy and come to their aid. At that time it was widely believed and rumored
that the blessed abbot Sturm had been removed from the abbey of Fulda at the
instance of Bishop Lull: all men without exception took this very ill and there
was no church in the eastern region that did not bewail his exile.

---

12. Sturm was in exile at Jumièges from 763 to 765. Matters were more complicated than Eigil
suggests. Pepin faced considerable aristocratic opposition in central Germany and Sturm, a Bavarian aristocrat himself, was considered dangerous for a time.

17

In the meantime Lull, by giving bribes, obtained from King Pepin permission to place the abbey of Fulda under his jurisdiction,[13] and when this power was granted he installed there as abbot a certain priest of his named Marcus who would obey him in everything; but since the feelings of the brethren were turned against him because of the love they bore to his predecessor, he remained a stranger to them, and their manners did not agree. And because of this disagreement in outlook, though they dwelt together in body, they were separated in mind. Living in this state of disharmony, the brethren were always thinking how, through the grace of God, they could recall their abbot Sturm, and at length, being unable to endure the friction any longer, they hit on the plan of expelling Marcus, whom they had unwillingly accepted as their abbot after Lull had appointed him. Therefore they unanimously agreed to consider him no longer as their superior. When he was removed, all the brethren wished to leave the monastery and go to the court of King Pepin to demand the return of their abbot Sturm. When Lull heard this, he tried to calm them by persuasive words, promising them the power to appoint as abbot any member of the community of their own choosing. As this proposal was acceptable, the brethren elected a monk named Prezzold, a true servant of God, possessed of every good quality, whom blessed Sturm had trained and loved since he was a small boy. They appointed him as their abbot but with the sole purpose in view of discussing together as the days went by how, with the help of the holy martyr Saint Boniface and the grace of Almighty God, they could induce King Pepin to restore to them their former master Sturm. Prezzold governed the brethren for no little time, uniting them together in charity and cooperating with them on the method of persuading King Pepin to recall their abbot to them.

18

At length, when Prezzold had given long consideration to the matter and the brethren were stricken with grief at Sturm's absence, they implored God in unceasing prayer to use His invincible power to bring their master back to them. And when they had done this for a long time and all the churches,

13. In 745 Pope Zachary granted Fulda exemption from episcopal jurisdiction. This was unusual at the time and it is not surprising that Lull of Mainz, in whose diocese Fulda lay, would have tried to restore his customary rights.

monasteries, and convents in the eastern parts had joined in continual prayer with them, God, the Comforter of the lowly, heard the prayers of His suppliants. And He put it into the heart of King Pepin to think about blessed Sturm. And he commanded him to be brought with honor from his place of exile to the palace. When he had come in haste to the palace he waited in the king's chapel for several days, praying to God and waiting on the king's pleasure. It happened one day that as the king was going out to hunt and, as was his custom, came at dawn to pray, the rest of the king's servants were taking their rest after morning vigils. Sturm was praying alone, and, seeing the king about to enter, opened the doors of the church for him and led him to the altar with a lighted candle. When the king had humbly prayed to God at the sacred altars, he rose and, gazing on Sturm, he said with a smile: "God has brought us together at this moment. What the accusation was that your monks made against you in my presence I cannot remember, and why I was enraged against you I cannot recall." Then without heistation Sturm answered: "Although I am not free from sin, never, O King, have I committed any crime against you." Then the king said: "Whether or not you have ever conceived an evil design against me or have done me any wrong, may God forgive you as I do from my heart. For the future, enjoy my favor and friendship all the days of my life." And taking a thread from his cloak, he let it fall to the ground and said: "Lo, as witness of perfect forgiveness, I cast this thread from my cloak on the ground that all may see that my former enmity against you is annulled." And so, reconciled and firmly united in friendship, the king set out on the expedition he had prepared.

19

After a short time, when Prezzold and the rest of the brethren learned that their beloved master Sturm had been received back into the king's favor and friendship, they thought of going to the court and asking for their master. They sent deputies to the palace, humbly asking the king to send their abbot back to them. As everything that God wills is done, they easily obtained their request. The king kindly acceded to their wishes and promised to send Abbot Sturm to them—a result, we are convinced, due to the many prayers of the servants and handmaids of God. After a short time the king summoned Sturm to his presence and commended to him the government of the abbey of Fulda, which he had held before. He released him from the jurisdiction of Bishop Lull and commanded him to return with all honor to Fulda, there to govern the monastery with the privileges that blessed Pope Zachary, the supreme pontiff, had formerly granted to Boniface. The privilege just mentioned is preserved to this day in the monastery. He also ordered him to consider the king as the abbey's sole protector. On receiving this power from the king, Sturm returned to the monastery, bearing with him the privilege that he accepted from the hands of the king.

The news spread at once throughout all the provinces that Sturm would shortly return, and wherever the monks and nuns heard of it they gave thanks to Christ. When the brethren were told of his approach to the monastery they took up a golden cross and the relics of the saints and went out in procession to meet him at some distance from the abbey. Then they greeted him and those who had accompanied him, and brought him to the monastery, rejoicing and singing hymns. And they raised God who had restored to them the abbot they had long desired. So there was great joy on all sides.

20

Sturm himself, having given much thought to the question of how to make a new start, began by correcting the faults of the brethren and restoring discipline. He put the administration of the abbey on a better footing, embellished the church that they had at that time, and repaired the monastic buildings by adding new columns, great wooden beams, and new roofs. Shortly afterward he began to wonder how he could carry out the prescription of the holy Rule that says that various crafts should be exercised within the monastery in order to obviate the necessity of the brethren's wandering abroad. So he collected together as many workmen as he could. Then with his usual ingenuity, having surveyed the course of the river Fulda, he drew off a stream from it at some distance from the monastery and made it flow through large canals underneath the abbey workshops, so that the stream of waters made glad the city of God. What great profit this enterprise conferred on the brethren and how great are the advantages it brings to us even at the present time is obvious both to those who see it and those who use it.

Over the tomb of the blessed martyr Boniface he built a ciborium[14] wrought of silver and gold, which we call a *requiem*, and which, as the custom then was,

14. A canopy, usually placed over an altar. The word also applies, but not here, to the chalice-like vessel for the distribution of the Eucharist to the faithful.

was a work of remarkable craftsmanship. It can be seen to this day, together with the altar of gold, over the tomb of the martyr of Christ.

21

Because this upright and perfect man of God was held in high esteem by all, and particularly by King Pepin, he asked the king, as a token of the intimate friendship that existed between them, to assign him the revenues and the royal possessions in Onamstat as an alms for the monastery. He also begged him to confirm the gift by charter according to the usual custom. On the death of Pepin in the year of the Incarnation seven hundred and sixty-eight, in the twenty-third year of his reign,[15] Charles,[16] his son, succeeded to the kingdom. Since the young king wished to gain the favor of all those who had been honored by his father, he bestowed large presents upon them. With the same end in view he summoned Sturm, renewed ties of friendship with him, and loaded him with honors and princely gifts. At a certain time he was inspired by God to consider his eternal welfare, and, calling Sturm to his side, he decided to transfer to the abbey of Fulda the vill of Hammelburg with all the revenues that pertained to it. This gift was gratefully accepted by the brethren, who even now pray to the Lord for his salvation. Thenceforward Saint Sturm enjoyed the favor of King Charles as long as he lived.

22

It was at this time that Sturm went on an embassy from King Charles to Tassilo, the head of the province of Noricum, and established friendly relations between them for several years.

After King Charles had reigned prosperously for four years he began to consider how he might gain the Saxon people to Christ, for they still remained savage and hostile to all their neighbors and were deeply attached to their pagan rites. He took counsel with the servants of God and asked them to pray that the Lord would grant his desire. Then he gathered together a mighty army, placed it under the patronage of Christ, and, accompanied by bishops, abbots, and priests and all true believers, set out for Saxony. His purpose was

---

15. He was king from 751 to 768. Eigil's mistake is inexplicable.
16. Charlemagne (747–814), king of the Franks after 768.

to bring this people, which had been fettered from the beginning with the devil's bonds, to accept the faith and to submit to the mild and sweet yoke of Christ. When the king reached Saxony he converted the majority of the people partly by conquest, partly by persuasion, partly even by bribes, and not long afterward he divided the whole of the province into episcopal sees and handed it over to the servants of God to evangelize and baptize.[17] The greater part of that territory with its people was entrusted to Sturm. He accordingly undertook the labor of preaching, employed every means in his power, and so gained a great harvest for the Lord. He seized every opportunity to impress on them in his preaching that they should forsake idols and images, accept the Christian faith, destroy the temples of the gods, cut down the groves and build sacred churches in their stead.

23

After he and his priests had spent much time in instructing them and had built churches in each of the districts, the Saxons, who are a depraved and perverse race, lapsed from the Christian faith and reverted once more to their former errors. Then, when they had mustered an army, they streamed across the borders and came as far as the Rhine, laying everything waste and slaughtering all the inhabitants. On their return march they put to the sword everyone they met with savage ferocity. Then they encamped near Lahngau at a short distance from the monastery and planned to send a picked band of warriors from the army to attack the abbey, to burn it to the ground with all its contents, and to slaughter all the servants of God. When this news came to the ears of Sturm he summoned the brethren, acquainted them with their imminent danger and advised them to take the body of the holy martyr (Saint Boniface) and hasten to Hammelburg. Sturm himself set off for Wedereib to see if he could possibly prevent the soldiers from putting their plain into effect. We, his disciples, took the body of the martyr from its tomb in which it had lain for twenty-four years and began to leave the monastery with all the servants of God. On the first night we rested at the next cell, where the waters of the Fulda and the Fleden meet. Then early next day we reached Sinner on the far side and there we pitched a tent in which we placed the sacred body of the martyr of Christ, while the monks encamped around it. After spending

---

17. As the *Life of Willehad* (below) shows, Eigil's account of the Christianization of Saxony is a bit too smooth.

three days in tents, messengers came to us on the fourth day telling us that some of our people in the district had banded themselves together and attacked the Saxons, and that the Saxons had been beaten and put to flight. At this news, we took up the bones of the blessed martyr and returned with joy to the monastery, where we interred them once more in the place they had formerly occupied. Then we gave thanks to the Lord Christ for restoring the peace and allowing us to dwell once more in our monastery.

24

Then King Charles set out a second time for that country to establish by force of arms the Christian faith that had taken root there. He ordered Sturm, now weak and weary with age, to remain with his companions at Heresburg and to keep guard over the city. When everything had been arranged according to his desire, the king, on his return, commanded the holy man to remain for some days in the city already mentioned. After this number of days had elapsed, the man of God returned to the monastery accompanied by the royal physician, named Wintanus, who was to attend him in his illness. One day he gave him some kind of potion as a remedy for his sickness, but instead of diminishing it rather increased it, so that the painful disease grew stronger and more virulent. Sturm began to say with some anxiety that the physician whose duty it was to cure him had inflicted great harm upon him. He therefore gave orders to his attendants to bear him quickly to the church, to summon all the brethren, and tell them that his death was imminent; then he asked them to pray earnestly for him. When the community had gathered together, he had them brought into the chamber where he was lying and addressed the assembled brethren with these words: "My brethren, you are well aware of my last wishes. You know how I have labored, even till the present day, for your profit and peace, particularly for the continuance of this monastery after my death, so that you may be able to serve God here with sincerity and charity according to the will of Christ. Persevere, then, all the days of your life in the ideal you have set before you. Pray to God for me; and if I have committed any fault among you through human frailty or wronged anyone unjustly, forgive me as I also forgive all those who have offended or wronged me, including Lull, who always took sides against me."

After these and some other good words, he bade farewell to the brethren and sent them away. After the brethren had departed, the holy man began rapidly to lose strength and to hasten above. All were filled with grief; great sorrow afflicted the hearts of the brethren, who implored God with tears to have mercy on him, and they commended the death of their holy and revered abbot to the Lord.

25

The next day, which was the seventeenth of December, his weakness increased and his end rapidly approached. While we stood around his bed and saw how quickly his end would be, one of us said: "Father, we have no doubt that you are going to God and that you will enjoy eternal life. Therefore, we beg Your Paternity to be mindful of us there and to pray for us, your disciples; for our confidence is great that it will be to our profit to have sent on before us so powerful a patron." And he, gazing upon us, said at once: "Show yourselves worthy and so conduct yourselves that I shall be justified in praying for you. Then I will do what you ask." After these words his holy soul was released from the flesh and freed from the prison of the body. Full of good merits, it passed to Christ, whose Kingdom endures for ever and ever, Amen.

Alcuin

THE LIFE OF SAINT WILLIBRORD

Translated by C. H. Talbot

Alcuin (c. 735–804) was one of the most famous and accomplished early medieval writers to turn his hand to hagiography. He was educated in the north of England in the rich intellectual tradition of which Bede is the outstanding representative. His master Archbishop Egbert of York was one of the most learned men of his day and built up a great library. When Egbert died in 766 Alcuin succeeded him as master of the school of York. In 781, while on a mission to Rome, Alcuin met Charlemagne in Italy and agreed to come to the court of the Frankish king. Apart from some visits to England, Alcuin was resident at the Frankish court from 782 to 796. From 796 to 804 Alcuin was abbot of Tours where he actively fostered learning and the production of manuscripts.

Alcuin was learned and versatile. His earliest work was a verse life of the saints of York. In later years much of his writing was geared to his responsibilities as a teacher. Thus he produced textbooks on a wide range of subjects and biblical commentaries. Alcuin also left behind more than three hundred letters that help to illuminate his age and his own interests, a substantial corpus of poetry that is always competent and sometimes moving, and several works that were written to respond to contemporary quarrels.

The *Life of Willibrord* was written in about 796. It was requested by Beornrad, or Berhnard, bishop of Sens from 792 to 798, who was also abbot of Echternach, a monastery founded by Willibrord and his final resting place. As we have seen, however, it was entirely conventional for a life to be written—or, sometimes, for an author to allege that it had been written—on someone else's request. With this life Alcuin introduced some interesting features. He prepared both a prose and a verse version. This had already been done by Bede for Saint Cuthbert. Alcuin now brought this Northumbrian tradition to the Carolingian court. The prose version was meant for liturgical reading at Echternach while the verse life was intended to be both morally edifying and intellectually stimulating. In the Middle Ages the verse life was much more popular and more widely disseminated. This life also treats kinsmen of Alcuin and focuses on the luminaries of Northumbria.

Put a little differently, Alcuin was subtly moving the emphasis away from Boniface and his circle. It is possible that both Northumbrian patriotism and rivalries in Charlemagne's court circle motivated Alcuin's approach. Boniface was a Wessex man whereas Alcuin's connections were all in the north of England. What is more, Alcuin stresses selfless missionary zeal to spread the Gospel and to save souls over the kinds of political and institutional concerns that seem to loom large in the corpus of Bonifatian materials. Finally, the Carolingian family appears much more prominently in this text than it does in the lives associated with Boniface and his circle. Interestingly, even though Alcuin was a patriotic Englishman—and of course Willibrord was English too—Alcuin's text is less Anglocentric than the texts that arose around Boniface. We get here more glimpses of the uses to which hagiography could be put and of the historical contexts in which hagiographical documents must be situated.

Willibrord, the "Apostle of Frisia," was born in 658 and lived until 739. He received his education at the monastery of Ripon in Northumbria and then spent twelve years in an Irish monastery. In 690 he decided on a missionary venture to still-pagan Frisia, a land about which Northumbrians would have had considerable knowledge through frequent commercial contacts. In 695 Pope Sergius I made him archbishop of the Frisians without a fixed see—an anticipation of Boniface's later situation. Pepin II, then the Frankish mayor of the palace, and father of Charles Martel who figures prominently in the *Life of*

Boniface, gave Willibrord land for a cathedral just outside Utrecht. In 698 Willibrord founded the monastery of Echternach, which is in modern Luxembourg. This house became an extension of Northumbrian art and learning as well as a major center of missionary activity.

Texts and References

The basic Latin text remains Alcuin, *Vita Willibrordi, archiepiscopi Traiectensis*, ed. Wilhelm Levison, Monumenta Germaniae Historica, Scriptores rerum Merowingicarum, 7:81–141. Of books on Alcuin, there is no end. The most readable and accessible is still Eleanor Shipley Duckett, *Alcuin: Friend of Charlemagne* (New York, 1951). Brilliant insights, with numerous references, can be found in chapters 4 and 5 of Donald Bullough, *Carolingian Renewal: Sources and Heritage* (Manchester, 1991). Not much has been written on Alcuin as a hagiographer but a good starting place is the introduction to Peter Godman's edition of Alcuin's *The Bishops, Kings, and Saints of York* (Oxford, 1982). On Willibrord the best study is Arnold Angenendt, "Willibrord im Dienste der Karolinger," *Annales des historischen Vereins für den Niederrhein* 175 (1973): 63–113.

Preface*

To the most distinguished, venerable, and praiseworthy Lord Archbishop Beornrad, Greetings from Alcuin, a humble Levite!

Your excellency's letters reached me and, I confess, they moved me to great joy when I recognized in them your zeal for the Lord and your day and night meditation on his law. But finally I considered myself far from able to carry out what you asked of me, seeing that I lack the necessary gift of eloquence. But charity, which ought never to deny anything, urges me on for indeed I should never dare to attempt anything on the basis of my poor powers.

And so, holy father, you have set before me your wish that, with God's grace and the help of the most saintly father Willibrord, I write with pious zeal about the life, character, and miracles of Willibrord. I have obeyed your command, and I have set down two books. One walking along in prose, can be

---

*This preface, omitted by Talbot, is translated by Thomas Noble.

read publicly by the brothers in church, if it seems worthy to your wisdom. The other, running with the muse of poetry, your pupils can read over and over again privately in their rooms.

On account of my daily responsibilities, both, the products of tiny stolen moments of thought, were dictated at night. As they were very little polished by their own author, they will need all the more defense from you. As it was my duty not to spurn your instructions, so it will be your task to defend the inexperience of the one who obeyed you.

I have also added one homily to the first book. May it be worthy for you to preach it to your people!

1

There was in the island of Britain, in the province of Northumbria, a certain householder of Saxon descent, whose name was Wilgils, living a devout Christian life together with his wife and family. This fact was later borne out by miraculous events, for after he had given up his worldly career he devoted himself to the monastic life. Not long afterward, as his zeal for the spiritual life increased, he entered with even more intense fervor on the austere life of a solitary, dwelling in the headlands that are bounded by the North Sea and the river Humber. In a little chapel there, dedicated to Saint Andrew, the Apostle of Christ, he served God for many years in fasting, prayer, and watching, with the result that he became celebrated for his miracles, and his name was in everyone's mouth. People flocked to him in great numbers, and when they did so he never failed to instruct them with sound advice and the Word of God.[1]

He was held in such high esteem by the king and the nobles of that nation that they made over to him, in perpetual gift, a number of small landed properties that lie near those headlands for the purpose of building there a church to God. In this church the reverend father gathered together a rather small but devout company of those who wished to serve God, and there also,

1. This opening is unusually personal, apart from the invocation of Beornrade. Alcuin's discreet references show him to have been a kinsman of Wilgils and Willibrord. It cannot be concluded from "wisest of teachers" that Willibrord taught Alcuin. The emphasis on the character of Wilgils is interesting in two respects. It reflects ancient traditions, which held that character was passed down through families. Thus, describing a father was a kind of shorthand for describing a son. Alcuin knew classical literature well and may have quite deliberately appropriated this idea. At the same time, this heritability of character traits appears in *Beowulf* and in many Scandinavian sagas.

after the many trials of his spiritual labors, going to his reward, his body lies at rest. His successors, who still follow the example of his holiness, are in possession of this church to the present day. It is I, the least of these in merit and the last in time, who am now in charge of this little chapel, which has come to me by lawful succession, and I am writing this account of Willibrord, the holiest of fathers and the wisest of teachers, at the request of you, Bishop Beornrade, who, by the grace of God, have succeeded him in the episcopate, in the line of family tradition and in the care of those sanctuaries, which, as we know, he built for the glory of God.[2]

2

Now, in order to relate more fully the facts concerning Willibrord's birth, and recall the signs that show that even while he was in his mother's womb he was chosen by God, I shall return to the point where I began. Just as the most holy forerunner of our Lord Jesus Christ, blessed John the Baptist, was sanctified in his mother's womb and preceded Christ, as the morning star precedes the sun and, as the Gospel tells us, was born of devout parents in order to bring salvation to many, so likewise Willibrord, begotten for the salvation of many, was born of devout parents. Wilgils, the venerable man of whom we have already spoken, entered upon the state of matrimony for the sole purpose of bringing into the world a child who should benefit many peoples. Thus it was that his wife, mother of holy Willibrord, beheld, at dead of night while she slept, a heavenly vision. It seemed to her as if she saw in the sky the new moon, which, as she watched, slowly increased until it reached the size of the full moon. Whilst she was gazing intently upon it, it fell swiftly into her mouth, and when she had swallowed it her bosom was suffused with light. Filled with fear, she awoke at once and went to recount the dream to a holy priest, who asked her whether during the night on which the vision came to her she had known her husband in the customary way. When she assented, he replied as follows: "The moon that you saw changing from small to great is the

2. Beornrade was bishop of Sens, one of the most important dioceses in Francia, from 792 to 798. The "episcopate" is a corporate order. Thus Alcuin is not implying specifically that Beornrade succeeded Willibrord as bishop of Utrecht but generally that he succeeded him as a bishop. Of course, Beornrade also succeeded Willibrord as abbot of the important monastery of Echternach. It was not unusual for great Carolingian churchmen to control monasteries along with their bishoprics. By this means the Carolingians rewarded loyal supporters and, through those very supporters, extended their own authority to the vast lands controlled by cathedrals and monasteries—or such was the design.

son whom you conceived on that night. He will disperse the murky darkness of error with the light of truth, and wherever he goes he will carry with him a heavenly splendor and display the full moon of his perfection. By the brightness of his fame and the beauty of his life he will attract to himself the eyes of multitudes." This interpretation of the dream was borne out by the actual course of events.

3

"And in due time" the woman "conceived and bore a son" (1 Sm 1.20) and at his baptism his father gave him the name of Willibrord. As soon as the child had reached the age of reason[3] his father gave him to the church at Ripon[4] to be instructed by the brethren there in religious pursuits and sacred learning, so that living in a place where he could see nothing but what was virtuous and hear nothing but what was holy his tender age should be strengthened by sound training and discipline. From his earliest years divine grace enabled him to grow in intelligence and in strength of character, at least as far as was possible at such an age, so that it seemed as if in our day there had been born another Samuel,[5] of whom it was said: "Now the boy continued to grow both in stature and in favor with the Lord and with men" (1 Sm 2.26).

Hence, in the monastery of Ripon, the youth who was to prove a blessing to many received the clerical tonsure[6] and made his profession as a monk, and, trained along with the other youths of that holy and sacred monastery, he was inferior to none in fervor, humility, and zeal for study. In fact this highly gifted boy made such progress as the days went by that the development of his intelligence and character so outstripped his tender years that his small and delicate frame harbored the wisdom of ripe old age.

3. In principle, about seven.

4. An important monastery was founded at Ripon in about 650 by King Aldfrid of Northumbria. In 661 Wilfrid, a key figure for two generations in Northumbrian church history, became abbot. Willibrord was well connected.

5. At Charlemagne's court, members of the inner circle used biblical and classical nicknames. Charlemagne himself was "David," Alcuin was "Flaccus" (= Q. Horatius Flaccus or Horace), and Beornrade was "Samuel." Thus, calling Willibrord "another Samuel" was a clever way of flattering Beornrade.

6. The shaving of a circular patch on the top of the head of a candidate for entry into the clergy or the monastic state who signified thereby his humility and his submission to ecclesiastical authority.

4

When this youth, as highly endowed with sacred learning as he was with self-control and integrity, reached the twentieth year of his age he felt an urge to pursue a more rigorous mode of life and was stirred with a desire to travel abroad. And because he had heard that schools and learning flourished in Ireland, he was encouraged further by what he was told of the manner of life adopted there by certain holy men, particularly by the blessed bishop Ecgbert, to whom was given the title of Saint, and by Wichtberct, the venerable servant and priest of God, both of whom, for love of Christ, forsook home, fatherland, and family and retired to Ireland, where, cut off from the world though close to God, they lived as solitaries enjoying the blessings of heavenly contemplation. The blessed youth wished to imitate the godly life of these men and, after obtaining the consent of his abbot and brethren, hastened quickly across the sea to join the intimate circle of the said fathers, so that by contact with them he might attain the same degree of holiness and possess the same virtues, much as a bee sucks honey from the flowers and stores it up in its honeycomb. There among these masters, eminent both for sanctity and sacred learning, he who was one day to preach to many peoples was trained for twelve years, until he reached the mature age of manhood and the full age of Christ.[7]

5

Accordingly, in the thirty-third year of his age the fervor of his faith had reached such an intensity that he considered it of little value to labor at his own sanctification unless he could preach the Gospel to others and bring some benefit to them. He had heard that in the northern regions of the world the harvest was great but the laborers few. Thus it was that, in fulfilment of the dream that his mother stated she had seen, Willibrord, fully aware of his own purpose but ignorant as yet of divine preordination, decided to sail for those parts and, if God so willed, to bring the light of the Gospel message to those

7. Northumbria had been Christianized by Irish missionaries working from bases such as Iona off the western coast of Scotland and also by Roman missionaries coming north from their original bases in Kent. In 664 the Synod of Whitby decided for Roman usages and many English, such as Ecgbert and Wichtberct, who were loyal to Irish customs, decided to depart for Ireland. Because they left friends and family behind, there remained close ties between Northumbria and Ireland. Moreover, Ireland long retained its attraction as a great center of learning. Important too is that Ecgbert had wanted to go to Frisia as a missionary and that Wichtberct had actually done so for two fruitless years.

people who through unbelief had not been stirred by its warmth. So he embarked on a ship, taking with him eleven others who shared his enthusiasm for the faith. Some of these afterward gained the martyr's crown through their constancy in preaching the Gospel, others were later to become bishops and, after their labors in the holy work of preaching, have since gone to their rest in peace.

So the man of God, accompanied by his brethren, as we have already said, set sail, and after a successful crossing they moored their ships at the mouth of the Rhine. Then, after they had taken some refreshment, they set out for the castle of Utrecht,[8] which lies on the bank of the river, where some years afterward, when by divine favor the faith had increased, Willibrord placed the seat of his bishopric. But as the Frisian people, among whom the fort was situated, and Radbod, their king, still defiled themselves by pagan practices, the man of God thought it wiser to set out for Francia and visit Pepin,[9] the leader of that country, a man of immense energy, successful in war, and of high moral character. Pepin received him with every mark of respect; and as he was unwilling that he and his people should lose the services of so eminent a scholar, he made over to him certain localities within the boundaries of his own realm, where he could uproot idolatrous practices, teach the newly converted people, and so fulfil the command of the prophet: "Break up your fallow ground and sow not among the thorns" (Jer 4.3).

6

After the man of God had systematically visited several localities and carried out the task of evangelization, and when the seed of life watered by the dews of heavenly grace had, through his preaching, borne abundant fruit in many hearts, the aforesaid leader of the Franks, highly pleased at Willibrord's burning zeal and the extraordinary growth of the Christian faith, and having in view the still greater propagation of religion, thought it wise to send him to Rome in order that he might be consecrated bishop by Pope Sergius,[10] one of the holiest men of that time. Thus, after receiving the apostolic blessing and

8. It was an old Roman military fort, probably in a state of disrepair.

9. The account here is rather compressed. Willibrord arrived in Frisia in 690. It is not clear just when he first visited Pepin who was Frankish mayor of the palace.

10. Pope from 687 to 701. Willibrord actually made two trips to Rome. Notice how Willibald says that Boniface decided on his own to go to Rome while Alcuin stresses that Pepin sent Willibrord there.

mandate and being filled with greater confidence as the pope's emissary, he would return to preach the Gospel with even greater vigor, according to the words of the apostle: "And how can men preach unless they are sent?" (Rom 10.15).

But when Pepin tried to persuade the man of God to do this he was met by a refusal.[11] Willibrord said that he was not worthy to wield such great authority, and, after enumerating the qualities that Saint Paul mentioned to Timothy, his spiritual son, as being essential for a bishop, asserted that he fell far short of such virtues. On his side, the leader solemnly urged what the man of God had already humbly declined. At length, moved by the unanimous agreement of his companions, and, what is of more importance, constrained by the divine will, Willibrord acquiesced, anxious to submit to the counsel of many rather than obstinately to follow his own will. Accordingly he set out for Rome with a distinguished company, bearing gifts appropriate to the dignity of the pope.

7

Four days before Willibrord arrived in Rome the apostolic father had a dream in which he was advised by an angel to receive him with the highest honors, because he had been chosen by God to bring the light of the Gospel to many souls: his purpose in coming to Rome was to receive the dignity of the episcopate, and nothing that he asked for was to be refused. The apostolic father, forewarned by this admonition, received him with great joy and showed him every courtesy. And as he discerned in him ardent faith, religious devotion, and profound wisdom, he appointed a day suitable for his consecration, when all the people would be assembled together. Then he invited venerable priests to take part in the ceremony, and, in accordance with apostolic tradition and with great solemnity, he publicly consecrated him archbishop in the church of blessed Peter, prince of the apostles.[12] At the same time, he called him Clement and invested him with episcopal robes, conferring upon him the sacred pallium[13] as a sign of his office, like Aaron with the ephod.[14] Moreover,

11. This humility topos is ubiquitous in hagiography. It is meant to show that the saint did not grasp after power, status, and prestige.

12. Bede, *Historia ecclesiastica*, 5.11, says that Willibrord was in fact consecrated in Saint Cecilia's in Trastevere. Alcuin surely knew this. Perhaps he was, by a small deceit, emphasizing the connection between Saint Peter, the pope, and the Franks. The date was 22 November 695.

13. On the pallium, see above, page 105, note 31.

14. A Jewish liturgical vestment of linen and gold worn by the high priest.

whatever he desired or asked for in the way of relics of saints or liturgical vessels the pope gave him without hesitation, and so, fortified with the apostolic blessing and loaded with gifts, he was sent back, duly instructed, to his work of preaching the Gospel.

8

Having received the blessing of the apostolic authority, the devoted preacher of God's Word returned with increased confidence to the leader of the Franks.[15] Pepin welcomed him with every mark of esteem and then dispatched him, armed with his authority to preach the Gospel, more especially in the northern parts of his dominions, where, owing to the scarcity of teachers and the obduracy of the inhabitants, the light of faith shone less brightly. The more clearly the man of God saw the need of overcoming the ignorance and arresting the spiritual famine in these districts, the more vigorously he preached the Word of God. How great was the success that, through the help of divine grace, attended his labors is attested to even in these days by the people whom in the cities, villages, and fortified towns he brought to a knowledge of the truth and the worship of Almighty God by his holy admonitions. Other evidence is to be found in the churches that he built in each place and in the communities of monks and nuns whom he gathered together in various localities.

9

The man of God tried also to propagate the Gospel teaching outside the boundaries of the Frankish kingdom. He had the boldness to present himself to Radbod,[16] at that time king of the Frisians and, like his subjects, a pagan. Wherever he traveled he proclaimed the Word of God without fear; but though the Frisian king received the man of God in a kind and humble spirit, his heart was hardened against the Word of Life. So when the man of God saw that his efforts were of no avail he turned his missionary course toward the fierce tribes of the Danes. At that time, so we are told, the Danish ruler was Ongendus,[17] a man more savage than any wild beast and harder than stone, who nevertheless,

15. Note again this glorification of the Franks.
16. This is the same Radbod who figures so prominently in the *Life of Boniface*.
17. Some scholars have suggested that Oengendus may be identified with the Ongentheow of *Beowulf*.

through divine intervention, received the herald of truth with every mark of honor. But when the latter found that the people were steeped in evil practices, abandoned to idolatry and indifferent to any hope of a better life, he chose thirty boys from among them and hastily returned with them to the chosen people of the Franks. On the journey he instructed the youths in the faith and baptized them, so that if they perished from the long sea voyage or through the ambushes of the savage dwellers of those parts he should suffer no loss in their regard. In this way he desired to anticipate the craft of the devil and to strengthen these redeemed souls by the sacraments of the Lord.

10

Now while this energetic preacher of the Word was pursuing his journey he came to a certain island on the boundary between the Frisians and the Danes, which the people of those parts call Fositeland,[18] after a god named Fosite, whom they worship and whose temples stood there. This place was held by the pagans in such great awe that none of the natives would venture to meddle with any of the cattle that fed there nor with anything else, nor would they dare draw water from the spring that bubbled up there except in complete silence. On this island the man of God was driven ashore by a storm and waited for some days until the gale died down and fair weather made it possible to set sail again. He set little store by the superstitious sacredness ascribed to the spot, or by the savage cruelty of the king, who was accustomed to condemn violators of the sacred objects to the most cruel death. Willibrord baptized three persons in the fountain in the name of the Blessed Trinity and gave orders that some of the cattle should be slaughtered as food for his company.[19] When the pagans saw this they expected that the strangers would become mad or be struck with sudden death. Noticing, however, that they suffered no harm, the pagans, terror-stricken and astounded, reported to the king what they had witnessed.

11

The king was roused to intense fury and had a mind to avenge on the priest of the living God the insults that had been offered to his deities. For three whole

18. Modern Heligoland.
19. Compare Boniface's cutting down of the sacred oak of Geismar.

days he cast lots three times every day to find out who should die; but as the true God protected his own servants, the lots of death never fell upon Willibrord nor upon any of his company, except in the case of one of the party, who thus won the martyr's crown. The holy man was then summoned before the king and severly upbraided for having violated the king's sanctuary and offered insult to his god. With unruffled calmness the preacher of the Gospel replied: "The object of your worship, O King, is not a god but a devil, and he holds you ensnared in rank falsehood in order that he may deliver your soul to eternal fire. For there is no God but one, who created heaven and earth, the seas and all that is in them; and those who worship Him in true faith will possess eternal life. As His servants I call upon you this day to renounce the empty and inveterate errors to which your forebears have given their assent and to believe in the one Almighty God, our Lord Jesus Christ. Be baptized in the fountain of life and wash away all your sins, so that, forsaking all wickedness and unrighteousness, you may henceforth live as a new man in temperance, justice, and holiness. If you do this you will enjoy everlasting glory with God and His saints; but if you spurn me, who set before you the way of life, be assured that with the devil whom you obey you will suffer unending punishment and the flames of hell." At this the king was astonished and replied: "It is clear to me that my threats leave you unmoved and that your words are as uncompromising as your deeds." But although he would not believe the preaching of the truth, he sent back Willibrord with all honor to Pepin, leader of the Franks.

12

The latter was delighted at his return and begged him to persevere in his divinely appointed task of preaching the Word of God and to root out idolatrous practices and sow the good seed in one place after another. This the devoted preacher strove to carry out with characteristic energy. He traversed every part of the country, exhorting the people in cities, villages, and forts where he had previously preached the Gospel to remain loyal to the faith and to their good resolutions. And as the number of the faithful increased day by day and a considerable multitude of believers came to the knowledge of God's Word, many began in their zeal for the faith to make over to the man of God their hereditary properties. These he accepted. Shortly afterward he ordered churches to be built there, and he appointed priests and deacons to serve them, so that the new converts should have places where they could assemble on feast days and listen to wholesome instruction and where they could learn the principles of the Christian religion from those servants of God who had baptized them. Thus the man of God, favored by divine grace, made increasing progress from day to day.

13

It came about, however, that Pepin, leader of the Franks, died, and his son Charles became head of the realm.[20] Charles brought many nations under the power of the Franks, and among these were the Frisians, whose lands were added to his dominions after the defeat of Radbod. At that time Saint Willibrord was officially appointed to preach to the Frisian people, and his episcopal see was fixed at the fortress of Utrecht. Being given greater scope for the preaching of the Gospel, he now attempted to bring into the church by baptism the people that had recently been won by the sword. He allowed no error or past ignorance to pass unnoticed and lost no time in shedding upon them the light of the Gospel, so that soon among that people the statement of the prophet was fulfilled: "In the place where it was said to them, 'You are not my people,' it shall be said to them, 'You are sons of the living God' " (Hos 1.10).

14

Many miracles were also wrought by divine power through His servant. While the ministry of preaching the Gospel is to be preferred to the working of miracles and the showing of signs, yet, because such miracles are recorded as having been performed, I think mention of them ought not to be suppressed; and so that glory may be given to God who vouchsafed them, I will insert them into this narrative, and in this way what we know to have been achieved in former times may not be lost to future ages. Thus, when the venerable man, according to his custom, was on one of his missionary journeys he came to a village called Walichrum,[21] where an idol of the ancient superstition remained. When the man of God, moved by zeal, smashed it to pieces before the eyes of the custodian, the latter, seething with anger, in a sudden fit of passion struck the priest of Christ on the head with a sword as if to avenge the insult paid to

20. In 714 Charles became mayor of the palace, but the transition was not so smooth as there were battles after Pepin died.
21. Walcheren.

his god. But, as God was protecting His servant, the murderous blow did him no harm. On seeing this, Willibrord's companions rushed forward to kill the wicked man for his audacity. The man of God good-naturedly delivered the culprit from their hands and allowed him to go free. The same day, however, he was seized and possessed by the devil and three days later he ended his wretched life in misery. And thus, because the man of God followed the Lord's command and was unwilling to avenge the wrongs done to him, he was vindicated all the more by the Lord Himself, just as He had said regarding the wrongs which the wicked inflicted upon His saints: "Vengeance is mine, I will repay, says the Lord" (Rom 12.19).

15

On another occasion, when the blessed man was on his way to a cell belonging to him called Susteren, from the name of the stream that flows past it, he took a narrow path running through the cornfields of a certain wealthy landowner. When the keeper of the fields saw this he was furious and began to revile the man of God. Those who accompanied him [Willibrord] wanted to punish the man for insulting him, but the servant of God mildly restrained them, not wishing that anyone should perish on his account, since his whole happiness lay in bringing salvation to all. When he found it impossible to calm the fury of the foolish man, Willibrord did not persist but returned by the way he had come. Next day, however, the wretch who had not feared to heap insults upon the servant of God was struck down on that very spot with sudden death before a crowd of onlookers.

16

While the divinely inspired man in his urgent desire to preach the Gospel was traveling through the coastal regions where the people were suffering from the lack of fresh water he noticed that his companions could hardly bear the pangs of thirst. So he called one of them and bade him dig a small trench inside his tent. There, upon his knees, he secretly prayed to God that He who "made water flow" for His people "from the rock" (Is 48.21) while they were in the desert, would with like compassion bring forth water for His servants from the sandy soil. At once his prayer was heard and a spring of sweet water straightway filled the trench. His followers on seeing this gave thanks to God, who in this manner had glorified His saint and condescended to hear his prayer. And when they had drunk their fill they took with them as much water as they thought would satisfy their needs on the journey that lay before them.

17

Again, when the holy priest of God was pursuing his way in a certain place, he saw twelve poor beggars asking alms from the passers-by. Being extremely kindhearted, he gazed on them with compassion and bade one of his companions take his own flask and give a drink to Christ's poor. All the twelve drank from it as much as they would, and the remarkable fact was that as the company went on their way they found that the flask from which so many had drunk was just as full as it was before of the most excellent wine. When they discovered this they all blessed the Lord, saying: "Indeed, the saying of Christ in the Gospels, 'Give and it will be given to you' (Lk 6.38) has been fulfilled."

18

Once, the saintly man came to his monastery[22] to make a visitation, and after praying to God, greeting the brethren and speaking peaceably with them, the holy father went round the cells of each one of the brothers to see if anything in them might be improved. On going into the storehouse, he found there only a small supply of wine in one cask, into which, as a sign of his blessing, he thrust his staff, praying the while, and then went out. The same night, the wine in the cask began to rise to the brim and then to overflow. When the steward noticed it he was astounded at the unexpected increase, and, knowing it to have been wrought by God's mercy through the blessing of His servant, he did not dare to keep it secret. Next morning, he ran after the holy father and, falling at his feet, reported what he had seen. Willibrord, as usual, gave thanks to God, but, bearing in mind our Lord's command to His disciples not to make public the glory of the Transfiguration before the day of the Resurrection, he forbade the steward to speak to anyone of the miracle he had witnessed until the day of his (Willibrord's) death.

22. Echternach: the land for this house was donated by Irmina and her daughter Plektrude, the wife of Pepin II, as well as by Pepin himself and his son Charles Martel. Here is another measure of the Carolingian connection with Willibrord and his mission.

19

A further miracle of the same kind was wrought by Christ our God through Willibrord's blessing. On one occasion the servant of God came with his companions to the house of a friend of his and wished to break the tedium of the long journey by taking a meal at his friend's house. But it came to his ears that the head of the house had no wine. He gave orders that four small flasks, which were all that his companions carried with them for their needs on the journey, should be brought to him. Then he blessed them in the name of Him who at the marriage feast of Cana changed water into wine—and, remarkable to relate, after this gracious blessing about forty people drank their fill from these small bottles, and with great thanksgiving and joyful hearts said one to another: "The Lord Jesus has in truth fulfilled His promise in the Gospel: 'He who believes in me will also do the works that I do, and greater works than these will he do' " (Jn 14.12).

20

Once, when this holy preacher was going in haste toward Frisia in order, as usual, to preach the Gospel, he wanted to pasture his horses, worn out by the fatigue of the journey, in the meadows of a certain wealthy landowner. The man, seeing horses feeding in his meadows, began to beat them and drive them out of his pastures with great arrogance. The man of God accosted him with peaceable words and said: "Brother, do us no harm. Our purpose in wishing to rest in these meadows is not to do you harm but to meet our own needs. We are under obligation to pursue the work of God, and you also might share in its rewards if, as far as lies in your power, you help us in a friendly spirit, mindful of the sweet promise of Christ: 'He who receives you receives me, and he who receives me receives him who sent me' (Mt 10.40). Be at peace, and rather as a friend take a drink with us by way of refreshment. Then when we have gone on our way, return to your house with the blessing of God." The man, however, persisted in his ill-will and would not listen to the reasonable words of the man of God, but, on the contrary, repeated his abuse and continued to insult him. "You ask me to drink with you," he said, "and make peace: be assured that I set no store whatever upon drinking with you." The man of God took the words out of his mouth and said: "If you will not drink with me, then do not drink at all." Thereupon, as soon as his companions were ready, he went on his way. The obstinate man also hurriedly went home, but was seized almost at once with a burning thirst which he tried in vain to assuage with wine, for the mouth that had cast reproaches upon the man of God was unable to swallow a single draught. Thus the man who would not of his own accord make peace with the servant of God was now compelled to bear within himself the penalty of his fault. Doctors were called to relieve his thirst and to restore to the sufferer his power of drinking. His whole being cried out for relief, but no one could get a drop of wine to reach his parched throat. At last, struck with remorse, he came to his senses, and, discovering that the saintly man he had reviled was Willibrord, he began to yearn intensely for his return. In the following year, Willibrord came back by the same way, and on hearing of his approach the sick man hurried out to meet him. Confessing his sin and telling him of the suffering he had endured, he besought him for the love of Christ to release him from it. The man of God was moved with pity, released him from his punishment and allowed him to drink from his own cup. Thereupon the man who was released drank and returned to his own house cured.

21

In the town of Trier[23] there is a convent of nuns, which in the days of Willibrord was visited with a terrible plague. Many of the nuns died of the infection, others were confined to bed by severe sickness, while the rest were in a state of extreme terror, expecting death at any moment. At a short distance from this town stands the monastery of the holy man, called Echternach, in which his body reposes to this day and which his successors are known to have held by lawful bequest of the said father and through the goodwill of pious kings. Learning that the holy man was coming thither, the women of the above-mentioned convent sent a deputation beseeching him to come to them without delay. When he heard their request, the man of God, instructed by the gracious example of Saint Peter, prince of the apostles, who went from Joppa to Lydda at the request of the widows of Christ in order to raise holy Tabitha to life (see Acts 9.36–42),[24] went to their assistance without delay. On arriving at the convent, he immediately celebrated Mass for the sick and then blessed water and ordered it to be sprinkled about the buildings and given to the nuns to drink. Through the mercy of God they speedily recovered and there were no more deaths in that convent from the plague.

23. On the Moselle River, very near Echternach.

24. Notice how, in relating this miracle, Alcuin draws a parallel between Saint Peter and Willibrord, strengthening thereby the connection between Petrine Rome and the Frankish world.

22

It happened that a head of a family and his household were afflicted by a terrible visitation of devilish sorcery, and it became quite obvious from the horrors and evil tricks that occurred there that the house was haunted by a wicked spirit. For it would suddenly seize food and clothing and other household goods and throw them into the fire. Once, indeed, while the parents were asleep, it snatched their little boy as he rested in their arms and hurled him into the fire, and it was only with great difficulty that the parents, roused by the child's screams, rescued him from the flames. Many were the ill turns that the family had to endure at the hands of this execrable spirit and no priest was able to exorcize it. Eventually the holy man Willibrord, at the father's urgent request, sent them some holy water and directed them to sprinkle it over all the furniture after it had been taken out of doors, for the man of God foresaw that the whole house would be consumed by fire. When they had done this, a conflagration broke out in the very place where the bed had stood, and, quickly enveloping the house, reduced it to ashes. After another house had been built on the site of the old one and blessed with holy water the family suffered no more from their former trial and thenceforth lived in peace, giving thanks to the Lord who had deigned to deliver them through the hands of His servant.

23

The same holy man, who was pleasing to God, also prophesied certain things that were subsequently verified by the course of events. He baptized Pepin the Short,[25] son of the valiant Charles Martel, leader of the Franks and father of the present illustrious Charles, who reigns over the Franks at the present day in triumph, dignity, and glory. Of Pepin, father of the last named, Willibrord uttered the following prediction in the presence of his disciples: "Know that this child will be highly exalted and renowned. He will be greater than all the leaders of the Franks who have gone before him." The truth of this prophecy has been fulfilled in our times and there is no need to prove what is universally acknowledged throughout the whole kingdom. For all the people know what wonderful victories this illustrious conqueror has gained, how widely he has extended the bounds of his empire, how devotedly he has promoted the Chris-

25. Pepin III, mayor of the palace (741–751), then king of the Franks (751–768). The reader has met him often in the lives of Boniface and Sturm. As Alcuin notes, he was the father of Charlemagne.

tian religion and how he has defended the Holy Church of God abroad. All these things can be more clearly seen with the eye than set forth in words.

24

Now this holy man was distinguished by every kind of natural quality: he was of middle height, dignified mien, comely of face, cheerful in spirit, wise in counsel, pleasing in speech, grave in character, and energetic in everything he undertook for God. His forbearance is shown by the actions we have recorded above. How great was his zeal in preaching the Gospel of Christ and how he was sustained in the labor of preaching by the grace of God we need not set forth in writing, since it is vouched for by the testimony of all. His personal life can be inferred from his vigils and prayers, his fasting and singing of psalms, the holiness of his conduct and his many miracles. His charity is made manifest in the unremitting labors which he bore daily for the name of Christ.

This holy man, who progressed every day of his life in the work of God, who was pleasing to God and friendly to all the people, was laid to his fathers in the time of the elder Charles, the valiant leader of the Franks. He was then an old man coming to the end of his days and was about to receive from God a generous reward for his labors. He forsook this world to take possession of heaven and to behold Christ for ever in eternal glory, in whose love he had never ceased to labor as long as he lived in our midst. On the sixth of November, that is, the eighth day before the Ides, he passed from this place of pilgrimage to the eternal country and was buried in the monastery of Echternach, which, as we have said before, he had built to the glory of God. There to this day, through the mercy of God, miracles of healing are constantly performed beside the relics of the holy priest of God. That some of these should be appended to our account of his life we regard as redounding to the glory of our Lord Jesus Christ, who so often deigned to perfom them at the request of His servant.

25

His venerable body was laid to rest in a marble sarcophagus, which at first was found to be six inches too short to hold the entire body of God's servant. The brethren were greatly concerned at this, and, being at a loss to know what to do, they discussed the matter again and again, wondering where they could find a suitable resting-place for his sacred remains. Wonderful to relate, however, through the loving-kindness of God the sarcophagus was suddenly discovered to be as much longer than the holy man's body as previously it had been shorter. Therein they laid the remains of the man of God, and to the accompaniment of hymns and psalms and every token of respect it was interred in the church of the monastery that he had built and dedicated in honor of the Blessed Trinity. A sweet and marvelous fragrance filled the air, so that all were conscious that the ministry of angels had been present at the last rites of the holy man.

26

The death of the holy man was revealed to one of his religious disciples who was stationed at some distance from the monastery as he was keeping watch in prayer. He testifies that he saw the soul of his saintly father surrounded by a bright radiance as it was being carried by a host of angels toward the realms above, all singing his praises. Likewise many of the brothers have testified that they have frequently seen a wonderful light over the bed on which he gave back his blessed soul to his Creator, and perceived there a ravishing fragrance and most sweet odor. From these signs one can only surmise that the denizens of heaven used to visit the spot from which his saintly soul had passed to the Lord.

27

Many sick persons, through the grace of God and assisted by their own faith, have been cured after being anointed with the oil from the lamp that burns over the relics of the holy man. Penitents also frequently came to the church wearing rings on their arms, as the custom then was, and the links were broken and they were loosed from their bonds. Evidence of this are the rings that hang in the church to this day.

28

There was a certain woman suffering from paralysis and who had been tormented for seven years with severe pain, whose infirmity had increased so much from day to day that she had completely lost the use of her limbs and had to rely upon the help of others. So frail was she that she could scarcely breathe. This woman was carried by her relatives to the church in which the saint of God lay at rest and placed near the casket of his relics. There, with many tears, she prayed that God in His mercy might have pity on her through the intercession of His holy servant. Her prayer was heard by the Lord our God, and suddenly she was delivered from all her infirmities and restored to health. And she, who had previously been carried into the church by others, ran home upon her own feet, joyfully giving thanks to God.

29

In like manner a young man afflicted with sickness was brought by his friends to the body of the blessed prelate. He trembled in every limb and was totally unable to raise his head, which lolled and twisted this way and that as if it had not been fixed on his neck. Sometimes, too, he became so inert as to appear completely lifeless. This young man, as we have said, was placed near the body of the saint by his friends, and through the mercy of God was so quickly cured, in the presence of all the onlookers, that no trace remained of his former infirmity and long-standing affliction.

30

A certain man who held the office of deacon in the church of the saint (though he was quite unworthy of it) did not scruple to steal, among other things that had been offered to the church, a golden cross that the holy man used to carry with him on his travels. The brethren were distressed at this, and, though ignorant of the perpetrator of this sacrilege, they felt confident that through the prayers of the saint of God so heinous a crime could not long be concealed. They tried, nevertheless, in their brotherly kindness to bring the culprit to repentance, not wishing to encompass his downfall. But the man who had committed the crime hardened his heart and despised his own salvation, even as, according to Solomon, "When wickedness comes, contempt comes also, and with dishonor comes disgrace" (Prv 18.3). The unhappy wretch thought that the deed, which had been committed in secret and unseen by others, would remain undetected, but it could not be hidden from the eye of God, to whom all things lie open and who is often not slow to avenge the wrongs done to His servants. For the miserable wretch who had not scrupled to commit the offense was suddenly seized with sickness and died a miserable death, and in his dying moments confessed his guilt to some of the brethren and divulged the place where he had hidden the stolen objects. You see, brethren, what a fearful judgment was visited upon the man who presumed to desecrate the church of God's saint by stealing. I beseech you, therefore, to keep your manner of life pure in this house, so that in His mercy and through the intercession of the apostolic man Saint Clement He may deign to hear your prayers when you make your petitions, just as we have already told you how he heard the prayers of the sick in this same church, enabling them to return home with the good health they had long yearned for. Nor need we doubt that just as he deigned visibly to heal their bodily diseases, so also through the intercession of the saint on our behalf, whose body rests here and whom we believe to be present in the spirit, listening to our prayers, he will continue daily to cure the hidden disorders of our souls, if with firm faith and sincere confession we pour out our hearts with tears in that place before the merciful face of Him who in His mercy is quick to pardon if we are not slow to ask. Praise and glory be His for ever and ever.

31

It only remains now to speak of blessed Wilgils, who, as we have said, was the father of this holy man, for as the first chapter of this story began with him, so the last must close with a reference to him. It was on the anniversary of the sacred death of Wilgils that the good abbot Aldberct, successor to the venerable archbishop, proposed to eat and rejoice with the brethren after the solemnities of the Mass and the thanksgiving due to God. In the monastery, unfortunately, there were left only two flagons of wine; and since one of them had been drunk at the midday meal, the other was put by for supper. Accordingly, after vespers had been sung in honor of that day the brethren returned to the refectory; and when they came to the end of the reading the abbot addressed the brethren with these words: "It is fitting, reverend Fathers, that we should celebrate the feast days of our venerable predecessors with spiritual rejoicing and should allow our bodies somewhat more indulgence than our usual strictness permits, not from motives of gluttony but of love. Now if there were anything in the monastery that I could offer you beyond this single flagon of wine that is left over from the midday meal I should certainly not withhold it from you. But God is able through the prayer of His saints to make even this prove more than sufficient for our needs, alike to honor them as to gladden us, and to demonstrate to us, unworthy as we are, the kindly power of Him who once through the blessing of our former father, the holy Willibrord, condescended to satisfy forty men from four flagons. Let us drink what we have with rejoicing and with hope."

After all the brethren had drunk from the bottle a first and a second time the server found it as full as before. When the abbot was acquainted with this he joined the brethren in giving thanks to God; and, doing honor to the divine mercy, they drank soberly but gladly that night as much as they desired.

O happy father to beget such a son and to be deemed worthy by God of having such an heir! In thee is fulfilled the blessing that is read in Deuteronomy: "Blessed shall you be and . . . blessed shall be the fruit of your body" (Dt 28:3–4).

Ardo

THE LIFE OF SAINT BENEDICT, ABBOT OF ANIANE AND OF INDE

Translated by Allen Cabaniss

In the long history of Benedictine monasticism Benedict of Aniane is second in importance only to the founder himself. Therefore Ardo's *Life* of the saint is a text of capital significance to historians. Its significance would be even greater if more were known about its author.

In his own prefatory remarks to Benedict's *Life* Ardo tells us almost all that we can now know about him. He was a monk of Aniane, he knew Benedict, and he had witnessed a number of the events about which he wrote. He was requested to write this text by some monks of Inde. Inde was a monastery situated very near to the Carolingian capital at Aachen. Louis the Pious (814–840), Charlemagne's son and successor, built the monastery for Benedict who was, from 814 to 821, Louis's chief adviser on religious affairs. The Inde monks had jotted down a few accounts of Benedict, including, it seems, many of the miracle accounts included by Ardo, and they passed them along to the monk of Aniane. Perhaps it was assumed that more information would have been available at Aniane, the monastery of which Benedict had been abbot since at least 782.

Why Ardo? We do not know. Not a single fact about his life, other than his authorship of this important *Life*, has come to light. Aniane was not a major intellectual center and Ardo's Latin is, one might say, unreformed. That is, while Ardo writes a Latin that is clear, vigorous, and perfectly capable of conveying his meaning without confusion or ambiguity, it is not the polished, even classicizing, Latin associated with major centers of the Carolingian Renaissance. The point is that even if Ardo was regarded as something of a scholar at Aniane, Aniane was evidently something of a backwater in terms of Carolingian culture. Even backwaters have their interest, however. Ardo's work is full of faint classical allusions. Some aspects of the Carolingian intellectual reform had obviously touched him even if they had not dramatically affected his syntax. Ardo was also very familiar with the major conventions of hagiography. Ardo's achievement in creating a hagiographical portrait of Benedict should not be underestimated.

Benedict (c. 750–821) was a nobleman who had a secular career before embracing the ascetic life. He twice changed his mode of spiritual existence, moving from extreme, individual asceticism to communal Benedictine monasticism. But Benedict did not live peacefully in his community. He was constantly drawn into the wider world of Carolingian public life. It is good for the modern reader, and revealing of Ardo's skill, that our author did not adopt one hagiographic model and, as if it were a procrustean bed, cut Benedict to fit it. Instead, he measured his subject against several models and in the process created a more interesting text and a satisfying portrait of a major historical figure.

Texts and References

The Latin text of Wilhelm Wattenbach, *Vita Benedicti abbatis Anianensis et Indensis,* Monumenta Germaniae Historica, vol. 15, part 1, pp. 200–220 is still standard. Virtually nothing has been written on Ardo. Franz Brunhölzl, *Geschichte der lateinischen Literatur des Mittelalters,* 2 vols. (Munich, 1975) 1:443–44 is useful as is Allen Cabaniss, *The Emperor's Monk: Contemporary Life of Benedict of Aniane by Ardo* (Ilfracombe, 1979), 30–37. Benedict of Aniane has not been the subject of a full-scale modern study. A good introduction is C. H. Lawrence, *Medieval Monasticism,* 2d ed. (London, 1989), 77–82. Standard encyclopedias and major church histories can also be relied upon to provide basic details on his life and achievements.

PREFACE

To the venerable masters, fathers, and brothers serving God Jesus at the monastery of Inde, Ardo, servant of Christ's servants, sends greetings.

A long time ago, my beloved brothers, your letters were delivered to me, letters full of love for the pious memory of our Father Abbot Benedict. They contained briefly but livingly an account of his death and departure to Christ. In them you deigned to suggest to my littleness that I write more elaborately for those who want to hear about the beginning of his manner of life. Thus far, however, I have demurred, being aware of the burden on my abilities.

If only by perceptive zeal care could be taken by those composing a life of persons who went before—a life respected for merits and famed for virtues— not to overlook profitable matters when led to do so by partiality; if they could write with fluent pen only matters scrupulously ascertained and confirmed by report of trustworthy witnesses, they would not embarrass the ears of scholars by offering the blemish of inelegance. They would present words savoring of witty urbanity and with polished language titillate the ears of detractors.

But conscious of my shortcomings, I have long maintained silence even though persuaded to acquiesce in your request. I have refrained so that it might be expressed by more learned persons, believing that it was surely unfair for me with inept verbiage to touch the life of so great a patron. I have deferred the appropriate task to more skillful writers. With flowing supply of words they can make clear (and even with a flourish) whatever they wish, since they have nothing to fear. They can steer the vessel between the sandbanks and avoid the bad odor of grammatical errors. Gifted with facility of language they have that abundance of speech that checks the tongues of detractors.

I was fearful that readers, irritated at what was badly constructed, might seek to correct clumsy composition. They would thus adjudge the content to be ignored, especially since I knew that you were present at the entrance to the sacred hall of the palace,[1] that you thirsted for no drink of boisterous streams, but eagerly drained the flow of wisdom from an unfailing watercourse of the purest fountain. Such reasoning restrained me for the space of a year.

In the meanwhile you brothers undertook to rouse my lethargic inclination with stinging words, you brothers whom with holy endeavor Benedict begot for Christ. You constrained me to bring him to life for you by tales of his life in religion. It is certain that you are absent from him only in fellowship with his bodily presence, not in fullness of charity. So I am finally about to unfold a

---

1. He means that Inde was very near the Carolingian capital at Aachen.

composition. Even the place, originally erected by him, and the brothers, who knew the beginning of his way of life, have given me a bold and favorable purpose. For what to some can scarcely be unheard, can by them hardly be unseen. Since the materials have been comprehensively assembled, we are ready to disclose more elaborately those that are suitable for the task. We severely confine as it were a seedbed as we are about to publish it more widely.

We humbly beg that if anyone finds this work distasteful he will leave it alone or correct it. Otherwise he may allow others to read and study it while he turns himself to reading the life of earlier fathers. But if he should find that this man did not stray from their path and influence, let him be glad. If he must refute it, let it not be a hasty judgment. Let him interrupt himself and refer it tearfully to the just and peaceful Judge.

Since I have obeyed your request, holy brothers, I ask you to aid me by prayers to God for pardon of my faults and for future readers to make progress by reading this book. I beg you to read it with watchful zeal. Correct in detail whatever you may show to be in error. If there are useful matters in it, cherish them in the secret of your breast. By removing the force of silence we have at your command provided a mood, if not an outward act. But you must attribute our speaking to yourselves, remembering that you compelled us to break silence.

Abbot Helisachar[2] clung to Benedict with a disposition of unique love as he left this world—so the abbot's letter, more precious than gold, addressed to us bears witness. For that reason, after you have examined this book, I think it should be presented to him in particular. Should he decide for it to be suppressed, I beg forgiveness for my error. But should he deem it useful, let those who freely obeyed Benedict when he was alive, now devote themselves to imitating his life although he is absent.

Every scholar knows, I suppose, that there is a very ancient custom, still practiced by kings, for matters that are done or events that occur to be committed to annals for the information of future generations. The mind becomes blind to various happenings when forgetfulness supervenes. We therefore believe it divinely planned for things to be preserved in records so that obliging forgetfulness and scurrying time may not efface them. Those who desire to read such chronicles take pleasure in them. They are gladdened and they turn themselves to expressions of gratitude. An author of such a record is not

2. He was abbot of the important monastery of Saint Riquier (in southern Flanders near the coast of the English Channel) and chancellor to Louis the Pious (r. 814–840), Charlemagne's son and successor. An Aquitainian like Benedict, he had long been associated with the new emperor.

judged rash by them even if it does not resound with polished words and even if an avid reading of it may require great exertion.

Let them agree with us both to read the life of those going before us and to entrust to posterity what in our own times we have seen or heard so as to spur souls on to progress. Let us who emit the odor of crudity not be condemned for unskilled language. We deem it sufficient to draw forth a salutary patter albeit with rude words and to exhibit delicious honey in rough honeycombs. Let each one take by his own choice what he finds acceptable to his mind.[3]

1

That venerable man, by name and merit Abbot Benedict, was sprung from the nation of the Goths in the area of Gothia.[4] Born of noble origin he was, but heavenly religion ennobled him by even greater brilliance of character. His father held the county of Maguelonne as long as he lived. With all his might he was loyal to the nation of Franks.[5] He was courageous and clever, and to enemies very dangerous. With vast slaughter, as everyone knows, he overthrew the Basques who entered the frontiers of the Frankish realm to lay it waste. None escaped except the one who was saved by precipitate flight. He entrusted his aforesaid son, while still in boyhood years, to the court of glorious King Pepin[6] to be brought up amid the queen's scholars.[7] Bearing his age with natural quality of mind, Benedict was beloved by his comrades in arms. He was of nimble wit and adaptable in everything. Later he received the office of cupbearer.[8] He performed military service in the days of the aforesaid king. After the latter's death and the accession of most glorious King Charles,[9] Benedict was attached to him in service.

3. Ardo's Latin culture may have been somewhat deficient, but this did not prevent him from drawing out his opening modesty topos to vast proportions.

4. A region lying astride the Pyrenees in southern Gaul and northeastern Spain. It got its name when many Visigoths fled into the area after the Muslim invasion of Spain in 711.

5. The Carolingian family in particular forged close bonds with many families from southern France.

6. Pepin III, 751–768.

7. Noble families often sent sons to the household of a more powerful person, partly for training and partly to grow accustomed to other youth of like age and background. Note how the role of Pepin's wife—Bertrada—is emphasized. In noble households, women had primary responsibility for educating the youth present.

8. It was normal for sons of aristocrats to be assigned largely ceremonial offices at court such as cupbearer, butler, doorkeeper, and the like.

9. Charlemagne, king of the Franks (768–800), emperor (800–814).

In the meanwhile divine grace enlightened him. He began to blaze with heavenly love to abandon this flaming world with all its exertions and to shun that perishable honor, which he realized one could attain with effort, but once gained could quickly lose. Brooding over this in his heart for a period of three years, he kept it secret except from God. He continued to associate himself in body, though not in mind, with activities of the world. During that interval he tried to grasp the pinnacle of continence, to deprive his body of sleep, to check his tongue, to abstain from food, to take wine sparingly, and to prepare himself like a skilled athlete for future struggle. While still in secular habit he pondered those matters he afterward fulfilled with devotion.

Although he wanted to divest himself of activities of the world, he hesitated about the ways in which that could be done: whether to assume the habit of a pilgrim, or perhaps attach himself to someone to take care of men's sheep and cattle without pay, or even to engage in the shoemaker's craft in some city and spend on poor folk whatever profit he might be able to gain. While his mind was vacillating in such debate, he turned himself to love of life under the Rule.

2

In the year that Italy was made subject to the sway of glorious King Charles,[10] Benedict's brother sought recklessly to ford a certain river, but he was caught up in the swelling waves. Benedict was sitting on his horse watching when he perceived his brother's peril, but he plunged headlong into the flood to rescue the drowning exile from danger. As his horse swam forward Benedict grasped his brother's hand. The brother took hold and held on desperately. He who wanted to rescue the drowning man barely escaped death. Then and there Benedict bound himself by a vow to God not to serve the world any further. He returned to his homeland but did not tell his father about his intention.

Now there was a certain religious named Widmar who lacked bodily sight, but in his heart shone with light. To him Benedict revealed his desire. Widmar kept the secret and offered salutary counsel. When everything was ready, Benedict undertook a journey as though to go to Aachen. But when he reached the house of Saint Seine,[11] he ordered his companions to return to their native country, then announced that he wanted to serve God the Christ in that monastery. He thereupon requested permission to enter. When that was ob-

10. 773–774.
11. In Dijon, in Burgundy.

tained, he soon laid aside the hair of his head[12] and put on the habit of a true monk.

When Benedict became a monk he proceeded to damage his body with incredible fasting for the space of two years and six months. In that way he was, of course, endangering his own flesh as if it were a bloodthirsty beast. He took scanty food, sustaining his body with bread and water to avert death but not hunger, shunning wine as if it were a noxious poison. When his mind was overpowered and he sought a little sleep, he would rest for a short while by lying down on a cheap quilt. Sometimes prostrate on the bare ground, he rested when excessively exhausted, but only in order to fatigue himself even more by such rest. Often spending the whole night in prayer he kept himself awake by standing with bare feet on the pavement in the icy cold. He devoted himself so completely to divine meditation that he would continue many days in sacred psalms without breaking the rule of silence.

While others were asleep he cleaned their shoes with water and oiled them, then returned them to their proper places. Certain ones, alas, like jeering madmen, threw their boots at him as he stood some distance away. Their insane foolishness he endured with lofty serenity and high purpose. In his own clothing he reduced himself with such disregard that it was scarcely possible for those, who did not know better, to be persuaded that it was as it appeared. He had a cheap old tunic that he did not change until many days had elapsed. Inevitably a colony of lice grew on his filthy skin, feeding on his limbs emaciated by fasts. His cowls were threadbare with extreme age. When the old threads were finally broken, he patched the rent with any available rag even if of a different color, a fact that rendered him somewhat unsightly. He was, therefore, ridiculed, shoved, spat upon by many people, but his mind, fixed upon heaven, sought even cheaper materials. On festal days, when others put on neater clothes, he wore his old ones without any timidity. During that period he never indulged his body in baths. Yet he employed himself for the cleanliness of the monastery as often as opportunity demanded.

The grace of compunction and divine help were granted to him in such large measure that he could weep at will. In fear of Gehenna[13] he was daily sustained by tears and groans as he sang lovingly the Davidic words, "For I eat ashes like bread, and mingle tears with my drink" (Ps 102.9). His face grew gaunt with fasting; his flesh was exhausted by privation; his shriveled skin hung from his

12. That is, he was tonsured. See above, page 194, note 6.

13. A word that appears frequently in the Bible signifying a cursed place; sometimes interpreted as hell, although this was not its original meaning.

bones like the dewlaps of cows. Not so much taming a young but ungovernable animal, as mortifying the body, he was compelled by the abbot to exercise rigor against himself more sparingly. But he did not in any way express agreement. Declaring that the Rule of blessed Benedict was for beginners and weak persons, he strove to climb up to the precepts of blessed Basil and the rule of blessed Pachomius.[14] However much the Benedictine Rule might regulate things for paltry people, our Benedict perennially explored more impossible things.[15] Dedicating himself wholly to penance and lamentation, he could not be imitated by anyone or only by a few. But divine favor decreed that he would become an example of salvation for many. He was inflamed with love of the Rule of Benedict, and like a new athlete just back from single combat he entered the field to fight publicly. In the meanwhile he undertook to correct the manners of some, to scold the negligent, exhort beginners, admonish the upright to persevere, and upbraid the wicked to turn from their ways.

After that it was enjoined upon him to supervise the cellar. There he committed to memory the Rule of the aforesaid Father Benedict. According to its regulations he sought with all his might to establish himself firmly, then without delay to be generous to those seeking lawful things, to deny those seeking in a bad way, and courteously to make excuse for those inquiring for impossible things. Because he did not freely provide them cups, he was not regarded with favor by many. The care of guests, children, and poor folk he exercised with assiduity. Moreover the abbot esteemed him with supreme fondness, because he was beneficial in everything, circumspect in his own life, solicitous for the salvation of others, prompt in ministering, infrequent in speaking, ready to obey, good-natured in serving. Divine pity conferred on him, among other virtues, the gift of understanding and a supply of spiritual eloquence.[16]

3

The space of five years and eight months having flown by in salutary manner, the abbot of that monastery departed from the world. With one mind and joint

14. See above, pages xi and 2–3.

15. In addition to describing Benedict's early preference for rigorous forms of monasticism, Ardo engages here in a bit of verbal play. The Rule of Saint Benedict itself is called by its author (chap. 73) "a little rule for beginners." It is a commonplace of monastic literature that the truly holy will strive for ever stricter regimes of personal renunciation.

16. This passage need not be taken literally as Ardo is simply attributing to Benedict the very qualities to which the Rule of Saint Benedict invites monks to aspire.

agreement all chose Benedict to be set over them. But knowing that there was no compatibility between their manner and his, he hurriedly set out toward his paternal soil. There, on property belonging to his father and himself, at the brook called Aniane near the river Saône, he along with Widmar and a few others erected for their residence a small hut close to the modest church of Saint Saturninus.[17] For several years he lived there in great poverty. For nights and days he entreated divine clemency with groanings and tears for his desire to effect powerful fruition. At the same time in that province there were certain active men of great holiness, namely, Atilio, Nibridius, and Anianus,[18] living a religious life, but unaware of supervision by the Rule. When Benedict became known to them, they held him in high esteem. When adverse influence tried to overcome him, he would saddle his little donkey quickly and hurry away to Atilio, his nearest neighbor.

At first many who abandoned the world attempted to live the religious life with him. But weak in spirit and afraid of a new manner of life when compelled to embrace an unheard-of way of abstinence, such as receiving bread by weight and wine by measure, they soon retraced their steps that they once set on the road to salvation, and returned like swine to mire and a dog to his vomit (see 2 Pt 2.22). The man of God observed their unsteady faith and being disturbed decided to go back to his own monastery.

For that reason Benedict approached Atilio for counsel. When he related his wish, Atilio scolded him, "It has been revealed to me from heaven that you are given to men as a lamp (see Acts 13.47). It would be fitting for you to complete the good work (see Phil 1.6) you have begun. This trouble has come to pass by deceit of the ancient enemy who always grudges, always hates good deeds. No concession should ever be made to him." Bolstered by Atilio's advice, Benedict fearlessly applied himself with ardent spirit to what he longed to accomplish. Not building upon another's foundation, he began with new endeavor to erect houses as well as to expound the strange new way of salvation.

4

A few brothers assembled about him, indeed flocked to him, when his belief become known; and the venerable Benedict began to flourish in holy religion

17. The foundation of Aniane, here recorded, must have taken place in about 780. Presumably five years and eight months had passed since Benedict, after his brother's accident in the year of Charlemagne's conquest of Italy (773–774), had decided to devote his life to God.

18. The lives of these three men cannot be reconstructed. They may have been fellow Gothic noblemen.

at that place. He was free to expound the heavenly road to those who wanted it and to labor with his own hands. Lest as he preached to others he should be found dishonest, he took care to fulfill what Atilio had warned him should be pursued. For he did not through fear of want give up the work he had begun. On the contrary, as the apostle says, beset by hunger and thirst, in cold and nakedness (see 2 Cor 11.27), he urged his subordinates to persist with untroubled heart, teaching that the way that leads to life is constricted and narrow (see Mt 7.14), that the sufferings of this time are not comparable to future glory that will be revealed to the holy ones (see Rom 8.18). Strengthened by his example, his students yearned to be exhausted by even heavier labors.

At that time they had no possessions, no vineyards, no cattle, no horses. There was only one small donkey. By its help the weariness of the brothers was relieved when it was necessary for them in turn to travel any distance. They received wine only on Lord's days and festivals. Their hunger was occasionally assuaged with milk brought by neighboring women. They wasted their bodies by dehydration, living only on bread and water. To ward off the constant cold, they used blankets when they attended divine vigils. They were indeed poor in possessions, but wealthy in merits. The more their bodies were impaired with want, the more their souls were fattened with virtues. They glowed with heavenly love; tears alone brought them consolation in their poverty. The ancient foe, observing their unconquered brotherly unity, strove to divide it by craft.

They had only one mill nearby in which they ground what provisions they might have. One night a visitor, goaded by mean thoughts, came to them. They made him as comfortable as possible in the donkey's stall. But, watching with evil intent, he got up as soon as they were asleep and left, taking along what he lay on, the jug from which he drank water, and even the tools of the mill, thus repaying evil for good. The next morning the students reported to the master the loss they had discovered. He taught them to endure with goodwill injuries inflicted on them and to consider losses as gain (see Phil 3:7f.), protesting to them rather to grieve for him who forgot faith while straining to take advantage.

5

In the meanwhile the band of students began gradually to increase. The fame of holy religion began by degrees to flit by the mouths of those dwelling nearby, spreading itself to places a long distance away. Because the valley in which he had made his first residence was very narrow, he undertook little by little to erect by new effort a monastery beyond its confines. Sometimes he labored with the brothers as they worked; sometimes he had his hands full with cooking food for them to eat, while at the same time he was also occupied even in the kitchen with writing a book. Often because of scarcity of oxen he carried wood on his own shoulders along with his students.

There was a building on the place where they were endeavoring to establish the monastery that they expanded and dedicated in honor of holy Mary Mother of God. Since they were flocking thither from everywhere, begging zealously to submit themselves to his superintendency, the fabric of the monastery was quickly completed. The place was endowed and increased with properties as various persons offered what they had. Benedict had given order not to cover or make the houses with ornate walls, red roof tiles, or painted panelings, but with thatch and cheap timber. Although the number of brothers was rapidly expanding, he still strove for cheaper and more modest materials.

If anyone wanted to bestow some of his possessions on the monastery, Benedict took it. But if a person pressed to attach servingmen and women to it, he refused. He moreover permitted no one to be delivered to the monastery by charter, but ordered them to be set free. For himself he preferred that vessels for the body of Christ not be of silver. To him first choice was wooden vessels, second glass, and finally tin. He refused to have a silken chasuble.[19] If some person gave him one, he immediately gave it away to others.

6

In the meantime in the same region or thereabout some religious men constructed monasteries and assembled monks, disciplining themselves according to the blessed man's example. Steeped in his instruction, they pruned away their former life and old errors. To them he was like a father, bringing assistance and support not only in spiritual matters, but also in material. Often visiting them he urged them not to abandon the work they had begun lest the spirit, oppressed by want and worn by terrors, might look backward. And so monasteries, sustained by wholesome testimony, became numerous and the multitude of monks was at a peak.

19. The outer vestment worn by a priest when celebrating mass.

7

At the same time a severe famine occurred.[20] Many poor folk, widows, and orphans began to pour upon him and to fill the gates and roads of the monastery. When he saw them languishing for lack of nourishment, almost swallowed up by death itself, he was troubled because he did not know how he could feed such a number. But since nothing is lacking to those who fear God, whatever new fruits they might lay hands on to suffice the brothers he ordered to be set aside separately. He then gave command to distribute the rest through brothers designated for each day. Meat of cattle and sheep was given out every day and even goat's milk provided sustenance. They made huts for themselves in suitable places where they could dwell until the new harvests.

When food began to fail, Benedict gave another order to measure out what he had commanded to be set aside for the brothers' use. That was done three times. Among the brothers the mood of pity was so strong that they would have weighed out everything if it had been permitted. What each one was entitled to withdraw for himself, he secretly allotted to those consumed with hunger. Even so they were barely rescued from the peril of famine, for several times a man was found dead although there was bread in his mouth.

8

I do not think one should maintain silence when at the same time the baneful doctrine of Felicianism[21] invaded that province. Unharmed by the noxious error of unbelief, Benedict avoided it inwardly by divine help and by his zeal rescued not only the lowliest, but also prelates of the church. Armed with javelins of debate he often joined battle against the infamous doctrine.

There was at that time also a band of brothers already numerous and inflamed with ardor for eternal life. They vied indeed who of them might be humbler, who prompter in obedience, who more zealous in abstinence, who more forward in vigils, who slower to speak, who cheaper in dress, and who more fervent in charity. Revelations were also made to certain ones.

20. Probably in 793.

21. Bishop Felix of Urgel (d. 818), taking his lead from his metropolitan bishop, Elipandus of Toledo (c. 718–802), taught what theologians call "Adoptionism," namely that Jesus Christ was the son of God by adoption after his birth rather than by conception by the Holy Spirit.

9

There was a certain brother who was by no means disposed to human honor. When Father Benedict noticed that he was making his way apparently negligently, he concluded the same rudeness in his spirit. But caught up in an ecstasy the man saw a flock of doves, some gleaming with marvelous whiteness, some distinguished by an amazing variety of colors, some marked with a repulsive color on the head. Soon he realized what this meant and the names of each were spoken: negligence made some black, zeal made some gleam brightly. Returning to himself (see Lk 15.17), he related to Father Benedict what he had seen and warned him not to despise him. Searching the deeds of each, Benedict then discovered the minds of the brothers distraught just as he learned from the ecstatic and therefore restored them to suitable pattern by imposing a kindly emollient of reproof.

10

The ancient foe tolerated with difficulty the unity and increase of the good flock. He tried to agitate the hearts of certain ones to make the good founder an exile from his own sheepfold. By his craft he drove many away from the monastery and unsettled others. Although he could not dismay the mind prepared for tribulation, he nursed back to life latent forces that were broken and about to perish, by inciting them to take away horses and cattle both secretly and openly. But he who has set God before everything loses without grief what he possessed without love. Certainly no one ever saw Benedict upset over anything that was lost; he never sought to recover what was destroyed; he never looked for what was stolen. If a thief was caught, Benedict offered kindness and quietly released him so he would not be caught again.

11

A certain one who stealthily removed the monastery's horses was captured by neighbors and wounded. When he was brought before Father Benedict, the latter furnished him expenses, summoned a physician, and sent him unharmed to the infirmary.

On another occasion, when the venerable father was making a journey in company with a brother, they met a man astride a horse stolen from the monastery. The brother stared inquiringly and recognized it as one that had been stolen. He immediately blurted out that it was the monastery's horse. But Benedict told him to keep quiet, "One horse is often similar to another." Aside he remonstrated with the brother, "I, too, recognized it, but I think it is better to remain silent than to create a sense of embarrassment."

12

Since Almighty God, who created all things, performs on suitable occasions miracles through His servants, I will compress into a brief narrative some that He wrought through Benedict.

Once upon a time a fire broke out in a house located near the basilica of the Blessed Virgin Mary. When the devouring flame licked at the dry thatch, the grieving brothers ran thither. They watched the house they had built with great labor as it was being consumed by the leaping flames. They busied themselves with earnest zeal to prevent the fire from spreading to the neighboring church, for the whole fury of the flame was tending in that direction. Father Benedict approached the spectacle. At once the brothers importuned him to help them with his prayers. Quickly complying with the brothers' urgency, he threw himself with tears before the altar of the Blessed Virgin Mary Mother of God. While he was praying, the fury of the fire suddenly turned with the aid of divine mercy in another direction.

13

At the same time, too, there was a great flight of locusts that hid the sun's rays with its thickness. They settled in massed attack on the vineyard that lay near the monastery to devastate it. The brothers were accustomed to receive their cups chiefly from it. The venerable man entered the basilica of the Blessed Mother of God and with tear-drenched face and voice implored divine aid. After a little while the locusts became restless and left.

14

By another chance fire attacked a neighboring mountain, licking at the dry straw, the branches, and the earth parched by the sun's heat. Moved by its own impetus, it threatened ruin to the vineyard and monastery. To extinguish it all the brothers gathered. With them came venerable Father Benedict. Suddenly the fire abandoned the path it had begun and quickly subsided on right and left. Except for Benedict's prayers, I think, it must be supposed that conflagration would have prevailed.

15

A certain brother was enjoined to guard the cattle. As he left the monastery to go to his duty, he sought Father Benedict for a blessing. "May the Lord protect you," said the latter as he bestowed the sign of the cross. When the brother reached the pasture, he encountered bandits in this manner. Approaching without any suspicion, he was halted by them. They seized the reins of the horse on which he was sitting. After peering at him a long time in silence, they let him go—and he left in a hurry. When he told the father, the latter remarked, "God's blessing did preserve you unharmed."

16

What I have personally seen should not be passed over in silence. A certain brother was made provost. Falling into pride, he was deposed from his office. At length he became so spiteful that he decided to leave the monastery and practice robbery. Thus it was that he decided to steal a horse surreptitiously from the monastery itself. When he tried to do so, Benedict commanded him to be driven away with his feet tied under the horse. But he began to bawl and swear that he would never depart from the monastery. Because of his folly, Benedict gave order to beat him lightly with switches. Thereafter he remained in the monastery, living properly and piously, as if he himself were the smitten malign foe.

17

Thus far what is said may suffice concerning the life of so great a father as, by the light of divine clemency, he abandoned the world and removed to the regions of Gothia to erect by new endeavor a monastery. Now by Christ's aid we may unfold with clearness how by Charles's command he constructed another monastery in the same place.

In the year 782, the fourteenth of King Charles the Great, Benedict, with dukes and counts aiding him, undertook to construct another large church in honor of our Lord and Savior, but differently. He no longer covered the houses with thatch but with tiles and adorned the cloisters with as many marble columns as possible placed in the porches. The place was furnished by them with such holiness that whoever might seek in faith would come not doubting in his heart, but believing that what he might need would come to pass.

Because it glistened with outstanding religious observance, we deem it appropriate to relate for future generations some things about the location of that place. Venerable Father Benedict decided upon pious reflection to consecrate the aforesaid church not by the title of one of the saints but in the name of the Holy Trinity. For it to be more clearly recognized, he determined that three small altars should be placed near the main altar so that by them the persons of the Trinity may be figuratively indicated. A marvelous arrangement it is: by the three altars the undivided Trinity is shown forth and by the single altar the true Godhead in essence is shown forth. The great altar is one solid surface on the front, but inwardly concave. In figure it suggests what Moses built in the desert. It has a little door behind where on ferial[22] days chests containing various relics of the fathers are enclosed. The foregoing statements suffice concerning the altar.

We now pass briefly to the furnishing of the building, in what order or number it is arranged. All the vessels that are kept in the building are consecrated to the number seven. For instance, there are seven candelabra curiously wrought by the craftsman's art. From the arms project branches, little spheres, with lilies, reeds, and bowls, after the manner of a nut tree, done like that which Bezaleel contrived with his wonderful skill (see Ex 31.2–5, 36.1, 37.17–24). In front of the altar hang seven lamps, marvelous and beautiful, spread with incredible effort, lighted in the manner of Solomon by trained persons eager to tend them.

In the same way other lamps, silver ones, hang in the choir in the form of a crown with containers inserted in circles. It was customary on special feasts to fill them with oil and light them. When they were lighted the whole church was aglow at night as if it were day. Lastly three further altars in the basilica were dedicated, one in honor of Saint Michael the archangel, another in devotion to the blessed apostles Peter and Paul, and a third in honor of good Stephen the protomartyr.

---

22. In ecclesiastical parlance ferial days are days of the week, other than Sundays, on which no church feast occurs.

In the church of Blessed Mary Mother of God which was first established, there are altars of Saint Martin and blessed Benedict. But that one that is built in the cemetery is distinguished in honor of Saint John the Baptist, than whom among those born of women none greater has arisen, as the divine oracles testify (see Mt 11.11). It is appropriate to ponder with what profound humility and reverence this place was feared by them, this place protected by so many princes. The Lord Christ is indeed the Prince of all princes, King of kings, the Lord of lords. Blessed Mary Mother of God is held to be queen of all virgins. Michael is placed over all angels. Peter and Paul are chiefs of the apostles. Stephen the protomartyr holds first place in the choir of witnesses. Martin shines as a gem of prelates. Benedict is father of all monks.[23] By the seven altars, by the seven candelabra, and by the seven lamps, the sevenfold grace of the Holy Spirit is understood.

18

Whoever he is who seeks to read or listen to this biography, let him realize that Aniane is the head of all monasteries, not only of those erected in the regions of Gothia, but also of those erected in other areas at that time or afterward according to the example of this one and enriched with the treasures of Benedict, as this document will hereinafter relate. He gave his heart to studying the Rule of blessed Benedict. To be able fully to understand it, he visited various monasteries and inquired of any skilled persons what he did not know. He assembled the rules of all the holy ones as he was successful in discovering them.[24] He taught a useful standard and wholesome custom for monasteries which he transmitted to his own monks to be observed. He established cantors, taught lectors, secured grammarians, and scholars in scriptural knowledge. From them certain ones became bishops. He collected a multitude of books, assembled costly vestments, large silver chalices, and silver offertory vessels.

Whatever he observed as needful for Divine Office he obtained with enthusiasm. He became known to everyone and the fame of his sanctity reached the ears of the emperor. Later he went to most glorious Emperor Charles for the benefit of the monastery. Moved by pious consideration, Charles granted the monastery to Benedict by charter, so that after the emperor's death the wit-

23. Martin of Tours and Benedict of Nursia.
24. His work of assembling rules resulted in the *Codex Regularum*, a large collection of rules on which he based his later studies of the monastic tradition.

nesses would not permit any disruptions by his successors. From Charles, Benedict soon received an "immunity" containing the following:

"In the name of the holy and undivided Trinity, Charles, by God's grace king of the Franks and Lombards and patrician of the Romans.[25] We believe that fortification of our realm will reach its greatest peak if, with well-wishing devotion, we concede suitable locations as benefits for churches. With the Lord's protection we decree them to endure without variations. Be it therefore known to all bishops, abbots, counts, viscounts, vicars, hundred men, judges, and all the faithful, present and future alike, how the venerable man, Abbot Benedict, came to our clemency from the monastery he himself built up by new effort and by his own right from the foundations in honor of our Lord and Savior, Jesus Christ, of the holy and ever-virgin Mary Mother of God, and of other saints, in the place called Aniane, in the countryside of Maguelonne, near the fortress of Montcalm. With complete purpose he assigned to our hands the aforesaid monastery with all properties and ornaments of the church, whether attached to it or adjacent, and committed that holy place to us to rule with our protection and government.

"At his special petition, therefore, we have granted for the sake of eternal reward a benefit to that holy place in this manner. In respect of churches, places, fields, or other properties of that monastery, which it rightly has in modern times by our gift and confirmation or that of other faithful ones, in whatever locations, whatever has been conferred there for the sake of divine love, whatever else holy religion may hereafter add in the right of that holy place, whether by us or others, we command them to receive. Moreover we pronounce a curse to the effect that no count, bishop, or any judicial authority dare at any time ever to enter or presume to force cases to be heard, taxes to be levied, habitations or provisions to be seized, sponsors to be taken away, people of that monastery, free or servants, who live on its lands to be removed, any cancelled sales or unlawful pretexts to be sought, or any property to be questioned.

"The abbot himself, his successors, and the monks, present or future, may rule the aforesaid place for the sake of God's name under complete immunity without disturbance or opposition by anyone whatever; and they may never dare for any reason to divert its property to anyone. We desire to confirm that holy place under our defense and government. We therefore declare and order that neither you nor your juniors or successors, or anyone with judicial authority shall ever, at any time, dare make disturbances or exactions in the churches,

---

25. In their capacity as protectors of the popes and of the Roman church, the Carolingian kings were named by the papacy "patricians of the Romans." The title did not confer specific rights.

places, fields, or other possessions of the monastery aforesaid or indeed make changes in any of the matters written above; but what for the sake of the Lord's name and of eternal reward we have granted to the aforementioned monastery, may it increase and progress.

"When, at the divine summons, the venerable Abbot Benedict mentioned above or his successors depart from this life to the Lord, that holy congregation wishes to choose an abbot from the monastery described above or from whatever place, an abbot of similar kind or better, one faithful to us in all matters, one able to govern that holy congregation according to Saint Benedict's Rule, they have permission to do so by this our authority and indulgence. Wherever they and their monks may wish to be regulated or by whatever prelate, they have authority by our precept and consent, so long as those servants of God belonging to God's household in that place may be pleased to pray constantly for the Lord's mercy upon us, upon our wife and children; and for the stability of the entire realm committed and spared to us by God."

19

Most glorious King Charles conferred that by precept upon the venerable man Benedict, but the latter also received from all directions through the imperial charter useful cattle and lands suitable for farming. Dowered by the emperor with great honor, that is, almost forty pounds of silver, he returned in peace to his monastery as quickly as possible. As soon as he reached his native sod, he dispatched the silver he bore, divided for the sake of blessing, to the several monasteries. In our times he had this singular gift beyond all others, namely, a kindly and pious respect for everyone and care for all the monasteries whether near at hand or at a distance. He visited them frequently and imbued them with the regulations of holy living.

Of those materials brought to him by the faithful, he transferred according to the number of inhabitants and according to their ability, more to those in greater want, less to those requiring little. For he knew monasteries of both kinds and he remembered their names. Since he could not distribute mantles to each one, he sent them divided and made into crosses. For of all the monasteries situated as well in Provence as in Gothia and the province of Novempalitana,[26] he was like a nurse cherishing and aiding. He was beloved by all as father, venerated as master, and revered as teacher.

26. Roughly Gascony, southwestern France.

A portion for the poor was separated with greatest enthusiasm and he did not allow widows' shares to be expended for other purposes. He knew of course the names of all the nuns and widows located roundabout. Ransom was joyfully provided for captives. No one departing left him without a gift and as far as possible everything was done for everyone. For that reason each person voluntarily brought provisions to him to be laid up for distribution to the poor, needy, widows, captives, and monks. From some people he might receive as much as four or five thousand *solidi* in vessels to be apportioned among those in want.

Benedict had great concern not only to refresh his own people with food of preaching, but also to nourish with heavenly bread whomever he happened to encounter. That they might not lose the salutary food through forgetfulness, he was accustomed to impress upon them to cling tenaciously to it in their heart. This he did with such words as, "Let it be," he said, "with chaste body and humble heart, because proud chastity and vain humility are not acceptable to God." On some he was in the habit of stressing this, "If most precepts are impossible for you to remember, keep at least this short one, 'Depart from evil and do good' " (Ps 37.27). That sentence was so habitual to him that near the time of his death, when he had assembled statements from all the fathers, he proposed to produce one book about it alone. At every hour, whether at nocturn, in chapter, or in refectory, he provided the food of life for all those subject to him.

20

While we have tried to unfold his goodwill, a number of his virtues stand out in plain view. We will, therefore, detail a small selection of them suitable for men who do not know about them, but desire the information. Everyone attached to his "family" knows this—that he surpassed all in charity. Never did he do anything for himself, but rather what he deemed beneficial to others. If he did otherwise, he quickly made reparation. Out of devotion to charity and in order to secure the salvation of many, he visited the cells of others and explained the obscurities of the holy Rule. Full of charity he spent days in Arles with many bishops, abbots, and monks, explaining the mysteries of the canons and expounding the homilies of blessed Pope Gregory to ignorant ones. Filled with charity he nurtured within his own monastery clergy and monks from different localities. Appointing a teacher for them, he saturated them with sacred interpretations. In charity he sent gifts to those who did injury to him. But we should not belabor that what everyone saw better, many experienced with complaisance.

21

Benedict turned away little by little from the rigor of his first way of life, for he had undertaken an impossible task, yet the same will remained. He plowed with plowmen, accompanied diggers, reaped with reapers. Although that region was scorched by the sun's heat, a heat as though of fire from a furnace, burning rather than heating, he rarely allowed his men, even when suffering from excessive heat, a cup of water before the hour of refreshment. Worn with labor, scorched by the heat, they desired cold water rather than wine. But no one grumbled against him, because he experienced the same. That fact brought them no little solace, for he acted more leniently toward them when he observed himself burning with thirst. Nor did any laborers dare to make noise by talking; their hands were occupied with work and their tongues with psalms. The mouths of those going to and returning from labor were attentive to divine meditations.

We, who tried to treat him more humanely in drink and food, often saw him giving away dates. We also saw him measure the dish set before him. Those who were in charge of the cellar related that he usually drank water while others were drinking wine, except on the Sabbath and the Lord's Day. We had to separate any fat from his food and special care was taken lest even a small particle of common cheese be found in it. From the day of his conversion to the end of his life he chose not to eat the flesh of four-footed animals. If any illness assailed him, he took a broth made from a chicken.

For many years in his earlier day he avoided fat, yet he provided for others what he denied himself as often as there was opportunity. So great was his solicitude that if a tiny grain of vegetables, small fragment of chicken, or leaves of cabbages were overlooked by anyone, a suitable discipline was meted out for him whose fault it was proven to be. If anyone drew water for washing and poured more than was necessary (as did happen), he had to acknowledge that he had sinned by not walking the road of discernment.

Benedict possessed an unusual gift: as soon as anyone with disturbed thoughts in his mind approached him, the tumultuous crowd of thoughts dissipated at his wholesome counsel. Often indeed when a person was bombarded by unsafe thoughts (so I learned from a true brother), he would say to himself, "I will go and reveal you to Lord Benedict." At that very moment the unsuitable confusion left him. If anyone was hindered by severer faults, he received soothing consolation when he opened up his heart to Benedict. If one was oppressed by the disease of melancholy, he soon departed in happiness after visiting Benedict.

22

The throng of monks engaged in God's service increased so that there were more than three hundred. Because of so large a congregation, Benedict gave order to erect a bigger house to hold a thousand or more men.[27] It was a hundred cubits in length and twenty in width. Moreover, because other places could not hold them, he constructed cells at convenient locations where he placed brothers with teachers to direct them.

23

About that time a rainstorm occurred while the brothers and their teacher were resting. Suddenly water rushed in from both doors and threatened to fill the house. The frightened brothers got up in a hurry. Latrines had been built with great effort over flowing water that began to rise and endanger them. The rivulets below began to surge with a roar and leaped up in waves at that moment to ruin the structure. Although it was nearly midnight the monks ran to the church. The father himself had already arrived there. He seized the bell rope and shouted to them to sing Lauds, to implore the suffrages of the saints, and to entreat God's mercy with tears. After much prayer they went out to see whether the building was overthrown. As the venerable man was going, night was so dark and gloomy that he ran into a bramble bush and hurt his legs. But he did not cease tearfully to beg God for the flood to abate. When they reached the location, the water was found to have subsided a whole foot. Relying on God's help they returned to their companions in the church. When they had related God's kindness, they blessed God together.

24

In the meantime some bishops who heard reports of Benedict's sanctity and the holy reputation of his flock, began to demand some monks from him to serve as examples. Among them Leidrad, bishop of Lyon,[28] wanting to rebuild the monastery of Île-Barbe, sought with persistence those who might display

27. This would have made it the largest monastery in Europe by far. The largest Carolingian monasteries had only two to three hundred monks.

28. Bishop, 798–814. Lyon was an old Roman city and remained important through the Middle Ages. It had a large Jewish community.

for him the beginning of the good life. Benedict thereupon selected about twenty students from his flock, set a director over them, and instructed them to take up residence in the region of Burgundy. With the Lord's assistance there has now been assembled in that area a large band of monks, thriving and flourishing in holy religion.

Theodulf, bishop of Orléans,[29] wanted to erect the monastery of Saint Maximin[30] and demanded of Benedict some experts in the discipline of the Rule. The latter quickly gave assent and dispatched to him twice ten monks with a teacher set over them. Since they continually vied in holy zeal, they added to themselves no small band of monks.

I will relate what occurred there when the venerable father approached them for a visit. Awaiting his arrival, they devoted their energy to procure an abundant supply of fish and foods not only out of love for him, but also for all the brothers. There was a meeting of the brothers; fishermen were dispatched; markets were searched; but the activity eventuated in difficulty. Nothing could be found for purchase; the fish would not bite. They were filled with great sorrow because of this barren result. In the meanwhile the master arrived. They received him joyously and he, rejoicing in their progress, greeted them in return. The brothers concealed their chagrin under cheerful countenances.

In the meanwhile a certain brother was diligently pursuing his effort beside the Loire River. Suddenly he spied a large fish, one they call a salmon, swimming near the bank. The brother made no delay in springing to catch it and bring it to the others. There was joy over this, but there was even more wonderment, for they all professed that this came about owing to the merits of venerable Benedict. Unless I am in error, I learned this from a faithful brother.

Alcuin, of the Angle nation,[31] a deacon in holy orders, venerable by merit of holiness, governing the monastery of blessed Martin (who had been bishop of Tours), was held worthy of all honor at the court of glorious Emperor Charles. When Alcuin heard and experienced the holiness of God's man, he joined himself to him in lasting charity. From his letters addressed to Benedict, a booklet has been compiled. When gifts had been offered, Alcuin resolutely demanded that some monks be given to him. The venerable father at once complied and Alcuin dispatched horses to fetch them. He located them in a monastery named Cormery which he had erected. There were, I think, twenty

29. C. 750–821; bishop of Orléans, c. 798–818. He was a fellow Goth and a great biblical scholar, theologian, poet, and ecclesiastical administrator.

30. The monastery of Micy, near Orléans.

31. This is the Alcuin already encountered as the author of Willibrord's life. The Angles had settled Northumbria, whereas the Saxons had settled parts of eastern and most of southern England.

with a teacher set over them. By their good example of life a great multitude of monks was assembled.

25

I do not think it amiss if miracles done by divine grace at this time are inserted in this treatise.

A certain brother was sent to carry from one cell to another a consecrated container in which relics of Saint Denis and other saints were put. With him he took along also some puppies, but returning after several days he negligently strove to bring back the consecrated container without having washed his clothes. He embarked hurriedly in a boat—for his cell was situated between a lake and the sea. As soon as he reached land he mounted a horse, settling the puppies first and then picking up the container to attach it. But divine punishment overthrew him: at that very moment the horse reeled in a circular motion so that the brother fell to the ground. The container slipped from his hands (it was later recovered unharmed); the horse died at once; and the brother who had fallen was knocked into unconsciousness. He remained that way a long time, but ultimately regained his health.

When the brothers learned what had happened, they sent back another brother to look for the relics. Being a priest he took along a cross in which some of the Lord's wood was embedded. As he entered the lake his boat was shaken by a mighty wind. But when he held up the cross, which he wore about his neck, to the swelling waves, the winds subsided. Earlier, while he was resting in his cell, he had seen in a dream a man of dazzling brightness who addressed him thus, "Unless you take with you the Lord's wood, you will never leave here at the time you want to leave." He was also warned to carry the relics on foot. But he did not obey and, when he recovered and returned them, he was stricken with severe illness. Afterward to the church from which the relics were removed he presented a lamp, in the vessels of which there was very little oil. But on the next day they were found to be filled. That happened three times. I learned this story from the brother who fell and fainted.

26

In the mountains where the brothers lived when they took care of feeding the sheep, they erected a small oratory for prayer. After the brothers departed from that place, some women entered it. Jeering at the residence of the monks, they said to one another, "You take the abbot's position and stand in his place." But as each one, who took turn in the prayer stall as though praying, knelt down, she had difficulty in rising. Those dwellings in which the monks lived remained vacant only during summertime. Suitable punishment overtook the women at once. They began to be wracked with jerks and twists. They were not rescued from the pain until their husbands followed the monks as they went down the mountain with the sheep and begged them to offer prayers for the rash women. As the brothers prayed, the women were instantly restored to health.

27

A certain man from some place came to the monastery with his parents leading him. He was placed in the basilica of Blessed Mary ever Virgin Mother of God. When the brothers poured out prayers for him with vigils, his health returned and he left in peace.

A woman filled with an unclean spirit came to the monastery. The brothers guarded her with vigils and prayers in the oratory of Saint John the Baptist, which is located at the cemetery. With God's help she, too, left in safe condition.

28

To the oratory dedicated in honor of Saint Saturninus the martyr, where venerable Benedict first lived, to it if anyone with fever went and slept a little while, he would return in sound condition to his own estates, if he did not waver in confidence.

Let it suffice to have said these few things about miracles done in our times. With God's aid let us return to the sequence we began.

29

Most glorious Louis,[32] then king of Aquitaine, but now by God's provident grace august emperor of the whole church in Europe, discovered Benedict's

---

32. Louis the Pious (778–840), king of Aquitaine (781–814), emperor (814–840). He was Charlemagne's sole surviving legitimate son. Benedict's association with Louis went back at least to the 790s.

way of holiness, loved him beyond measure, and freely obeyed his counsel. The emperor set him over all the monasteries in the realm to exhibit to all a wholesome standard. For there were certain monasteries observing canonical institutes, but unaware of the precepts of the Rule. Obeying Louis's commands, Benedict traveled around the monasteries of each kind not once or twice only, but many times, showing the admonitions of the Rule and discussing it with them chapter by chapter, confirming what was known, revealing what was unknown. By God's foresight it therefore came to pass that almost all the monasteries located in Aquitaine accepted the plan of the Rule.

But he who hates good deeds, the opponent of innocence and enemy of peace, deemed it unfair not to inflict damage if Benedict persisted a long time in the pious king's friendship, if their love remained undivided. Since the devil lost the glory of his nature by pride, he is on guard with all his prowess lest a human be introduced into those good things that he lost. He takes offense that a human can be recovered by God's pity. It is no wonder that the ancient foe is tortured by the uprightness of pious persons and that he persecutes those whom he observes to be invincible in their progress. Nonetheless there are many who emulate Satan's wicked works. Although it is to be deeply lamented, many burn with alien practices; they are armed with hatred of those who choose not to follow their example.

When the aforesaid deeds were recognized as outstanding and meritorious to God, Satan, overwhelmed by their number, armed with weapons of envy, set forth to fight them with evil. First he fired the spirits of the clergy to minimize them. Then he invaded the hearts of knights of the royal court. He subverted the minds of certain counts. All equally inflamed with the faggot of envy, not secretly but openly vomiting the venom of a pestilent mind, they clamored loudly that he who always prayed for their souls was a "wandering monk,"[33] greedy for property, and invader of other people's estates. Their mad fury exploded to such enormity that they tried to arouse the most serene Emperor Charles against Benedict.[34]

But God's man with sure conscience was neither dismayed by the detractions nor frightened by false declarations. He therefore approached the palace because of that matter. As he entered no one tried to prevent him, because it

33. The point of the accusation is that the Rule of Saint Benedict had severely criticized wandering monks.

34. Benedict aroused opposition from monastic communities that did not want to adopt strict Benedictine usages, preferring either the more relaxed status of canons or the continuation of their long-standing mixed rule status. Laymen had long enjoyed the use of monastic property and Benedict was proposing to end this practice.

was supposed that if he appeared in the emperor's presence he would not be allowed to return to his homeland, since imperial anger would be aroused against him. He went in, however, without trepidation, relying on God's pity and putting his hope in Him for love of whom he strove without reluctance. If he should be sentenced to undergo pain of exile, so be it. It would make his mind freer to serve God. If he should be removed from office, he explained that with deep yearning he had long desired that boon. But when he appeared in the emperor's presence heavenly piety inclined Charles's mind to such great peace that as soon as he saw Benedict he embraced him and with his own hand extended a cup to him. Thus he, whom envious men had said would be an exile from his own soil, returned to it with high honor. And so, with divine mercy overriding, those who tried to defame him actually praised him and showed him, whom they sought to render odious by lies, not only revered by the least, but also by the greatest.

30[35]

Count William,[36] who was more outstanding at the emperor's court than all others, clung to blessed Benedict with such fondness that he scorned the dignities of the world and chose him as his leader in that way of salvation by which he might attain to Christ. Permission to be converted was finally received and he bestowed on the venerable man vast amounts of gold, silver, and costly vestments. William endured no delay in allowing his hair to be shorn. On the birthday of the apostles Peter and Paul [29 June], he laid aside clothes woven of gold and put on the habit of Christians, rejoicing that he was so quickly added to the number of heaven-dwellers.

There was a valley about four miles away from blessed Benedict's monastery. It was called Gellone. There the aforesaid count, hitherto so high in the world's dignity, gave order to construct a cell wherein he committed himself to serve Christ for the duration of his life. Although born of noble origin, he was zealous to make himself Christ's by embracing a nobler poverty. For Christ he rejected the highest honor he had inherited.

35. This chapter of the *Life*, which may well contain some authentic information, was nevertheless added to the text in, probably, the eleventh century.

36. Or Duke William of Toulouse, as this cousin of Charlemagne is usually known, helped the Carolingians to defend the Pyrenees frontier against Muslim raiders from Spain. He became an ardent admirer of Benedict, converted to the monastic state, entered a monastery at Gellone near Aniane, and died around 821. Rich legends grew up around him.

I think it worthwhile to relate, for those who do not know, some of the religious deeds of his manner of life. In the aforesaid cell Father Benedict had already placed his monks. Imbued with their example, within a few days William excelled in virtues those by whom he was taught. With the aid of his sons whom he had set over his counties and of neighboring counts, he quickly brought to completion the fabric of the monastery he had begun. That place was so remote that he who dwelled there could not wish for solitude. On all sides it was surrounded by cloud-covered mountains. No one had access to it but one whom a willing spirit drew there for the sake of prayer. It was bathed in such pleasantness that one could desire no other place if he decided to serve God. Vineyards were there that William ordered planted, an abundance of gardens, a valley packed with different kinds of trees. He acquired a great many possessions.

At his request, the most serene King Louis expanded it with a spacious boundary, granting from his own treasure funds to work the areas. The king gave many holy vestments, furnished silver and gold chalices and vessels for the offertory, brought along many books, clothed the altars with gold and silver. Into this cell William entered, dedicated himself wholly to Christ, abandoning all trace of worldly ostentation. He was of such profound humility that seldom if ever could a monk whom he happened to meet bow low enough not to be surpassed by him in abjection. We often saw him mount his donkey to carry flagons of wine to the barn, himself seated thereon bearing a chalice over his shoulders on his back, visiting the brothers of our monastery at harvest time to slake their thirst. He was so wakeful at vigils that he surpassed everyone. At the mill he worked with his own hands unless another occupation hindered or illness impeded him. He completed the baking in his turn. In dress he wore the standard vesture of deepest humility. He was a lover of fasting, constant in prayer, unwearying in compunction. Scarcely ever did he receive the body of Christ without streams of tears falling to earth. He greedily sought harshness of bed, but because of his poor health Father Benedict had a blanket spread beneath him although he did not want it.

Some say that for love of Christ, William often had himself flogged with whips, but no person other than the one who was present was aware of that practice. Often during the middle of the night and known only to God, he remained in the oratory that he had erected in honor of Saint Michael; although shivering with the icy cold and clad with one thin cloak, he was absorbed in prayer. For a few years he was full of these and other virtues. Then he realized that the day of death was threatening him. He ordered it to be made known in writing to almost all the monasteries in Lord Charles's realm when he had departed from this world. In this manner, bearing a supply of virtues, he left the world when Christ summoned him. For those desiring to know, these matters are sufficient. Let us again return to the work we undertook.

31

Most pious King Louis, knowing how usual it is for evil persons to resent advancement of upright persons, associated himself more and more with Benedict in loving esteem as the venerable abbot was ridiculed more and more by madmen. The queen, too, cherished him with pious disposition. Because Louis had come to know the good man, he willingly paid attention to him and very often bestowed gifts on him. When the multitude of students grew and the place where Benedict dwelled was unfruitful, the ground almost barren, and scorched with the sun's heat, Louis gave him the monastery situated in the Auvergne that Saint Menelaus, scion of royal origin, had founded and where his body lay. Thither Benedict directed twelve monks, setting over them as abbot a man of highest respect named Andoar, a man approved and worn by many toils, who had been with him from the earliest day of his conversion. As they labored and strove with holy zeal, seventy or more joined them to practice monastic life as fully as possible.

On one occasion the eminent Abbot Benedict went to that monastery to visit the brothers. While the abbot and brothers were awaiting his arrival at a particular place, it happened that Benedict entered that cell of the monastery where the church in honor of God and our Savior is located. The brothers had indeed at first made residence there, but because it was a narrow place the most serene king had soon transferred them to the monastery mentioned above. The brothers who were left behind to care for the cell were delighted when they saw Abbot Benedict approaching with some of his monks. They were embarrassed, however, because they were so poor. But where charity is, there is enough, so he who presided over the brothers ordered one of them to fetch wine. He replied that there was none in the vessel. The other brothers had left with them only two small vessels in which there was just enough wine with which they could say Mass or sip small amounts on Lord's days.

The master of that cell was downcast when he heard there was no wine in the vessel. But he spoke confidently, "Go and bring it to us. Those who are going ahead to meet him should drink out of respect for the father. It will not fail them." The brother went and turned the spigot—and wine came out!

When he had first tried to get some and did not succeed, he had returned. But now he told them what was occurring. Those who were present glorified God and declared that it was accomplished by the merits of Lord Benedict. They drank, therefore, at will and took some with them to refresh the travelers. Lord Benedict and his monks arrived and accepted what was needful. Some of it he carried with him on his journey. Immediately thereafter the vessel again ceased to yield wine. I learned this from those very brothers who told me what they saw. There are some witnesses still living.

32

At another time Benedict went back to the same monastery. When he was getting ready to depart after a long sermon and holy conversation, he offered a kiss of peace to the brothers. Among them a certain brother approached for the embrace. When the man of God saw him he stopped at once and for a moment refused the kiss of peace. Then, after a suitable rebuke at which we wondered, he kissed the brother. Another brother then presented himself. Benedict did the same to him. Finally after a last farewell he left the brothers. On the morning after he went away it was discovered that those two brothers had decided to desert. Then we knew why the venerable abbot was, under the Holy Spirit's revelation, slow to embrace them. Even if he did not openly betray their perverse intention, he nevertheless did upbraid their disturbed consciences with salutary words.

33

At length the most glorious king gave Benedict another monastery, where I believe he sent twenty monks and an abbot. That monastery was situated in the region of Poitiers and dedicated in honor of Saint Savinus. While the brothers placed there sweated away diligently in holy zeal, no small band of monks were joined to them. Again Louis conferred on him another monastery located in the region of Bourges. There Benedict settled about forty monks and an abbot. Since the place was founded as an entirely new effort, he provided assistance and gave them books and vestments. While they were flourishing in the practice of holy religion, displaying a standard of holy life, and preserving unity of spirit in the bond of peace (see Eph 4.3), they assembled into Christ's sheepfold a very large flock of monks.

34

An illustrious nobleman, Wulfar by name, kinsman of Count William, gave them by charter a place to erect a monastery in the confines of Albi. Thither Benedict sent about twelve monks with an abbot ordained for them. Since they had enough to do to complete by new effort the fabric of the monastery they had undertaken, Benedict gave them also a great many books, provided them sacred vestments, and managed a silver chalice, offertory vessels, a cross, and everything he saw would be needful for them. As they struggled both in construction of material buildings and in edification of souls by the regulations of the holy Rule, they acquired a large congregation of religious brothers in the service of Christ God.

35

After the death of most serene Emperor Charles and after his son, King Louis of Aquitaine, assumed care of the empire, the latter ordered Benedict into the region of Francia. Louis appointed Marmoutier in Alsace where Benedict located many followers of his kind of life from the monastery of Aniane. Since the aforesaid place was at such a distance from the palace that Benedict could not meet at a suitable time when he was summoned, and because he was required by the emperor for many occasions, it pleased Louis to provide him a convenient place not far from the palace where he could live with a few monks. Thus an abbot was set over the brothers at Marmoutier, while Benedict himself went with several in obedience to the emperor's wish.

There was a neighboring valley which is, I think, not more than six miles from the palace. It was pleasing in the eyes of God's man. There the emperor gave order to erect with amazing effort a monastery called Inde, the name of the valley itself and derived from the little river. The emperor was present for dedication of the church and he endowed it abundantly from his own treasures. He gave it "immunity" in a document and decreed that thirty monks should dwell there in the service of Christ. To complete the number, the venerable *abba* commanded brothers selected from noted monasteries to come, whom he might instruct by his example to be lessons of salvation to others, until animated by divine grace, secular pomp abandoned, and seeking knightly service for the eternal King, others might in time be selected from that province.

After that God's man began to wear away the palace floors and, for the profit of many, to endure troubles he had once set aside. All who suffered from injuries of others or who sought imperial opinions came to him. He received them with gladness and embraced them. At an opportune moment he brought their complaints set down in documents to the emperor. The most serene emperor, plucking at his napkin or sleeves, received them, read them as he found them, and decided as usefully as he knew how after becoming acquainted with them. But sometimes he put them away and forgot them. Yet the emperor willingly listened to complaints of this kind and for that reason ordered Benedict to be at the palace as unremittingly as possible.

There were many who consulted the abbot about direction of the realm, about disposition of provinces, and about their own advantage. No one in fact had such compassion on the miseries of the afflicted; no one revealed to the emperor the needs of monks as he did. Benedict was an advocate of the wretched, but a father of monks; a comforter of the poor, but a teacher of monks. He provided the food of life for rich people, but he inculcated the discipline of the Rule upon the minds of monks.

36

The emperor therefore set Benedict over all monasteries in his realm, that as he had instructed Aquitaine and Gothia in the standard of salvation, so also might he imbue Francia with a salutary example. Many monasteries had once been established in the Rule, but little by little firmness had grown lax and regularity of the Rule had almost perished. That there might be one wholesome usage for all monasteries, as there was one profession by all, the emperor ordered the fathers of monasteries to assemble with as many monks as possible. They were in session for many days. When all had come together, Benedict elucidated obscure points to all as he discussed the entire Rule; he made clear doubtful points; he swept away old errors; he confirmed useful practices and arrangements. He presented decisions of the Rule and questionable points with keen result, as well as practices the Rule did not mention. Everyone gave assent. Benedict then prepared for the emperor a chapter by chapter decree for confirmation to enjoin observance in all monasteries of his realm. We refer the inquiring reader to that document.[37]

37. This was a decisive moment in the history of Benedictine monasticism. Charlemagne, and now even more vigorously Louis the Pious, imposed the observance of the Rule of Saint Benedict, and indeed of Benedict of Aniane's understanding of that Rule, on all monasteries. The precise reference here is slightly ambiguous. It could mean Benedict's *Concordia Regularum*, a detailed commentary on the Rule prepared in light of the materials collected for the *Codex Regularum*, or

Louis appointed inspectors for each monastery to oversee whether those practices that were enjoined were observed and to transmit the wholesome standard to those unaware of it. By the aid of divine mercy the work was happily accomplished. All monasteries were returned to a degree of unity as if taught by one teacher in one place. Uniform measure in drink and food, in vigils and singing, was decreed to be observed by all. Since Benedict established observance of the Rule throughout other monasteries, he instructed his own at Inde so that monks coming from other regions might not engage in the noisy conversation to which they were accustomed, but might see the standard and discipline of the Rule portrayed in usage, walk, and dress of the monks at Inde.

37

Because of the indiscreet warmth of many, the unwarranted tepidness of some, and the obtuse sensibility of those with less capacity, Benedict determined a boundary and gave to all an arrangement to be observed, restraining some from seeking superfluous exertions, commanding others to shake off sluggishness, admonishing still others to fulfill at least what they did know. He ordered many things in conformity with the Rule. But there are a great many matters demanded in daily practice about which the Rule is silent. Yet by them a monk's habit is adorned as if with jewels and without which it appears to be careless, monotonous, and disorganized.

For the sake of unity and concord or perhaps for the sake of honorable appearance or even out of consideration for human frailty, Benedict commanded some matters that are not inculcated in the Rule. Hence the venerable abbot of holy memory ascertained what should be observed without delay or under pretext of excuse and ordered them fulfilled. Those matters that for certain reasons should be remitted or changed, he did not consider but entrusted them to his students to be observed in some measure as he could differentiate according to possibility or according to place. Where any page of the Rule explains less lucidly or remains altogether silent, he established and supplied with reason and aptness some matters on which, with divine help, I will touch briefly as follows.

---

it could point to the extremely detailed ecclesiastical legislation, much of it bearing on monasticism, issued between 816 and 819.

38

First, how the bell was to be rung for the night hours. Benedict ordered that a small bell in the brothers' dormitory be tapped, so that the congregation of monks maintained by prayer might first occupy their own place. Later, when the doors of the church were opened, entry might be permitted to guests. Rising quickly, as the Rule orders, the brothers should sprinkle themselves with holy water and run humbly and reverently to all the altars, then go to their places so that when the third bell is rung they may stand without delay, with ears attuned, awaiting the priest designated to begin the office.

During this interval no one allowed to enter was permitted to stand in corners of the church, but stationed in choir they were to intone quietly the prescribed psalms. Benedict ordered them to sing five psalms for all the faithful living throughout the whole world; then five for all the faithful departed; and five for those who were recently deceased. He decreed that the last five be sung comprehensively, for there was no reason regularly to mention specific deceased persons. When those last five psalms were completed, one might prostrate himself in prayer, commending to God those in general for whom he sang; and only then begin to petition for particular persons. As one's body lies on the earth there should be no reluctance to supplicate the eternal King in specially prescribed psalms. One should not fear to bow his head at designated words along with others able to do so, since in this manner divine grace is suitably invoked and the warmth of compunction is aroused.

In summertime, when the office of matins is over, Benedict ordered the monks to go outside the church if they were sleepy. Putting on their sandals and washing their faces, they could then return fully aroused and as before go around the altars with reverence, sprinkle themselves with holy water, and then go to the places allotted to each to complete the day office in an honorable manner, as well as those offices which are, according to Roman use, rendered with Psalm 119. He ordered the bell to be rung a long time: while it was ringing everyone could rush, but when it stopped the priest was to begin the "Hour." When prime was over, they could disperse to assemble in chapter. When that was completed, they could then go out to the task imposed on them either in silence or in singing psalms. Those who remained at the monastery must not be occupied in idle stories but two by two or even singly they were to sing psalms whether in kitchen, mill, or cellar. But he decreed that after compline no one might go outside freely or even linger in the oratory.

In wintertime they should sing ten psalms; in summer, five. Then, when the last bell is rung, all should walk together around all the altars in the aforesaid manner, and thereafter go to sleep, each on his own bed. At those three times each day he commanded them to go around all the altars. At the first one they should say the Lord's Prayer and the creed; at the others, the Lord's Prayer; or they should confess their sins. At the day hours for prayer, each should go to his own place to pray. If, however, one had peculiar reason to pray alone, he should do so only by permission and only at whatever hour he was not otherwise occupied. Benedict established those three stations of prayer so that those who were sluggish, slow, or not in a mood to pray might at least do under compulsion what they did not want to do freely and thus not abandon the appointed hours, while those who were aflame with extreme love might be restrained from indiscreetly seeking extra hours. Thus it came to pass that they were not worn away with excessive or indiscreet vigils during the course of one night and hence preoccupied at the hours when one should be intent on divine psalms, since one cannot fulfill the divine requirement while sleepy.

The practice of many had in the past caused them also to dress differently. The cowls of some hung down to their ankles. God's man therefore instituted a uniform style to be worn by all monks: the length should not extend more than two cubits or reach to the knees. Out of necessity he conceded beyond what the Rule decrees: two woolen shirts, pants, leather cloaks and coverings, and two copes. Whatever he observed as necessary to diminish evasion by any pretext, he conceded and allowed.

In a letter to the emperor, Benedict gave his opinion on those matters that the Rule directs but that for good reason remained untried, as well as on those matters on which it was silent but which were usefully introduced. He directed his desire toward observance of the Rule; it was his greatest study that nothing might escape his knowledge. Consequently he interrogated minutely those whom he found to be expert, whether living nearby or at a distance. Those who came into these parts on their way to Monte Cassino he asked to collect not only what they heard, but also what they saw. Because of his love of knowledge, anyone who might unfold something new to him he received without delay, with humility, and chatted with him without awe.

Even so he could not learn all the hidden meanings of the Rule. With everyone (not with novices, of course, but with wise persons) he would make it clear that he learned new and unheard-of matters not only from learned people, but also from simpler ones. He caused a book to be compiled from the rules of various fathers, so that blessed Benedict's Rule might be foremost in the minds of all. He gave orders to read it all the time in the morning at assembly. To demonstrate to contentious persons that nothing worthless or useless was set forth by blessed Benedict, but that his Rule was sustained by the rules of others, he compiled another book of statements culled from other rules. To it he gave the title, *Harmony of the Rules*. Statements in agreement with blessed Benedict's book were added to show that the latter was obviously foremost. To it he joined another book from the sermons of holy teachers. These were presented for exhortation of monks. It he ordered read all the time at the evening assemblies.

39

Perceiving that some men panted with all their might to acquire monasteries of monks and strove not only with petitions, but also with money, to obtain them; perceiving, too, that monastic expenses were being sequestered by them for selfish purposes; and perceiving that in that way some monasteries were being destroyed and others secured by secular clergy after the monks were driven away, Benedict went to the most pious emperor and pressed him with supplications to ban clergy from contentions of this kind and set the exiled monks free from this danger. The most glorious emperor gave consent and decreed that all monasteries in his realm where there were regular abbots be enumerated. By charter he ordered that they remain unchanged for all time; he sealed that charter with his ring. Thus he stripped the greed of many and at the same time relieved the anxiety of the monks.

Certain monasteries were employed for secular burdens and for military service. They had reached such dire poverty that both food and clothing were lacking to the monks. Considering that, the most pious king, at the aforesaid man's suggestion, gave order to relieve them as much as possible so that nothing might be lacking to God's servants. For this alleviation they gladly prayed to God for the emperor, his children, and the pious establishment of the entire realm. Those monasteries that remained under canonical authority he arranged separately so they could live according to the Rule, but the rest he granted to the abbot.[38]

38. The Carolingians had long attracted and rewarded followers by assigning them monastic properties and/or by naming them lay abbots of monasteries. Through such practices some houses had been impoverished. Benedict worked with Louis to assess the value of monasteries and then to assign only very wealthy ones to lay abbots, and even then to require that an inviolable portion of the monastery's revenues be set aside solely for the support of the monks. Poorer monasteries made small cash payments to the emperor or simply rendered prayers. It is interesting to see that Benedict was concerned about both the spiritual life and the economic well-being of monasteries.

40

I think I should not overlook what happened by God's will once when Benedict was going to a general assembly at the emperor's order. Although worn by illness and severe fever, he was on his way in obedience to the king's order. Attended only by the weapons of charity, he was prepared to accomplish the benefit of many persons. But the enemy, who always envies holy deeds and seeks to bring detriment to the salvation of pious people, strove by any craft to slow him down on the path he had undertaken through vast forests. Driving away the horses on which Benedict was traveling, he confused the guides and rendered the way unfamiliar to them. But God's man was not discouraged by grief over the lost horses and he soon reached the royal gates. When the losses on the monasteries and monks were reported to the emperor, he, who had great, constant, and holy solicitude for them, replenished the number of horses. Yet after an interval of a month the lost horses were returned. Thus by divine action it came to pass that Benedict received double reward because he had not grieved over what was lost.

Thereafter he began to wear away with differing ailments: the constant vigils through many years, streaming tears, severe fasts, and prolonged meditations. He undertook, therefore, to prepare his frail, worn body for a new struggle, so that he, who had gained the pinnacle of virtues by subduing vices, might be girded with weapons of patience to strive against infirmities and gain the victor's double palm from his King after his foes were overthrown. The more vigorously he was mauled by illness, the more intently he pursued over and over again prayers and readings. No one found him idle, no one found him sluggish at Divine Office, no one found him indulging in vain and frivolous stories. He persisted either in reading by himself or in listening attentively to someone else reading. Who ever found him alone except also weeping? Who ever entered his place unannounced and found his cheeks dry and him not prostrate on the ground or standing with hands outstretched to heaven or catching his tears in his hands lest a page of the sacred volume be stained with them?

The powers of his flesh wasted, but his purpose of spirit was firmer than iron. He endured in the hardness he had begun. Not since the day of his conversion did Benedict eat the flesh of four-footed animals. Even in his last days when he was worn by listlessness he scarcely ever indulged in a bath. He was accustomed to change his clothes only after forty days or more. He ordered brothers to read the life and death of the holy fathers to him. Refreshed by that reading his spirit endured even stronger. O good Jesus, drenched with what sighs and tears did his spirit seethe with desire to be released and be with Christ, but he never refused to perform a duty if it was helpful to the brothers.

When illness grew stronger, he appealed directly to the emperor to be borne to his monastery. Delivering a farewell address to the brothers, he spent the whole night in prayers and psalms, then went to the regular office of that day. On a later day when he completed the regular office and tried to reach the door, a phrase recurred to him, "Righteous art thou, O Lord" (Ps 119.137). Reciting that versicle, he said, "I am fainting," and added, "Deal with Thy servant according to Thy steadfast love" (Ps 119.124). Thus amid words of prayer he breathed out his spirit adorned with virtues.

His letters, sweeter than all riches, are here. The day before he departed from the world he dictated them with his own mouth to the brothers stationed at Aniane. In them he testified that they would see his face no more. Certain ones declare that at the very hour he departed to Christ, his death was revealed to Bishop Stabilis of Maguelonne. Rising from sleep the latter quickly related to his men what had occurred. We have, therefore, touched upon his death cursorily for brothers who were present at that time have unfolded it more extensively as the following pages indicate.

42

"Abbot Benedict, born in the province of Gothia, lived there from infancy to adolescence in the days of Pepin, king of the Franks, and after his death, in the days of his son Charles. Later abandoning the palace, he took the habit of a true monk at the monastery of Saint Seine in the province of Burgundy. There he served in God's knighthood zealously for two and a half years. But since he found little practice of the Rule there, he removed to the regions of Gothia. At first he built with his own hands a cell on the river Aniane and afterward, with the help of brothers who for love of Christ came under his government, a monastery of new foundation. Not long thereafter he had three hundred monks under his authority.

"When Emperor Charles died and his son Louis received the empire, the latter caused the venerable man Benedict to come with several students to Francia. At first Louis granted Benedict Marmoutier in the countryside of Alsace, but later for love of him erected a completely new monastery for him on the river Inde near the palace of Aix. It was through Benedict that the Lord Christ restored the Rule of Saint Benedict in the entire realm of the Franks. He had under his government twelve monasteries: Aniane, Gellone, Casa Nova, Île-Barbe, Ménat, Saint Savinus, Saint Maximin, Massay, Cormery, Celle-neuve near Toulouse, Marmoutier in Alsace, and Inde. The last was erected by the emperor's authority for Benedict and his students and endowed from the royal treasuries. For all these Benedict dispatched monks and abbots of his own teaching. He had the greatest concern for the entire ecclesiastical order, whether monks, canons, or layfolk, but especially for monks.

"The emperor listened to all his counsel willingly and accomplished it. For that reason Louis was called by some 'the Monkish.' For love of the holy man he always called the monks "his own" and after Benedict's decease he went so far as to declare himself openly 'abbot' of this monastery. The holy man continued up to his death in the king's palace for the benefit of all the faithful, although not for earthly profit. The monastery in which he dwelled was nearby. On the fourth day before his demise and while he was still well he repeated to the emperor everything that he was in the habit of saying to him. On that day, however, he returned to his own dwelling racked with fever. On the next day all the emperor's magnates heard about that and came to visit him. So great was the throng of bishops, abbots, and monks that we, who were keeping watch over him, scarcely had space to get close to him. Abbot Helisachar came first and remained with him until he died.

"Benedict grew sicker on the fifth *feria*. On the sixth *feria*[39] at nightfall the emperor sent Tanculf, his chamberlain, ordering that we should convey him that very night to the monastery. Lifting him up, we bore him before cockcrow in company with Helisachar, his men, and ours to the monastery at the first hour of the day [prime]. When the third hour of the day [terce] came, Benedict ordered everyone to leave him and he remained alone until the sixth hour [sext]. After that Abbot Helisachar and our provost entered and inquired how he was feeling. He replied that he had never been so well and added, 'Until now I have been standing among the choirs of holy ones in the Lord's presence.' On the next day he summoned the brothers, gave them reminders of salvation, then confided to them that in the forty-eight years since he had been a monk he had eaten no food on any day until he poured out tears before God.

"On the same day he sent a note of admonition to the emperor and directed others to various monasteries. In them the venerable man noted every office he had performed during the five years and two months before his death, as we found in his records after his death. While still alive he spoke of certain offices to be sung for him. He died in his seventies on the third day before the ides of

39. The fifth *feria* is Thursday; the sixth, Friday.

February[40] in the year of the Lord's incarnation 821, the fourteenth indiction, first concurrent, fourteenth epact, ninth year of most pious Emperor Louis. We prepared his grave on the third day afterward and put him in a stone coffin that the emperor had had prepared. As we covered his face, we noticed on the forehead, above his eyes, and on his lips such ruddiness as he never had while alive.

"These matters having been thus indicated and thus delivered, we, servants of the monastery of Inde, namely, Deidonus, Leovigild, Bertrad, and Desiderius, desire for you, Master Ardo, health in the Lord and we beg your charity to compose and send to us, according to your God-given wisdom, a little book about the life of our Father Benedict. All our brothers greet you and do you greet all your brothers for us. Amen."

43

"For George, abbot of the monastery of Aniane, of supreme beatitude and felicity in the Lord Christ, and for all our sons and brothers who live well and watchfully under the standard of Benedict, Benedict, least of all abbots, already at his end, desires health.

"Above all things and before all matters that burn my spirit and require care is this: that I am intensely solicitous for your order in the regular life. In no way am I unaware that you sweat nobly. You are loyally mindful of us and are in no wise wanting in words of encouragement. Set in my last stages, not knowing whether I can see you again, but since my love turns my spirit toward you, I have taken care to address some words to you through faithful persons as well as through letters. You know how with all possible labor I have availed as long as I could. Solicitous for you I have exhibited patterns of life and exhortation. Now, therefore, my sons, I pray to God and call Him to witness that you may be of one mind in the bond of charity (see Eph 4.3), and that you may be discreet. Do not hold anyone as 'foreigner' whom I have had with me. I have not sent people anywhere to seek another example or another reason. Whoever may wish to return to you from among them and live with you under the Rule, you will receive in holiness and kindness as brothers, for that is fitting.

"Thanks to God, material aid will not fail you. To all in general, but especially to those whom you know to be joined with us in friendship, always offer

40. 11 February 821, a Monday.

an attentive disposition so far as you can. Minister to poorer monasteries the necessities that are more than sufficient for you. Give aid to Abbot Modan, of the monastery of Saint Thibery, in those matters in which he may be in want. After my death do even more for these and others than you did in my lifetime. Many monasteries are still corrupt even though they have, through God's largess, received some correction from us. So beware in every way lest (may it not be!)—I pray you, merciful Lord—the sinister way . . . that may be able to hold at all times. You at the monastery of Inde, be united as very special brothers.

"Consider Helisacher (who before others upon earth has always been a loyal friend of canons) and his brothers in my place and may your refuge always be in him. I now advise you thus because I do not know whether I may see you again in this present world. Already on the seventh day before the ides of February[41] with a very sharp pain, Christ granting his mercy . . . I am smitten. I await nothing other than the last day of my summons speedily."

Lord Benedict ordered the foregoing to be written on the fourth day before the ides of February[42] while he was still living. He died on the third day before the ides of the same month.[43] Here ends the letter.

> The divine seed has been sown; may it avail
> for new ones,
> Drenched with dew from heaven, to plow the
> planting of teachers,
> And the rich fruit of the heart produce fruit
> a hundredfold [see Mk 4.8].

44

"Abbot Benedict, least of all abbots, to Archbishop Nibridius,[44] venerable father in Christ, I wish health and eternal felicity in the Lord. O man of God, may charity, love, and good will be evident now as always. By yourself in person or through a servant or friend transmit a message throughout all monasteries wherever you can, that they not cease to pour out prayers for me to the Lord together with psalms and masses, because such intercession is now

41. 7 February.
42. 10 February.
43. 11 February.
44. Of Narbonne in the south of France.

profoundly necessary for me. Know, beloved father, that I am now struggling at my end, that my soul has left my body, and that I can no longer see you in the light with eyes of the body. May He who can make a clean person out of an unclean one, a just person out of a sinner, and a holy one out of an irreligious person, cause us to enjoy the eternal realm there to sing the new song with all the holy ones.

"I beg, dear father, that as you have always had an interest in the brothers dwelling at the Aniane monastery, so always keep them more and more in your holy love until your holy soul leaves your body. I commend to you all my friends, servants, and relatives in those areas. In your own monastery, I believe, you work with all your efforts. Be zealous to labor for them with perseverance. Ever use your mouth to all, rich and poor alike, in accord with that statement that the Lord deigned to speak through His blessed apostle Paul, "convince, rebuke, and exhort" (2 Tm 4.2). May your holiness know well whom to convince, whom to rebuke, and whom to exhort. I therefore say to you, father, may no peril remain in you whereby you might be forever damned. With free voice may you be able to say with the psalmist, 'I have not hid Thy saving help within my heart, I have spoken of Thy faithfulness and Thy salvation' (Ps 40.10). Do everything, however, with charity and discretion. May the Holy Trinity guard you and grant you bountifully the eternal reward. Amen."

Rudolf

THE LIFE OF SAINT LEOBA

Translated by C. H. Talbot

Rudolf, the author of this *Life,* is usually assumed to be identical with the Fulda monk who was chancellor—chief recordkeeper—of the monastery in 812. If this identification is correct, then Rudolf must have been born well before 800. Rudolf died at Fulda in 865 as a very old man, unless of course we are dealing with two different Rudolfs.

Rudolf was a pupil of Hrabanus Maurus (c. 780–856), the greatest of Alcuin's many students, master of the school of Fulda, abbot of that important monastery (822–847), and archbishop of Mainz (847–856). Rudolf became master of Fulda's school when Hrabanus became abbot, and accompanied Hrabanus to Mainz in 847, although he soon returned to Fulda.

In addition to writing the entries for the years 839–863 in the *Annals of Fulda,* the major narrative source for the eastern kingdom of the Franks, Rudolf wrote a number of hagiographical works, and he collected, forged, and interpolated a number of Fulda's charters. Despite having held important positions and having authored a substantial corpus of writings, Rudolf remains a shadowy figure.

Rudolf tells us that he was asked to write this *Life*. There is nothing unusual in that, but it is interesting to note that in accomplishing his task he had access to four accounts of Leoba's life by some of her disciples. This piece of information, provided quite incidentally by Rudolf, permits us to wonder if Huneberc was the only woman of her time to have written a saint's life. Another interesting feature of Rudolf's text is its unusually long and detailed account of Leoba's youth, and of the English convent she entered as a little girl. Other texts in this collection do not dilate on the youth of their subjects, preferring instead to focus on the details of a life lived in public. Rudolf was in a bit of a quandary. His account makes it clear that he personally favored the strict claustration of women, but he had to write of a woman who traveled widely and frequently. Perhaps the account of Wimbourne was meant to establish Leoba's credentials as a recluse, and also to establish Rudolf's preferences, in light of a career that was anything but reclusive. This suggests that many accounts of female sanctity may stress seclusion precisely because their subjects were not secluded. It is also worth drawing attention to the emphasis placed on female learning in this text. Finally, it is intriguing to note that Rudolf depended heavily on the *Life of Germanus* in composing his *Life of Leoba*. This has led some to wonder how reliable his account is.

This work survives in very few manuscripts and seems not to have been very influential. One recent study has shown that of some 2,200 known saints from the early Middle Ages, only about 300 were women. Perhaps Leoba's *Life* was relatively uninfluential because sanctity was mainly controlled not only by men but more particularly by men of Rudolf's point of view.

Texts and References

The Latin text of Rudolf's *Vitae Leobae abbatissae Biscofesheimensis* was edited by Georg Waitz in Monumenta Germaniae Historica, Scriptores, 15:118–31. For very basic details on Rudolf it is necessary to consult Max Manitius, *Geschichte der lateinischen Literatur des Mittelaltens*, 3 vols. (Munich, 1911–31), 1:668–73 and Franz Brunhölzl, *Geschichte der lateinischen Literatur des Mittelaltens*, 2 vols. (Munich, 1975), 1:343–44. Leoba's career and Rudolf's account of it are engagingly treated in Stephanie Hollis, *Anglo-Saxon Women and the Church* (Woodbridge, 1992), 274–75 and passim. Some perspective on both Leoba and her *Life* can be gained from Jo Ann McNamara et al., eds., *Sainted Women of the Dark Ages* (Durham, N.C., 1992), a collection of seventeen lives of women saints who lived between the fifth and the seventh centuries.

The small book which I have written about the life and virtues of the holy and revered virgin Leoba has been dedicated to you, O Hadamout,[1] virgin of Christ, in order that you may have something to read with pleasure and imitate with profit. Thus by the help of Christ's grace you may eventually enjoy the blissful reward of him whose spouse you now are. Most earnestly do I beg you and all the nuns who unceasingly invoke the name of the Lord to pray for me, so that I, Rudolf, a monk of Fulda and a wretched sinner, in spite of my unworthiness to share the fellowship of the elect of God, may through the merits of those who are pleasing to Him receive pardon of my sins and escape the penalties due to them.

PROLOGUE

1

Before I begin to write the life of the blessed and venerable virgin Leoba, I invoke her spouse, Christ, our Lord and Savior, who gave her the courage to overcome the powers of evil, to inspire me with eloquence sufficient to describe her outstanding merits. I have been unable to discover all the facts of her life. I shall therefore recount the few that I have learned from the writings of others, venerable men who heard them from four of her disciples, Agatha, Thecla, Nana, and Eoloba.[2] Each one copied them down according to his ability and left them as a memorial to posterity.

One of these, a holy priest and monk named Mago,[3] who died about five years ago, was on friendly terms with these women and during his frequent visits to them used to speak with them about things profitable to the soul. In this way he was able to learn a great deal about her life. He was careful to make short notes of everything he heard, but, unfortunately, what he left was almost unintelligible, because, while he was trying to be brief and succinct, he expressed things in such a way as to leave the facts open to misunderstanding and provide no basis for certainty. This happened, in my opinion, because in

1. As with the Angildruth who requested the *Life of Sturm*, nothing is known about Hadamout.

2. These women cannot be identified except, probably, as nuns of Bischofsheim.

3. A monk and priest of Fulda whose death occurred in 831, which dates this text to 836.

his eagerness to take down every detail before it escaped his memory he wrote the facts down in a kind of shorthand and hoped that during his leisure he could put them in order and make the book more easy for readers to understand. The reason why he left everything in such disorder, jotted down on odd pieces of parchment, was that he died quite suddenly and had no time to carry out his purpose.

Therefore it is not from presumption but in obedience to the command of my venerable father and master, Abbot Hrabanus, that I have tried to collect together all the scattered notes and papers left by the men I have mentioned. The sequence of events, which I have attempted to reconstruct for those who are interested in knowing them, is based on the information found in their notes and on the evidence I have gathered from others by word of mouth. For there are several religious men still living who can vouch for the facts mentioned in the documents, since they heard them from their predecessors, and who can add some others worthy of remembrance. These latter appeared to me suitable for inclusion in the book and therefore I have combined them with material from the written notes. You will see, then, that I have not only reorganized and completed the work set on foot by others but have written something on my own account. For it seems to me that there should be no doubt in the minds of the faithful about the veracity of the statements made in this book, since they are shown to be true both by the blameless character of those who relate them and by the miracles that are frequently performed at the shrine of the saint.

But before I begin the narration of her remarkable life and virtues, it may not be out of place if I mention a few of the many things I have heard about her spiritual mistress and mother, who first introduced her to the spiritual life and fostered in her a desire for heaven. In this way the reader who is made aware of the qualities of this great woman may give credence to the achievements of the disciple more easily the more clearly he sees that she learned the elements of the spiritual life from so noble a mistress.

2

In the island of Britain, which is inhabited by the English nation, there is a place called Wimbourne,[4] an ancient name that may be translated "Winestream." It received this name from the clearness and sweetness of the water

---

4. In Dorset near the south coast.

there, which was better than any other in that land. In olden times the kings of
that nation had built two monasteries in the place, one for men, the other for
women, both surrounded by strong and lofty walls and provided with all the
necessities that prudence could devise. From the beginning of the foundation
the rule firmly laid down for both was that no entrance should be allowed to a
person of the other sex. No woman was permitted to go into the men's
community, nor was any man allowed into the women's, except in the case of
priests who had to celebrate Mass in their churches; even so, immediately
after the function was ended the priest had to withdraw. Any woman who
wished to renounce the world and enter the cloister did so on the understanding that she would never leave it. She could only come out if there was a
reasonable cause and some great advantage accrued to the monastery. Furthermore, when it was necessary to conduct the business of the monastery and to
send for something outside, the superior of the community spoke through a
window and only from there did she make decisions and arrange what was
needed.

3

It was over this monastery, in succession to several other abbesses and spiritual
mistresses, that a holy virgin named Tetta[5] was placed in authority, a woman
of noble family (for she was a sister of the king), but more noble in her conduct
and good qualities. Over both the monasteries she ruled with consummate
prudence and discretion. She gave instruction by deed rather than by words,
and whenever she said that a certain course of action was harmful to the
salvation of souls she showed by her own conduct that it was to be shunned.
She maintained discipline with such circumspection (and the discipline there
was much stricter than anywhere else) that she would never allow her nuns to
approach clerics. She was so anxious that the nuns, in whose company she
always remained, should be cut off from the company of men that she denied
entrance into the community not merely to laymen and clerics but even to
bishops. There are many instances of the virtues of this woman which the
virgin Leoba, her disciple, used to recall with pleasure when she told her
reminiscences. Of these I will mention but two examples, so that from these
the rest may be conjectured.

---

5. She was a sister of King Ine of Wessex (688–725) and ruled Wimbourne—a double monastery like Heidenheim—in succession to her sister.

4

In that convent there was a certain nun who, because of her zeal for discipline and strict observance, in which she surpassed the others, was often appointed prioress and frequently made one of the mistresses.[6] But as she was too incautious and indiscreet in enforcing discipline over those under her care, she aroused their resentment, particularly among the younger members of the community. Though she could easily have mollified them and met their criticisms, she hardened her heart against taking such a course of action and went so far in her inflexibility that even at the end of her life she would not trouble to soften their hearts by asking their pardon. So in this stubborn frame of mind she died and was buried; and when the earth had been heaped over her, as the custom is, a tomb was raised over her grave. But this did not appease the feelings of the young nuns who hated her, and as soon as they saw the place where she was buried they reviled her cruelty and even climbed onto her tomb, as if to stamp upon her corpse, uttering bitter curses over her dead body to assuage their outraged feelings. Now when this came to the ears of the venerable abbess of the community she reprehended the young nuns for their presumption and vigorously corrected them. She went to the grave and noticed that in some extraordinary way the earth that had been heaped over the corpse had subsided and lay about six inches below the surface of the surrounding ground. This sight struck her with great fear. She understood from the subsidence of the ground how the dead woman had been punished, and judged the severity of God's sentence upon her from the sinking of the grave. She therefore called all the sisters together and began to reproach them for their cruelty and hardness of heart. She upbraided them for failing to forgive the wrongs they had suffered and for harboring ill feelings on account of the momentary bitterness caused by harsh discipline. She told them that one of the fundamental principles of Christian perfection is to be peaceable with those who dislike peace, whereas they, far from loving their enemies as God had commanded, not only hated their sister while she was alive but even pursued her with their curses now that she was dead. She counseled them to lay aside their resentment, to accept the ill-treatment they had received and to show without delay their forgiveness: if they wished their own sins to be forgiven by God they should forgive others from the bottom of their hearts. She begged them to forget any wrongs inflicted by the dead woman before her death and to join

---

6. The prioress was second in command to the abbess. Mistresses were responsible nuns who supervised groups of younger sisters.

with her in prayer that God, in His mercy, would absolve her from her sins. When they had all agreed to follow her advice, she ordered them to fast for three days and to give themselves earnestly to watching, prayer, and the recitation of psalms for the repose of her soul.

At the end of the fast on the third day she went with all the nuns into the church, singing litanies and invoking the Lord and His saints; and after she had prostrated herself before the altar she prayed for the soul of the deceased sister. And as she persevered in prayer, the hole in the grave, which previously had appeared to be empty, suddenly began to fill in and the ground rose, so that the moment she got up from her knees the grave became level with the surface of the ground. By this it was made clear that when the grave returned to its normal state the soul of the deceased sister, through the prayers of Tetta, had been absolved by divine power.

5

On another occasion it happened that when the sister who looked after the chapel went to close the door of the church before going to bed after compline she lost all the keys in the darkness. There were very many of them belonging to various things locked away in the treasury of the church, some of silver, others of bronze or iron, all fastened together with a metal clasp. When she rose at the sound of the bell for the morning office and could not find the keys for opening the doors of the church, she lit a candle and carefully searched all the places in which there was any hope of finding them; and as if one search was not enough, she went over the same ground again and again looking for them. When she had done this several times without success, she went to the abbess, who as usual had anticipated the hour for the night office and was deep in prayer, while the others were still at rest. Trembling with fear, the nun threw herself at the feet of the abbess and humbly confessed the negligence of which she was guilty. As soon as the abbess heard it she felt convinced that it was the work of the devil, and, calling the sisters together, she recited the nighttime vigils and the morning office in another building. When this was ended, they all gave themselves to prayer. At once the wickedness of the old enemy was brought to light, for, while they were still at prayer, a little dead fox was suddenly seen at the doors of the chapel holding the keys in his mouth, so that what had been given up as lost was found. Then the venerable mother took the keys and ordered the doors to be opened; and going into the church accompanied by the nuns, who at that time were about fifty in number, she gave thanks to God in hymns and praise for mercifully hearing His servants who had trusted in Him and for putting the wicked spirit to confusion. For he who had said, "I will exalt my throne above the stars of God" (Is 14.13) was transformed for his pride into a beast, and he who would not humbly submit to God was unmasked as a fox through the prayers of the nuns and made to look foolish.

Let these instances of the virtues of the venerable mother Tetta suffice. We will now pursue our purpose of describing the life of her spiritual daughter, Leoba the virgin.

6

As we have already said, her parents were English,[7] of noble family and full of zeal for religion and the observed of God's commandments. Her father was called Dynno, her mother Aebba. But as they were barren, they remained together for a long time without children. After many years had passed and the onset of old age had deprived them of all hope of offspring, her mother had a dream in which she saw herself bearing in her bosom a church bell, which on being drawn out with her hand rang merrily. When she woke up she called her old nurse to her and told her what she had dreamed. The nurse said to her: "We shall yet see a daughter from your womb and it is your duty to consecrate her straightway to God. And as Anna offered Samuel to serve God all the days of his life in the temple, so you must offer her, when she has been taught the Scripture from her infancy, to serve Him in holy virginity as long as she shall live." Shortly after the woman had made this vow she conceived and bore a daughter, whom she called Thrutgeba, surnamed Leoba because she was beloved, for this is what Leoba means. And when the child had grown up her mother consecrated her and handed her over to Mother Tetta to be taught the sacred sciences. And because the nurse had foretold that she should have such happiness, she gave her her freedom.

7

The girl, therefore, grew up and was taught with such care by the abbess and all the nuns that she had no interests other than the monastery and the

---

7. The date and place of Leoba's birth are unknown.

pursuit of sacred knowledge. She took no pleasure in aimless jests and wasted no time on girlish romances, but, fired by the love of Christ, fixed her mind always on reading or hearing the Word of God. Whatever she heard or read she committed to memory, and put all that she learned into practice. She exercised such moderation in her use of food and drink that she eschewed dainty dishes and the allurements of sumptuous fare, and was satisfied with whatever was placed before her. She prayed continually, knowing that in the Epistles the faithful are counseled to pray without ceasing. When she was not praying she worked with her hands at whatever was commanded her, for she had learned that he who will not work should not eat. However, she spent more time in reading and listening to Sacred Scripture than she gave to manual labor. She took great care not to forget what she had heard or read, observing the commandments of the Lord and putting into practice what she remembered of them. In this way she so arranged her conduct that she was loved by all the sisters. She learned from all and obeyed them all, and by imitating the good qualities of each one she modeled herself on the continence of one, the cheerfulness of another, copying here a sister's mildness, there a sister's patience. One she tried to equal in attention to prayer, another in devotion to reading. Above all, she was intent on practicing charity, without which, as she knew, all other virtues are void.

8

When she had succeeded in fixing her attention on heavenly things by these and other practices in the pursuit of virtue she had a dream in which one night she saw a purple thread issuing from her mouth. It seemed to her that when she took hold of it with her hand and tried to draw it out there was no end to it; and as if it were coming from her very bowels, it extended little by little until it was of enormous length. When her hand was full of thread and it still issued from her mouth she rolled it round and round and made a ball of it. The labor of doing this was so tiresome that eventually, through sheer fatigue, she woke from her sleep and began to wonder what the meaning of the dream might be. She understood quite clearly that there was some reason for the dream, and it seemed that there was some mystery hidden in it. Now there was in the same monastery an aged nun who was known to possess the spirit of prophecy, because other things that she had foretold had always been fulfilled. As Leoba was diffident about revealing the dream to her, she told it to one of her disciples just as it had occurred and asked her to go to the old nun

and describe it to her as a personal experience and learn from her the meaning
of it. When the sister had repeated the details of the dream as if it had
happened to her, the nun, who could foresee the future, angrily replied: "This
is indeed a true vision and presages that good will come. But why do you lie to
me in saying that such things happened to you? These matters are no concern
of yours: they apply to the beloved chosen by God." In giving this name, she
referred to the virgin Leoba. "These things," she went on, "were revealed to
the person whose holiness and wisdom make her a worthy recipient, because
by her teaching and good example she will confer benefits on many people.
The thread that came from her bowels and issued from her mouth, signifies
the wise counsels that she will speak from the heart. The fact that it filled her
hand means that she will carry out in her actions whatever she expresses in her
words. Furthermore, the ball which she made by rolling it round and round
signifies the mystery of the divine teaching, which is set in motion by the
words and deeds of those who give instruction and which turns earthward
through active works and heavenward through contemplation, at one time
swinging downward through compassion for one's neighbor, again swinging
upward through the love of God. By these signs God shows that your mistress
will profit many by her words and example, and the effect of them will be felt
in other lands afar off whither she will go." That this interpretation of the
dream was true later events were to prove.

9

At the time when the blessed virgin Leoba was pursuing her quest for perfection in the monastery the holy martyr Boniface was being ordained by Gregory, bishop of Rome and successor to Constantine, in the Apostolic See. His
mission was to preach the Word of God to the people in Germany. When
Boniface found that the people were ready to receive the faith and that, though
the harvest was great, the laborers who worked with him were few, he sent
messengers and letters to England, his native land, summoning from different
ranks of the clergy many who were learned in the divine law and fitted both by
their character and good works to preach the Word of God. With their assistance he zealously carried out the mission with which he was charged, and by
sound doctrine and miracles converted a large part of Germany to the faith. As
the days went by, multitudes of people were instructed in the mysteries of the
faith and the Gospel was preached not only in the churches but also in the
towns and villages. Thus the Catholics were strengthened in their belief by

constant exhortation, the wicked submitted to correction, and the heathen, enlightened by the Gospel, flocked to receive the grace of baptism.

10

When the blessed man saw that the church of God was increasing and that the desire of perfection was firmly rooted he established two means by which religious progress should be ensured. He began to build monasteries, so that the people would be attracted to the church not only by the beauty of its religion but also by the communities of monks and nuns. And as he wished the observance in both cases to be kept according to the holy Rule, he endeavored to obtain suitable superiors for both houses. For this purpose he sent his disciple Sturm, a man of noble family and sterling character, to Monte Cassino, so that he could study the regular discipline, the observance and the monastic customs which had been established there by Saint Benedict. As the future superior, he wished him to become a novice and in this way learn in humble submission how to rule over others. Likewise, he sent messengers with letters to the abbess Tetta, of whom we have already spoken, asking her to send Leoba to accompany him on this journey and to take part in this embassy: for Leoba's reputation for learning and holiness had spread far and wide and her praise was on everyone's lips.[8] The abbess Tetta was exceedingly displeased at her departure, but because she could not gainsay the dispositions of divine providence she agreed to his request and sent Leoba to the blessed man. Thus it was that the interpretation of the dream that she had previously received was fulfilled. When she came, the man of God received her with the deepest reverence, holding her in great affection, not so much because she was related to him on his mother's side as because he knew that by her holiness and wisdom she would confer many benefits by her word and example.

11

In furtherance of his aims he appointed persons in authority over the monasteries and established the observance of regular discipline: he placed Sturm as abbot over the monks and Leoba as abbess over the nuns. He gave her the

---

8. Boniface was consecrated bishop in 722. If Leoba was already then famous "for learning and holiness" she must have been born early in the century. Perhaps, in reality, her reputation was less important than her kinship to Boniface's mother.

monastery at a place called Bischofsheim,[9] where there was a large community
of nuns. These were trained according to her principles in the discipline of
monastic life and made such progress in her teaching that many of them
afterward became superiors of others, so that there was hardly a convent of
nuns in that part that had not one of her disciples as abbess. She was a woman
of great virtue and was so strongly attached to the way of life she had vowed
that she never gave thought to her native country or her relatives. She expended all her energies on the work she had undertaken in order to appear
blameless before God and to become a pattern of perfection to those who
obeyed her in word and action. She was ever on her guard not to teach others
what she did not carry out herself. In her conduct there was no arrogance or
pride; she was no distinguisher of persons, but showed herself affable and
kindly to all. In appearance she was angelic, in word pleasant, clear in mind,
great in prudence, Catholic in faith, most patient in hope, universal in her
charity. But though she was always cheerful, she never broke out into laughter
through excessive hilarity. No one ever heard a bad word from her lips; the
sun never went down upon her anger. In the matter of food and drink she
always showed the utmost understanding for others but was most sparing in
her own use of them. She had a small cup from which she used to drink and
which, because of the meager quantity it would hold, was called by the sisters
"the Beloved's little one." So great was her zeal for reading that she discontin-
ued it only for prayer or for the refreshment of her body with food or sleep:
the Scriptures were never out of her hands. For, since she had been trained
from infancy in the rudiments of grammar and the study of the other liberal
arts, she tried by constant reflection to attain a perfect knowledge of divine
things so that through the combinations of her reading with her quick intelligence, by natural gifts and hard work, she became extremely learned. She read
with attention all the books of the Old and New Testaments and learned by
heart all the commandments of God. To these she added by way of completion
the writings of the Church Fathers, the decrees of the councils and the whole of
ecclesiastical law. She observed great moderation in all her acts and arrangements and always kept the practical end in view, so that she would never have
to repent of her actions through having been guided by impulse. She was
deeply aware of the necessity for concentration of mind in prayer and study,
and for this reason took care not to go to excess either in watching or in other
spiritual exercises. Throughout the summer both she and all the sisters under
her rule went to rest after the midday meal, and she would never give permis-

---

9. On the Tauber River, a tributary of the Main, about 100 miles southeast of Mainz.

sion to any of them to stay up late, for she said that lack of sleep dulled the mind, especially for study. When she lay down to rest, whether at night or in the afternoon, she used to have the Sacred Scriptures read out at her bedside, a duty the younger nuns carried out in turn without grumbling. It seems difficult to believe, but even when she seemed to be asleep they could not skip over any word or syllable while they were reading without her immediately correcting them. Those on whom this duty fell used afterward to confess that often when they saw her becoming drowsy they made a mistake on purpose to see if she noticed it, but they were never able to escape undetected. Yet it is not surprising that she could not be deceived even in her sleep, since He who keeps watch over Israel and neither slumbers nor sleeps possessed her heart, and she was able to say with the spouse in the Song of Songs: "I sleep, and my heart watcheth" (Song 5.2)

She preserved the virtue of humility with such care that, though she had been appointed to govern others because of her holiness and wisdom, she believed in her heart that she was the least of all. This she showed both in her speech and behavior. She was extremely hospitable. She kept open house for all without exception, and even when she was fasting gave banquets and washed the feet of the guests with her own hands, at once the guardian and the minister of the practice instituted by Our Lord.

12

While the virgin of Christ was acting in this way and attracting to herself everyone's affection, the devil, who is the foe of all Christians, viewed with impatience her own great virtue and the progress made by her disciples. He therefore attacked them constantly with evil thoughts and temptations of the flesh, trying to turn some of them aside from the path they had chosen. But when he saw that all his efforts were brought to nought by their prayers, fasting, and chaste lives, the wily tempter turned his attention to other means, hoping at least to destroy their good reputation, even if he could not break down their integrity by his foul suggestions.

There was a certain poor little crippled girl, who sat near the gate of the monastery begging alms. Every day she received her food from the abbess's table, her clothing from the nuns, and all other necessities from them; these were given to her from divine charity. It happened that after some time, deceived by the suggestions of the devil, she committed fornication, and when her appearance made it impossible for her to conceal that she had conceived a child she covered up her guilt by pretending to be ill. When her time came, she wrapped the child in swaddling clothes and cast it at night into a pool by the river that flowed through that place. In this way she added crime to crime, for she not only followed fleshly sin by murder, but also combined murder with the poisoning of the water. When day dawned, another woman came to draw water and, seeing the corpse of the child, was struck with horror. Burning with womanly rage, she filled the whole village with her uncontrollable cries and reproached the holy nuns with these indignant words: "Oh, what a chaste community! How admirable is the life of nuns, who beneath their veils give birth to children and exercise at one and the same time the function of mothers and priests, baptizing those to whom they have given birth. For, fellow citizens, you have drawn off this water to make a pool, not merely for the purpose of grinding corn, but unwittingly for a new and unheard-of kind of baptism. Now go and ask those women, whom you compliment by calling them virgins, to remove this corpse from the river and make it fit for us to use again. Look for the one who is missing from the monastery and then you will find out who is responsible for this crime." At these words all the crowd was set in uproar and everybody, of whatever age or sex, ran in one great mass to see what had happened. As soon as they saw the corpse they denounced the crime and reviled the nuns. When the abbess heard the uproar and learned what was afoot she called the nuns together, told them the reason, and discovered that no one was absent except Agatha, who a few days before had been summoned to her parents' house on urgent business: but she had gone with full permission. A messenger was sent to her without delay to recall her to the monastery, as Leoba could not endure the accusation of so great a crime to hang over them. When Agatha returned and heard of the deed that was charged against her she fell on her knees and gazed up to heaven, crying: "Almighty God, who knows all things before they come to pass, from whom nothing is hid and who has delivered Susanna from false accusations when she trusted in You, show Your mercy to this community gathered together in Your Name and let it not be sullied by filthy rumors on account of my sins; but may You deign to unmask and make known for the praise and glory of Your Name the person who has committed this misdeed."

On hearing this, the venerable superior, being assured of her innocence, ordered them all to go to the chapel and to stand with their arms extended in the form of a cross until each one of them had sung through the whole psalter, then three times each day, at tierce, sext, and none, to go round the monastic buildings in procession with the crucifix at their head, calling upon God to free them, in His mercy, from this accusation. When they had done this and they were going into the church at none, having completed two rounds, the blessed Leoba went straight to the altar and, standing before the cross, which was being prepared for the third procession, stretched out her hands toward heaven, and with tears and groans prayed, saying: "O Lord Jesus Christ, King of virgins, Lover of chastity, unconquerable God, manifest Your power and deliver us from this charge, because the reproaches of those who reproached You have fallen upon us." Immediately after she had said this, that wretched little woman, the dupe and the tool of the devil, seemed to be surrounded by flames, and, calling out the name of the abbess, confessed to the crime she had committed. Then a great shout rose to heaven: the vast crowd was astounded at the miracle, the nuns began to weep with joy, and all of them with one voice gave expression to the merits of Leoba and of Christ our Savior.

So it came about that the reputation of the nuns, which the devil had tried to ruin by his sinister rumor, was greatly enhanced, and praise was showered on them in every place. But the wretched woman did not deserve to escape scotfree and for the rest of her life she remained in the power of the devil. Even before this God had performed many miracles through Leoba, but they had been kept secret. This one was her first in Germany and, because it was done in public, it came to the ears of everyone.

13

On another occasion, when she sat down as usual to read the Scriptures to her disciples, a fire broke out in a part of the village. As the houses have roofs of wood and thatch, they were soon consumed by the flames, and the conflagration spread with increasing rapidity toward the monastery, so that it threatened to destroy not only the buildings but also the men and beasts. Then could be heard the mingled shouts of the terrified villagers as they ran in a mob to the abbess and begged her to avert the danger which threatened them. Unruffled and with great self-control, she calmed their fears and, without being influenced by their trust in her, ordered them to take a bucket and bring some water from the upper part of the stream that flowed by the monastery. As soon as they had brought it, she took some salt that had been blessed by Saint Boniface and that she always kept by her, and sprinkled it in the water. Then she said: "Go and pour back this water into the river and then let all the people draw water lower down the stream and throw it on the fire." After they had done this the violence of the conflagration died down and the fire was extinguished just as if a flood had fallen from the skies. So the buildings were saved.

At this miracle the whole crowd stood amazed and broke out into the praise of God, who through the faith and prayers of his handmaid had delivered them so extraordinarily from a terrible danger.

14

I think it should be counted among her virtues also that one day, when a wild storm arose and the whole sky was obscured by such dark clouds that day seemed turned into night, terrible lightning and falling thunderbolts struck terror into the stoutest hearts and everyone was shaking with fear. At first the people drove their flocks into the houses for shelter so that they should not perish; then, when the danger increased and threatened them all with death, they took refuge with their wives and children in the church, despairing of their lives. They locked all the doors and waited there trembling, thinking that the last judgment was at hand. In this state of panic they filled the air with the din of their mingled cries. Then the holy virgin went out to them and urged them all to have patience. She promised them that no harm would come to them; and after exhorting them to join with her in prayer, she fell prostrate at the foot of the altar. In the meantime the storm raged, the roofs of the houses were torn off by the violence of the wind, the ground shook with the repeated shocks of the thunderbolts, and the thick darkness, intensified by the incessant flicker of lightning that flashed through the windows, redoubled their terror. Then the mob, unable to endure the suspense any longer, rushed to the altar to rouse her from prayer and seek her protection. Thecla, her kinswoman, spoke to her first, saying: "Beloved, all the hopes of these people lie in you: you are their only support. Arise, then, and pray to the Mother of God, your mistress, for us, that by her intercession we may be delivered from this fearful storm." At these words Leoba rose up from prayer and, as if she had been challenged to a contest, flung off the cloak that she was wearing and boldly opened the doors of the church. Standing on the threshold, she made a sign of the cross, opposing to the fury of the storm the name of the High God. Then she stretched out her hands toward heaven and three times invoked the mercy of Christ, praying that through the intercession of holy Mary, the Virgin, He would quickly come to the help of His people. Suddenly God came to their aid. The sound of thunder died away, the winds changed direction and dispersed the heavy clouds, the darkness rolled back and the sun shone, bringing calm and peace. Thus did divine power make manifest the merits of His handmaid. Unexpected peace came to His people and fear was banished.

15

There was also another of her deeds that everyone agrees was outstanding and memorable, and that I think it would be wrong to pass over in silence. One of the sisters of the monastery named Williswind, of excellent character and edifying conduct, was attacked by a grave illness; she suffered from what the doctors call hemorrhoids, and through loss of blood from her private parts was racked by severe pains of the bowel. As the ailment continued and increased from day to day in severity, her strength ebbed away until she could neither turn over on her side nor get out of bed and walk without leaning on someone else. When she was no longer able to remain in the common dormitory of the monastery because of the stench, her parents who lived close by asked and obtained permission for her to be taken on a litter to their house across the river Tuberaha. Not long afterward, as the sickness gained hold, she rapidly drew near her end. As the lower part of her body had lost all sense of feeling and she was barely able to breathe, the abbess was asked by her parents not to come and visit the sick nun but to pray to God for her happy decease. When Leoba came, she approached the bed, now surrounded by a weeping throng of neighbors, and ordered the covering to be removed, for the patient was already enveloped in a linen cloth, as corpses usually are. When it was taken away she placed her hand on her breast and said: "Cease your weeping, for her soul is still in her." Then she sent to the monastery and ordered them to bring the little spoon which she usually used at table; and when it was brought to her she blessed milk and poured it drop by drop down the throat of the sick nun. At its touch, her throat and vitals recovered; she moved her tongue to speak and began to look round. Next day she had made such progress that she was able to take food, and before the end of the week she walked on her own feet to the monastery, whence she had previously been carried on a litter. She lived for several years afterward and remained in the service of God until the days of Louis,[10] king of the Franks, always strong and healthy, even after the death of Leoba.

16

The people's faith was stimulated by such tokens of holiness, and as religious feelings increased so did contempt of the world. Many nobles and influential

---

10. Louis succeeded his father Charlemagne as king and emperor from 814 to 840.

men gave their daughters to God to live in the monastery in perpetual chastity; many widows also forsook their homes, made vows of chastity, and took the veil in the cloister. To all of these the holy virgin pointed out both by word and example how to reach the heights of perfection.

17

In the meantime, blessed Boniface, the archbishop, was preparing to go to Frisia, having decided to preach the Gospel to this people riddled with superstition and unbelief. He summoned his disciple Lull to his presence (who was afterward to succeed him as bishop) and entrusted everything to his care, particularly impressing on him a solicitude for the faithful, zeal for preaching the Gospel, and the preservation of the churches, which he had built in various places. Above all, he ordered him to complete the building of the monastery of Fulda,[11] which he had begun to construct in the wilderness of Bochonia, a work undertaken on the authority of Pope Zachary[12] and with the support of Carloman, king of Austrasia.[13] This he did because the monks who lived there were poor and had no revenues and were forced to live on the produce of their own manual labor. He commanded him also to remove his body thither after his death. After giving these and other instructions, he summoned Leoba to him and exhorted her not to abandon the country of her adoption and not to grow weary of the life she had undertaken, but rather to extend the scope of the good work she had begun. He said that no consideration should be paid to her weakness and that she must not count the long years that lay ahead of her; she must not count the spiritual life to be hard nor the end difficult to attain, for the years of this life are short compared to eternity, and the sufferings of this world are as nothing in comparison with the glory that will be made manifest in the saints. He commended her to Lull and to the senior monks of the monastery who were present, admonishing them to care for her with reverence and respect and reaffirming his wish that after his death her bones should be placed next to his in the tomb, so that they who had served God during their lifetime with equal sincerity and zeal should await together the day of resurrection.

11. These details are related more fully in Eigil's *Life of Sturm*.

12. Pope, 741–752.

13. Austrasia was the easternmost portion of the old Frankish kingdom. Neustria, from the Paris basin to the Atlantic coast, along with Burgundy, were the other two regions. Carloman was mayor of the palace (741–747) but not king.

After these words he gave her his cowl and begged and pleaded with her not to leave her adopted land. And so, when all necessary preparations had been made for the journey, he set out for Frisia, where he won over a multitude of people to the faith of Christ and ended his labors with a glorious martyrdom. His remains were transported to Fulda and there, according to his previous wishes, he was laid to rest with worthy tokens of respect.

18

The blessed virgin, however, persevered unwaveringly in the work of God. She had no desire to gain earthly possessions but only those of heaven, and she spent all her energies on fulfilling her vows. Her wonderful reputation spread abroad and the fragrance of her holiness and wisdom drew to her the affections of all. She was held in veneration by all who knew her, even by kings. Pepin, king of the Franks, and his sons Charles and Carloman treated her with profound respect, particularly Charles, who, after the death of his father and brother, with whom he had shared the throne for some years, took over the reins of government.[14] He was a man of truly Christian life, worthy of the power he wielded, and by far the bravest and wisest king that the Franks had produced. His love for the Catholic faith was so sincere that, though he governed all, he treated the servants and handmaids of God with touching humility. Many times he summoned the holy virgin to his court, received her with every mark of respect, and loaded her with gifts suitable to her station. Queen Hildegard[15] also revered her with a chaste affection and loved her as her own soul. She would have liked her to remain continually at her side so that she might progress in the spiritual life and profit by her words and example. But Leoba detested the life at court like poison. The princes loved her, the nobles received her, the bishops welcomed her with joy. And because of her wide knowledge of the Scriptures and her prudence in counsel they often discussed spiritual matters and ecclesiastical discipline with her. But her deepest concern was the work she had set on foot. She visited the various convents of nuns and, like a mistress of novices, stimulated them to vie with one another in reaching perfection.

14. Pepin's two sons Charles (Charlemagne) and Carloman inherited jointly in 768 but Carloman died in 771 and Charlemagne ruled alone until 814.
15. The third of Charlemagne's four wives, she died in 783.

19

Sometimes she came to the monastery of Fulda to say her prayers, a privilege never granted to any woman either before or since, because from the day that monks began to dwell there entrance was always forbidden to women. Permission was only granted to her, for the simple reason that the holy martyr Saint Boniface had recommended her to the seniors of the monastery and because he had ordered her remains to be buried there. The following regulations, however, were observed when she came there. Her disciples and companions were left behind in a nearby cell and she entered the monastery always in daylight, with one nun older than the rest; and after she had finished her prayers and held a conversation with the brethren, she returned toward nightfall to her disciples whom she had left behind in the cell. When she was an old woman and became decrepit through age she put all the convents under her care on a sound footing and then, on Bishop Lull's advice, went to a place called Scoranesheim, four miles south of Mainz. There she took up residence with some of her nuns and served God night and day in fasting and prayer.

20

In the meantime, while King Charles was staying in the palace at Aachen,[16] Queen Hildegard sent a message to her begging her to come and visit her, if it were not too difficult, because she longed to see her before she passed from this life. And although Leoba was not at all pleased, she agreed to go for the sake of their long-standing friendship. Accordingly she went and was received by the queen with her usual warm welcome. But as soon as Leoba heard the reason for the invitation she asked permission to return home. And when the queen importuned her to stay a few days longer she refused; but, embracing her friend rather more affectionately than usual, she kissed her on the mouth, the forehead, and the eyes and took leave of her with these words: "Farewell for evermore, my dearly beloved lady and sister; farewell, most precious half of my soul. May Christ our Creator and Redeemer grant that we shall meet again without shame on the day of judgment. Never more on this earth shall we enjoy each other's presence."

16. Charlemagne did not in fact begin construction of his palace at Aachen until 788, after both Leoba and Hildegard were dead.

21

So she returned to the convent, and after a few days she was stricken down by sickness and was confined to her bed. When she saw that her ailment was growing worse and that the hour of her death was near she sent for a saintly English priest named Torhthat, who had always been at her side and ministered to her with respect and love, and received from him the Viaticum [Holy Eucharist] of the body and blood of Christ. Then she put off this earthly garment and gave back her soul joyfully to her Creator, clean and undefiled as she had received it from Him. She died in the month of September, the fourth of the kalends of October.[17] Her body, followed by a long cortège of noble persons, was carried by the monks of Fulda to their monastery with every mark of respect. Thus the seniors there remembered what Saint Boniface had said, namely, that it was his last wish that her remains should be placed next to his bones. But because they were afraid to open the tomb of the blessed martyr, they discussed the matter and decided to bury her on the north side of the altar, which the martyr Saint Boniface had himself erected and consecrated in honor of our Savior and the Twelve Apostles.

After some years, when the church had grown too small and was being prepared by its rectors for a future consecration, Abbot Eigil, with permission of Archbishop Heistulf, transferred her bones and placed them in the west porch near the shrine of Saint Ignatius the martyr,[18] where, encased in a tomb, they rest glorious with miracles. For many who have approached her tomb full of faith have many times received divine favors. Some of these that occur to me at the moment I will set down plainly and truthfully for my readers.

22

A certain man had his arms so tightly bound by iron rings that the iron was almost covered by the bare flesh that grew up around it on either side. One of these had already come off one arm and had left a deep scar that was plain to see. This man came to the church and went round the shrines of the saints, praying at each altar. When he reached the tomb of the holy virgin Leoba and began to pray some hidden force expanded the iron ring and, breaking the clamps, cast it from his arm, leaving it all bloody. With joy and gladness he

17. She died 28 September 779.
18. A second-century Christian whose relics were transferred to Fulda in the ninth century.

gave thanks to God, because by the merits of the blessed nun he, who until that moment had been bound in fetters on account of his sins, was released.

23

There was another man from Spain, who for his sins was so afflicted that he twitched most horribly in all his limbs. According to his own account he contracted this infirmity through bathing in the river Ebro. And because he could not bear his deformity to be seen by his fellow citizens he wandered about from shrine to shrine, wherever he had a mind to go. After traveling the length of France and Italy, he came to Germany. When he had visited several monasteries to pray there, he came to Fulda, where he was received into the pilgrim's hospice. He stayed three days there, going into the church and praying that God would be appeased and restore him to his former state of health. When he entered the chapel on the third day and had gone from altar to altar praying, he automatically came to the shrine of the holy virgin. He ended his prayer there and then went down to the western crypt above which the body of the holy martyr Boniface lies at rest. Prostrate in prayer, he lay like one asleep, but not twitching as he usually did when he slept. A saintly monk and priest named Firmandus, who used to sit there because he had an infirmity that prevented him from standing, noticed this and was struck with astonishment. He ordered those who wished to lift him not to touch him, but rather to wait to see what would happen. Suddenly the man got up and, because he was cured, he did not twitch. On being questioned by the priest, who, as an Italian, understood his language, he said that he had had an ecstasy in which he saw a venerable old man, vested in a bishop's stole, accompanied by a young woman in a nun's habit, who had taken him by the hand, lifted him up and presented him to the bishop for his blessing. When the bishop had made the sign of the cross on his breast an inky-black bird like a raven had flown out of his bosom and through the hood of his tunic; as soon as it alighted on the ground it changed into a hen and then transformed itself into the shape of a very ugly and horrible little man, who emerged from the crypt by the steps of the north entrance. No Christian man can doubt that he was restored to health through the prayers of the holy virgin and the merits of the blessed martyr. These two, though they do not share a tomb, yet lie in one place and never fail to look on those who seek their intercession with the same kindliness now they are in glory as they did when they lived on earth and showed pity and compassion on the wretched.

Many other marvels did God perform through the prayers of the holy virgin, but I will not mention them lest by prolonging my story I inflict tedium on the reader. But I recall these two, because several of the brethren who are still alive have borne witness in words that are not lightly to be disregarded that they saw them. I also was present when they occurred. I write this, then, for the praise and glory of the name of our Lord Jesus Christ, who glorifies those who glorify Him and who grants to those who serve Him not only the kingdom of heaven but also in this world nobility and honor. To whom be glory with the Father and the Holy Spirit forever and ever, Amen.

Anonymous

THE LIFE OF SAINT WILLEHAD

Translated by Peter J. Potter and
Thomas F. X. Noble

Although called by a good scholar "one of the most important saint's lives of the Carolingian period," this life of Willehad is little known or studied. Its author is unknown. Early manuscripts present this life together with a collection of tales about Willehad's miracles. Because the famous Scandinavian missionary Anskar (801–865) wrote the latter, it was long assumed that he wrote the life too. Careful research has shown this not to be the case, but no alternative has yet been suggested. The date of the composition may, on one reading of internal evidence, be put between 838 and 847. Others think a date in the 850s is more likely. Mysteries abound.

What is important or distinctive about the text? On historical grounds, two things. This work takes us into the time of Charlemagne's conquest of Saxony and of his attempts to procure order and organization there. Moreover, Willehad's hagiographer is the first person to mention explicitly the "*Translatio imperii*," that is the transfer of the imperial title from the Byzantines to the

Carolingians. We get here a nice reminder of the way in which cultural ideals and historical events can be recorded in a wide array of source materials.

On hagiographic grounds Willehad's life is conventional in many ways but it also illustrates well a particular Carolingian preoccupation. It will be recalled that Boniface was concerned about religious eccentrics in Germany. Charlemagne, in his massive program of ecclesiastical reform, tried hard to establish uniformity and conformity. It will, therefore, be noticed in this text that the spiritual powers of Willehad are fully recorded but just as fully attributed to God alone. There was no room in the Carolingian scheme of things for uncontrollable charismatics.

The date of Willehad's birth is unknown. He died in 789. He was an Anglo-Saxon and he received his education at York. He was probably a slightly older contemporary of Alcuin and may well have known him. Around 770 he, like so many of his countrymen before him, went over sea as a missionary, beginning his work at Dokkum in Frisia—an area still imperfectly Christianized. At some point Willehad became known to Charlemagne who sent him to Saxony in about 780 to found churches, introduce priests, and organize the conversion of the countryside. Between 782 and 785 Willehad had to flee Saxony because of a massive rebellion against Carolingian rule. While away from Saxony, Willehad went to Rome and met Pope Hadrian I (772–795). It is interesting that, in comparison to Boniface, Willehad received no instructions or episcopal office from the pope. Charlemagne was very much in control. Indeed, in 787 Willehad was consecrated at Worms as the first bishop for Saxony. It was the plan for Willehad to establish his see at Bremen but it took until 789, the year of his death, for him to bring the plan to fruition.

Texts and References

The best edition remains Albert Poncelet, ed., *De sancto Willehado primo Bremensis episcopo et inferioris Saxoniae apostolo*, *Acta sanctorum*, (Brussels, 1910), 3 Nov.:842–846. Poncelet's excellent introduction (pp. 835–842) remains the soundest overall treatment of the work. Useful is the introduction and annotation to a German translation by Andreas Röpke, *Das Leben des heilige Willehad Bischof von Bremen und die Beschreibung der Wunder an seinem Grabe* (Bremen, 1982). The only significant scholarly work on the life is Gerlinde Niemeyer, "Die Herkunft der Vita Willehadi," *Deutsches Archiv* 12 (1956): 17–35.

PROLOGUE

A religious disposition produces praises for the saints and acts from the faithful. To preach Christ truly in the saints, therefore, is to glorify Christ. For the saints have been made victors by the strength of him through whose grace they had been shown faithful in their good conversion. In fact, according to the apostle, the saints are what they are by the grace of God (see 1 Cor 15.10). And since his grace is always good, through it they are made men of good will. Indeed, this grace of God brings it about that this very goodwill, which has already begun to exist, increases in goodness so that in growing it might be multiplied. Consequently, any just man should be able, when he wishes, to keep the divine commandments fully and perfectly.

Therefore, if the saints are to be praised for their accomplishments, how much more should Christ be praised, whose grace the saints received so that they might become good and holy. Still, praises should be shared with the many faithful people who are living with piety and devotion in this life, but it is better and more sensible to praise those holy people who have well completed and happily finished their perilous life in this world. Further, it is fitting to extol and proclaim their most potent sanctity when neither he who is being praised can be tempted to elation nor he who is doing the praising can be given credit.

For this reason, the holy church has developed the most fitting custom of committing to writing the miracles, good works, and devotion to the faith of those saints whose very lives stood out so that posterity might have an example of virtue to imitate. In the saints the faithful have an example of divine mercy to follow so that, when they see works accomplished by the saints, they themselves will not despair of being able to do these same things, which perhaps might seem impossible. Even those who are fragile and bound by the flesh can accomplish exceptional and wonderful things with divine help. Indeed, everyone ought to strive toward this end since this right has been guaranteed by all the holy faithful, namely, those citizens of that most blessed heavenly country through whom we confidently believe that we have special protection aiding and guiding us. Therefore, even we are led to write down the life of our holy father Willehad, the first bishop of the church in Bremen, who was religious and devout in all things before God. By describing the triumph of his virtue and revealing the divine glory that was in him, we set forth the example of his sanctity for others to imitate.[1]

---

1. Notice that this author opens with a theological justification for writing a saint's life, not a rhetorical justification for his own efforts.

1

There was a venerable man from Northumbria, of the race of the Angles, named Willehad, who was taught sacred letters from infancy and who was instructed in spiritual discipline. He began most zealously to live in the ways of God, and by means of fasts, vigils, and prayers both day and night he showed himself to be keenly devout in the service of Almighty God. And in the eyes of all those living there his acts were as good and honorable as they were pleasing and praiseworthy. When he grew older, having the support of all, he was promoted to the priesthood by the grace of election. He especially strove to augment and adorn his priestly office more and more through the merit of holiness and the extraordinary exercise of good works.

Finally, after he had been ordained priest, he heard that the Frisians and Saxons, peoples who up until then had been pagan unbelievers, had rejected the worship of idols and had just begun to seek in small measure the mysteries of the Catholic faith and desired to be cleansed of their former blemishes through the sacrament of baptism. Thus, when he heard this, the man of God was filled with delight, and, burning with an inward love, he began to investigate how he might transfer himself to those lands. Because this servant of God was inflamed with such zeal day after day by the divine spark of the Spirit, the burning candle could not be hidden under the bushel in darkness but rather was placed on a candlestand so that it might shine openly to all those who were then, or would be in times to come, in the house of the Lord (see Mt 5.15).

Therefore, Willehad approached the king who was ruling over the Angles at the time, Alchred[2] by name, and told him with many tears that he was burning with desire to serve the Lord. He asked that he be permitted to go to preach the word of the Lord in those lands that had been brought to his attention. When the king had learned of his most holy desire, he convened no small council of bishops and other servants of God and openly pointed out to all of them Willehad's most fervent devotion. And with the mutual consent of all (naturally since the holiness of that blessed man had long since been demonstrated) he appointed Willehad, who had been commended by heavenly grace, to preach the word of the Lord in the aforementioned places.[3]

---

2. King, 765–774.

3. This may or may not have happened. What is striking is the emphasis on royal authority.

2

With a most willing heart, Willehad then began his journey, crossing the narrow sea that lay nearby. He arrived in Frisia, at a place called Dokkum[4] in the district of Oostergoo, where the lord Bishop Boniface had already been crowned with martyrdom. Willehad was received with great honor because many of the people there had once been instructed in the faith through the preaching of this martyr. He lived there for quite some time teaching them the things of God. Several noblemen handed their children over to him to be educated, and he inspired them to divine love by both the word of his teaching and the piety of his behavior. Many who once had strayed from the faith he called back to a true and Catholic understanding, and he showed himself to be the brightest light of heavenly brilliance in that place. Indeed, he baptized as great a number of pagans as possible, having instructed them by the word of his holy preaching.

3

Moving on, he traveled up the river Lauwers and came to a place called Humsterland.[5] There he began to preach to the barbarians in the name of the Lord and to persuade them that they should give up the superstition of idols and receive the news of the one true God so that they might merit pardon from their sins through the washing of holy baptism. He told them that it was mad and pointless to seek help from stones and to expect solace from deaf and dumb idols. But hearing these words, this fierce and deeply idolatrous people were all stirred to great wrath, and they gnashed their teeth at him, saying that anyone who presumed to pronounce such sacrilegious words against their unconquered gods ought not to live any longer; indeed, he ought to be put to death. Nevertheless, some among them persuaded the others, through wiser counsel, pointing out that this rule of religion was unknown to them and should therefore be tested to see if it might be from divine will, and that the man himself was in fact guilty of no crime and therefore should not die an ambiguous death. Thus, they suggested that lots be cast, which would prove by heavenly sign if he was deserving of destruction or if they should set him free. In this way, they themselves would not be responsible for any man's fate. So, it was done as these men had urged, and, according to the custom of the people,

4. On the northern coast of Frisia.
5. He was moving inland toward Germany.

they cast lots to see if Willehad should live or die. But, under the direction of divine providence, the lot of death could not fall upon him, wherefore they did not dare to hurt him in any way.[6] And so, after taking counsel they let him leave them unharmed.

4

Departing, Willehad came to Drenthe,[7] where, when he preached the word of the Lord, a great multitude of the people believed and received the sacrament of baptism. He decided to stay longer in this place because he was eager to teach unbelievers and to confirm those who already believed in the way of truth both through his words and through his earnest example. And a great many people, imitating the good life of the teacher, began to hold in hatred the errors of unbelievers and to venerate with fervent devotion the Christian religion that they now professed.

Then it happened that certain of his disciples, moved by divine passion, began to destroy the temples that had been erected throughout the region according to pagan custom and, insofar as they were able, to raze them to the ground. Consequently, those barbarians, who up to this point had stood watching in disbelief, were suddenly overcome with rage and descended at once upon the disciples with force, hoping to destroy them utterly. They fell upon the fallen servant of God with clubs, inflicting many wounds, and one of them, having unsheathed his sword, rushed at Willehad and tried to cut off his head. But, at that very moment, the blessed man had a small box of holy relics hanging about his neck, and when the blow struck his neck it cut the chain holding up the box, but he himself was not harmed in the least. Frightened by this miracle, the pagans allowed him and his company to depart unmolested, not daring to harm them in any way.

5

After this, Charles, the most glorious king of the Franks, who had already worked hard among the Saxons to convert them to the Christian religion (even though these hard-hearted people were always abandoning their new faith and

6. Compare Willibrord's experience (see pages 199–200).
7. In the Westphalian region of Saxony, just west of the River Ems.

returning to their old errors) heard of the fame of the man of God and instructed Willehad to come see him. When he arrived, Charles received him reverently and honorably, and he turned his attention willingly to his conversation and to his teachings. When he found Willehad's ways holy and his faith constant, Charles sent him to Saxony to the region that is called Wigmodia,[8] where, on royal authority, he might build churches and extend to the people the doctrine of his holy teaching and proclaim the way of eternal salvation to all people living there.

Because Willehad accomplished his task with duty and devotion, and because he made regular rounds throughout his entire diocese, he converted many to the faith of Christ through his teaching so that by his second year all the Saxons and Frisians who lived in the circuit of his travels promised that they would become Christians. This occurred in the year of the Lord's incarnation 781, the fourteenth year of the reign of the most serene prince, Charles, who had not yet been raised up to the imperial honor. This would occur in the thirty-forth year of his reign, when with reverence and joy the Catholic Church of Europe, itself resting upon Christ, accepted Charles as emperor, consecrated by the hands of the most reverend apostolic Leo. After the reign of the most pious Augustus Constantine, and right down to that time, the imperial power had resided among the Greeks at Constantinople. Then, with men of the royal family lacking there and with the state being administered by a woman's authority,[9] in the time of Charles the empire was translated to the rule of the Franks through the election of the Roman people and especially by a council of bishops and other servants of God. This happened because Charles himself was seen to hold that city that had been the head of the empire and also many other lands and provinces throughout the world. Therefore, he was rightly deemed worthy to be called emperor. Anyway, during the reign of Charles, the servant of God, Willehad, began to construct churches throughout Wigmodia and to ordain priests for them who freely shared with the people the words of salvation and the grace of baptism.

6

In the following year, a certain Widukind, inspired by the devil who envies everything good, conceived a foul plan to rebel against King Charles. He

8. Beyond the River Oder, to the east of where he had already been working.
9. The Empress Irene, 797–802.

assembled a great multitude of Saxons, and all the rebels began to persecute and punish those whom they perceived to be constant in the faith of Christ. They even began to disperse the servants of God, scattering them throughout the land and forcing them to flee beyond their borders. As the persecution flared up, it moved the servant of God to heed the command given by the Lord: "When they persecute you in one city, flee to the next" (Mt 10.23). He crossed from Wigmodia and came to Rustringerland where he boarded a boat and traveled by sea along the coast of Frisia. And so, assisted by the grace of Christ, he escaped the persecution. Meanwhile, the Saxons, with ever-growing wrath, visited that cruelty on Willehad's disciples that they had been unable to wreak on the teacher himself. Indeed, out of hatred for the Christian name, they struck down with their swords Folcardus the priest, and Counts Emmiggus in the district called Laras and Benjamin in Rustringerland, also the cleric Atrebanus in Ditmarschen and Gerwalus with his company in Bremen. And while those who shed their blood were summoned happily to the kingdom of heaven, the storm of persecution raged on long afterward at the hands of the rebellious Saxons.

7

The man of God, knowing that there would be no opportunity to preach during this time, set out to see King Pepin[10] of the Lombards and then went on most eagerly to Rome. Earnestly and devoutly seeking divine clemency in Rome, he commended himself and all his company of faithful to the most holy see of the blessed Peter, prince of the apostles, with many tears and prayers. He especially remembered those in Saxony who, having received Christianity, might now be totally destroyed by diabolical machination. Thereafter, strengthened not a little by the consolation of the venerable Pope Hadrian, the servant of God departed and returned joyfully to Francia.

During his journey, it happened that divine power was demonstrated through him. A servant of the man of God, called Aldo, who regularly procured food for his master, had a certain wooden plate (which is commonly called a *scutella*) that he would always place, clean and shiny, on the table before his master. However, on one day he discovered that the plate was

10. Actually Pepin was Charlemagne's son. He was made king of Italy, not of the Lombards, by his father in 781 and ruled until his death in 811. It is hard to explain why Willehad should have conceived a desire to go to see Pepin.

accidentally broken. Therefore, at dinnertime, when the man of God needed the plate, the servant did not want to hide his negligence. When he told him that the plate was broken, Willehad immediately commanded him to bring it to him just as it was. But the servant, returning to the place where it lay, indeed, where he had left it broken, found it whole as if it had never suffered damage. So when he returned with the plate and placed it before his master, he who a few moments earlier had been trembling for fear of the wrath of just correction, was happy and cheerful. He had no doubt that this heavenly act happened on account of the grace of the holy man, but Willehad himself rejected exaltation, wishing the matter to be kept secret rather than made public.

Upon returning from his journey, Willehad went to the place which is called Epternach,[11] where his disciples, who had been scattered all over for fear of persecution, joined him again. Reviving them with kindhearted consolation so that they might remain steadfast in all things for the faith of Christ, he was careful to admonish them tenderly. Meanwhile he remained in this same place for almost two years, choosing to live a solitary life as a recluse. He did not, however, live a life of ease but gave himself continuously to reading and prayer, and during the day he was especially dedicated to writing. He inscribed the Epistles of the blessed Paul, and many others too, into one volume that has been kept as a monument to his holy memory by his successors; it remains intact to this day. Furthermore, through his example and his admonitions many others in this place were brought to a higher life and inflamed to take up the Lord's service courageously.

8

Later, the venerable priest of the Lord, Willehad, went again to King Charles, who was then encamped in a fortress at Eresburg[12] in Saxony. He explained to Charles his most fervent desire to spread the gospel of peace, and he sought Charles's most beneficial counsel in this matter. As support for his work and to provide for his followers, Charles gave to him in benefice a certain cell in Francia, called Justina, and he instructed him to return again to the parish where he had begun his work. Graciously and devoutly accepting the benefice, Willehad returned to Wigmodia where he preached the faith of the Lord to the

11. Not far from Trier in the very heartlands of Carolingian territory.
12. In southern Saxony, near the border with Hesse.

people openly and forcefully. He also restored the destroyed churches and appointed proven people in each place who could deliver the words of salvation to the people. In that same year, it was God's will that the Saxons should once again accept the Christian faith, which they had earlier abandoned. What is more, in that same year the author of all evil and the instigator of treachery, Widukind, submitted himself to King Charles and received the grace of baptism. So for the moment the evils that had been spawned by his wickedness subsided. In fact, after this time when all seemed peaceful and the necks of the barbarous Saxons had been forced into the gentle yoke of Christ, the excellent prince Charles, then in the city of Worms,[13] had Willehad consecrated bishop there on 13 July 787. He appointed him pastor and rector over Wigmodia, Laras, Rustringerland, and Ostringen, as well as Norden and Wangerland so that he might lead the people there with episcopal authority and, just as he had already begun, strive to lead them to salvation by his teaching and by his outstanding labors under the watchful eye of God. And so this Willehad became the first bishop of the diocese.

But his installation was delayed a long time because the people frequently resisted the divine faith, even under compulsion. They refused to permit priests among them, not tolerating episcopal authority, even backed by royal authority. So he returned where he had begun seven years before, though now he was called bishop, not priest; and, as far as he was able, he arranged everything possible by his episcopal authority. Having received pontifical consecration, he began to conduct himself even more devoutly in all things, and that keenness for virtue that he had earlier cultivated he accumulated in vastly greater degree.

9

From the days of his youth, he was a man of great self-control, and he served the omnipotent Lord devoutly from an early age. He did not drink any wine or cider or anything that might make him drunk. For his food he ate bread and honey and fruit and vegetables. He abstained from meat and milk and also from fish until the above-mentioned apostolic Hadrian told him that, at his age and for the sake of his health, he should eat fish. Obeying the pope's advice, Willehad reluctantly began to eat a little fish.

Almost no day passed when Willehad did not celebrate the solemn sacred

13. On the Rhine in central Germany.

mass with much weeping and contrition of heart. He was always eager to read and meditate on the holy teachings, and, equally mindful of the psalms, he used to chant the entire psalter almost daily, and sometimes twice or three times a day. By the practice of these and other good works, he set before the people the great grace of the Lord in his own example. His teaching, therefore, was a prophecy that shone forth in two ways: what he taught by his word he confirmed by his example.

This blessed man of God traveled in circuit throughout his diocese confirming the Christian people whom he had once baptized and caused erring hearts to repent and take to the path of salvation through his preaching. He also built a house of God of marvelous beauty in a place called Bremen and established his episcopal see there and dedicated it on the first day of November in honor of our Lord Jesus Christ and under the name of Saint Peter.[14]

10

Later, when with piety and zeal he was making one of his frequent circuits throughout his diocese, teaching those things that are of God so that he might strengthen many in the faith, he came to the place that is called Blexen. While staying there, his body began to shake from a severe fever, and he grew weaker day by day so that his disciples who were with him began to despair for his life. One of them, named Egisrik, who was in the habit of speaking intimately with the blessed man, approached him with tears and laments and let him know that they greatly feared his death. Pointing out the grave loss this would be to his people, the very people who were under his pastoral guidance and who were just then beginning to obey the divine will, Egisrik said: "Venerable priest, do not abandon so quickly those whom you have recently brought to the Lord. Do not leave behind so soon the people and clergy assembled through your earnest efforts lest the flock, which is still tender in the faith, should be devoured by hungry wolves. Do not deprive your humble dependents of your holy presence lest they should wander aimlessly like sheep without a shepherd" (see Mt 9.36).

Hearing this, the blessed man was filled with sorrow and responded with these words: "Do not, my children, keep me any longer from the sight of my Lord. Do not bring down upon me the troubles of this world through your plaintive cries. I neither seek to live any longer nor am I afraid to die. I wish

14. Note again the Carolingian connection with Saint Peter.

most to pray to my God whom I have always loved with all my heart and whom I have served with fullest devotion, that he, being compassionate and merciful, might deign to confer upon me whatever he sees fit as the just recompense for my labors. The sheep, however, whom he has entrusted to me, I commit to him for safekeeping because if I have accomplished anything good, I have done it through his power. His compassion will not fail you whose mercy fills all the earth" (see Ps 32.5).

Therefore, with pious devotion this man of the Lord, whose gaze was always fixed on heaven and whose prayers were always ascending to God, indeed, this confessor of the Lord, rested in the name of Christ on Sunday morning, the eighth day of November.[15] Hearing of his death, devout people from everywhere rushed to the funeral procession and carried off this most blessed father and doctor to Bremen, all the while singing hymns and praises. With fitting honor and reverence they placed him in the sepulcher in the new basilica which he himself had built.

11

Many signs have been seen in this place that truly demonstrate that this blessed man was a chosen soldier of the Lord. Unfortunately, through neglect and indifference they have not been written down anywhere, but there may be those, not a few in number, who would admit that divine power had manifested itself in that same place. But later he was translated into another basilica (this happened in the time of his successor of good memory, Bishop Willerich)[16] and when this basilica was dedicated, Willehad worked even more miracles through divine power, but no one has set these down either, even though the assertion of many people proves them to have been true miracles. One should now shroud in silence and keep locked away in the church of Bremen what God has revealed to the glory of the blessed man. For example, after the blessed man's death, his followers kept the staff, which he used to carry according to episcopal custom, and, out of devotion to him, placed it in a certain chest. It once happened that the building in which this very same chest resided suddenly went up in flames, and the building along with the chest and everything that had been placed in it was almost totally consumed. But the fire was completely unable to touch that staff in any way, and it was actually found

15. For centuries the feast of Saint Willehad has been important in northern Germany.
16. Bishop of Bremen, from 804–805 to 838.

in the midst of where the fire had been, but the flames had left no sign on it. Wherefore, Almighty God is to be praised in his saints, for even in little things he reveals the merit of his disciples to his faithful.

Another thing happened, which equally showed that this blessed man was truly worthy of great merit in the sight of the Lord. The most devoted affection of his disciples led them to keep in a certain secret place his chalice, the very one with which he regularly offered sacrifice to the Lord. But, when the devouring fire consumed everything, and its heat turned into liquid anything that had been made of metal, the chalice was found whole, even though it was made of silver. Remarkable indeed is the power of the Lord that while the blessed man lived his heart was kindled by the first of divine love, but after he died earthly fire had no power whatsoever over his relics. For creation, being subject to the rule of the creator, loses even the power of nature when it attends to the power of God. Nor, even when nature wills it, can it accomplish anything bad since the force of everything in nature depends on the absolute will of the creator.

The blessed Willehad, chosen priest of God, remained in the office of bishop for two years, three months, and twenty-six days. Having fought the good fight, he happily departed to be with the Lord, to whom be honor and glory and power and dominion, forever and ever. Amen.

Odo of Cluny

THE LIFE OF SAINT GERALD OF AURILLAC

Translated by Gerard Sitwell, O.S.B.

Odo, second abbot of the great monastery of Cluny, was born, possibly in Le Mans but maybe in Aquitaine, in 878 or 879. He died in Tours in 942. He was educated for secular service at the court of Duke William of Aquitaine, the actual founder of Cluny. In his background he was, thus, much like Benedict of Aniane and Gerald of Aurillac himself.

When he was about nineteen Odo decided to abandon secular life. He became a canon of Saint Martin's at Tours. Not long after this he became a Benedictine monk. Odo also studied for a time in Paris under the renowned master Remigius of Auxerre (c. 841–c. 908). When he was around thirty Odo went to Baume, to whose abbot, Berno, William had entrusted the foundation of Cluny. By 924 Berno had named Odo as his successor at Baume, Cluny, and other monasteries that had come under his control in the meantime. Until his death Odo was one of the major figures in Europe, friend and adviser to popes, kings, and magnates from many lands. We noted already some tensions in the careers of activist ascetics from Anglo-Saxon England. Those tensions are also evident in the work of Benedict of Aniane. With Odo they are magnified many times.

Odo seems not to have known Gerald, although he was a younger contemporary from the same general area of France. He wrote this *Life*, as he tells us, on the request of Abbot Aymo of Saint-Martial in Limoges. Stories about Gerald were circulating widely and Odo was requested to look into them. While visiting Tulle, a monastery not too far from Aurillac into which he had introduced strong Benedictine usages, Odo decided to investigate Gerald's life and deeds. Odo repeatedly states his concern to get at the truth. This concern to establish a verifiable historical account is not unique to Odo's text, but it takes on clearer proportions here than anywhere else previously. Odo was also abbot of Aurillac, the chief monastery in the town that had been the center of Gerald's county. Odo is well attested to in many historical sources and was himself the subject of a full-length *Life* by John of Salerno.

For Gerald was a count, and that is the prime, though not the only, interest of this text. It was, in the early Middle Ages, even rarer to write the life of a layperson who was not a king than the life of a woman. Odo investigated Gerald's life and found him to be entirely worthy of the sainthood that had been popularly attributed to him. But it was sainthood with a difference. Odo describes a holy life lived entirely in the bumptious world of human activity. In other words, Odo held up Gerald as a model to those who would remain in the world and carry out their duties there. We have already encountered ascetic texts that oppose monastic virtues to the vices that are most likely to afflict monks. Odo also produces an account of warring virtues and vices—a literary form that reaches far back into both Christian and pagan antiquity— but he focuses on the special virtues required by a layman to meet the challenges of life in the world.

Apart from the adjustments made necessary by Gerald's lay status, Odo accomplished his work in quite traditional ways. The text is on the whole well written, clear, and vigorous. Odo is much more the product of the Carolingian Renaissance than Ardo. Odo certainly knew the Bible extremely well, as his many allusions and quotations show. In others of his voluminous writings Odo shows himself to have been learned in classical and, especially, patristic writings. Perhaps because this text was aimed at a lay audience Odo did not put his learning on display in it.

Gerald himself was born in about 855 and lived to 909. He came from an important family of the Auvergne region of France. His parents were nobles and the family held extensive properties scattered over a wide area. Gerald's family was one of the last south of the Loire River to continue acknowledging the authority of the kings of the West Frankish kingdom—the lands that evolved into France. This text makes clear the extent to which power was fragmenting and falling into the hands of local potentates. It was, then, in very uncertain times that Gerald lived out his extraordinary life.

Texts and References

No serious work has been done on the text of Odo's *De vita Sancti Geraldi Auriliacensis comitis Libri Quattuor,* and it is still necessary to consult the old edition in *Patrologia Latina,* vol. 133, cols. 639–703. Although this *Life* has been of keen interest to historians, it has not received a full and careful scholarly analysis. Odo, as abbot of Cluny and European statesman, has received abundant attention but Odo as author has been all but ignored. For a start see Max Manitius, *Geschichte der lateinischen Literatur des Mittelalters,* 3 vols. (Munich, 1911–31), 2:20–27 and Franz Brunhölzl, *Geschichte der lateinischen Literatur des Mittelalters,* 2 vols. (Munich, 1975), 2:206–9. Basic details on Odo and his writings may be found in the article of D. Verhelst, "Odo," *Lexikon des Mittelalters* (Munich, 1993), 6: cols. 1357–58. On Gerald, see J.-C. Poulin, "Geraldus von Aurillac," *Lexikon des Mittelalters* (Munich, 1988), 4:1297–98.

Dedicatory Epistle of the Author

To the Father Abbot Aymo in affectionate remembrance of his merits, Odo the servant of the brethren, everlasting salvation in Christ. I am undertaking, venerable Father, as best I can and with much trepidation, the little book that you recently urged me so strongly to write concerning the life and miracles of the holy man Gerald. On the one hand I fear to be presumptuous in undertaking something beyond my capacity; on the other hand, in not doing it I fear greatly to be contumacious by being disobedient. I undertake the task, however, relying on the obedience and the goodness of Christ, and I beseech you to implore His mercy, that for the love of His servant Gerald He would deign so to guide what I say, that it may not be entirely unworthy of the man He has seen fit to glorify, and that to me it may not be a cause of transgression. To avoid such transgression I pass over some things for which perhaps you will blame me, and set down those things only that were made known to me by sure authorities and when you also were present. Farewell.

PREFACE

Many doubt whether the things that are said about the blessed Gerald are true, and some think that they are certainly not true but fantastic. Others, as though seeking excuses for their sins, extol him indiscreetly, saying that Gerald was powerful and rich, and lived well, and is certainly a saint. They strive indeed to excuse their luxurious lives by his example. It seemed to me therefore that I ought to reply a little to these according to my ability. For I too, formerly, hearing the fame of his miracles, was nevertheless in doubt, and for this reason chiefly, that stories get about here and there, through I know not what channels, and are then gradually discredited as empty. But when cause arose that I should visit the community of the monastery at Tulle, I was glad to go to his tomb, and then having summoned four of those whom he had brought up, namely the monk Hugh, the priest Hildebert, and two wellborn laymen, Witard and another Hildebert, along with many others, I investigated his behavior and the quality of his life in detail. Now with the others, now alone, I carefully investigated what each one said and whether they agreed, silently pondering if his life was one in which miracles frequently occurred. Having learned how religiously he lived and that God had shown this man to be in His grace by many signs, I could no longer doubt of his sanctity. I marvel rather, that in this age of ours, when charity has almost entirely grown cold, and the time of Antichrist is at hand, the miracles of the saints should not cease, but He is mindful of the promise, that He makes by Jeremiah: "I will not turn away from doing good to [my people]" (Jer 32.40). And of this good that He has done the apostle bears witness, when he says that God, not leaving Himself in any age without a witness (see Acts 14.16), in His kindness fills the hearts of men with joy. If, therefore, it pleases the divine goodness, that He who did wonderful things for our fathers, should be glorified also in our times, we ought by no means to be incredulous. For it seems that the divine dispensation performs these things in our age and through a man of our time, because everything that the saints did or said in the past has been forgotten. And since, as in the days of Noah, a man of God was found, who lived according to the law, God set him up as an example to those who saw him, that their hearts should be inspired to imitate one who was their neighbor, and whom they saw to live a just and pious life. And let not the observance of the commandments of God seem hard or impossible, since it is seen to have been achieved by a layman of great position. For nothing more encourages mental cowardice than that the retribution of good or evil works, that is to follow in the next life, should not be meditated upon in the present. And against this Scripture warns us that in all our actions we should remember our last end (see Sir 7.36). God, therefore, exalts on earth in the sight of his contemporaries the servant whom He rewards in heaven, so that by that which is done outwardly the contemners of God may see inwardly that God is not served in vain, but that as He Himself testifies, He will glorify those who glorify Him, and bring down in shame those who despise Him. Since, therefore, I believe this man of God to have been given as an example to the mighty, let them see how they may imitate him as one of themselves held up for their example, lest perchance, as the Queen of the South the Jews, he shall condemn them in the Day of Judgment. Taking occasion from his actions, I have added something by way of admonition to those same mighty ones, where opportunity has arisen, as you asked me. And indeed Bishop Turpio[1] and the venerable Abbot Aymo,[2] who is most dear to me, with many others, have driven me with urgent prayers to undertake this. When I would have put forward the true excuse of lack of skill, they said that they preferred matter such as this to be put forth in an unpolished style, and I, considering that a grandiose style little fitted a humble man, have put my faith in the words of witnesses, who have recorded not many of the miracles that ordinary men think of great moment, but rather a disciplined way of life, and not a few works of mercy pleasing to God. For in the judgment the king will say to many who prophesied and who did great things: "I do not know you" (Mt. 25.12). But those who execute justice, in which Gerald excelled, are to hear "Come, O blessed of my father" (Mt. 25.34). And in truth the things that were done by Job, David, and Tobias, and many others, and through which they are blessed, are not those that Gerald is shown to have done. Having considered all this I was persuaded to believe that Gerald (through whom the heavenly Giver of gifts deigns to work miracles) is worthy of the company of the saints. But in making this apology in the preface I have spoken too long; now in the name of Christ let us come to the beginning of our tale.

BOOK 1

1

The man of God, Gerald, took his origin from that part of Gaul which was called by the ancients *Celtica*,[3] in the territory that borders the Auvergne and

---

1. Turpio (or Turpin) was bishop of Limoges in the early tenth century. He was the brother of Abbot Aymo who asked Odo to write this *Life*. He died in 944.
2. The date of Aymo's birth is unknown. He was abbot of Saint-Martial from 937 until his death in 943.
3. Celtic Gaul was, to the Romans, the central region of what is now France.

the regions of Cahors and Albi, in the town or village of Aurillac. His father was Gerald, his mother Adaltruda. He was so illustrious by the nobility of his birth, that among the families of Gaul his lineage is outstanding both for its possessions and the excellence of its life. For it is said that his parents held modesty and religion as a sort of hereditary dowry. Two witnesses among his ancestors are themselves sufficient to prove the point: namely Saint Caesarius, the bishop of Arles,[4] and the holy Abbot Aredius.[5] And because the Lord is in the generation of the just, the generation of Gerald is of those who seek the Lord; and so the righteous generation is blessed. And indeed the great quantity of estates endowed with serfs, lying in various places, which came to Gerald by right of succession, testifies to the extent of their riches. But in him the beauty of mind that he inherited from his parents shone forth much augmented. With what grace were his parents endowed, who merited to beget so excellent an offspring!

2

His father was so careful to conduct himself chastely in his marriage, that he frequently slept alone far from the marriage bed, as though for a time giving himself to prayer according to the apostle (see 1 Cor 7.5). He is said to have been warned in sleep on a certain night that he should know his wife, because he was to beget a son, and they say that it was announced to him that he should call his name Gerald, and that he would be a man of great virtue. When he awoke he was full of joy at the vision. Having fallen asleep again it seemed to him that a rod grew up from the big toe of his right foot, which gradually grew into a great tree, which burst into leaf and spread itself on all sides. Then seeming to call workmen he ordered props in the form of forks or poles to be put underneath it. And even when it grew very great, he felt no weight on his toe. In truth visions of dreams are not always vain. And if faith is to be put in sleep, it seems that this vision agrees in its result with future events. He knew his wife, who conceived a son as the vision foretold. The dream may perhaps be doubted, but the mark of virtue evidently followed.

---

4. Caesarius (c. 470–542) was bishop of Arles from 502. He left behind a huge collection of sermons. There is no certain evidence that Gerald was related to him.

5. Aredius was born in Limoges to noble parents in the early sixth century. He was abbot of Attane, now Saint-Yrieix (Dépt. Haute Vienne). As with Caesarius, there is no evidence that Gerald was related to Aredius.

3

When his mother was near to giving birth, on the ninth day before he was born, it happened that she and her husband were lying awake. And while they were talking about I know not what, the child cried out so that both heard it. Lost in astonishment, they were dumbfounded as to what it might be—yet they could not but know that the voice sounded in the womb of the mother. The father called the waiting-woman and ordered her to search with a light for the place where the crying came from. When, equally astonished, she protested that there was no child present to have uttered the cry, the child cried a second time. And after a short interval it cried a third time, as a child recently born is accustomed to cry. Three times, therefore, he was heard in the womb of his mother, and assuredly this is a strange thing that certainly happened against the course of nature. And because it happened not by chance but by the dispensation of God, the Ruler of nature, perhaps that voice presaged that his actions in the prison of his mortality were to be of great moment. For as the child in the womb of his mother lives indeed, but is not conscious, so after the guilt of the first man the whole human race on earth is confined as in the narrowness of the womb, and although by faith it lives in the hope of the glory of the sons of God, nevertheless it scarcely performs, except in a languid manner, any act of the senses like seeing, nor can it make use of the senses in the way that the first man did before sin, or the saints do after this life. Gerald therefore did well to cry in the womb of his mother, because acting in the faith of the Holy Trinity beyond the common vigor of men, he signified by that small voice the happy fame with which he was to fill the world.

4

When he had been born, then, and weaned, and had come to that age in which the character of children may usually be discerned, a certain pleasing quality began to show itself in him, by which those who looked closely conjectured of what virtue the future man should be. For at an early age, as we often see, children through the incitements of their corrupt nature are accustomed to be angry and envious, and to wish to be revenged, or to attempt other things of this sort. But in the child Gerald a certain sweetness and modesty of mind, which especially graces youth, adorned his childish acts. By the grace of divine providence he applied himself to the study of letters, but by the will of his parents only to the extent of going through his psalter; after that he was instructed in the worldly exercises customary for the sons of the nobility; to ride to hounds, become an archer, learn to fly falcons and hawks in the proper manner. But lest given to useless pursuits the time suitable for learning letters should pass without profit the divine will ordained that he should be a long time sick, though with such a sickness that he should be withdrawn from worldly pursuits but not hindered in his application to learning.[6] And for a long time he was so covered with small pimples that it was not thought that he could be cured. For this reason his father and mother decided that he should be put more closely to the study of letters, so that if he should prove unsuited for worldly pursuits, he might be fitted for the ecclesiastical state. So it came about that he not only learned the chant, but also learned something of grammar. And this was afterward of much use to him, since, perfected by that exercise, his wits were sharpened for whatever he might wish to apply them to. He had a lively and discerning mind, and was not slow to learn anything to which he set himself.

5

While he was growing up his bodily strength consumed the harmful humors of his body. So agile was he that he could vault over the backs of horses with ease. And because, endowed with bodily strength as he was, he became very active, it was demanded of him that he accustom himself to military service. But the sweetness of the Scriptures, to the study of which he was greatly attracted, held his mind in pledge, so that, although he excelled in military exercises, nevertheless it was the charm of letters that attracted him. In the former by a voluntary sloth he was a little slow, in the latter he was assiduous. I believe now he began to perceive that according to the testimony of Scripture, "wisdom is better than strength" (Wis 6.1),[7] and that nothing is more precious. And because it is easily perceived by those that love it, wisdom took possession of his mind to reveal itself to him and to be the sweet expression of his thought. Nothing was able to hinder Gerald from hastening to the love of learning. So it came about that he learned almost the whole series of the Scriptures and surpassed many clerical smatterers in his knowledge of it.

6. The clear implication is that lay boys, even aristocrats, were not educated. In fact, many boys were given at least a rudimentary education at home by their mothers.

7. This verse is Vulgate, not RSV.

6

After the death of his parents, when he attained full power over his property, Gerald was not puffed up, as youths often are who boast of their grown-up mastery, nor did he change the modesty that was springing up in his heart. His power of ruling increased, but the humble mind did not grow haughty. He was compelled to be occupied in administering and watching over things that, as I have said, came to him by hereditary right, and to leave that peace of heart, which he had to some extent tasted, to take up the weariness of earthly business. He could scarcely bear to leave the inner solitude of his heart, and he returned to it as soon as he could. But while he seemed to fall headlong from the heights of contemplation to the occupations of earth, as the chamois in its fall saves itself from death by its horns, so, turning to the divine love and the meditation of Holy Scripture he escaped the ruin of spiritual death. Inspired, as I think, by the very spirit of David, in his fervor he gave no sleep to his eyes, until freed from daily activities he might find within himself a place for the Lord and exulting in it secretly he "tasted the kindness of the Lord" (1 Pt 2.3). Perchance Christ, the rock, poured forth rivers of oil for him, in accordance with the saying of Job (see Jb 29.6), lest many waters should be able to extinguish in him the light of charity.

Dragged down to earth, he yearned for this spiritual refreshment, but his household and dependants demanded that he should break into his repose and give himself to the service of others.

7

He admitted these gnawing cares unwillingly for the sake of the complaints of those who had recourse to him.[8] For his dependants pleaded querulously, saying: "Why should a great man suffer violence from persons of low degree who lay waste his property?" adding that, when these discovered that he did not wish to take vengeance they devoured the more greedily that which was rightfully his. It would be more holy and honest that he should recognize the right of armed force, that he should unsheath the sword against his enemies, that he should restrain the boldness of the violent; it would be better that the

---

8. The reader might find it interesting to read this and the following chapters, indeed much of the rest of the work, in close juxtaposition with a copy of the Rule of Saint Benedict. It is clear that Odo traced his picture of Gerald on the prescriptions of the Rule, allowance having been made for Gerald's lay status. That Odo chose to construct Gerald's character in this way does not necessarily vitiate the picture that emerges.

bold should be suppressed by force of arms than that the undefended districts should be unjustly oppressed by them. When Gerald heard this he was moved, not by the attack made on him but by reason, to have mercy and to give help. Committing himself entirely to the will of God and the divine mercy, he sought only how he might visit the fatherless and widows and "keep oneself unstained from the world" (Jas 1.27) according to the precept of the apostle.

8

He therefore exerted himself to repress the insolence of the violent, taking care in the first place to promise peace and most easy reconciliation to his enemies. And he did this by taking care, that either he should overcome evil by good, or if his enemies would not come to terms, he should have in God's eyes the greater right on his side. And sometimes indeed he soothed them and reduced them to peace. When insatiable malice poured scorn on peaceful men, showing severity of heart, he broke the teeth of the wicked, that, according to the saying of Job, he might "make [them] drop the prey from [their] jaws" (Jb 29.17). He was not incited by the desire for revenge, as is the case with many, or led on by love of praise from the multitude, but by love of the poor, who were not able to protect themselves. He acted in this way lest, if he became sluggish through an indolent patience, he should seem to have neglected the precept to care for the poor. He ordered the poor man to be saved and the needy to be freed from the hand of the sinner. Rightly, therefore, he did not allow the sinner to prevail. But sometimes when the unavoidable necessity of fighting lay on him, he commanded his men in imperious tones, to fight with the backs of their swords and with their spears reversed. This would have been ridiculous to the enemy if Gerald, strengthened by divine power, had not been invincible to them. And it would have seemed useless to his own men, if they had not learned by experience that Gerald, who was carried away by his piety in the very moment of battle, had not always been invincible. When therefore they saw that he triumphed by a new kind of fighting that was mingled with piety, they changed their scorn to admiration, and sure of victory they readily fulfilled his commands. Fot it was a thing unheard of that he or the soldiers who fought under him were not victorious. But this also is certain, that he himself never wounded anybody, nor was wounded by anyone. For Christ, as it is written, was at his side (see Ps 118.6), who seeing the desire of his heart, saw that for love of Him he was so well disposed that he had no wish to assail the persons of the enemy, but only to check their audacity. Let no one be worried because a just man sometimes made use of fighting, which seems incompatible with religion. No one who has judged his cause impartially will be able to show that the glory of Gerald is clouded by this. For some of the fathers, and of these the most holy and most patient, when the cause of justice demanded, valiantly took up arms against their adversaries, as Abraham, who destroyed a great multitude of the enemy to rescue his nephew and King David who sent his forces even against his own son. Gerald did not fight invading the property of others, but defending his own, or rather his people's rights, knowing that the rhinoceros, that is, any powerful man, is to be bound with a thong that he may break the clods of the valley, that is, the oppressors of the lowly. For as the apostle says, the judge "does not bear the sword in vain, for he is the servant of God to execute his wrath" (Rom 13.4). It was lawful, therefore, for a layman to carry the sword in battle that he might protect defenseless people, as the harmless flock from evening wolves according to the saying of Scripture (see Acts 20.29), and that he might restrain by arms or by the law those whom ecclesiastical censure was not able to subdue. It does not darken his glory, then, that he fought for the cause of God, for whom the whole world fights against the unwise. Rather is it to his praise that he always won openly without the help of deceit or ambushes, and nevertheless was so protected by God, that, as I said before, he never stained his sword with human blood. Hereafter, let him who by his example shall take up arms against his enemies, seek also by his example not his own but the common good. For you may see some who for love of praise or gain boldly put themselves in danger, gladly sustain the evils of the world for the sake of the world, and while they encounter its bitterness lose the joys, so to speak, which they were seeking. But of these it is another story. The work of Gerald shines forth, because it sprang from simplicity of heart.

9

The old deceiver had made trial of the virtue of the youth, and having found I know not what of the divine in him, burst out in envy, and for this reason strove to overthrow him by all the tricks of temptation that were in his power. But Gerald had learned to flee in prayer to the bosom of the divine love, and relying on the grace of Christ to refute the fabrications of the evil one. But insatiably envious, the enemy, when he had found by experience that he could exercise no power over him through the delectation of the flesh, raised up the tempest of war against him by means of wicked men, as I have described above, so that by this means he might capture the citadel of his heart, into which by himself he was in no way able to enter. To return to his youth—the cunning foe was most actively inflamed against that chastity which Gerald earnestly loved. For it was something new and unaccustomed to him that a

youth should have avoided completely the shipwreck of his purity. He constantly suggested lustful thoughts to him therefore, for that is his first and
greatest means of leading mankind astray. When Gerald completely repelled
them, the enemy suffered tortures, because he could not introduce them even
to the portals of his heart. And so he repeated the old fraud and had recourse to
the instrument of deception by which Adam and his posterity are most often
led astray—I mean woman. He brought, it is said, a certain girl before his eyes
and while Gerald incautiously took notice of the color of her clear skin, he was
softened to take delight in it. O, if he had at once understood what lay hidden
beneath the skin! For the beauty of the flesh is nothing but the thin disguise of
the skin. He averted his eyes but the image impressed on the heart through
them remained. He was tortured therefore, allured, and consumed by a blind
fire. Overcome at length, he sent word to the mother of the girl that he would
come by night. He followed the messenger, violently hastened to the death of
his soul. Meanwhile, as captives in chains remember with groans their former
liberty, with sighs Gerald remembered the familiar sweetness of the divine
love. And though but weakly, he asked God that he should not be entirely
swallowed up by this temptation. Gerald came to the agreed place, and the girl
entered the room; because he was cold he stood at the hearth facing her; divine
grace looked on him, and this same girl appeared to him so deformed that he
did not believe it was she whom he saw, until her father asserted that it was so.
Understanding that this did not happen without the divine assent, that the
same girl should no longer have the same beauty in his eyes, he soon betook
himself once more to the mercy of Christ, and sighing deeply he got onto his
horse, and giving thanks to God rode away musing. Perhaps he who had
allowed himself to be on fire for a whole night, was now assailed by too great
coldness, that a harsh frigidity might punish the warmth of a slight delectation. He ordered the father forthwith to give the girl in marriage, presented
her with her liberty, and granted her a small holding. Perhaps suspecting his
weakness, he had her marriage hurried on, and this was the reason that, as an
alms, he gave her the dowry of her liberty, lest her marriage should be delayed. You who were to grow into a cedar of paradise, how could you be so
agitated? Surely that you might learn what you might be, left to yourself. For
your patron, the prince of the apostles[9] to whom afterward you committed
yourself and all you possessed, would not have had sufficient knowledge of
himself, if the critical moment of temptation had not come upon him. But now
that you know by experience what a man may be by himself and what by the

9. That is, Saint Peter. Cluny was dedicated to Saint Peter and to the pope.

grace of God, do not scorn to have compassion on the weakness of your supplicants. We know that it is not unusual for the saints to be tempted, for the vices inherent in their corrupt nature come to life, that wherever they strive they may conquer, and conquering be crowned. For there is a difference between one who feels the delight of vice and gives way, and one who fighting against it conquers, and occupying his mind rather with the pleasure of virtue drives out the poison of an evil delight, which perhaps he has for a time imbibed, with the antidote of pious supplication. And the youth, more discreet for the experience of this danger, like a man who has knocked his foot in a slippery place, walked more cautiously, being careful that the eyes should announce nothing to the heart, by means of which death might find entrance through the windows of the soul.

10

For the rest, the kind and just Lord, who by the attractiveness of holiness, kept his servant Gerald from defilement, did not omit to punish his concupiscence by a just punishment. A few days after He struck the offender for a year and more with blindness from cataract, so that the eyes that had looked on unlawful things should not for a time be able to see even that which was lawful. And indeed not the slightest evil could penetrate his eyelids. Those about him knew of the blindness and they concealed it from the peering eyes of strangers with the greatest care. But he, humiliating himself under the chastising hand of the Lord, as though prepared for His scourges, was silent. He neither refused bodily medicines, nor eagerly sought them, but waited patiently for the time and the manner in which his Lord might see fit to remove the scourge, and no longer desire to strike him. For he knew that every son is chastised. The judger of hearts indeed purges even the smallest stains in His elect in this life, lest afterward there should remain in them anything which might offend His eyes. And for this reason God brought on this affliction, that the youth's mind might be cleansed from that which was past, and be kept more pure in the future. When, therefore, God had fulfilled His will in him, He removed the affliction and restored the sight to his eyes.

11

With his senses as it were dried up by suffering, Gerald led an upright life, and departed neither to one side nor the other from the middle path of discretion, so that he neither failed in the duties of his worldly affairs, nor diverted himself from the practice of religion by earthly occupations. He surrounded himself with the better type of men and with clerics of good name, with whom whether at home or abroad he performed the divine office either in common or privately. On a certain Sunday he had to attend a meeting of the law court that had been arranged and to which certain nobles were going to come. Lest he should keep them waiting by coming late, he took care to go on horseback and set out before dawn. For he was on his guard on this grand court-day not to show himself slow or difficult to anybody, as is now the custom with some, who as though coming from a wedding give themselves to drunkenness before they show themselves to their friends—contrary to that saying of Scripture: "Woe to those who rise early in the morning, that they may run after strong drink" (Is 5.11). But with Gerald it was not so. Very unworthy he thought it, that he who was the lord of many people should become a slave to the domination of vices. He went fasting to the law court, lest failing in temperance he should be unable to give a reasonable judgment. For he sought what was of Christ, what was of peace, what might further the common good. After the night office, if he was to go anywhere, the solemnity of mass followed, and so, committing himself and his followers to the divine mercy he set out. On the above-mentioned Sunday, since it was necessary to start before dawn, he omitted the mass, hoping to hear one after the court, but it was nowhere possible. He went away therefore very sad looking for a place where there might be some hope of finding a mass, but when he could not find one, he called the clerics who happened to be present and with them all the soldiers who would sing psalms, saying, "It is my fault that this holy day passes uselessly for us. But there is something that we may do for the praise of God, lest we should seem to have spent the holy day quite in vain." After saying this he went through the psalter from the beginning with them, singing no mortal song. And he made it now his custom to recite the psalter almost daily. And when he had finished it, he was seen to rejoice as though spiritually refreshed, as a man is accustomed to rejoice when he has fulfilled his ambition.

12

It seems to be useful to say something of his bodily appearance. For although "the flesh is of no avail" (Jn 6.63) and although beauty is a deceiving grace, because it is often the cause of lust and pride, nevertheless in this man it is to be praised, because it was both attractive and free from the foulness of lust. Gerald, therefore, was of medium height and well proportioned. And while beauty encompassed all his members, his neck was of such shining white and so adorned to suit the eye, that you would think you had hardly seen another so beautiful. His beauty of mind further adorned the beauty of his body, so that the nature of his disposition shone forth in his appearance. And Scripture gives testimony of this, saying that "open-mouthed laughter" (Sir 19.30) and the movement of the face show the inner nature of a person. For he had "tasted the kindness of the Lord" (1 Pt 2.3) and "tasted" that the embrace of the celestial spouse "is good" (Ps 34.8). For that reason he did not allow the beautiful image of his soul to be enticed by carnal knowledge before the gaze of that same spouse. People were accustomed to delight in kissing him on the neck. Nor did he object, because pride, which is always intractable, found no place in him. His bodily agility made him very quick in his movements, and he was very strong. What is especially noteworthy, because it shows how admirable he was, is that, having matter for pride, he kept himself humble. How blameworthy are those on the other hand, who, possessing little or nothing, are yet puffed up with pride. After he applied himself more closely to intellectual studies his bodily activity began to fail. It was then that he began to take especial pleasure in conversation, and to give profound advice for the handling and arranging of affairs, and although he avoided words of buffoonery his serious talk was of such a nature that even in that he was pleasing to his hearers. He was neither unduly menacing in his threats, nor tenacious in nursing injuries. But neither was he too easy in conferring benefits, nor changeable in taking away those that he had given. Whatever he said he would do he carried out unhesitatingly, unless by chance he learned that there was sin in it.

13

He attached such importance to sobriety, that he preserved not only himself but also his household from drunkenness. For those of his household were neither great eaters nor great drinkers. He never compelled his guests to drink, nor was drink brought to him more frequently than to his household. He so ordered his meals that the company rose from them without having drunk too much but at the same time suitably refreshed. And when sometimes he had made his guests, to whose welfare he gave himself entirely, dine early, he himself did not take anything before the third hour, and on fast days not before the ninth. This blessed prince observed the precept of Scripture by eating "at the proper time, for strength, and not for drunkenness" (Eccl 10.17). For what might he guard against more fittingly than drunkenness, which apart from the fact that it is the death of the soul and, by the testimony of the apostle (see 1 Cor 6.10) excludes, like homicide, from the kingdom of God, also does much harm to the body. For from this come lack of strength, shaking of the limbs, lack of perception in the senses, premature old age. Sight, speech, appearance are all debauched, and the beauty of religion quite disfigured. No one can be filled at once with wine and the Holy Spirit, and by no treaty can Jerusalem be saved from the fire of fornication, if she is not willing to keep Nabuzardan, the prince of cooks, from besieging her.

14

Chairs for the poor were always placed in his presence and at intervals meals were put in front of them, that he might see for himself what and how much food was given to them. Nor was he limited to receiving a certain number, but when more happened to be present, at least of those who seemed deserving, more were brought in to him. No one was ever turned away from his door without alms being given. His servants so arranged that he always had dishes at hand that he might give. Drink also was brought, which he distributed after inspecting and tasting it, so that those might first drink to whom he gave a portion of his bread. Believing that he received Christ in the poor, and reverently honoring Him in them, he brought Christ to himself in their persons, whose delight it is, according to the prophet, to "give rest to the weary" (Is 28.12). How much do those diminish the merit they receive who send out their alms but do not bring in the poor to themselves. For in this way they exclude from their houses Christ Himself, who says "I was a stranger and you welcomed me" (Mt 25.35). In order to surpass the justice of the Pharisees, as the Lord commanded (see Mt 5.20), he had a ninth part of the produce of his fields set apart. From this the poor were fed in certain of his houses, and clothes and shoes were provided for them in these places. To those who met him he gave coins that he carried for this purpose, and that he gave secretly either himself or through a reliable servant; sometimes when money was bequeathed for some man, he received it along with the needy, rejoicing and choosing to be joined to the poor; he distributed it at once and compensated those who had given by a generous performance of the divine office in return for the small gift.

15

At mealtimes great respect was paid to him. Chattering or buffoonery had no place at his table but the talk was of necessary or virtuous subjects, or indeed of religious ones. At all times of the year he dined once in the day, unless perhaps in the summer when he had a supper of something simple and uncooked. At his table there was always reading for some time to begin with; but for the sake of the seculars present he used to suspend the reading at intervals, and ask the clerics what had been said in it—those whom he knew to be able to reply. He had noble clerics at his board to whom he eagerly imparted both good behavior and learning. To the adolescent he showed himself more austere, saying that that age was very dangerous, when a youth put off the voice and appearance of his mother and began to assume the voice and appearance of his father; and one who took care to guard himself at that time, he said, might easily overcome thence-forth the movements of the flesh. When those whom he asked about the reading requested that he should rather speak himself, he used to offer them not a pompous dissertation, but a speech of learning and simplicity. When those were present who would bring forward something facetious or jocular, as used to happen, he restrained them not with biting indignation, but as though by joking also. But he never allowed idle talk to be protracted in his presence. For he knew that it is commanded to all Christians in general that each should eat his bread in silence. At the end of the meal the reader always repeated what had been read. So Gerald spent the greater part of mealtimes speaking with God, or with God speaking to him through the reading. Let them look to this example of his who, against the reproof of the prophet, have the harp and the lyre to play at their banquets. They rejoice in the playing and exult at the voice of the organ. They look not at the work of the Lord, because among the voices of those who make a great noise they do not hear the cry of the poor. What then? That is true which Christ, who is the truth, said, that "out of the abundance of the heart the mouth speaks" (Mt 12.34). It is clear what those who are always speaking of worldly things, and little or rarely of God, love most, and what abounds in their hearts. Would that, like Gerald, they might look to the last things, and that "whether they ate or drank" they might, according to the precept of the apostle, "do all to the glory of God" (1 Cor 10.31). On three days in the week and during the whole time when abstinence is ordered, he abstained from meat. But if one of the annual feasts occurred in these days he so broke the abstinence that he abstained on some free ferial day in place of that which he had broken. And he used then to give a meal to one poor man over and above the usual number in view of the feast. But if a fast occurred on a Sunday, he by no means broke or neglected it on this account, but he kept the fast on the Saturday preceding. And if this should seem incongruous in the holy man, let him who may think so know that to the clean all things are clean (see Ti 1.15), that is, to those who eat without the vice of greed. The Judger of Hearts does not look to the quality of the food, but to the necessity or the appetite with which it is taken. The prophet Elias, and Esau, show this by their example. It was lawful, therefore, for a layman, and especially one so just, to make use of things that are not lawful to those whose profession forbids them. For the Tree of Paradise did not bring death because it was evil, but because it was presumptuously eaten against God's command.

16

He always wore woolen or linen clothes of the old fashion, and not in that which the sons of Belial, who are without restraint, have devised and follow in our day. His were so made that they neither suggested pompous affectation, nor drew attention by plebeian rusticity. He took care not to adorn himself more than usual with silken or precious garments either because of the occurrence of any feast or the presence of any dignitary, and he would not change or renew his sword-belt for twenty years if it would last so long. What shall I say of the belts, the twisted cinctures, the buckles, the decorated medallions for horses, when he not only forbade himself to wear gold, but even to possess it? For it was not in gold nor in the multitude of riches that he believed his strength to lie, but in God. Even those who profess religion, harassed by an unashamed and untiring care for the body after which they strive with every effort, scheme to obtain from those who see them the respect that they have lost by their morals through the display at least of a fine coat. It would be more use to these people to spend their time in the cultivation of the soul, which can equally grow more beautiful.

17

The poor and the wronged always had free access to him, nor did they need to bring the slightest gift to recommend their cause. For the more fully anyone brought his necessity to his notice, the more closely did he attend to his need. And now his goodness was heard of not only in neighboring, but also in distant regions. And because everyone knew his kindness to all, many found the solution of their difficulties in him. Nor did he disdain either personally or through his officials to interest himself in the affairs of the poor, and, as occasion offered, to give help. For often when he knew that there was fierce strife between litigants, on the day on which the cause was to be heard he had mass said for them, and implored the divine assistance for those whom, humanly speaking, he could not help. Nor did he allow any lord to take benefices from a vassal because he was angry with him.[10] But when the case was brought forward, partly by entreaty, partly by command, he allayed the exasperation. You might think the vigor of his justice severe in this one thing alone, that whenever a poor man was brought before a more powerful man, he was at hand to uphold the weaker, in such a way that the stronger was overcome without being hurt. For the rest, truly hungering after justice, he insisted on its being carried out not only among his own people but even among strangers.

18

The thirst for justice burned in him, and hunger too. Neither simplicity nor kindness was lacking to the asperity of his zeal, but neither was the asperity of zeal lacking to the kindness of his simplicity. For as it is said of Job that he "was blameless and upright" (Jb 1.1), so Gerald, although he had much care for the poor, was never slow in punishing the guilty. He was aware that it was divinely granted to some that they should wash away crime, which cannot remain unpunished, by temporal suffering. So King David, when he was dying, ordered Joab and Semei to be punished.

Robbers had taken possession of a certain wood, and plundered and murdered both passers-by and those who lived in the vicinity. Gerald, hearing of this, immediately gave orders for them to be captured. It happened, however, that a certain countryman was driven by fear to join them. But the soldiers who captured them, fearing that Gerald would either release them, or blame them for showing him the prisoners unpunished, forthwith put out the eyes of all of them. And so it came about that this countryman was blinded. Later he went into the district of Toulouse, and a long time afterward, when Gerald heard that he had not been a companion of the robbers, he was very grieved, and asked if he was still alive, and where he had gone. Having learned that he had gone to the province of Toulouse, he sent him, so they say, a hundred shillings, ordering the messenger to ask pardon for him from the man.

19

How he mercifully consoled the afflicted, and often spared the guilty, may be seen from an example. His neighbors had afflicted a certain priest with increas-

---

10. Vassals pledged homage and fidelity to lords, and agreed to perform certain services, usually military, in return for something of value, called a benefice. Often that benefice was a parcel of land called a fief, whose Latin name, *feudum*, yields the word "feudalism." Lords and vassals struggled continuously over the terms of their mutual obligations.

ing quarrels, to the point that they put out his eyes. The count consoled the man greatly by his words, urging him to be patient. But lest the consolation of words should seem meager, he handed over to him a certain church in his jurisdiction by formal deed. After a little time one of those who had done violence to the priest was taken by the officers and shut up in prison, and this was forthwith announced to the count as something over which he would rejoice. And he in haste, as though with the desire of punishing the man, went to the prison. But other cases arose that it was necessary to deal with on the next day, and so he ordered the accused to be kept till then. In the evening when the officers had gone home, he secretly ordered the jailer to refresh the man with food and drink. And because he had no shoes he allowed shoes to be given to him and permitted him to escape. On the next day when those who were attending the court came to the count, he ordered the accused to be brought forth, and some men whom the jailer had prepared to act on his behalf announced trembling that the accused had escaped. Gerald, wishing to conceal the truth, made as though to threaten the jailer, but soon he said, "It is well, for the priest has now forgiven the injury done to him."

20

So, two men in chains were presented to him accused of a great crime. The accusers insisted that he should order them forthwith to be hanged. He dissembled, because he did not wish to free them openly. For he so conducted himself in any good work, that the goodness did not appear too much. Looking therefore at the accusers, "If," he said, "they ought to die, as you say, let us first give them a meal in the customary manner." Then he ordered food and drink to be brought to them, and ordered them to be unbound so that they might eat. When they had eaten he gave them his knife saying, "Go yourselves and bring the osier with which you must be hanged." Not far away was a wood that grew up thickly with saplings. Going into this as though looking for osiers and gradually penetrating further they suddenly disappeared, and so escaped the moment of death. Those who were present, understanding that it was with his consent, did not dare to search for them among the bushes. He punished either with fines or branding the accused who were, as far as could be judged from their appearance, confirmed in evil. But those who had done wrong not through seasoned malice but inadvertently, he set free uncondemned. It was unheard of, nevertheless, that anyone was punished by death or maiming in his presence.

21

Of the many things he did let me recall a few particular examples that will suffice to show certain acts of goodness that are known to me. For this reason, too, I insert certain small facts through which his great zeal may be illustrated, as, for example, the following. Once while he was going along by the road, a countrywoman was guiding the plow in an adjoining field. He asked her why she was doing a man's work. She replied that her husband had been long ill, that the time of sowing was passing, she was alone and had no one to help her. Having pity on her calamities, he ordered as many coins to be given her as there were days of sowing left over, so that on each day she might hire a laborer and she herself cease from doing the work of a man. Nature flees from everything artificial, as Ambrose[11] says, and its author, God, abhors what is unnatural. This is a small thing in itself, but the attitude of a just man in agreement with the laws of nature makes it become great.

22

On another occasion as he was going along the road a peasant was reaping chickpeas nearby. Some of his retinue, who were in front, took some of it and began to eat it. When he saw this, spurring his horse, he came at full speed to the man, asking if his followers had taken the chickpeas. "I gave it to them freely," he said. "May God reward you!" Gerald replied.

23

An incident of the same kind is that which occurred when his servants were preparing a meal under the shade of some cherry trees. He bought for silver from a peasant who was claiming them some branches that were hanging down loaded with ripe fruit, which the servants had broken off before he came. Perhaps someone will say that these things are not worth relating: but I am showing the mind of this God-fearing man in small things, that indirectly it may be understood that he who did not despise little things, was not able to be

11. Ambrose (c. 339–397) was the Church Father and bishop of Milan whom we met in Possidius's *Life of Augustine*.

brought low by great ones. Was not the goodwill of the widow with two small coins approved by the Lord?

24

To his vassals he was so kind and peaceable that it was a matter of wonder to those who saw it. And they frequently complained that he was soft and timid, because he permitted himself to be injured by persons of low degree as though he had no authority. Nor was he easily or lightly annoyed, as lords generally are, by his critics. On one occasion he met a number of countrymen who had left their holdings, and were moving into another province. When he had recognized them and inquired where they were going with their household goods, they replied that they had been wronged by him when he had given them their holdings. The soldiers who were accompanying him urged that he should order them to be beaten and made to go back to the holdings from which they had come. But he was unwilling, for he knew that both he and they had one Lord in heaven, who was accustomed rather, in the words of the apostle, to "forbear threatening" (Eph 6.9), and who was not used to raise the hand of His might "against the fatherless" (Jb 31.21). He therefore permitted them to go where they thought they would be better off, and gave them permission to live there. Not without shame I recently heard some idle tattle that he used not to remit the debts of a man who was in pledge to him, but that is quite false, as those bear witness who often saw him remit not only the interest but also the capital.

25

His tenants and clerics, who loved him dearly as a father, often brought him bundles of wax, which he with many thanks accepted as great gifts. And he did not allow any of this wax to be burned for his own use, but he ordered it all to be burned in lights before the altar in the relics of the saints, which he had carried about with him. The servants of his bedchamber, when it happened that there was no wax ready for his service, prepared birch bark or pinewood torches. But how could one who was so careful that private people should not use the gift that had been freely given him, exact strict payment from those who had pledged themselves? Rather, he often remitted to the debtors more than they owed to him by right. In the same way, according to the precept of the apostle, he "forbore threatening" (Eph 6.9) his servants. Sometimes he was defrauded, and according to the precept of the same apostle (see 1 Cor 6.7), he suffered his goods to be seized.

26

To prove this by an example: a thief once entered his tent at night; a candle was burning before his bed as was usual and Gerald happened to be awake, for it was his custom in bed to be nourished with the love and the sweetness of Christ through the practice of prayer. Curiously peering about, the thief was looking to see if there was anything that he could carry away. He saw a little cushion with a silk cover and stretching out his hand drew it to him. "Who are you?" said Gerald. The thief was terrified and hesitated in a dazed way. Then Gerald said, "Go on with what you are doing, and depart carefully lest anyone hear." So he persuaded him that he might lawfully depart with what he had stolen. Who except Gerald would have done this? Certainly it seems to me that this is much more worthy of admiration than if he had caused the man to grow stiff in a stone prison.

27

How careful he was to fulfil that command of the apostle "that no man transgress and wrong his brother" (1 Thes 4.6) in business will be clear from this example. Once on his way back from Rome as he was going past Pavia he made his camp not far from the city. The Venetians[12] and many others hearing of this immediately went out to him, for he was quite the most celebrated traveler on that road, and was known to all as a religious and generous man. When therefore the traders, as their manner is, were going about among the tents and inquiring if anybody wanted to buy anything, some of the more considerable among them came to Gerald's tent and asked the retainers whether the lord count (for so they all called him) would order some cloaks or spices. He himself called them and said, "I bought what I wanted in Rome; but I should like you to tell me whether I bought wisely." Then he ordered the cloaks that he had got to be brought out. Now, one of them was very valuable, and a Venetian looking at it, asked what he had given for it. When he had learned the price, "Indeed," he said, "if it was at Constantinople it would be worth even more." When the count heard this he was horrified, as though in dread of a great crime. Afterward, therefore, when he met some Roman pilgrims whom he knew, he gave them as many shillings as the Venetian had said the cloak was worth more than the price he had given for it, telling them

12. The Venetians were the foremost traders in western Europe. Presumably they had a commercial colony in Pavia.

where they could find the seller of the cloak. Truly, while men are accustomed to have compunction for other kinds of sin, and to consider amendment, rarely or never will you see anyone except Gerald who regrets having transgressed in a sin of this kind. But indeed he knew that God is offended by all sin, and he did not wish to offend even in the smallest things Him whom he loved with his whole heart.

28

Not unmindful that the justice of Christians ought to surpass the justice of the Pharisees, when all his produce had been rightly tithed, he ordered a ninth part to be set aside so that it might be used to buy various necessaries for the poor, and from this, as occasion demanded, clothes also were bought for the needy who presented themselves from time to time. In addition he always carried money with him, of which he secretly gave as much as he could to poor people whom he met, either himself or through somebody who knew of the case. And though the returns from his fields and vineyards were large, it was never heard that his stewards lent anything. He himself never bought land, except one small field that happened to be surrounded by one of his properties. Some rich men become very ardent over this, forgetting the terrible threat of the prophet: "Woe to those who join house to house, who add field to field" (Is 5.8). For Gerald, according to the precept of the Gospel, was contented with his wages (see Lk 3.14). And as he never injured or calumniated anyone, so, like the Lord, the Disposer of all things, he kept those things that were his by right safe from the wicked and perverse. For he was lord of so many estates in different provinces, that in those places in which he had full authority he might truly be said to be rich. Nor did the number of his properties make him proud, for as the psalmist says, other than the Lord, "there was nothing on the earth" (Ps 73.25) that he desired. And the Lord indeed added all these things to him, because he sought first the kingdom of God (see Mt 6.33). By the grace of God he so prospered, and went on his way so safely and unharmed, that the saying of Job would seem to apply to him: "Thou hast put a hedge about him . . . and his possessions have increased in the land" (Jb 1.10).

29

Let me relate this fact as an example of how he used "to overcome evil by good," following the precept of the apostle (Rom 12.21). When he came on one occasion to Piacenza, a certain cleric arrived who was in charge of the port. [13] As is usual there, this man was expecting very lucrative passage-money from the Roman pilgrims. For some reason he was in a very bad temper, and was flinging angry words about, attacking the bishop of Rodez[14] and other distinguished men in opprobrious terms. The man of God happened to be standing opposite him, and, fearing a quarrel would start, restrained his fellow travelers from using hard words in reply. But the cleric he subdued by gentle words, and gave him some small gifts. Noticing the graceful words with which Gerald restrained the bishop and the others from replying to his insults, the cleric returned to a more gentle frame of mind, and asked who he was. When Gerald replied that he was from Aquitaine and a person of moderate position, the cleric, noting his appearance and his speech, gave way entirely to his graciousness. He remitted whatever was owed of passage-money for all his company, and filled his flasks and bottles and those of all his party with wine. For the count had this gift from God, that both he and what he said were most pleasing, and not only to chance persons, but to great men. Even by kings he was always liked and respected.

30

And rightly indeed was he loved by all, for he himself loved everybody. Let me relate what he did for a certain fugitive as for a friend. On this same journey he found a man who had left his protection some years before. This man was considered to be rich and of some standing by the people among whom he dwelt. Gerald's retainers finding the man brought him trembling and in great fear into his presence. But Gerald privately inquired of him how things were going with him, and when he had learned that he was held in no small esteem in that place, he replied, "And neither will I bring you into discredit." He ordered his men not to betray what the man had been in his own country, and then in the presence of his neighbors he gave him some little gifts and paid him considerable respect in talking to him and at table, and sent him away in peace. Who but Gerald would have done this? Yet this is what he did who was no servant of avarice, but had dedicated himself entirely to mercy.

---

13. Piacenza was a moderately important city on the Po River. It was located due south of Milan and was a stopping point for persons bound to and from Rome.

14. Rodez is about fifty miles south of Aurillac. This passage is rich with irony. Gerald, not the bishop, is called "man of God," and the layman "teaches" the cleric.

31

Again on this same journey, a certain man from the neighborhood of
Bourges[15] had broken his hip not far from Rome. Abandoned by his companions, he remained alone with his wife. One of Gerald's soldiers, a certain
Boniface, found him by chance, and hearing of his necessity brought him to
Gerald saying: "Look, my lord, I have found something after your heart's
desire that I present for your pleasure: here is a man needing help." The
man of God joyfully took him into his protection and supplying all his wants
conducted him to Brioude.[16] Then he gave him ten shillings more with which
he might get back to his own people. This and similar facts witness to the
desire of showing mercy with which he was generously filled by divine
inspiration.

32

We know indeed that the corn for the harvest must grow along with the cockle
and the grain of wheat be kept down by the straw above it for a time; so it was
necessary that the malicious Cain should exercise the just Abel in patience.
Gerald also, who like Job may be said to have been the brother of dragons and
the companion of ostriches, was often attacked by certain men of his provinces. For, the state being in a most disturbed condition, the marquises in their
insolence had subjected the royal vassals to themselves.[17] But it had been
proved by experience in many cases that, as has been said, the Almighty
opposed the enemies of Gerald. He appeared so invincible to them that the
trouble that they strove to make for him came back rather on their own heads,
as it is written: "He who digs a pit" for his neighbor "will fall into it" (Prv
26.27). Duke William of Aquitaine,[18] indeed, a good man and praiseworthy for
many things, when he had already become very powerful, urged Gerald not by
threats but by entreaties to leave the king's service and *commend*[19] himself to
him. But Gerald would not agree for he had only recently acquired royal favor

15. Bourges was an important town lying between the Loire and Cher Rivers to the northwest
of the Auvergne.

16. Brioude was a town in the eastern Auvergne about fifty miles from Aurillac.

17. Odo here sounds what became a traditional Cluniac theme: loyalty to the king. Marquises
were minor royal officials who were often, as here, neglecting their allegiance to the king.

18. William II, "the Pious," who came to power in 886 and died in 918, styled himself "Duke
of the Aquitanians." His father had really founded the fortunes of the house of Auvergne and
Aquitaine during the breakup of the Carolingian West-Frankish kingdom.

19. *Commend* is the technical term for a person becoming the vassal of another.

as count. He commended his nephew, Rainald, to him, however, with a great number of his men. But the same William was not at all annoyed with him, remembering that his father Bernard had recommended him as a youth to this same Lord Gerald for the love he bore him. And therefore he always held him in great veneration and as a dear companion. When the matter came up William went to talk with him, and, always delighted by the gentleness of this gracious man, by force of entreaties exacted that he should remain with him for some time. And in discussing what was to be done he often made him walk for a long time with him.

33

It happened once, since the occasion demanded it, that he spent a long time with William in a district to which he had gone to wage war. During this time the pay, which was carried on Gerald's packhorses, gradually gave out, and the army turned to looting. Under the pretext of pursuing William's enemies it laid waste the whole region, with the result that the inhabitants, fearing for their safety, left their property and fled, and no one could be found to pay Gerald's retainers. As they found nothing to buy, and they were not allowed to touch any of the booty, they suffered great want in that expedition. For he would not allow anything to be received from those who were plundering, lest by participating with them he should be party to sin. He stayed, however, in the company of his friend, and in spite of his troubles did not desert him. Some mocked, because he and his men were in want while others enjoyed the booty, but many, who were sensible, blessed him lamenting greatly that they were not fit to imitate such an example. From this he earned the name of Gerald the Good, by which he was afterward always known.

34

William thought so well of him that he wished to give him his sister in marriage, and their mother, Ermengard, desired it also without delay, for she loved this man with great affection. But Christ, the Son of the Virgin, had ever imbued him with the love of chastity, which he so embraced from his earliest years that he would not allow himself to be diverted from it even by the prospect of so excellent a marriage. The horror he felt for carnal obscenity may be judged from the fact that he never incurred a nocturnal illusion without grief. Whenever this human misfortune happened to him in sleep, a confidential servant brought him privately a change of clothes, kept ready for this emergency, and cloths and a vessel of water. When the servant had brought these, he immediately retired and shut the door, for Gerald would not allow him to see him naked. This follower of interior purity so fled from the staining of the body that he washed away what happened to him in sleep not only with water but with tears. This may seem foolish, but only to those whose unclean minds reek with the foulness of vice, and who, when they soil themselves naturally or voluntarily, disdain to wash away their uncleanness. But Gerald knew the Scripture, "keep your heart with all vigilance" (Pr 4.23), as well as "he who despises small things will fail little by little" (Sir 19.1). Only consider how great this man is to be held who, placed amidst worldly riches and at the height of earthly position, preserved chastity. What could he have done more splendid? One could demand nothing more, or more excellent, for as Saint Martin asserts, nothing is to be compared with virginity.

35

Count Ademarus[20] was very insistent that Gerald should give him his allegiance, but he was not able to extract any agreement from him. Gerald refused to commend himself not only to Ademarus but even to Duke William, who had greater possessions, and I believe he had in mind Mardochai who scorned to submit himself to the proud Aman and to show to princes an honor due to God. Indeed, when he was enjoying the friendship of William and apparently in peace, that persecution might not be lacking to one living in Christ, Satan stirred up the above-mentioned Count Ademarus against him whom he had tried to reach by many and various temptations, but whom he had never been able to subject to himself. On one occasion it happened that Gerald camped at night in a meadow with a few soldiers, and Ademarus, having sent a spy, ascertained where he was and how many he had with him. Delighted at having found an opportunity of capturing him, he collected a force of armed men, and directed it to the place. Gerald, it is said, was asleep with all his men in a part of the meadow. But He who guards Israel did not sleep in guarding an innocent man. As it is written of the prophet Jeremiah that the Lord hid him on the way (see Jer 36.26), so God concealed Gerald, and the men, having made a circle round the whole meadow, and then a smaller one in the center, were not able to find him. Ademarus, his effort having been foiled, and with regret that his wickedness was brought to nothing, departed. "The righteous man," as it is written, with "clean hands grows stronger and stronger" (Jb 17.9) to praise the Lord.

20. It is not clear who this man was.

36

In the same way the followers of Count Ademarus occupied his castle. When Gerald heard this he took a few soldiers who happened to be with him at the time, and hastened to the place. Ademarus, with a strong body of troops, prepared to follow the attackers. But when the troops that Gerald was leading were not far from the castle, Ademarus held back his hastening army, saying, "We must find out by how many fighting men this Gerald is defended, who has dared to come before us and lay siege to the castle, for he would not have put himself into this danger unless he had been guarded by forces from the countryside." He then sent some evil vassals to investigate. Night came on, and the spies hastened without delay and carefully sought out the nature of Gerald's encampment. But as happens at night, they mistook some white stones seen at a distance in the uncertain light for the tents of the besiegers. They forthwith returned, pale and trembling, to Ademarus and told him that they had seen an enormous encampment. On their way back they passed a certain married woman to whom they told the same thing, and it was through her that what had appeared to the spies was afterward made known to the man of God. Ademarus, therefore, his army having been overthrown by the divine will, returned to his own part of the country, and when the invaders of the castle learned next day that he was no longer present, they sought peace from Gerald, begging that he would permit them to retire without disgrace. And that the man of God, Gerald, immediately did. But his soldiers, who were greatly roused, would hardly suffer them to go unless they were despoiled of their arms. The goodness of Gerald, however, prevailed, and he compelled his men to stand aside while the fleeing enemy came out through a postern. Nevertheless he ordered two of his men to stand there armed, and see that no one dared to take any of their belongings as they went out. In this way Gerald triumphed without bloodshed over his discomfited enemy, and Christ, as His manner is, brought greater honor to His soldier through this adversity.

37

Godfred, the count of Turenne[21] on one occasion collected a force of troops and hastened to provoke the man of God to war, and to lay waste the districts under him. But it happened that he was so wounded by the very sword with which he had armed himself, that he was not able to carry out the expedition

21. Turenne is about forty-five miles west of Aurillac. Godred's identity is unknown.

322 SOLDIERS OF CHRIST

he had undertaken. Understanding at length that he had been wounded on account of the wrong to the man of God, he gave up his malice, rightly seeing that the saying of Moses held good: "let us flee from before Israel; for the Lord fights for them against us" (Ex 14.25).

38

Nevertheless, the brother of the aforesaid Ademarus secretly broke into the castle that overlooks the monastery. But because he had learned from the experience of others that, with God on his side, Gerald always prevailed over his enemies, he did not dare to remain there. Nevertheless, he took everything that could be carried away, before fleeing as fast as he could. Not long afterward he gave back everything to some honest men who were reproaching him for his crime, and coming to the man of God he asked pardon for his boldness. For Gerald was held in such reverence by all who knew him that anyone who injured him, as though he had committed a sacrilege, might be assured that he would not prosper. Although the sons of darkness molested the son of light in the ways that I have related and in many others, he did not fail to protect the poor wherever he was able. He pardoned those who injured him so easily that you would think that he was more willing to pardon than they were to be reconciled. The harder case for him was always one involving the poor, since he had much sympathy for them, and he could more easily neglect his own interest than theirs. Like a skillful doctor who chances to be wounded himself but is careful to heal the wounds of others, he did not fail to protect the weak even when he was suffering injury himself.

39

He was so invincible to his enemies that the harm which they tried to inflict on him came back rather on their own heads, as may be seen from what has been said above and from the following example. Count Adalelmus, the brother of Ademarus, apart from the injury that he did to Gerald when he attacked the castle of Aurillac (which injury Gerald gladly forgave him), was still inflamed with malice and was persistently driven to harm the holy man. Having collected, therefore, a force of his followers he tried to break into the castle at a time when Gerald happened to be hearing mass. When he was still some distance off, those inside saw him coming and quickly shut the gate. A great noise of people shouting arose in the castle and the soldiers who were at mass with the count wanted to go out, but he stopped them with a word and would not allow them to go until mass was finished. Meanwhile the followers of Adalelmus, going round the castle walls, found nothing except seven horses, which they drove off, and seeing they had made their attack to no purpose they began shamefacedly to retire. It is said that the man of God, after he had restrained his soldiers, took his psalter and straightway went up above the gate and recited I know not which of the psalms to the Lord. The tyrant who had made the heart of the just man to mourn (see Ezek 13.22) was nevertheless permitted to retire rejoicing. I am about to relate marvelous things and almost unbelievable, unless they had been asserted on such good testimony. Nearly sixty of their horses died in a short time, and Adalelmus after fourteen days died so terrible a death, that in whatever place he was buried a violent whirl-wind uncovered his body. Adalbert bears witness to this, that same monk who preaches the word of God to the people at Limoges. He used to look after the treasury of Saint Martial at Turenne,[22] when it had been moved there for fear of the pagan peoples. Seeing what had happened, the robbers sent back to the man of God the horses that they had taken.

40

Sometimes he was compelled unwillingly to show his strength and to bow the neck of the wicked by force of arms, as happened in the case of a most evil man called Arlaldus. This man held a certain small castle which is called Saint Céré,[23] and coming out from this like a wolf in the evening he made attacks on the retainers of Gerald, who as a peaceable man talked to him who hated peace, and also gave him some little gifts, and arms for his soldiers, as though to soften his fierce manners by kindness. But the foolish and brutal man, attribut-ing this not to goodness but to cowardice, acted still more audaciously against his retainers. At length Gerald, considering that he could not restrain the madness of the foolish man without punishing him, collected a force of soldiers and went to his castle. And by a remarkable stroke of victory, he drew the beast from his lair without killing any of his men. When Arlaldus stood before him full of confusion, Gerald, as befitted him, spoke not abusively but reason-ably. Trembling, he replied with humble and appealing words, and the man of God said to him: "Now you have learned that you and your forces cannot resist me: be careful therefore how you rage, be careful how you continue to

22. This refers to the treasures of Saint-Martial of Limoges, whose monks had fled west to escape Viking incursions up the Loire.
23. This little town is about twenty-seven miles southwest of Aurillac. Arlaldus is a mystery.

act with malice, lest something worse comes on your head. I will let you go without troubling to take a hostage or an oath from you. Nor will I permit any of your goods to be taken in compensation for the booty that you habitually take." So he sent the man away with a rebuke, and he henceforth was careful not to presume to injure Gerald's people.

41

Now, as I said above, his adversaries, dismayed by the fear of God, gave in, for although, following the example of Job, he was "a brother of jackals and the companion of ostriches" (Jb 30.29), the beasts of the field were peaceable to him. He had a freehold property at Pousthomy, and from there his estates so lay that in going and returning from the Puy de Griou he was always able to stay at his own chapels.[24] Moreover he did not need to commend any village to another lord for its safety, except one small place called Talizat, which was situated far from the rest of his property among bad neighbors. The officers permitted him, though he was unwilling, to commend this to a certain Bernard for safety. He bore this patiently with a certain amusement, saying: "It is well that I should learn that 'it is better to take refuge in the Lord than to put confidence in man' " (Ps 118.8). It is good to relate this, so that it may be seen that whenever God permitted something to happen for his trial, he did not let it lead to sadness but to humility. This demonstrates that he lived by faith, and knowing how to subject everything to the divine dispensation, was aware that "affliction does not come from the dust" (Jb 5.6).

42

I have now treated of his external actions and his ordinary way of life, from which it may easily be seen, that he was a man who cultivated justice, and, according to the apostolic precept, lived a "sober, upright and godly" (Tit 2.12) life. Since therefore he fulfilled uncomplainingly all that justified him in the eyes of the Lord it ought not to seem incredible that the Lord multiplied His mercies on him. For this reason I exhort those to whom all that report says of this holy man seems unworthy of credence to reconsider his case more cautiously and more diligently. For if it seems to be a difficulty, that he was a man of great position in the world, it is to be considered that the man is especially

24. It is nearly one hundred miles from Pousthomy to Puy de Griou. Gerald's personal holdings were obviously vast.

worthy of praise who has matter for pride and attains the height of power but is nevertheless humble. For power is only from God, who, according to the Scripture, does not cast away the mighty, whereas He himself also is mighty (see Jb 36.5). Although Gerald was raised on high by the glory of the world, it ought not to seem incredible that God should glorify the man who glorified Him in the observance of His commandments. Were not King David, Ezechias, and Josias mighty and warlike? The same things have been heard in this age of those who took care to glorify Him by keeping His commandments, and whom God honors with miracles, as King Oswald of the English.[25] For in every age the divine mercy does many things to foster religion, which has been despised and forgotten. Whence the apostle says that God leaves no age without a witness of Him (see Acts 14.16), and this is sometimes given by the wicked, as under Moses they performed many signs, of whom it is written, that with most of them God was not well pleased. Faithful witnesses assert things that are hardly to be believed, as Saint Jerome[26] of a man who was formerly violent and a robber, that after he had been converted to Christ he made the sun to stand still so that he might complete his journey, and then entered in to his disciples in bodily form through a closed door. If therefore God, who did wonderful things for the fathers, even in our time deigns to work miracles in order to revive enthusiasm for downtrodden religion through a man who, as in the days of Noah, was found just, it ought not to seem incredible. But He rather is to be glorified who, leaving no time without a witness of His goodness, and mindful of His promise, does not cease to do good to His people. Keeping for the next book what has to be said about the actions of this man after he had given himself entirely to the cult of the divine service, let me bring this one to an end in the name of the Lord.

Book 2

Preface

Those who rashly dispute about Gerald's merits may satisfy themselves if they will consider the nature of his life. As if seated on a judgment-seat they may determine whether he ought to be a saint or not; for this depends upon the will

25. Oswald (c. 605–642) was king of Northumbria. He led a saintly life that is vividly recounted in the pages of Bede's *Ecclesiastical History*.
26. Jerome (342–420) is the Church Father best known for the Vulgate Bible.

of God, which brings it about that even by the reprobate marvels are often performed for the benefit of the good. Let them therefore be satisfied by the testimony of the miracles that Christ deigned to work through him both in his lifetime and after his death. To those who find satisfaction in remarking that Gerald was both a man of great position and holy, I would point out (lest they congratulate themselves on this) that unless they become poor in spirit and, as he did, season their power with religion, their little house will not be able to stand. They will be condemned by a comparison with him, for they could have lived righteously as he did, but they would not. There are some professed religious, great eaters and drinkers, who making excuses for their own sins assert in their cups that Gerald used to eat meat and yet was holy, but their profession clearly condemns them. For many things are lawful to a layman that are not lawful to a monk. Adam was condemned, not because the tree in Paradise was evil in itself, but because he did that which had been forbidden. Gerald was quite justified in using those things that are allowed to his state in life, for he both abstained from what is not allowed and took his food with the poor. He knew that wine was made to be drunk soberly. Elias too ate meat and was worthy of being carried up into heaven. But through the greed that drives some men Esau lost his first birthright for a pottage of lentils. Gerald's case therefore is different from these. But let those who say foolishly that he can neither be called a martyr nor a confessor know that he can be called both, and not only he but all those who carry the cross by resisting vice, or who glorify God by doing good. God indeed is confessed by deeds, as John bears witness: "And by this we may be sure that we know him, if we keep his commandments" (1 Jn 2.3). By deeds also he is denied as the apostle says of some: "They profess to know God, but they deny Him by their deeds" (Ti 1.16). Since therefore a confessor is so called because he confesses, and God is either denied or confessed by deeds, Gerald can all the more truly be called a confessor as he confessed God by more righteous deeds. What do those who, like the Jews, seek signs, do about John the Baptist, who is not reported to have worked any miracle after his nativity? With regard to this man, although miracles are by no means absent, I say one thing, that he did not put his hope in money or riches, for, as it is written "he has done wonderful things for his life" (Sir 31.9).

1

The athlete of the heavenly hosts long struggling in the arena of this earthly life fought manfully against the forces of evil. And indeed keeping the word of life in the midst of a wicked nation, he shone out as a lamp. And since it was necessary that he should be tested in the darkness of the storm, the malignant enemy tried by all the tricks in his power to put out this light both directly and through his ministers. But as a flame fanned by the wind burns more fiercely, so the fire of divine love, which glowed in the heart of Gerald from his youth, could not be extinguished by the rain of temptation. On the contrary, as he grew more mature, and any vices that he had were gradually suppressed, he daily grew stronger in virtues. Now he set his heart on rising upward, now according to the saying of the prophet he towered above "the heights of the earth" (Is 58.14). You may see the dawn of his sanctity break on the festival day, you may see the lily spring up among the thorns, and that the nearer he came to maturity the more did the flowers of his virtue unfold. And therefore as though resting on the highest point, he had fixed the desire of his mind on the happiness of heaven. And since through this desire of heaven an inward light illuminated him, he was able to distinguish the darkness of earthly desire. Should I not have called earthly desire a darkness that blinds the lovers of the world, so that they love vanity? But Gerald had learned to distinguish the precious from the valueless, and though it very unworthy that he should lick the dust who knew himself to be called to the banquet of the heavenly Lamb. He grieved much over those whose love of the world makes them enemies of God. And after he had "tasted the kindness of the Lord" (1 Pt 2.3), he disdained to drink of the stolen waters that are sweeter. He lamented rather those who, according to the saying of Job (see Jb 30.4), run eagerly to gnaw the roots of juniper, that is, a cupidity full of thorns. He scorned worldly power, which was abundantly offered to him. But nevertheless, as it is the part of the wise to turn all things to their use, he took thought how he might so dispose of his temporal possessions that they might profit him in eternity.

2

He called, therefore, the venerable and most praiseworthy Bishop Gausbert,[27] with some other honest men, and told them privately what was in his mind. For this Gausbert was very dear to the man of God, and he and Gerald were intimate friends, united as they were by the common bonds of holiness. Gerald, therefore, stated that he was weary of the life he was leading, that he desired to enter religion, to go to Rome, and to make over his property by will to the blessed Peter, prince of the apostles. When the matter had been discussed for a long time, the holy man Gausbert, considering the case more

---

27. Bishop of Rodez from at least 888 to 922, referred to above, book 1:29.

deeply, finally recommended that for the sake of the general welfare he should continue to wear secular dress, but that he should dedicate the property to the blessed Peter as he wished. And so as not to appear disobedient by adhering obstinately to his plan Gerald agreed. Mindful of that saying of the apostle (see Rom 2:28–29) that the Jew (which is interpreted as *one who confesses*) becomes greater and better in secret than in public, he was tonsured in such a way that it remained hidden from men, though known to God. For he shaved off part of his beard, and continuing round his head shaved off part of his hair in the form of a tonsure. But in order that this should be quite unknown, he bound some of his chamberlains, who were aware of it, by an oath, that as long as he lived they should never betray the fact. He seems in the end to have won a double reward by this action of his, for on the one hand, glowing with the love of the Lord, he showed to God the sign of his conversion, on the other, filled with the love of his neighbor, he compelled himself against his inclination to remain for his sake in a dress which he did not desire. For what way of life could he show more pleasing to God than that in which he neither neglected the help of his fellow men nor diminished the perfection of his own life? And what way of life could be more valuable? For it was useful to many, and known only to God, who according to the Scripture, so directed his purpose that, although He made him enter into marriage with Lia, He did not deprive him of the desired embraces of Rachel (see Gen 29 and 30).

3

He easily found a means of hiding his tonsure. He shaved off his beard as though it were troublesome to him, since the hair from the back of his head hung down, and he concealed the tonsure on the top of his head by wearing a cap. He wore clothes of skin above his linen ones, because both clerics and laymen are accustomed to use clothes of this sort. But he never had two skin garments at once. When a new one had to be got, he ordered the old one to be given away immediately. When he rode his sword was carried in front of him, but he himself never laid a hand on it. From early on he had a golden cross made for his belt, and he never rode a horse adorned with medallions. In ways like this it appeared how much he studied moderation and despised the trappings of his position.

4

After he had freed himself from everything to serve God, he went to Rome to consecrate his possessions to the Lord, and assigned the notable property of

Aurillac to the blessed Peter,[28] prince of the apostles, by formal will, with as many additional properties as would suffice the monks he had decided to gather there for their whole income. For he very much desired to establish a monastic foundation in that place, where the monks might lead the common life with an abbot of their order. He assigned also dues to be paid each year at the tomb of Saint Peter. And what he had conceived in the fervor of his heart he carried out according to plan, and by the favor of God he performed what he had decreed. When he got back he ordered quarrymen and masons to be collected from all around, and commanded the foundation to be laid for a church in honor of Saint Peter. But Satan, envious of all good, by what device I know not, made the judgment of the masters to err. For they laid the foundation unsoundly and, when a great sum of money had been spent and the walls raised to a considerable height, the joining of the dressed stones suddenly came apart, and they fell to the ground. But Gerald was not unduly saddened by this. As it is written, "no ill befalls the righteous, but the wicked are filled with trouble" (Prv 12.21). For he had complete trust that, although the work would be retarded by this happening, the reward of the wasted effort would by no means be lost. He saw that this collapse came about with the permission of God, for it almost always happens that when anything pleasing is offered to God, it is carried through with difficulty. And certainly in natural things that which grows most quickly withers most quickly; that which grows with difficulty lasts longer.

5

The season of Lent had arrived and the milder weather favored the building operations. One morning after he had finished his accustomed prayers Gerald went out from the castle that overlooks the site, and when he had gone a little way, looking about here and there, he began to consider where he could best lay the foundations of a church. Eventually by the will of God he chose the destined place. So he ordered workmen to come once more and to set about making plans to start the interrupted work again. When they had begun, they were to carry on wisely and to build a church of suitable size and in rounded form, such as his father had formerly built in honor of Saint Clement. For, as I have said, his father was a religious man, as befitted one descended from a religious stock.

28. He founded Saint Peter of Aurillac in 894. There were precedents (for example, Fulda) for placing monasteries under direct papal protection.

6

While he went on with building the monastery he was always turning over in his mind where to find monks of good character who would live in the place according to their rule. But when the rareness with which they were to be found brought home the difficulty of his task, he became anxious and did not know what to do. Then he sent some noble youths to the monastery at Vabres,[29] where a fervent regular observance was growing up, that they might be trained in the rule with the community there. One of them still survives and he states, and also in writing, that he has himself witnessed those actions that I have ascribed to blessed Gerald. When these same youths were ordered to return, they became relaxed with a feminine softness through lack of masters, and neglected the rigor of their rule, and so the plan came to nothing. Compelled, however, by necessity he put one of them in charge of the rest. But when this man led a dissolute life, the man of God was much troubled, because he was not able to correct him, and he did not have another whom he could put in his place. When he saw him and his associates entering on the path of a corrupt life, sighing profoundly, he repeated that saying of David, "You will defeat for me the counsel of Ahithophel" (2 Sm 15.34).

7

Sometimes he broke out in lamentation at the sight of men giving themselves to evil. In his disgust he sighed complainingly that these men were perishing through love of the world, that piety was failing and iniquity abounded, that innocence had almost entirely departed from the hearts of men, and truth from their lips. He did not wish to be involved in their quarrels, but prayed that Almighty God would bring peace to all, ordering masses to be said, frequently repeating that saying of Hezekiah: "There will be peace and security in my days" (Is 39.8) and "There is no longer any that is godly; for the faithful have vanished from among the sons of men" (Ps 12.1).

8

He hoped that the desire by which he aspired after heavenly things and despised those of earth might be a consolation to him, if he found some to share in it. Consequently his mind was in a turmoil day and night, and he

---

29. A monastery near Toulouse founded in 866.

could not forget his wish to gather a community of monks. He often spoke of it with his household and friends. He was so moved by his desire for this that sometimes he exclaimed, "O, if it might be granted me by some means to obtain religious monks. How I would give them all I possess, and then go through life begging. I would make no delay in taking the necessary steps." Sometimes his friends would say, "Are there not many monks to be found in these regions from whom you can choose a community at will?" But speaking with great vehemence he would reply, "If monks are perfect, they are like the blessed angels, but if they return to the desire of the world they are rightly compared to the apostate angels, who by their apostasy did not keep to their home. I tell you that a good layman is far better than a monk who does not keep his vows." When they rejoined, "Why then have you been accustomed to show such favors not only to neighboring monks, but to those from a distance?" making little of his deeds, with his usual humility he would reply, "What I do is nothing; but if, as you say, I do anything, I am certain that He is true who promised to reward a cup of cold water given in His name. Let them understand what they are in the eyes of God. Certainly it is true that he who receives a just man in the name of a just man shall receive the reward of a just man." These and similar words of his make it clear that he despised the pleasures of this present life, that he burned with the desire of heaven, that he wished to leave all his possessions, if there had been anyone to whom he could reasonably hand them over. The common saying that the will is taken for the deed is true. Whence it comes also that he who hates his brother is considered a murderer, and John the Evangelist drank the chalice of the passion (Mt 20.22) though he died in peace. If therefore the will is taken for the deed, Gerald is certainly not to be deprived of the reward promised to those who give up all things.

9

It was against his will, therefore, that he was kept in the world. And although companions were lacking with whom he might renounce the world, he occupied himself entirely in a wonderful way with the work of God. To such an extent was he occupied alternately listening to reading and saying prayers, now with others now alone, that the marvel was how he could devote so much effort to this, and that he always wanted to say such a large number of psalms, especially as he got through much other business in the meantime. He was not obstinate in absenting himself unduly from necessary cases, but giving himself to these for a little as occasion demanded he soon hurried back to the sweetness of the psalmody. How reverent he was in church cannot be adequately expressed, for he appeared to be contemplating divine things and with rapt expression imitating that saying of the prophet, "As the Lord . . . lives before whom I stand" (1 Kgs 17.1). To make this clear from an example: the festival day of Our Lord's ascension had come round and he went to celebrate it, as it is a great feast, at the monastery of Solignac.[30] He would not suffer the office of so great a festival to be recited other than solemnly, nor did he allow, as many do, the service to be shortened in celebration. The monks, therefore, came and prepared a throne and a *prie-dieu*[31] arrayed as was fitting for so great a person, and when he had come to this after visiting the altars, the brethren began to say the office in a protracted manner as the custom is. The count stood so lost in contemplation that he neither sat nor reclined, or only very slightly, until it was finished, showing by the immobility of his body the devotion and constancy of his mind. With us it is not so, for we sing the divine praises before the face of God as though concealing the fact that we are praying, with a pompous voice rather than with simplicity of heart. And when the understanding of the mind ought to be in harmony with the voice, we make the voice keep pace with the quickness of the mind. But Gerald, recalling the saying of the apostle, "what we are is known to God" (2 Cor 5.11), so comported himself as in the sight of the Judge who sees all things.

10

That it might honor him in the sight of men, who honored God before the wicked by carrying out His commandments—although the time of Antichrist is now at hand and the miracles of the saints ought to cease—the divine mercy, mindful of the promise that says "for those who honor me I will honor" (1 Sm 2.30), deigned to honor this His servant with the gift of healing. And the manner of healing was such, that although he refused through humility to lay hands on the sick, he nevertheless frequently helped them, although he was absent and was not desiring to do so. The sick used to steal the water with which he had washed his hands; and many were cured. That this may seem more credible it is right that certain persons should be called to mind. For a certain countryman near the monastery of Solignac had a son who was blind, and lamenting for a long time that he was oppressed by both blindness and

---

30. A town near Limoges (Dépt. Haute Vienne) that had an important monastery founded by Saint Eligius in the seventh century and restored by Louis the Pious in the ninth.

31. "Pray-God": An individual prayer kneeler with, usually, a flat desklike surface.

poverty, he was warned in a vision that he should go to the count Gerald and bathe the eyes of his son with the water in which he had washed his hands. The man believed the vision, and coming made known the content of his dream. When the count heard this he was much afraid and troubled in his mind, and refusing to be so presumptuous said it was an illusion that had deceived the man and would deceive him, that he might attempt things that had not been granted. The man was in error in asking such things with a vain hope. The father, made anxious by the blindness of his son, burst forth in lamentations, and understanding that the holy man would not agree out of humility, pretending to go away he obtained the water from one of the servants. Returning home and invoking the name of Christ he bathed the blind eyes of his son, who received his sight. And another deed followed this one.

11

A certain boy in Aurillac was lame, and he was handed over to a smith to learn a trade by which he might live. Warned in sleep that he should beg the water in the same way, the smith, who had to obtain it, knowing that the man of God was very strict in this matter, did not dare to ask for the water openly, but got it secretly from the servants. He sprinkled the useless member with the water, and the divine power immediately restored it to its proper use. When the report of this fact became gradually spread abroad, it eventually reached the ears of the count. Struck by the strangeness of the event, he said it had not come about by his merits, but by the faith of those who had given the water to the smith. This had been kept secret from him, and unable to discover who had given it, he was moved to violent threats that no one should presume to do such a thing again, saying that if a serf did it he should be maimed, if a free man should be reduced to servitude. For he feared nothing more than praise. And while he was kind to his enemies, he was severe to those who praised him.

12

At Pousthomy, a considerable freehold property of his, a blind woman received her sight from the water in which he had washed his hands. This became known to all, but was most carefully concealed from him for the sake of one of the servants who had given the water to the woman. For his people could not make light of the mutilation that he had threatened, knowing that he would not yield in the matter of punishment, if he caught the man who had given it.

13

Again, he was staying at a chapel near the village called Crucicula,[32] when another woman, who was one of his servants, was given her sight by the water from his hands. When he learned this he urgently interrogated the man, Rabboldus, who had given the water, found out that he had done it, and immediately dismissed him from his service. After a little time, however, a certain nobleman called Ebbo came to reason with the count, saying that perhaps he was acting against the will of God, when he neglected a grace given from heaven under the pretext of indiscreet humility, and sent away in sadness those whom he might have helped. It was better to give those who asked what they needed, since perhaps this grace was given to him for their sakes. There was no fear of pride, since he was not covetous of praise; nor of presumption, because those who asked for help had stated that they were divinely urged; and a special reason for granting it was that it had been proved by experiment that the gift of health asked from him had often been granted, though without his knowledge. He set all this out in a very reasonable way. But with sighs and tears Gerald replied that he feared it might rather be a deceit of the devil wishing to make use of the occasion to deceive him, and plotting to deprive him of the reward of any good he had done. At length, convinced by reason and by entreaty, he took back the man he had dismissed, and ordered the woman to be given twelve coins.

14

Knowing that the condition of the mind is best preserved by alternate reading and prayer, he had the Scriptures read to him, as I have said. And so it was that he adopted the practice of having reading at his dinner, and this was not omitted even if guests were present. At intervals he graciously ordered the reader to stop, and to ask the meaning of the reading from those who might know. When those whom he asked used to beg him rather to speak himself, he would reply clearly and knowledgeably, as one well versed in the subject, but in such a way as not to put his clerics to shame. When the meal was finished and the others had departed, he generally had those passages that were left over from the lessons recited in church read to him. While he was listening to reading no one easily presumed to break in on him for any reason. For he was awe-inspiring to those set beneath him and, according to the saying of Job,

---

32. Probably Croisette, a village near Argentat (see note 45 below).

"the light of his countenance was not turned to the earth" (Jb 29.24). It is wonderful to recall his words and talk. When he spoke from a joyous mind his words were most pleasing, but when he spoke rebukingly, they seemed like goads and were feared almost more than mere words. He was slow to give anything, but when he had once given it, he did not take it back. If he heard a priest was of evil repute, he did not disdain his mass, because he knew that the sacred mystery cannot be invalidated by a man who is a sinner.[33] And whereas he judged the deeds of others severely or mildly as the case deserved, he held his own deeds to be of little value, and the less value he attached to them the more he commended them to the divine regard.

15

Because he gave himself wholeheartedly to the desire of heaven, his mouth was so filled from the abundance of his heart that the law of God sounded almost continuously on his lips. For he had marked certain holy words that seemed to fit bodily duties. Thus, before he spoke in the morning he said: "Set a guard over my mouth, O Lord, keep watch over the door of my lips" (Ps 141.3). And there were other sayings of this sort which he adapted to particular actions, for example when he awoke, when he got out of bed, when he put on his shoes, his clothes, or his belt, or certainly when he went on a journey or began any other action, so that in the words of the apostle he seemed to "do everything in the name of the Lord" (Col 3.17). Sometimes when he happened to be sitting with few companions or alone, he meditated on I know not what for long in silence, and, bathed in tears, he sighed from the depths of his heart so as to shake his whole body; it was easy to see that his mind dwelt on other things and he found no consolation in the present time. His speech and his silence were such that his mouth declared the praise of the Lord and the meditation of his heart was always in His sight.

16

His followers knew that he greatly desired to be a religious, but being a prudent man and realizing that those who set a high ideal before themselves only fall the more grievously when the love of the world corrupts them, he judged it better to remain as he was than to attempt so difficult an undertaking without tried assistants. If therefore one considers his desire, he was true to

---

33. Compare this remark with the Donatist problem in Augustine's North Africa.

the monastic profession through his devotion to Christ. And it is indeed high praise for a man in secular dress to keep the rule of religious, as on the other hand it is a very shameful thing to follow the world in the habit of a monk. Since, therefore, as I said above, he had no brethren with whom it was good to live together in unity, life on earth was irksome to him. But as, long ago, Noah's dove, not finding where she might rest, returned to Noah in the ark, so this man, amid the waves of the world, retiring into his inmost heart, took his rest in the joy of Christ. He did not, like the crow, settle on the carrion of bodily pleasure, for his soul refused to be consoled with this life's glory, but took its delight in the memory of its God, and coming back to the sanctuary of the heart as though to the ark, gave voice to its joy. For he did not allow iniquity to dwell in his heart, fearing lest the Lord should be unwilling to hear him. Rather, the sins that human nature cannot escape and that, though slight to us, seemed great to him, he was always careful to keep before his eyes, so that he might with confidence look to receive from the mercy of God forgiveness for the evil dispositions of his heart. And so his King and Lord mercifully directed his ways in His sight, and kindly hearkened to the voice of his prayer. He took so much trouble always to have his lodging next the church that for many years he went to the oratory every night, except once on the feast of the Innocents on account of a journey. A number of clerics always accompanied him and with these he labored at the work of God. All the ecclesiastical equipment necessary for the service was carried with him, and with this he performed the divine service with great care and reverence, especially on the festivals. For the night office he used to come to the oratory a long time before the others, and when it was finished he remained alone. And then all the more sweetly as it was more in private he tasted the savor of internal sweetness. After a time he came out joyous and brisk, and either went to his bed or joined his household. He had established such a way of life that any wise man must have marveled at the great grace which had come to him. He so clung to this manner of life in externals, that his servants knew how he would conduct himself at every season of the year.

17

He established a custom of going frequently to Rome. It is said that he went there again and again; my informants are certain of seven times. For it is a quality of human nature always to wish to see the light, and being a spiritual man, he went to gaze spiritually on those two lights of the world, Peter and Paul. And since he was not yet able to contemplate them directly, he often visited their tombs and shrines, and he made over his possessions to Saint Peter. He made it a rule to go every second year to their tombs as a serf with ten shillings hung round his neck that he might pay them as a due to his lord. Who can describe the devotion with which he performed this? He was so good to those in want, that his bounty hardly passed a poor man by, and they abounded in that place, for he was confident that he himself would be heard, if he heard the cry of the poor. He gave generously also to the monasteries that lay on the road, and the fame of his great generosity sounded far and wide, so that monks, as well as pilgrims and the needy who were his guests, used to inquire anxiously, at the time when the pilgrims to Rome are accustomed to pass by, if and when Count Gerald was coming. Even the Marruci,[34] the fierce inhabitants of the Alps, thought nothing more profitable than to carry Gerald's baggage through the pass of Mont Joux.[35]

18

Once when he was making this journey and came to the city of Asti,[36] a thief made off with two of his packhorses, but coming to a river he was not able to get them across before he was taken by Count Gerald's men. Having got back the packhorses he took no action against the thief.

19

Another time when he was going that way he had a certain monk called Aribert with him, a man of great abstemiousness. For it was always a sweet companionship for him, when he found men of religious life, and he used to take great delight in their company. Now it happened on one occasion that there was none of the food that this abstemious man ate with his bread. The count asked carefully whether the servants had prepared the usual food for him, and when they replied that they had nothing except bread, he became most anxious saying: "What has happened to us today? We have all we want to eat, and this servant of God will go short." It was an abstinence day; the time to wash hands had arrived, and Samuel, who tells the story, running to fetch the water, found a small fish lying gasping on the bank, which had

34. The Moors, or Saracens—Muslims actually—who had established a base for piratical raiding on Saint-Tropez off the south coast of France. They raided high into the Alps, preying on merchants and pilgrims alike.
35. The place cannot be identified with certainty.
36. The first city on the Italian side of the Alps on the road between Lyon and Turin.

jumped out of the water when it saw him. He caught it and returned joyfully to the count. "Look," he said, "God sends you this fish; for I found it lying near the water." "Thanks be to God," he replied. And while it was being cooked he went into his tent and kneeling down prayed for a while in tears. His character was such that he preferred nothing to Christ, but rather devoutly returned thanks to Him for everything that happened. When he arose from prayer he cheerfully joined himself to the company. The abstemious man, however, sitting down at table with the rest, ate till he was satisfied, and since there was still a part of the fish left over, the count urged him, saying, "Why do you hold back, brother, from eating the little fish, when you will have nothing else?" When he replied that he had already had enough, the count took some to try its quality. Finding it to be of excellent flavor he ate as much as he wanted, and to all those present he gave a morsel as a token of devotion. All gave thanks to God, recognizing the divine gift both in the finding of the fish and in the amount that was left over. For it had been six inches long.

20

In the same way, when he was going to Rome and arrived at the city of Tuscany called Lucca, a certain woman came up to him saying that she had been warned in a vision that he would give back his sight to her son. When he heard this he rebuked the woman, and setting the mule he was riding in motion, he fled, much disturbed. The woman asked everyone she could find how she might obtain the hoped-for benefit from the man of God. Perhaps it was one of the servants who told her that miracles had been worked by the water from his hands. But the count had been put on his guard by the woman, and whenever he washed his hands had the water poured out on the ground in front of him. Still she kept on following him, until he became less careful about the water being poured away. At length she obtained some without his knowledge and bathed the eyes of her blind son, who immediately received his sight. When, therefore, the holy man came back from the city, the woman presented him with his son, now able to see. And when all were praising this deed, Gerald went away silent and in tears, nor did anyone dare to refer to this or anything of the kind in his hearing.

21

What I am going to relate is remarkable, and it may seem incredible, but I believe the two witnesses who assert it. They say that this same holy man was returning from Italy by the road which goes to Lyon from Turin.[37] He had crossed the Alps, and the way led through some country that, they state, is without water. It happened too that the supply of wine ran out. There was no water, and, since the district had long been laid waste by the Saracens, wine could not be found there either, so the party began to suffer greatly from thirst. They tried as best they might to get over this part of the journey quickly, but they were short of servants and packhorses, so the count had to order a short halt. The dispirited men threw themselves on the turf, while the packhorses, driven by thirst, wandered in all directions over the grazing-ground. When one of the clerics, not wishing to continue the halt, went to collect and saddle them again, he found a little hole full of some liquid. He was very surprised, and wishing to find out what it was, stooped down. The liquid smelled to him like wine. Greatly rejoicing, he ran back to the count and told him that he had discovered something like wine. "What, are you mad?" said the count: "I wish you might have found water. Where could wine come from here?" The cleric, however, taking a vessel, drew some of this liquid and brought it to him. That which was brought certainly had the color and smell of wine. Then the count ordered his chaplains to take the cross and the reliquaries and to say the exorcism for the blessing of water over the hole with the liquid. Then he ordered that in the name of Christ they should find out what it was by tasting it. When they found it was wine the holy man joined them all in giving thanks to God with great admiration and joy, and before he drank himself, he ordered it to be given to all the others, but he did not allow any of it to be put into flagons. I have related this on the word of those who say they saw it. Nevertheless, those things that now happen at his tomb persuade one to believe everything that one hears of him.

22

The holy man often took this road [to Rome]. It was not that he wished to approach the palaces of kings, or the halls of marquises, and certainly not the assemblies of princes, but it was the heavenly rulers Peter and Paul, as I said before, that he was on fire to see more frequently. But he sought out too with keen devotion other holy places, namely the tomb of the most holy Saint Martin, and of Saint Martial. I believe he saw in contemplation how the ranks

37. One of northern Italy's two great cities; Milan is the other. It is approached via the Saint Gotthard pass.

of the blessed rejoice in the court of heaven. With those to whom he was soon
to be joined he had to some extent a foretaste of the joy of his Lord.

23

On the other side of Sutri,[38] next to the town, there is a rushy field called Saint
Martin's, where the Roman pilgrims are accustomed to camp. The servants
had put up the tents there, and the count happened to be standing alone, when
a blind man had himself led up to him. Begging suppliantly he asked if he
would deign to give him some water that had touched his hands. The count
ordered him to remain where he was and be silent. Then he went into his tent
and prayed for a little time before the relics of the saints. The servants were
going about their work, and while they were occupied, seeing that he would be
unobserved, he called up somebody to lead the man in unnoticed. Then he
carefully washed his hands, and soaked his fingers in the water, and made the
sign of the cross over it with the holy relics. When the blind man poured it on
his sightless eyes, he was immediately able to see. The man of God stopped
him from crying out, and joined him in giving thanks to the divine majesty.
He then clothed him with one of his garments, a tunic, and had him conducted
in secret from the tents.

24

It was the same when he came back from the city. He arrived one Saturday at a
certain church, at the place where heaps of sulfur are to be seen. When his
people wished to go on the next day, he kept them back, saying that out of
reverence of the Lord's day they should stay at least till none. And this delay
was not without even a temporal advantage, for when the High Mass was over
and they were setting out on their journey after having something to eat, a
man came in mounted on a broken-down horse, who had got lost on his
journey, and Count Gerald ordered him to be received without charge to the
resident priest. Before they had reached Abricola,[39] a blind man sitting by the
roadside asked them as they passed, if there was anybody in the company
called Gerald. One of our brethren, who at that time was still a canon, happened to be traveling in Count Gerald's party, and out of devotion he was
traveling on foot. Being weary he came up to the blind man, and to his inquiry

38. A modest town about twenty-five miles north of Rome.
39. This site cannot be identified.

about Count Gerald answered that he was following behind. "But why are you seeking him so earnestly?" he said. "I have been afflicted with blindness of nine years, and last night I was warned in sleep to come here and seek Gerald, the pilgrim of Saint Peter, that I might ask him to wash his hands, and then pour the water on my blind eyes." When the cleric heard this, he stood still till Count Gerald came up. Now it was Gerald's custom to ride alone with his head covered that he might be more free to say his psalms. When he came up, therefore the cleric whispered to the blind man, "Here he is," and the latter asked him if he would mind stopping for a short time, and he added what he had been told in sleep. The count blushed, and with a changed countenance rejecting what he heard, started to go on. But the blind man, adjuring him strongly, begged him to stop and help a man in misfortune, and not to refuse the hoped-for benefit. Those who were present implored the same thing. But he, deliberating a little, and remembering, as I think, that according to the saying of the apostle (see 1 Tm 4.14), he ought not to neglect the grace that was given to him, replied with his usual words, saying, "Help me, you saints of God," and stopped. And since, as is usual among those small hills, a stream flowed by, water was forthwith brought.

He dismounted and washed his hands saying, "The will of God be done." Then, much moved, he started to go on. The blind man did not delay in taking the water, nor did the outcome of the miracle fail him. He received his sight so promptly that he immediately ran after Gerald crying, "O holy Gerald, O holy Gerald, thanks be to God I see." But Gerald put spurs to his mule so as not to hear the cries of those who were praising him, and passed through Abricola, nor could his fellow travelers catch up with him for two days! Indeed, it is not hard to believe that those hands through which this power of healing was conferred shone with purity and were without stain, and that every gift was shaken from them. On the other hand how unhappy are "those whose right hands are full of bribes" (Ps 26.10), for it is written that "fire consumes the tents of bribery" (Jb 15.34).

25

Other things are related of his journeying that I pass over for fear of being too lengthy, but let me add one, because it shows a miracle of another sort. On one of his journeys to Rome, when he was already in Italy, he heard the voice of a man crying out and announcing his death. It seemed to him that it was the voice of a certain Girbald whom he had left at home. So he called some of his followers and asked them if they knew anything of Girbald. They replied that he was sick when they left him. He ordered the time to be noted, and the psalms for the dead to be recited for him. When he came home and inquired about this man, he found that he had died on the very day that the voice had been heard.

26

After his journey of devotion he liked to go to some quiet place, as though to fulfil that word of the psalmist that says: "I would fly away and . . . I would wander afar, I would lodge in the wilderness" (Ps 55.6–7). He wished to rest from the comings and goings of the world and the noise of the law courts, that he might give himself more freely to the service of God. Now when he was staying for this reason at the chapel called Catuserias,[40] on the feast of Saints John and Paul a certain countrywoman came into the garden to do some work or other, when suddenly a great drop of blood appeared on her hand, which immediately began to swell. The terrified woman ran lamenting to the man of God, and showing him her hand begged him to have mercy on her. He immediately ordered clerics to come and say mass for her, and then to bless water and to wash away the drop of blood with it. He himself stood aside out of humility, lest the miracle should be attributed to his virtue. When the woman's hand was washed, the blood and the swelling disappeared, and she went away healed.

27

Because that place, which I have said was dear to him, was remote and little known, he often stayed there. On one occasion he had been celebrating the Assumption of the holy Mother of God, Mary, in this church, and after mass he went out to his followers, for it was his custom after long-continued prayers to give himself to general conversation, so that anyone who had cause to speak with him might have the opportunity of doing so. When he had gone out among his people, therefore, the man who was in charge of the preparation of the food said to him: "We are very sorry, my lord, that we cannot find anything for your meal on this feast except salted meat." "Do not let that worry you," he said, "for if it pleases the Mother of God we shall not lack on her feast." He spoke, and from a rock that overhung the place a stag threw

40. Catus, ten miles northwest of Cahors (Dépt. Lot) and sixty-five miles southwest of Aurillac.

itself down. Rejoicing and lost in admiration the servants seized it, and from it, as the flesh of stags is tender at that season, they prepared a delicate meal for the count. And it should not seem incredible that the divine bounty provided him with food in this unexpected manner, because he ate his morsel with the poor, acting according to the apostle, "to the glory of God" (1 Cor 10.31). As those of his followers who are still here attest, he never turned his ear from the cry of the poor. The holy man, according to the saying of the psalmist, "Blessed is he who considers the poor" (Ps 41.1), when he heard the voices of those who cried out, used to sigh deeply and reply with words of compassion.

28

You knew Count Raymund, the son of Odo.[41] This man treacherously held captive Count Gerald's nephew, Benedict, who was viscount of Toulouse. But his brother, Rainald, gave himself up as a hostage and won him back his freedom. When Count Gerald heard that Rainald had given himself up in his brother's place, he did all he could to help his nephew. But Raymund delayed making restitution, secretly plotting to capture Benedict again and hold them both. Seven months had passed without the holy man Gerald's being able to make any progress in the rescue of his nephew, and one day he complained to his sister, Avigerna, about this: "Why do you cease to implore Christ for your son? Certainly, either we are lacking in faith, or what is more true, we do not deserve to be heard"—and he wept as he said the words. From that time on Gerald gave himself wholeheartedly to the Lord in prayer. And he also sent Abbot Rudolf to Raymund at once, but he was not able to make any headway and soon returned. But on the following night it seemed to Raymund that the holy man Gerald stood beside his bed and struck him with his hand, saying, "Why do you not listen when I ask so often? Know for sure that if you hold the hostage any longer, misfortune will come upon you." At these words Raymund woke up and was greatly terrified by the memory of the vision. He called his household and told them what he had dreamed. One of them, from whom up till then most opposition had come, was for some reason equally afraid, and urged him to grant Count Gerald's petition at once, saying that otherwise they would certainly die. Raymund immediately sent to the lodging of Abbot Rudolf and ordered him to come back. When he did so, he told him plainly how the man of God had terrified him in a vision, forthwith gave back

41. He may have been the count of Toulouse who was contemporary with Duke William the Pious of Aquitaine.

the hostage, and humbly asked Rudolf to bring him back into the good graces of Count Gerald. So by the help of God Gerald prevailed, and according to the word of Scripture humbled the great ones of the earth (see Is 45.2: Vulgate).

29

Once when he was going to meet this same Count Raymund and was approaching the river Aveyron,[42] someone happened to mention that he had no fish to eat that day. While they were speaking of this those who were walking with the count saw a fish called a mullet swimming toward them. One of them, who tells the story, threw out a cast-net and wounded it. When it was wounded it withdrew a little and then came again to the bank toward which it had been swimming, and there it remained till one of them put out his hand and caught it. It was of no small size. The holy man giving thanks to God tried to make the others, who were extolling the fact as a miracle, keep quiet; as though it had happened by accident. And perhaps someone may say that this could have happened by accident, but I think he will not remember having seen a fish in a broad river like the Aveyron rushing in to men on the bank.

30

If it is rightly considered a miracle, either that a fish should have jumped out of the water, or a stag fallen unexpectedly from a rock, so should it that a fish in a river offered itself to be caught. But much more wonderful is something that the divine agency brought on another occasion to bring food to the man of God. Not far from the monastery of Figeac[43] there is a hamlet dedicated to Saint Gregory, in charge of which was a certain priest called Gerald, who on account of his sanctity was a very dear friend to the man of God, and who before the end of his life went to live as a recluse. Gerald, therefore, on one occasion turned aside to visit this man, and after they had prayed together and kissed each other, he said, "What are you going to give us to eat, Brother Gerald? For we have come to have dinner with you." He spoke like this on account of the easy relations that this priest had with him. But with pleasure the priest replied, "If it pleases your piety, my lord, you shall not go away fasting. Nevertheless I have only bread and wine to put before you, but I will see if by chance I can find some cheese or eggs." "Do not trouble yourself," the

42. A river about forty miles south of Aurillac in the Quercy region.
43. A small town some thirty miles southwest of Aurillac.

count said, "because it is an abstinence day and it will be good for us to eat more sparingly on this occasion, since there is nothing to provide a banquet." The priest hurried away to prepare, and going into his inner room he saw a fish lying on a plate. Astounded, he asked his servant privately who had brought it. The servant replied that he did not know, and said that nobody had been there who could have done so. The priest, therefore, going out to the count asked him if he would mind coming into his inner room, and when he followed him in showed him the fish. Astonished and full of admiration, Gerald joined the priest in giving thanks to God. But he bound him and his servant, nevertheless, under oath not to betray this fact to anyone during his lifetime. But gradually the fact did become known to many, for the divine dispensation, which glorifies holy men, sometimes makes them known against their will. Truly the Lord is still mindful of His promise and does not deprive of all good those who seek Him (see Ps 34.10). For the rest, this should not seem incredible, since we often read that God has deigned to supplement the food or the drink of his servants miraculously.

31

Not far from Aurillac in a district called Marcolez,[44] there is to be found a naturally round stone. On one occasion when Count Gerald was passing through the district, one of his followers called Adraldus told his companions that he could jump onto the top of the stone, and he forthwith did so to the amazement of all. But it was said that this Adraldus had a knowledge of incantations and magic. When the count came up, those in front stopped and pointed the jump out to him. He thought that it could not possibly have been made by any natural agility, and raising his hand he made the sign of the cross. After that the man, though he tried many times, was quite unable to jump onto the stone. And so it was manifest that this activity of his was the result of an incantation, which could no longer aid him after the sign of the cross, and that the power of Count Gerald was great, since the power of the enemy had no force against his sign.

32

Since I have related this about his making the sign of the cross, let me add something else that he did in this way. It was the feast of Saint Laurence and

---

44. A little town about ten miles south of Aurillac.

he was keeping it in a certain chapel not far from Argentat.[45] Now one of his serving-women there was grievously afflicted. Since he had already prayed for her, and in the midst of the people, as she was, she was still mouthing and raving, they asked if the man of God would deign to make the sign of the cross over her. Out of his usual humility he was unwilling to do this for a long time, but as she never stopped raving, and those who were present asked more insistently, he at length raised his hand and made the sign of the cross over her, and she, vomiting forth blood and matter, was straightway healed. When all were sounding the praises of God and glorifying His servant, Gerald ordered them with many reproaches to be quiet, saying that they should glorify God alone, and Saint Peter whose church it was. For it is that same church at which he was stopping when the blind woman mentioned above received her sight from the water in which he had washed his hands.

33

A man called Herloard fell from his horse and badly damaged one of his knees. The pain was such that for six days he went without eating. Not being able to find a remedy he sent to Capdenac[46] and had some of the water from Count Gerald's hands secretly brought to him. Wonderful to relate, as soon as he had sprinkled this water on his knee, he got up cured and free from all pain. Other things are told of him that deserve both to be related and admired, but because they rest on common report and not on the four witnesses I mentioned, I prefer to keep silent about them, for I am not ignorant that he did many things that none, or few, know about. Like all pious and good men he was careful always to guard humility as the apple of his eye, and for that reason, as far as he could, he concealed his good works. But of those that became known against his will he would hear no praise.

34

Let this suffice for his miracles, and it may satisfy those who assess the glory of a saint not from the amount of his good works, but from the number of the signs that he performed. To such as these perhaps his sanctity would have seemed less, if they had heard nothing about the miracles that he did in his lifetime. But the righteous works that he performed will be more pleasing to

45. A small town about thirty miles south of Aurillac.
46. A little town near Figeac.

those who are held by his holy love, and who revere him with a discerning admiration. But since both are to be found in him, namely, a holy justice and the glorification of miracles, they honor him with a more secure and lively devotion. If he had happened to have the spirit of prophecy, no one, I think, would have denied that he was a saint. But he accomplished more than this, because he conquered avarice. For what profit was it to Balaam that he prophesied so profound a mystery, when he was rejected on account of avarice? Do not look for any great miracle in Gerald, therefore, because this is he "who did not go after gold" (Sir 31.8). This is he, who, as I have said, did wonderful things. So rarely will you find one who does not put his hope of happiness in riches, that on account of that very rarity the divine word must have interposed. Who is such a one? When he is found he is worthy of praise, and as the text goes on, we will praise him for he has done wonderful things in his life (see Sir 31.9). There is much evidence for the wonderful things which Gerald did. For it is well known that he preserved those things that were given him by his parents and by kings, so that he might dispense them not as to servants but as to masters, that he increased his property without injuring anyone, that he laid up treasure for himself in heaven, that he was exalted in power but nevertheless remained poor in spirit. For this reason it should seem neither wonderful nor unbelievable, if, as the text goes on, "his property will be established" (Sir 31.11). Although by far the most outstanding of his deeds is that he preserved his chastity to old age. For it is chastity alone that imitates the purity of the angels. Since, therefore, he overcame lust, which is Satan's chief weapon, it is not remarkable that he had power over Satan, whom he conquered in preserving chastity. It is not incredible that he who cast the Prince of Mammon out of his heart by overcoming avarice now frees those who are possessed by devils. Rightly is the spirit of pride now subject to him, who at the very summit of earthly power showed himself humble.

Book 3

Preface

Since what I have already said has shown clearly that the venerable man, Gerald, was outstanding for the power of working miracles, it remains now for me to describe by way of conclusion how he gave up his spirit from its bodily habitation. It is beyond doubt that, although he had brought his bodily appetites into subjection through spare living, he had great vigor. Nor, when his strength failed, did he lack fortitude. But when, in view of his age, the time approached for him to be freed from the service he had faithfully performed, he began gradually to lose his accustomed vigor. The fact was not hidden from him, and indeed the loss of his strength made it clear that he was failing. When he looked around at the many who were habitually in close attendance on him, he began to speak with deep sighs and failing breath: "Alas, my poor followers and most dear friends, do you not see that I am without my former strength? Know that the time of my death is approaching, when my spirit at the will of its Creator will be transferred to its destined habitation, and weak nature will return to dust." Suffering and weakness did not keep him from his usual abstinence. It is a remarkable thing, but the feebleness that normally takes possession of old people was not able to move his indomitable spirit out of its usual course. The weakness of the flesh was by no means able to relax the strictness of his mind. While, therefore, the soul was increasing in virtues, his bodily strength was ebbing away. But since, thinking meanly of himself, he did not recognize his own virtues, he did not rightly understand whence his bodily weakness sprang. For the power of the spirit, which was always growing in him, had almost cut off his bodily strength. And indeed this is the way with the saints, for the divine power would have been less strong in them, if the bodily power had not grown weaker. So Daniel, seeing the vision of angels, was sick for many days, and Jacob became lame when he wrestled with an angel. For he who is filled with spiritual grace is deprived of bodily strength. So the exterior man failed, while the interior was renewed from day to day.

1

One day he was in the castle that overlooks Aurillac, and looking at the monastery he wept copiously. When one of his followers asked why he wept, he replied, "Because I can by no means bring into effect the desire which I have long had for this place. For 'this is my resting place for ever' here I will dwell' " (Ps 132.14). By the help of God I have easily provided all those things for the use of monks; only the monks are missing; they alone could not be found, and so alone and bereaved I am worn out with sorrow. Nevertheless I hope that Almighty God in His own good time will deign to fulfil my desire. Nor is it strange if I, a sinner, am left with my desire unfulfilled, since King David was forbidden to build the temple of the Lord, while God provided the one who was to carry out the work after him. And though I may not see it in my lifetime, the mercy of Christ will grant what I long for when it pleases

Him, for you know my desire that the walls of this house may be too narrow for all those who will come to it." How he came to this knowledge he did not say. But seeing the place full of people as he foretold, those who know him to have made the remark have formed the opinion that he was inspired to say what he did by the power of God. For truly his mouth was filled from the abundance of his heart, that the law of God might ever resound in it. For the rest, according to the example of David aforesaid, he foresaw all that would be necessary for the future inhabitants, and took care to provide for them in relics of the saints, ornaments, and vestments for the church, and in the produce of the fields.

2

And truly, as the Scripture says that he who is holy shall be sanctified (see Rev 22.11), it was fitting that this man of God should be brought to naught through suffering before his death. To him it happened as to blessed Job and Tobias that he was chosen to be proved by trial. And so for seven years and more he lost the sight of his eyes. But so sharp-witted was he that it was unbelievable that he suffered from blindness. He not only did not grieve over this affliction, but even rejoiced in the Lord that He had deigned to scourge him. For he knew, indeed, that not every one who is chastised is a son, but nevertheless there is no son who does not suffer the rod. And this was a consolation to him, that the Judge on high should raise His hand to strike him, and that his sins, without which no man may live, should be punished in this life. For assured of the mercy of the Lord, he trusted that He would deign to free him whom He had deigned to afflict in this life from everlasting chastisement. If it had been possible to add to his previous practices, the more he retired from exterior activity by reason of his blindness the more attentively he gave himself to prayer. In proportion as he was not able to gaze on the face of the world, by so much he contemplated more clearly the true light of the heart. Outside business ceased, and he applied himself entirely to the practice of prayer and reading.

3

Two years before he died he had the church solemnly consecrated. So many relics of saints were enclosed within the altars that those who knew the number were amazed. To those who only know by hearsay it may seem incredible. For this holy father set himself to collect them from all sides, whenever opportunity offered, during his whole life. He obtained them at Rome and everywhere, for he was pleasing in speech and manner, generous in the price he paid and, what is more, supported by divine grace in whatever he undertook. It is known that in obtaining relics he often gave precious tents and well-conditioned horses, as well as great sums of money. He placed the tooth of Saint Martial at the right-hand side of the altar with the relics of Saint Martin and Saint Hilary. None of the benefactors had been able to loosen this tooth from the holy man's jaw, though they had long tried, but after praying he withdrew it at once. In connection with this same altar a marvelous thing happened on the day of the consecration. Crowds of people were pressing around and a boy took the covering from it to give to one of the ministers. Those who were standing near told him not to do so, but he did not let go of it, and was forthwith seized by violent pains. First the skin came off his hands, then gradually off his whole body, so that he had scarcely recovered in six weeks. Gerald, as he had formerly decided, handed the church over to the control of monks, of whom up till then few were living there.

4

While he still lived he took the greatest care to ensure that he should leave all those dependent on him in peace, lest any occasion of strife should arise among them. The farms and estates that he had not handed over to Saint Peter[47] he left to relations and soldiers, and even serfs; to some of them in such a manner that after their death they should return to Aurillac. At this time he only gave their liberty to a hundred serfs, but they are innumerable whom he emancipated at different times and places. Many through their love of him refused their liberty and preferred rather to remain as his serfs. It shows how mild a dominion he exercised over them that they sometimes preferred being his serfs to being free. He was warned by some of his followers that as far as concerned his household, and it was very large, he should not free a greater number from the yoke of servitude. "It is right," he said to these, "that the civil law should be observed in this, and therefore the number appointed in that law should not be passed." Let this be told that hence it may be clear how closely he adhered to the divine precepts, when he submitted in this way to legal and human ones.

47. That is, Saint Peter of Aurillac.

5

When the time of his departure drew near he was staying at Cezerviacum,[48] a certain church that belonged to him, dedicated to Saint Siricius. More than usually full of compunction he sighed profoundly, so that it was evident that his heart's desire was elsewhere and that he would never have consolation in the present life. Tears were mingled with the sighs, and with eyes raised to heaven he prayed that he might be freed from this world, repeating often the invocation "Help, you saints of God." This expression had always been familiar in his mouth, and it was what he was accustomed to exclaim at any unexpected event. Not long after this he lost much strength by a convulsion, and the strength of his limbs and the harmony of the whole body gradually disappeared. Knowing that the time of his dissolution was at hand he ordered Bishop Amblardus[49] to be called that he might fortify him in death by his prayers, and that the pastor might hand over the sheep seeking the pastures of paradise to Christ the Pastor of all. Meanwhile, with his faculties clear and no lack of memory, he arranged everything necessary for his funeral and the needs of those he was leaving. When swift fame suddenly spread all around the rumor that the man of God, Gerald, was near his end, men came together as though lamenting a common loss, crowds of clerics and monks with nobles mingling among them, groups of the poor, and people from the countryside; all these by their lamentations incited the grief of others. They broke out into sighs and tears as though they had a grievance. They raised their voices in lamentation over his piety, his charity, his care for the poor, his protection of the weak. In tears some declared, "How great a comfort is the world losing," others, "O Gerald, rightly called good, who will help the needy as you have done? Who will be a father to orphans or the defender of widows? Who will give such comfort to the sorrowful? Who will use your great authority on behalf of the poor? Who will consider the necessities of individuals and help them as you did? Most indulgent father, how kind, how gentle you always were! You won the thanks of all; the fame of so great goodness drew to you the affections even of those who were unknown to you." Expressions of this sort, which a great sorrow usually elicits among the sighs, poured in with such deep lamentation that you would think these tears could never cease. So it went on each day until the end of his time on earth arrived. To the last he could not give up his custom of ordering alms to be given to all wishing to receive them.

48. Now Saint Cirgues (Dépt. Cantal) southeast of Aurillac.
49. Forty-third bishop of Clermont; his regnal dates are unknown although he signed Cluny's foundation charter in 910.

6

Truly I may call that man blessed and happy whose character was such that even on earth he did not lose the love due to his good works, and in heaven is received in the love of the saints. Truly he is happy who, although at the height of worldly power, nevertheless injured none, oppressed none, and against whom none brought the smallest complaint. For if Nathanael is called a true Israelite because guile was not found in him, rightly may I call this man an Israelite whom, in the words of blessed Job (see Jb 29.11), the ear that heard blesses, to whom the eye that saw gives testimony. When, therefore, all were mourning, he alone continued joyous, as one indeed who knew that the splendor of the noonday shall arise in the evening for those who hope in the Lord, and when He has given them sleep, this is their inheritance. Therefore, although the flesh might fear on account of its mortal state, the spirit, confirmed in the sight of glory, exulted, trusting that it would now receive in fact the hope so long desired. For as it is written that the just man has confidence in his death (see Prv 14.32), so you would judge that he was confirmed in hope and had no fear of death. He seemed joyous therefore, since not the slightest word betrayed that he feared. During the whole time of his illness he forced his failing limbs to the divine service, so that he would not allow the night office to be celebrated once except in church. Placed before the altar he always heard both the mass of the day and a black mass.[50] And indeed when his limbs became too stiff and he was no longer able to walk by himself, the fervor of his spirit was such that it forced the body to be carried by the hands of bearers to the oratory; moreover, as if extending the tunic of good works to the heels, he sang the praise of God's might to the end.

7

At dawn on a Friday, feeling himself grow worse he ordered his chaplains to recite the night office in his presence, while the bishop was reciting it in church with his. He himself sang the psalms with the others, and after Lauds he finished the day hours also. Then as he came to the end of compline he armed himself with the sign of the cross and adding, the expression so long familiar to him—"Help, you saints of God"—for the last time, he closed his eyes in silence. Seeing that he had ceased to speak, those who were present called the bishop. They clothed his holy limbs in sackcloth, and while the rest were

---

50. A funeral mass, so called because the celebrant wore black vestments.

singing the psalms for the dying, one of the priests celebrated Mass and brought him Holy Viaticum.[51] Some were saying that he was already dead, but he still retained the use of his senses and opening his eyes showed that he was still alive. Then of his own will he received the body of the Lord for which he was waiting, and so that happy soul departed to heaven. It is as though the order of the day in the week symbolized his own situation, for it showed that the good work, which is proper to the number six, had been completed, and that he had passed on to the true Sabbath that signifies rest. And he, as we believe, now sees what he craved for, now possesses what he hoped for. But to many his passing meant no little grief, and although it was relieved by a certain sweetness inasmuch as they knew that for him rejoicing rather than grief was called for, nevertheless they lamented loudly that they were deprived of his companionship, the like of whom they did not hope to see again. They, because of their human nature, were sad, but the angels, as we believe, rejoiced. For if there shall be joy among the angels on one sinner doing penance, how much more for this just man who grew old in performing works of virtue. Faith sees the joy of the Lord in which he is received by the angels, but this is hidden from the bodily eyes, which have only seen the body paying its debt of death; and it has not yet appeared how greatly the soul is glorified in heaven. Gerald dies therefore, by no means as cowards are accustomed to do, but, according to the saying of David (see Wis 5.5), his lot is among the saints. And although Gerald fulfilled the saying of the psalmist, "Nevertheless you shall die like men" (Ps 82.7), the previous verse likewise applies to him, "I say 'you are gods, the sons of the Most High' " (Ps 82.6). The evangelist also bears witness: "We are God's children now; it does not yet appear what we shall be" (1 Jn 3.2). Happy, then, Gerald who distinguished the precious from the worthless. After he had tasted how sweet the Lord is, he gave himself not at all to the pleasures of this life to the contempt of the Lord. Life on earth, which is precious to the reprobate, he held to be of little value, and death, which to them is the worst of evils, he found precious. Truly blessed is he whose days passed in sorrow and whose years in lamentation, because he has now experienced "how abundant is the goodness" (Ps 31.19) that the Lord has in store for those who fear Him. And even in the sight of men he demonstrates this to some extent by daily signs. How great is the difference between him and the evil rich! To him tears were as bread and he had "tears to drink in full measure" (Ps 80.5). These live their days in good things and have their consolation, according to the saying of the Gospel, in this life. But he with the

51. The Eucharist, received at the moment of death.

voice of exultation has passed over to the tabernacle of God. Of them it is said that in a moment they are brought down to hell. For the rest, even if anyone should be able to say anything worthy of his external way of life, none of us could, I do not say expound, but even touch, the meaning of the delights that fill him everlastingly in the right hand of the Lord, unless perchance somebody feels in himself what it is to delight in the salvation of God.

8

But since God is wonderful in his saints, in whom we are commanded to praise Him, by the saying of Scripture, "Praise the Lord" (Ps 150.1) in his saints, therefore, O blessed Gerald, as far as we can we will praise God for you. I will praise Him because He chose and justified you, because He made glorious His mercy in you, and led you "in paths of righteousness" (Ps 23.3), because He made known the fruit of your labor, and did not desert you even to old age, and what is more, because He counted you among the sons of God, and finally glorifies you in the sight of all. And because praise becomes the saints, to the glory of God I also praise you, because according to the saying of Jeremiah you bore the yoke of Christ from your youth (see Lam 3.27), and did not spurn the grace of His calling; because you did not give anything in exchange for your soul, and did not receive His salvation in vain; because you did not expose the secret thoughts of your heart, which you conceived of the love of Christ, and did not fail in the hour of temptation; because you did not give yourself to the external joys of this life, and did not falter in doing good. But, nevertheless, do You, O Lord, pardon my presumption through him. For I fear to exaggerate in what I say, because I have attempted what I was by no means fitted to do. For although he in whom You are praised is worthy of praise, I, O Lord, am unworthy to give it, because "a hymn of praise is not seemly on the lips of a sinner" (Sir 15.9). Let the saints, therefore, bless You, as it is written (see Ps 145.10), and let Your works confess You. But because Your eyes see the imperfect being of the church, and its stones shall have pity on the earth, we beg that those who on account of the solidity of their morals are called stones may deign to help us who, because of our wickedness, are earth; that we who have not the garment of justice may embrace the stones and be able to cover our nakedness with their merits. May this servant of Yours direct to us the loving mercy with which Your charity endowed him, and may he look lovingly from the eternal court of heaven, in which he resides among the heavenly rulers, into this vale of tears that he has left. May he hear the prayers of each, and with You may he meet the necessities of all, Our Lord Jesus Christ Your Son assisting, who with You and the Holy Spirit lives and is glorified, God forever and ever. Amen.

9

Swiftly, as happens in the case of people of great virtue, the news of his death was spread far and wide. A vast multitude of men soon began to come together from all sides, nobles in great numbers, innumerable crowds of countrypeople and the poor, many monks, and bands of priests. All of them mourned him with a brotherly and tender devotion, and wept for him with I know not what divine instinct of compunction and love, because they knew that he was pleasing to God.

10

When his body had been stripped for washing, Ragembertus and other servants who were performing the duty put both his hands on his breast, when suddenly his right arm extended itself, and his hand was applied to his private parts so as to cover them. Thinking this had happened by chance they bent the hand back to the breast. But again it was extended in the same way and covered his private parts. They were amazed, but wishing to understand the matter more carefully they bent the arm back a third time and put the hand back with the other on his breast. Immediately with lightning speed it sought the same parts and covered them. Those who were laying him out, struck at once by admiration and fear, realized then that this was not happening without divine power. Perhaps it was being divinely shown that this flesh when alive was always anxious to preserve the modesty of chastity. They quickly covered the body, and when it had received a covering the hand no more stretched out.

11

With great crowds accompanying them his people carried the holy body to Aurillac, as he had ordered, and placed it under a stone monument on the left-hand side of the church—near and to the right of the altar of Saint Peter.

But let me bring this little book to an end lest it should displease both by its unpolished style and its length. If anything in it has pleased the reader, let him attribute that to the merits of Count Gerald. Whatever is displeasing he shall put down to my lack of skill, but let him find in it nevertheless an occasion for forgiveness. And for this reason, and in view of the fact that I only presumed to undertake the work by order, I humbly beg that he may intercede for me with Him who judges the hearts of men.

12

For blessed Gerald it is more than enough that the faithful Witness in heaven, whom he always sought to please, recompenses him in paradise, but nevertheless this same Witness, Christ, deigns to manifest outwardly how great is the glory that he possesses within. For it is written that God renews His witnesses against us (see Jb 10.17), and whoever keeps His commandments is His witness against us, that we too are able to keep those same commandments but are not willing. For to speak of people like myself, we scorn to read all the sayings of holy men and neglect to imitate their example, while nevertheless we are tirelessly occupied with idle and worldly speech. But acting in this way we prove ourselves to be those of whom the apostle says, they "will turn away from listening to the truth and wander into myths" (2 Tm 4.4). And so to reprimand somewhat our laziness and other manifestations of vice Christ, the Ruler of the Ages, raises this witness of His against us, making him glorious in our sight with many miracles, so that, because we close our eyes, as has been said, to the consideration of the example of holy men, we may turn our gaze to the splendor of this man, as to one resplendent with His own merits. In our own day he kept the divine precepts, but because the dead quickly depart from our hearts, we forthwith forget this, and not remembering the reward due to his good works we are sinfully slothful in imitating them. And for this reason He deigns to work miracles, which occur perhaps for a time, that so we may understand the glory which he has within, and may turn our minds to those recently performed works by which he attained that glory, and that we may strive to grow strong to imitate them. But now with the help of God let me say something of these same miracles, as may seem reasonable.

Book 4

1

On the Sunday after his death he was carried to Aurillac, as I said, with great crowds accompanying him. While the choir was singing the psalms round the bier during the night, a certain noble called Gibbo placed his daughter, who was afflicted with epilepsy, under the bier, and afterward she suffered no more from her infirmity. She is now the mother of a family and her perfect health bears witness to this miracle.

2

A certain man living on the estate called Grimaldus saw himself in a dream trying to lift the lid off the coffin. When he woke up he found his hands and arms from the elbow downward withered, so that he could do nothing with them. Remaining stricken like this for nearly a fortnight, he came as a suppliant to the tomb and was immediately healed.

3

The lunatic maid of a certain man called Lambert was warned in a dream that she should come as a suppliant to his tomb. She told this to her master, but he, fearing that it was an illusion and that he would be ridiculous, if no miraculous result followed the vision, forbade her. But warned a second and a third time in a vision she again asked her master to be allowed to go there, and this he now granted. The woman went, and after praying at the tomb departed completely healed.

4

In the meantime a little round plot of grass appeared before the crypt. Although the plot was covered with grass, the earth round about was bare and dusty. When those who passed through the cemetery saw the little plot and the dusty path that surrounded it, they were astonished, for they knew that neither man nor beast had trodden out the path. For a time it was there and then it disappeared. Next summer the same thing was seen in the same place, but much larger. There was a dusty path worn round as before. The third summer in the same way a round plot of grass surrounded by a dusty path appeared, but it was larger still. And thenceforth it was seen for many years gradually spreading itself outward. Those who considered the cause carefully believed it to be some prodigy, and conjectured that the green circle was perhaps a symbol of the fame of the blessed Gerald full of the greenness of virtue. This fame spreads itself around among the people, who are barren of good works and signified by the dusty circle, and makes them fertile by its good example. When for love of him they gladly undertake the labor of pilgrimages, when they offer gifts, and some of them return new men, they are like the circle extending itself forward and partly replacing the aridity of the circle of dust. Whether it really signified this the Ruler of all things knows, but it is certain that nothing is done on this earth without a cause.

5

There was a certain cleric of good name who lived in the city of Rodez. This man, if faith is to be put in dreams, saw the following vision. There was as it were a high place from which a great light shone forth, and four steps led up to this light. Before the first step was a footpace of iron, before the second one of brass. The third had a footpace of silver, the fourth of gold. He saw two men, glorious in appearance and dress, come to the first step, and they were followed by two more who were leading a third between them by the hand. It was revealed to the cleric who saw this that the first two were Saint Paul and Saint Martial, the two who followed Saint Peter and Saint Andrew, but the third whom they were leading was Saint Gerald, whom the cleric had not known in this life. But when afterward he described the figure and face he had seen, those who had known Gerald recognized the likeness. When these had come to the first step they appeared to recite a psalm, after which Saint Peter said a collect to which the others replied Amen. This was done a second, a third, and a fourth time. With the others still standing Saint Peter went toward the bright light mentioned above, and having prostrated himself on the earth lay for a little while in adoration. Then he got up and prostrated three times, and a voice replied from the light asking what he wanted. "Lord," he said, "I beg Thy mercy for Thy servant Gerald." And then one, I know not who, holding a book, seemed to recite his life story. When he had been reading for a little time the cleric was only able to distinguish the words, "He 'had the power to transgress and did not transgress, and to do evil and did not do it' " (Sir 31.10). Then the voice was heard to say, "Do what you will with him," and a scepter was brought forth and given to Saint Peter, and he had the power of raising Gerald with it. The cleric heard the voice of Him who gave, but saw only the scepter. Then Saint Peter returned rejoicing to those who were waiting, and a steep path leading up to heaven appeared at the place where they were standing. Saint Peter, taking the beloved of God, Gerald, by the hand and beginning to go up the steps, intoned in a loud voice *Te Deum laudamus*,[52] and so singing they departed into heaven with him.

And another sign from his tomb followed this vision.

52. This was a hymn to the Father and to the Son in rhythmical prose. It goes back to the fifth century but its origins are obscure. The charming legend that Ambrose composed it for Augustine's baptism appears baseless.

6

In the seventh year after his death the coffin began gradually to rise above the ground, but the earth that surrounded it did not seem to be either raised or depressed. Those who dwelt in the place had not yet noticed this, but a certain cleric coming from the district of Limoges asked the monks whether the coffin of Count Gerald had come out of the ground, and added that he had been warned in a dream to come to his tomb, because his coffin had begun to appear. Then the monks going with him to the tomb and taking away the hanging with which it was covered found all as the cleric had seen in his sleep. At that time it stood out a while, now considerably more. Whoever knows this cannot but be aware of some divine power. After this miracles began to occur frequently.

7

The feast of the Circumcision[53] had come round, and a certain vassal called Adraldus ordered a witch's fire to be kept all night in his house. But in the dead of the night demons attacked the guardians of the fire and did such harm to them that they killed one and deprived the other of the use of his limbs. Afterward this man, who eked out his living by begging, was carried to Aurillac. When a few days later some lawless men made an attack upon the place, and the monks began to sound the alarm and to recite litanies, the maimed man begged that those around him should carry him to the tomb of Count Gerald. When they had done this, he prayed that the saint would deign to help him, and in a short time he arose healed, and with all his limbs instantly restored he had his full health. Miracles followed and the fame of Gerald's virtues became more widely and better known. If anyone doubts the facts, for in the sick the same things are often repeated, he can put them to the test with his own eyes and so gain credence of the past. I omit what the divine mercy often deigns to repeat in those who are afflicted by various diseases, for fear of being too long, but I have touched lightly upon some things that redound to the glory of this blessed man, lest I should seem to have passed over them thoughtlessly.

---

53. The Feast of the Circumcision—that is the circumcision of Jesus—was, until recently, in the Roman Catholic Church celebrated on January 1.

8

It is known that this same holy man in his lifetime brought many relics of the saints to Aurillac. Indeed, as was said before, he was most assiduous in this cause, and he had no small help from God to obtain what he wished. Among other relics of the saints that were there is a certain relic of the true cross that was known by frequent trial to have such power that if a man who was carrying it rode on horseback, the horse shortly died, or if he perjured himself he became an epileptic. Not a few became epileptics on account of this sin. The inhabitants of that region had truly ferocious habits but gradually by his example and the reverence they have for the holy man they seem to be gentler. When they make any agreement or solemn oath in law they have the relic brought by some monk or cleric, who, however, comes on foot.

9

Some disputing rashly about the glory of Saint Gerald assert that this grace of healing was conferred not through his merits, but through the power of these relics. Considering the case carefully, I believe that the benefits of health are conferred through the holy relics in such a way as not to deny the cooperating virtue of Saint Gerald. The nature of the things that happen suggests this, for he himself is accustomed to appear in a vision to the sick, and the benefit of health is especially conferred before his tomb, as happened in the case of the son of John, the viscount of Auvergne. Bringing the boy, who was deaf and dumb and had a withered hand, the father prostrated himself before the tomb and gave himself to prayer. In the middle of the night blood burst forth from the child's ears, and reaching out his hand he put it healed round the neck of his father, and speaking for the first time he asked for bread. The church was filled with the voice of the father giving thanks for his son, and he made over a freehold property of his to the saint. I mention names in this case because the miracle, being performed for a person of standing, came to the notice of many. Different miracles, or those of another kind, were noted by the inhabitants, but since the number grew very great no care was taken to keep count.

10

In the castle of Aurillac there was a mounting-block before the doors of the church from which he used to mount his horse. The sick who kiss this for love of him recover their health, and for this reason the inhabitants have now moved it into the church and covered it with a hanging like an altar. Not far from the town that the countrypeople call *Mulsedonum*,[54] the man of God had a small country-house. Some citizens of the town agreed together that they would take his table, which was still there, to eat their meals off, and this they did. The bearers chanced to set it down in front of a certain house, and in the middle of the day a man tried to go to sleep on it, but he was immediately struck blind and senseless, and when a dog jumped on the table it immediately became paralyzed. Nobody realized as yet the cause, and someone else threw himself on the table, but he too was immediately struck blind. Understanding at length that these things were happening because the table had been consecrated by the many meals of the holy man, they carried it covered with a linen cloth into the church of Saint Martin which is nearby, and it is to be seen there to this day suspended from the roof. A certain priest, with some of his neighbors, came to hold a feast on another of his tables that was in the village of *le bex*.[55] When they were chattering and making jokes among themselves as is customary, suddenly a great fear struck them all, so that, stopping their jesting, they went to eat in another place. But the table they carried into an oratory that had been built in a place where the bearers had put down the bier [of Gerald] to change the pall. (When some grazing cattle came on the little space where the bier had been set down they immediately began to be tormented and some of them died. The natives realized the cause of what had happened to the cattle, and built this oratory in the place.) It is certain that from that time many sick people recovered their health there. And moreover a remarkable and almost unbelievable thing happened, if experience had not proved it, for a little spring burst forth in that place sufficient for wayfarers to drink from.

11

While he was still living the man of God bound Rainald,[56] whom he suspected, by an oath, but Rainald broke his oath and with his followers greatly troubled the community that Gerald had assigned to the monastery. In the pillaging that they were suffering some invoked the name of Count Gerald, and one night it seemed to Rainald that he saw the man of God standing by him and demanding that he kept his oath, at the same time warning him to cease from

54. A town about two miles from Argentat (see note 45).
55. A village near Aurillac.
56. Apparently this is Gerald's nephew whom we met twice already (books 1:32 and 2:28).

troubling the community any more. Roused by the vision he told it to his wife, and she persuaded him that having been warned in this way he should keep the oath. Full of compunction, he related this in due course to his followers, ordering them, but in a halfhearted way, not to molest the community, but they in a short time returned to their accustomed rapacity. Nor did Rainald stop them, for he was prone to evil, and although he was a blood relation to the holy man, he was very far from having his piety. Then the holy man appeared to him again in a threatening manner, and full of anger reproached him with the good he had done to him, for which he had received only evil, and striking him on the head he threatened him with death to follow.

12

In the province that is called Alemannia[57] a certain noble was possessed by demons. His parents and retainers took him to many relics of the saints, that at least by their intercession the divine grace might liberate him. But the Giver of all goods, who had decreed to glorify His chosen one, reserved this miracle for him. The name of the blessed man had not yet been heard in that province, and when the parents took their son to the bodies of the saints, the demons often exclaimed that they would never go out of him but through the intercession of Saint Gerald. The parents of the demoniac went in all directions to see if they could hear of the province in which Saint Gerald was. It may have been one of the Roman pilgrims, or another, who told them the province and the place. They hurried to Aurillac and as soon as they came to the tomb the demons began to cry out through the possessed man, "O Gerald, for what reason do you make game of us? For what reason do we burn in your power?" Forthwith the man fell to the ground and spewed them out together with a quantity of blood. Ever after he remained sound.

57. The area of southwestern Germany and northern Switzerland that included Basel, Zurich, and the foothills of the Jura.

GUIDE TO FURTHER READING

Peter Brown, *The Cult of the Saints: Its Rise and Function in Latin Christianity* (Chicago, 1981) is an extraordinarily exciting and readable work, one that has not only charted the social context and importance of sanctity in the world of late antiquity, but has laid the foundations for most later scholarly work that uses hagiography as a source for social history. Clare Stancliffe provides a thorough examination of the work of Sulpicius Severus in *Saint Martin and His Hagiographer: History and Miracle in Sulpicius Severus* (Oxford, 1983). Aline Rousselle, *Croire et guérir: La foi en Gaule dans l'Antiquité tardive* (Paris, 1990) presents a sensitive and provocative reading of the transition from Roman to Christian culture in Gaul, and of the role of Martin and his cult in that transition. A summary of her argument may be found in "From Sanctuary to Miracle-Worker: Healing in Fourth-Century Gaul," in *Ritual, Religion, and the Sacred*, ed. Robert Forster and Orest Ranum (Baltimore, 1982), 95–127. Sharon Farmer's exemplary study of twelfth-century social history, *Communities of St. Martin: Legend and Ritual in Medieval Tours* (Ithaca, N.Y., 1991), studies the function of Martin's cult in a later period.

The chief hagiographer of early medieval Italy was Gregory the Great. A fine introduction to his work may be found in Carole Straw, *Gregory the Great: Perfection in Imperfection* (Berkeley and Los Angeles, 1988). More specifically on his hagiography, see Joan Petersen, *The Dialogues of Gregory the Great in Their Late Antique Cultural Background* (Toronto, 1984). It was the Franks who adopted orthodox Christianity and its notions of sanctity most quickly among the Germanic peoples. The essential foundation to all other treatments of hagiography in the early Frankish kingdom remains Frantisek Graus, *Volk, Herrscher und Heiliger im Reich der Merowinger. Studien zur Hagiographie der Merowingerzeit* (Prague, 1965). In English, see J. M.

Wallace-Hadrill, *The Frankish Church* (Oxford, 1983); Raymond Van Dam, *Leadership and Community in Late Antique Gaul* (Berkeley and Los Angeles, 1985), and *Saints and Their Miracles in Late Antique Gaul* (Princeton, 1993); Paul Fouracre, "Merovingian History and Merovingian Historiography," *Past and Present* 127 (1990): 3–38. On the role of the cult of the saints in that society, see Peter Brown, "Relics and Social Status in the Age of Gregory of Tours," in *Society and the Holy in Late Antiquity* (Chicago, 1982), 222–50 and Ian Wood, "Early Merovingian Devotion in Town and Country," *Studies in Church History* 16 (1979): 61–76. Relatively little exists in English on hagiography in Visigothic Spain, but see Jacques Fontaine, "King Sisebut's *Vita Desiderii* and the Political Function of Visigothic Hagiography," in *Visigothic Spain: New Approaches*, ed. Edward James (Oxford, 1980), 93–129. For a guide to the extensive literature in Spanish, see Roger Collins, *Early Medieval Spain: Unity in Diversity, 400–1000* (London, 1983), 280–82.

The literature on hagiography and sanctity in Anglo-Saxon England is enormous. Fortunately David Rollason has provided a comprehensive overview, with full bibliography, in *Saints and Relics in Anglo-Saxon England* (Oxford, 1989). Further guidance to the sources may be found in Michael Lapidge, "The Saintly Life in Anglo-Saxon England," in *The Cambridge Companion to Old English Literature*, ed. Malcolm Godden and Michael Lapidge (Cambridge, 1991), 243–63. Henry Mayr-Harting, *The Coming of Christianity to Anglo-Saxon England*, 3d ed. (University Park, Pa., 1991) provides a useful introduction to the conversion of England, as well as many interesting observations on Anglo-Saxon saints both in England and on the Continent. For a wide-ranging introduction to the most famous of all Anglo-Saxon hagiographers, see Peter Hunter Blair, *The World of Bede*, 2d ed. (Cambridge, 1990). Gerald Bonner, David Rollason, and Clare Stancliffe, eds., *Saint Cuthbert, His Cult and His Community to A.D. 1200* (Woodbridge, 1989) treats one important Anglo-Saxon saint and his cult. On the development of the cults of Anglo-Saxon royalty, see Susan Ridyard, *The Royal Saints of Anglo-Saxon England: A Study of West Saxon and East Anglian Cults* (Cambridge, 1988), although it primarily treats the texts composed after the Conquest. Wilhelm Levison, *England and the Continent in the Eighth Century* (Oxford, 1946) remains essential on Boniface and other missionaries.

Nora Chadwick, *The Age of the Saints in the Early Celtic Church* (London, 1961) and Kathleen Hughes, *Early Christian Ireland* (Ithaca, N.Y., 1972) provide good introductions to the piety and hagiography of the Celtic lands. For more scholarly detail, one can consult J. F. Kenney, *The Sources for the Early History of Ireland: An Introduction and Guide*, vol. 2, *Ecclesiastical*

(New York, 1929), and Richard Sharpe, *Medieval Irish Saints' Lives* (Oxford, 1991) on Ireland; Elissa Henken, *The Welsh Saints: A Study in Patterned Lives* (Woodbridge, 1991) on Wales; and Julia Smith, *Province and Empire: Brittany and the Carolingians* (Cambridge, 1992), chap. 6 on Brittany. For a comprehensive guide to the sources, see Michael Lapidge and Richard Sharpe, *A Bibliography of Celtic-Latin Literature, 400–1200* (Dublin, 1985). Lisa Bitel, *Isle of the Saints: Monastic Settlements and Christian Community in Early Ireland* (Ithaca, N.Y., 1991) makes innovative use of hagiographic sources to consider the wider religious history of early Ireland. Julia Smith, "Oral and Written: Saints, Miracles, and Relics in Brittany, c. 850–1250," *Speculum* 65 (1990): 309–43, contrasts Celtic ideas of sanctity with those prevalent in Carolingian Europe.

A number of good introductions to Carolingian history and culture exist, among them two works by Pierre Riché, *Daily Life in the World of Charlemagne*, trans. Jo Ann McNamara (Philadelphia, 1978) and *The Carolingians: A Family Who Forged Europe*, trans. Michael Allen (Philadelphia, 1993). Wallace-Hadrill, *The Frankish Church*, 258–390, has much of interest to say about the role of the church and of the saints in the Carolingian empire. Patrick Geary has provided an entertaining and absorbing study of one aspect of the cult of saints in this period in *Furta Sacra: Thefts of Relics in the Central Middle Ages* (Princeton, 1978; 2d ed., 1990). The most wide-ranging study of Carolingian hagiography, however, remains Joseph-Claude Poulin, *L'Idéal de sainteté dans l'Aquitaine carolingienne d'après les sources hagiographiques (750–950)* (Quebec City, 1975). Suzanne Wemple has also used hagiography to study the history of women in *Women in Frankish Society: Marriage and the Cloister, 500–900* (Philadelphia, 1981). On the importance of the papacy and the institutional church in the formation of the Carolingian order, see Thomas Noble, *The Republic of St. Peter: The Birth of the Papal State, 680–825* (Philadelphia, 1984). For an exemplary study of the iconography of a hagiographic text from this period, see Cynthia Hahn, *Passio Kiliani . . . Passiio Margaretae: Faksimile-Ausgabe des Codex . . . Ms. I 189 . . . aus dem Besitz der Niedersächsichen Landesbibliothek Hannover* (Graz, 1988).

On the conversion of Scandinvia, see Dag Strömbäck, *The Conversion of Iceland* (London, 1975) and Birgit Sawyer, Peter Sawyer, and Ian Wood, eds., *The Christianization of Scandinavia* (Alingsaas, 1987). On the conversion of the Slavs, see Francis Dvornik, *The Making of Central and Eastern Europe* (London, 1949) and A. P. Vlasto, *The Entry of the Slavs into Christendom* (Cambridge, 1970).

On Europe after the collapse of the Carolingian empire, see Jean-Pierre Poly and Eric Bournazel, *The Feudal Transformation, 900–1200*, trans. Caroline Higgitt (New York, 1991) and Heinrich Fichtenau, *Living in the Tenth Century: Mentalities and Social Orders*, trans. Patrick Geary (Chicago, 1991). Both have perceptive comments about saints and their cults; the former also has an excellent bibliography. A study of the cult of saints that spans the Carolingian and post-Carolingian periods in one important region may be found in Thomas Head, *Hagiography and the Cult of Saints. The Diocese of Orléans, 800–1200* (Cambridge, 1990). Little is available in English on Ottonian hagiography, but see Patrick Corbet, *Les Saints ottoniens: Sainteté dynastique, sainteté royale et sainteté féminine autour de l'an mil* (Sigmaringen, 1986).

Numerous relevant primary sources are available in English translation. Translations of the early acts of martyrs, both Greek and Latin, may be found in *The Acts of the Christian Martyrs*, ed. Herbert Musurillo (Oxford, 1972). Many works of late antique Greek hagiography exist in translation. Some of the more important include Palladius, *The Lausiac History*, trans. Robert Meyer (Washington, D.C., 1964); Gregory of Nyssa, *Life of St. Macrina* in *Ascetical Works*, trans. V. W. Callahan (Washington, D.C., 1967); Athanasius, *The Life of Antony*, trans. Robert Gregg (New York, 1980). *Holy Women of the Syrian Orient*, ed. Sebastian Brock and Susan Harvey (Berkeley and Los Angeles, 1987) and *Three Byzantine Saints*, ed. Elizabeth Dawes and Norman Baynes (Crestwood, N.Y., 1977) both contain representative works of hagiography from the Christian east.

All the hagiographic works of Gregory of Tours have been translated: *Life of the Fathers*, trans. Edward James (Liverpool, 1986); *Glory of the Martyrs*, trans. Raymond Van Dam (Liverpool, 1988); *Glory of the Confessors*, trans. Raymond Van Dam (Liverpool, 1988); *The Suffering and Miracles of the Martyr St. Julian* and *The Miracles of the Bishop St. Martin* in Raymond Van Dam, *Saints and Their Miracles in Late Antique Gaul* (Princeton, 1993). The latter work also contains other works relating to the cult of the saints in Merovingian Gaul. A number of lives of female saints from the Merovingian kingdom are to be found in *Sainted Women of the Dark Ages*, ed. Jo Ann McNamara and John Halborg, with E. Gordon Whatley (Durham, N.C., 1992). The subjects of these lives all lived in the late sixth or seventh century; some of the works, however, date to a much later period. The only life of one of the male *Adelsheilige* from the Frankish kingdom currently available in English is the *Life of St. Amandus* in Hillgarth, *Christianity and Paganism*. For the life of the most important Celtic monastic reformer active on the continent, see Jonas, *Life of Columbanus* in *Monks, Bishops, and Pagans:*

Christian Culture in Gaul and Italy, 500–700, ed. Edward Peters (Philadelphia, 1975). That collection also contains numerous excerpts from the works of Gregory of Tours, Gregory the Great, and other hagiographers. There are numerous translations available of Gregory the Great's *Dialogues,* particularly of the second book, which concerns the life of Saint Benedict of Nursia; perhaps the best is that by Odo Zimmerman (The Fathers of the Church 39; Washington, D.C., 1959). The only other hagiography from early medieval Italy readily available in English is the early section of the *Liber Pontificalis: The Book of Pontiffs (Liber Pontificalis),* trans. Raymond Davis (Liverpool, 1989) and *The Lives of the Eighth-Century Popes (Liber Pontificalis),* trans. Raymond Davis (Liverpool, 1992). The single most important piece of hagiography from early medieval Spain, and the only easily available in English, is *The "Vitas sanctorum patrum Emeritensium,"* ed. and trans. Joseph Garvin (Washington, D.C., 1946).

Most of the Latin hagiographic works composed in Anglo-Saxon England are avilable in English translation. Three collections are particularly useful: C. W. Jones, ed. and trans., *Saints' Lives and Chronicles in Early England,* (Ithaca, N.Y., 1947); Clinton Albertson, ed. and trans., *Anglo-Saxon Saints and Heroes* (New York, 1967); David Farmer, ed., *The Age of Bede,* (Harmondsworth, 1983). A number of individual works have been edited and translated by Bertram Colgrave: *The Life of Bishop Wilfrid by Eddius Stephanus* (Cambridge, 1927; repr. 1985); *Two Lives of Saint Cuthbert* (Cambridge, 1940; repr. 1985); *Felix's Life of St. Guthlac* (Cambridge, 1956; repr. 1985); *The Earliest Life of Gregory the Great by an anonymous Monk of Whitby* (Lawrence, Kans., 1969). Several Old English hagiographic works may be found in modern English in *Anglo-Saxon Poetry,* ed. and trans. R. K. Gordon (London, 1926 and reprints).

Similarly, much Irish hagiography (both Latin and Celtic) has been translated, but often in versions that are now quite dated: *The Tripartite Life of Patrick, with Other Documents Relating to that Saint,* ed. Whitley Stokes (Rolls Series 89; London, 1887); *Lives of the Saints from the Book of Lismore,* ed. Whitley Stokes (Oxford, 1890); R. A. Stewart Macalister, "Life of Saint Finan," *Zeitschrift für celtische Philologie* 2 (1899): 545–65; *Miscellanea hagiographica hibernica,* ed. Charles Plummer (Brussels, 1925); *St. Patrick: His Writings and Life,* trans. Newport White (London, 1920); *St. Patrick: His Writings and Life,* trans. Newport White (London and New York, 1920); M. A. O'Brien, "The Old Irish Life of St. Brigit," *Irish Historical Studies* 1 (1938–39): 121–34 and 343–53; *Vitae sanctorum Hiberniae,* and W. W. Heist (Brussels, 1965); *St. Patrick: His Writings and Muirchu's Life,* ed. and trans.

A. B. E. Hood (Totowa, N.J., 1978). For an excellent, recent translation, see Adomnan, *Life of Columba*, ed. Alan Anderson and Marjorie Anderson, 2d ed. (Oxford, 1991). Collections of Scottish and Welsh lives may be found respectively in *Ancient Lives of Scottish Saints*, trans. W. W. Metcalfe (Paisley, 1895) and *Vitae sanctorum Britanniae et genealogiae*, ed. A. W. Wade-Evans (Cardiff, 1944). An intriguing piece of hagiography from Brittany is included in Caroline Brett, ed., *The Monks of Redon* (Woodbridge, 1989).

Many lives from the eighth, ninth, and tenth centuries are included in this volume. Another important work is Alcuin, *The Bishops, Kings, and Saints of York*, ed. Peter Godman (Oxford, 1982). Some other representative works from the tenth century may be found in *Three Lives of the Last Englishmen*, trans. Michael Swanton (New York, 1984); Wulfstan of Winchester, *Life of St. Aethelwold*, ed. Michael Lapidge and Michael Winterborrom (Oxford, 1991); *St. Odo of Cluny*, trans. Gerard Sitwell (New York, 1958); and *The Dramas of Hrotsvit of Gandersheim*, trans. Katharina Wilson (Saskatoon, 1985). On the conversion of the Slavs in central Europe, see *The Origins of Christianity in Bohemia: Sources and Commentary*, ed. and trans. Marvin Kantor (Evanston, Ill., 1990) which contains several interesting tenth-century hagiographic works translated from both Latin and Old Church Slavonic.

Although not all technically works of hagiography, the lives of Charlemagne and his family provide excellent comparisons to the works included in the present volume: *Two Lives of Charlemagne*, ed. Lewis Thorpe (Harmondsworth, 1969); *Charlemagne's Cousins. Contemporary Lives of Adalhard and Wala*, trans. Allen Cabaniss (Syracuse, N.Y., 1967); *Son of Charlemagne. A Contemporary Life of Louis the Pious*, trans. Allen Cabaniss (Syracuse, N.Y., 1961). Of similar use are tenth- and early eleventh-century royal biographies from Anglo-Saxon England and Ottonian Germany: Abbo of Fleury, *Passion of St. Edmund* in *Corolla Sancti Eadmundi. The Garland of St. Edmund, King and Martyr*, trans. Francis Hervey (London, 1907); Asser, *Life of Alfred* in *Alfred the Great*, ed. Simon Keynes and Michael Lapidge (London, 1983); *Encomium Emmae reginae*, ed. and trans. A. Campbell (Camden Society 3.72; London, 1949); Hrotsvit of Gandersheim, *The Deeds of Otto* in *Hrosvitae, Liber tertius*, trans. Sister Mary Bernardine Bergman (St. Louis, Mo., 1942); Liutprand of Cremona, *A Chronicle of Otto's Reign* in *The Works of Liudprand of Cremona*, trans. F. A. Wright (London, 1930; reprint, 1993); Wipo, *Deeds of Conrad* in *Imperial Lives and Letters of the Eleventh Century*, ed. and trans. Theodor Mommsen and Karl Morrison (New York, 1962).

In comparison to the lives of saints, relatively few texts concerning their posthumous cult during the Anglo-Saxon, Carolingian, Capetian, or Ottonian periods have been translated. Some exceptions are Einhard, *The History of the Translation of the Blessed Martyrs of Christ Marcellinus and Peter*, trans. Barrett Wendell (Cambridge, 1926); selections from Ermentarius, *Translation and Miracles of St. Philibert* in David Herlihy, ed., *The History of Feudalism* (New York, 1970); and the *Translation of St. Germain of Paris* in Donald Bullough, *The Vikings at Paris* (Manchester, 1992); Letaldus of Micy, *The Journey of the Body of S. Junianus to the Council of Charroux* in *The Peace of God: Social Violence and Religious Response in France Around the Year One Thousand*, ed. Thomas Head and Richard Landes (Ithaca, N.Y., 1992).

No adequate general guide to the history, study, and use of hagiography exists in English. See instead René Aigrain, *L'Hagiographie: Ses sources, ses méthodes, son histoire* (Paris, 1953); Réginald Grégoire, *Manuale di Agiologia: Introduzione alla Letteratura Agiografica* (Fabriano, 1987); and Jacques Dubois and Jean-Loup Lemaitre, *Sources et méthodes de l'hagiographie médiévale* (Paris, 1993). One of the foundational works in the modern study of hagiography, however, has been translated into English: Hippolyte Delehaye, *Legends of the Saints*, trans. V. M. Crawford (London, 1907; repr., South Bend, Ind., 1961). For a collection of exemplary essays, see Stephen Wilson, ed., *Saints and Their Cults* (Cambridge, 1983). It includes an excellent bibliography on pages 309–417. Another useful bibliography is to be found in Sofia Boesch Gajano, ed., *Agiografia altomedioevale* (Bologna, 1976), 7–48. Handy guides to information about specific saints can be found in the following: Donald Attwater, *The Penguin Dictionary of Saints* (Harmondsworth, 1965), David Hugh Farmer, *The Oxford Dictionary of Saints*, rev. ed. (Oxford, 1992), and the volumes of the *New Catholic Encyclopedia*. Unfortunately the well-known work by Alban Butler entitled *The Lives of the Saints* (revised edition by Herbert Thurston and Donald Attwater [London, 1926–38; repr., New York, 1956]) is largely based on secondary sources and remains unreliable. For those beginning to undertake serious research into hagiographic sources, further references and bibliography may be found in Iosepho Vizzini et al., eds., *Bibliotheca Sanctorum*, 13 vols. (1961–69); *Vies des saints et des bienheureux par les reverends pères bénédictins de Paris*, 13 vols. (1935–59); André Mandouze, André Vauchez et al., eds., *Histoire des saints et de la sainteté chrétienne*, 11 vols. (Paris, 1986–88); and the relevant volumes of "Typologie des sources du moyen âge occidental."

INDEX OF SCRIPTURAL
CITATIONS

SUBJECT INDEX